LOST VOICES OF THE
ROYAL AIR FORCE

Also by Max Arthur

The Busby Babes: Men of Magic
Above All, Courage
Northern Ireland Soldiers Talking
Men of the Red Beret
Forgotten Voices of the Great War
Symbol of Courage: A History of the Victoria Cross
Forgotten Voices of the Second World War
Lost Voices of the Royal Navy

LOST VOICES

OF THE ROYAL AIR FORCE

MAX ARTHUR

HODDER

First published in Great Britain in 1993 by Hodder and Stoughton
A division of Hodder Headline
This edition published in 2005

A Hodder paperback

9

A CIP catalogue record for this title is available from the British Library

ISBN 978 0 340 83813 6

Typeset in Monotype Sabon by
Rowland Phototypesetting Ltd,
Bury StEdmunds, Suffolk

Printed and bound in the UK by
CPI Mackays, Chatham ME5 8TD

Hodder Headline's policy is to use papers that are natural,
renewable and recyclable products and made from wood
grown in sustainable forests. The logging and manufacturing
processes are expected to conform to the environmental
regulations of the country of origin.

Hodder and Stoughton Ltd
A division of Hodder Headline
338 Euston Road
London NW1 3BH

Originally published as THERE SHALL BE WINGS: The RAF from
1918 to the Present

This book is dedicated to all who have served
and are at present serving with the Royal Air Force,
and in particular those who gave their lives.

An Eighteenth-Century Prophecy

The time will come, when thou shalt lift thine eyes
To watch a long-drawn battle in the skies.
While aged peasants, too amazed for words,
Stare at the flying fleets of wondrous birds.

England, so long mistress of the sea,
Where winds and waves caress her sovereignty
Her ancient triumphs yet on high shall bear,
And reign, the sovereign of the conquered air.

> Translated from *Luna Habitabilis*
> by Thomas Gray (1716–71)

Contents

PART ONE

THE EARLY YEARS
1918–1939

1

THE RFC AND AN INDEPENDENT
AIR FORCE

The first British air force, the Royal Flying Corps, was created in 1912 with a Naval Wing, a Military Wing and a Central Flying School. Inevitably perhaps, the concept of an air arm for both naval and military purposes withered and died between the Admiralty and the War Office and in 1914 Britain went to war with the Royal Naval Air Service (RNAS) and a separate Royal Flying Corps (RFC) which belonged to the Army. Most of the Great War was fought with no central direction, little co-ordination and great rivalry between the two air arms. The government finally took action in late 1917. The Air Force Bill created the Air Ministry in January 1918 and, on 1 April 1918, the Royal Naval Air Service and the Royal Flying Corps were amalgamated to form the Royal Air Force.

The RAF thus became the world's first independent air service. It inherited the aggressive and inspiring traditions of airmanship forged in battle by the RNAS and RFC: from mid-1916 to the Armistice, 7,054 enemy aircraft had been claimed destroyed, 6,942 tons of bombs had been dropped and ten-and-a-half million rounds of ammunition fired at ground targets during 900,000 operational flying hours. It had also produced several 'aces' who had become household names – Ball, Mannock, McCudden and Leefe Robinson.

A mighty weapon by the time of the Armistice, the RAF had 188 operational squadrons, 199 training squadrons, 12 squadrons with the Navy and 291,000 personnel. But air power, in terms of the capabilities of the day, was still seen as a tactical adjunct of the Navy or Army and the fledgling RAF had to struggle to remain independent. By 1920 post-war reductions and Treasury constraints had cut the RAF to 25 operational, 11 training and 5 naval squadrons, and 28,300 personnel. Indeed, for a spell in 1920 the fighter defence of the United Kingdom was a single squadron of Sopwith Snipes.

Sir Hugh Trenchard, reappointed Chief of the Air Staff in 1919, nevertheless laid down foundations on which to build a major new service: the RAF College at Cranwell (1920), the Aircraft Apprentice School at Halton, Buckinghamshire (1920), the Air Staff College at Andover (1922), and the reserve Auxiliary Air Force (1924).

Ironically, the government's demands for economy helped ensure the RAF's independent survival. A few squadrons of aircraft could 'police' the troublesome corners of the Empire far more cheaply than scores of battalions of troops. Dissidents would face deterrence, intimidation and, if necessary, swift retribution from the air rather than from military expeditions. In particular, in the mandate of Iraq (formerly Mesopotamia) the RAF took over operational responsibility from the Army in late 1922, deploying eight squadrons. By 1925, the RAF's independent survival was probably assured. (However, the RAF at sea was renamed the Fleet Air Arm in 1924 and transferred to the Royal Navy in 1937. The Admiralty also coveted coastal patrol and maritime aircraft but the RAF retained what became Coastal Command.)

Aerial policing of the Empire was one assertion of the RAF's independence. In a way, so was the first of the famous RAF Pageants at Hendon in 1920. More significantly, the concept of strategic bombing, which became the RAF's central purpose in the next war, was developing.

By 1927 the RAF at home had twelve fighter squadrons using aircraft not much advanced from those of 1918. Government parsimony in defence stemmed from its belief that there would be ten years of noticeable threat before any new multi-nation European war – which in the event was true enough.

In Iraq in 1924, a Turkish-inspired 'jihad' was subdued by bombing and a Turkish Army incursion was halted by air attack.

There were intense if intermittent operations between 1925 and 1932, with rebels and raiders warned off by leaflet or, later, by airborne loudspeaker, or bombed or strafed. Troops were transported and supplied, and casualties evacuated, by air. The RAF presence remained when Iraq became self-governing in 1932 and five squadrons were still there when war broke out in 1939.

Throughout the period between the wars, the handful of squadrons in India were involved in operations of varying intensity on the North-West Frontier. Notable incidents included: an RAF Handley Page V/1500's six-hour flight to bomb the Afghan capital, Kabul, during the 1919 Third Afghan War; the airlift from Kabul to India in 1928 to evacuate 586 people of various nationalities from an Afghan conflict; intensive operations against the Fakir of Ipi's rising in 1927; and dispersing a Pathan invasion of Afghanistan in 1938.

By 1930 the RAF had 57 operational squadrons, 22 of them overseas, plus nine squadrons of the Auxiliary Air Force. Its latest fighter, the Hawker Fury biplane, could just top 200mph. By mid-1934, however, German rearmament had provoked major expansion plans for the RAF. The fighters planned for 1937–38 would include fast, eight-gun monoplanes with enclosed cockpits and retractable undercarriages, the Hurricane and Spitfire – which drew upon the technological advances of the Schneider Trophy racing seaplanes of 1931. The best of the new monoplane bombers, the Wellington and Hampden, would manage close on 250mph. Four-engined 'heavies' would follow.

The RAF was reorganised in 1936 into a new Command structure: Training, Bomber, Coastal and Fighter Commands, with Air Marshal Sir Hugh Dowding as commander-in-chief of the latter. A new RAF Volunteer Reserve of trained aircrew was formed. The air defence of Britain was replanned, giving crucial importance to the new radar and for the first time government expenditure on the RAF exceeded that on the Army.

Private Phyllis Chambers, RFC

Before I joined the Royal Flying Corps in 1915, when I was twenty-one, I worked in a munitions factory in Birmingham. We got good money on munitions and, because I worked nights, I got even more.

My mother and father were dead. My mother died when I was fifteen months and my father died when he was forty-five, so I didn't know either of them. My aunt and uncle brought me up, and they were monied people. I don't know what they did; in those days when you were a child you had to be seen and not heard. I'd never met any of my family, but my brother, who lived in Grantham, asked me to come and live with him.

Of course I had to work for my living, so I went to the Labour Exchange to see if they had any clerical work. They said, with my education I could do well in the Royal Flying Corps. I talked it over with my sister-in-law and she thought it the best thing I could do.

They sent me to Harlaxton and gave me a uniform which wasn't measured, it just fitted where it touched and went down to our ankles. First they sent me to the pay office, and then I went to be clerk to a Captain. He was a very nice man, very quiet, he just told me what to do and that was that.

To get to Harlaxton from Grantham we had to go by lorry and they picked us up at the same place every day. We had to climb on the wheel and over the side of the lorry. The New Zealand troops who were in Grantham at the time used to congregate at the corner wanting to see a bit of leg! But they were a very decent bunch of men, they were very young. We used to go to the dances with them and dance the military two-step, the Lancers and waltzes. They used to write in my autograph book, decent things of course.

Then the Captain was called to the front. He said he would like to give me a little present, and he gave me a fountain pen. Then he asked me if I would like a little flight. He said we'd have to keep it a secret, or he'd get into trouble. So I said, 'Yes, I'm game enough.' We went up in this little plane, I don't know what type it was but the boys had to swing the propeller and push the plane along until it connected. It was an open cockpit, the sky was coming down and the earth was coming upwards. We only just went round the airfield at Harlaxton which wasn't very far, but it was far enough for me. I was glad to get out.

After that I was sent to Cranwell to work in an office. They used to phone from down south to tell me how many planes had gone over Germany, and then later to say how many had come back. It was so distressing to hear how many had gone over and how few had come back. They used to keep the casualty list very quiet. I didn't like that part of the job. Then I went on the telephone exchange.

At Cranwell we had wooden huts which had an old stove. There was no such thing as a 'perm' in those days, so we would warm up the poker in the fire to curl our hair. We had two uniforms which we had to keep very clean and tidy. I'd often cycle into Grantham and stay with my sister-in-law for the day and she would wash my uniform. We had stockings issued and one pair of shoes which we had to keep for a long time. The hat was a peaked cap, but we also had a round hat. The Sergeant-Major used to call you something if you hadn't got the strap in the right place on your chin. We never had gloves unless we provided our own so we often used to buy khaki or blue wool and knit them.

The food was bad, a lot of us couldn't eat it, so when we got paid, we'd catch the steam train into Sleaford and eat a meal. Then we had to get the train back or walk, because if we didn't get back by nine o'clock we were in trouble.

But we were always laughing over something. There were three of us who went everywhere together. In those days all the girls had boy's names. I was Billy; my special friends were Mickey and Teddy.

We used to have dances where the officers mixed with the girls. Then of course, some of the officers started to go out with the girls, so it was given out that girls were not to be seen with officers in uniform. I was going out with an officer at the time, so I phoned him to tell him I wouldn't be allowed to see him on Sunday. But he borrowed his batman's suit and we went to his cottage. His batman was supposed to be on weekend leave, but he came back unexpectedly and there we were having tea when he walked in!

We kept in touch for a long time and then he was called to the front. I had several letters and then they suddenly stopped, so I presume he'd been killed. I never heard from him again.

They had the NS11 airship at Cranwell and we got to know all the boys. When it went off we waved farewell and shouted good luck. Unfortunately, it got struck by lightning over the North Sea. We all went into mourning for them, we were so sorry.

But we had funny moments as well. When the Duke of York (later King George VI) visited we all wanted to sleep in the bed that he had vacated. The other silly thing was pay day. When I was in the pay office I used to sit at a table with an officer and a Sergeant. The girls used to step forward when their name was called, pick up their money, take a step backwards, salute and go. When it came to my turn, I had to get up from the table, walk round, stand in front of the officer, pick up my money, salute and then go back round the table to get the money ready for the next girl!

But towards the end of the war things were a bit easier. We went on the back of motorbikes. We'd wrap our skirts round us and sit on the back. The men used to lend us goggles and we'd sit with our arms around their waists. I used to cycle a lot too in those days. Instead of going to bed after working nights, I used to go out into the country cycling. A lot of the girls used to go swimming, but I'd got into a canal once when I was twelve and drank dirty water and I've hated water ever since. I won't drink it, even now.

I did get across to France before the war was over, but the Germans advanced so I was sent back. A lot of girls served in France and I lost two friends out there.

In 1918 General Trenchard got us all together and said, 'I want to do away with the Royal Flying Corps, but we must have a Royal Air Force.' The uniform changed to blue. I think he could see the Second World War coming up, especially at the end. He was a very nice man and sympathised with the girls saying that he hoped the Air Force wouldn't lose us, as they needed us as much as the men.

I did get engaged to a young pilot, I knew him for a couple of years. He was killed in the last months of the war. He was Scottish – Alexander MacDonald – and lovely.

We had a big dance on Armistice Day and all the officers came including the women officers, too. They usually used to stand and watch, but that night they all joined in.

It was sad as well, because now I would be on my own.

Captain Gwilym Lewis, RFC

When the First World War broke out, I was at Marlborough School. I didn't do particularly well, but I was rather good at rugger, and played for the House whilst I was still a fag.

When I reached my eighteenth birthday, with the help of my father I got a commission in the Northampton Regiment. My father knew the old chap who commanded it, and it sounds silly, but it was quite hard to get into a regiment. I was there for about two or three weeks and I found it too much like hard work. They used to go in for long walks for days on end, carrying packs and everything, which was very tiring. So I went to the Colonel and said that I wanted to fly. Well he was frightfully angry. I suppose he saw me as a promising young subaltern. However, I applied for a transfer to the Royal Flying Corps and was interviewed by a Major Warner. He said, 'I'm sorry, young fellow, but we don't have any openings now.' He saw how disappointed I was and advised me to go to a civilian flying school to get my ticket (flying certificate).

I went to my father and said, 'I want to go flying.' He said,

'That's very silly, son.' And I said, 'You haven't heard the whole story, it's going to knock you back a hundred quid.' I think he felt he had rather a tiresome family, but he gave me the money.

I got my ticket and joined the RFC. On 3 January I went to Farnborough which was a bloody good station. Then I was moved off to Central Flying School at Upavon where I got my wings on 23 April. I had quite an experience there in a de Havilland 2 (D.H.2). I got into a spin at 3,000 feet; I tried everything all the way down. Fortunately, there was a hollow in the ground which gave me another 20 feet, and somehow I got control.

I then joined 32 Squadron as their youngest pilot and we flew over to France in D.H.2s and were sent down to the middle of 2nd Army front. We then got a shout to move down to the Somme early in July and a jolly good move it was too, because we had been there quite a time and had got settled and comfortable. Trenchard came out to meet us. 'I hear great things about you,' he said, 'but you will have to fight jolly hard, jolly hard.' That same day, our Commanding Officer, Lionel Rees, got his VC.

I wrote home to my parents and said I don't know what will happen, but I certainly won't run away from a Hun. I was perfectly certain of that. We had been out in France just a short time, and I was doing a line patrol. That's to say I was flying up and down the line without going over it. The sky was pretty empty in those days and I could see in the distance another aircraft coming along at the same level. I assumed it was one of our own, but in case he wasn't I got between him and the lines. I felt an absolute novice – couldn't fly the machine very well. Suddenly I saw his markings as he came nearer and my heart jumped into my mouth. He was a two-seater, a very effective two-seater fighter. The gunner was sitting up behind looking backwards with his gun ready – I could see his goggles and all his details. So I let him have a good burst; and he didn't fire back. Then he turned and I was after him again and put another burst into him. He turned under me and dived for home, so I thought I've won, I've won, I've sent him home! I felt very pleased with myself. But when I got back to the squadron, Rees wasn't at all pleased. He told me I had fired at much too long a range and had missed a chance.

The big day of that autumn period was 15 September 1916, when Haig launched a major offensive south-west of Bapaume and our tanks went into battle for the first time. It was an incredible sight. We were going to win the war! All the Infantry chaps were moving. They were actually cheering the tanks, because the Huns didn't know what to do. We certainly saw that no German aircraft were going to interfere with them. We were up in the air as soon as we could fill our tanks with petrol. We dominated the skies – the Infantry the ground. But it was all so short-lived. The casualties were terrible. I don't know how they stood it.

Later that month we had a particularly exciting offensive patrol. I was well above the rest when a Roland passed right over me. I couldn't see his crosses until he was right over, then I could see the observer looking over the side with his gun pointing straight down at me. I went as white as a ghost, but for some reason he forgot to fire. I sat there watching him, when I suddenly caught sight of a BE12 fighting for his life with two Huns. I dived down to 4,000 feet and to my horror saw three other Huns coming down too. I had to fight for my life, I don't think I was ever quite so frightened. I got close up behind the Roland and emptied a drum into it, and he went down in a spin. I put another drum on in a desperate hurry, but a bullet jammed. I soon got over that but as I looked around I saw another fellow on my tail. I did a hurried turn on a wing tip and gave him a drum and he went down. We had scared the Huns off, we'd done very well and we all waved to each other. Those dogfights were wildly exciting, but towards the end of 1916 I was beginning to get tired. I was longing to go home. I went down with an attack of appendicitis and was taken back to England. While I was recovering I received a letter from one of my ground crew which really summed up the affection they had for both pilot and plane.

32 Squadron, RFC, Christmas Eve, 1916.

Dear Sir

Really I don't know how to thank you for your great kindness in writing to us as you did. Medals and decorations have little chance of finding their way to the rank and file of the RFC, but personally I am quite content if the war brings me nothing more than your letter. It will be my most treasured 'souvenir' of 'The Great War'. We are all very, very sorry indeed to lose you – nowadays *good* pilots are few and far between – and the news that you are making a good recovery from your regrettable illness is very acceptable to us all. We hope you will soon be able to show them how flying should be done in England, for if the efforts of the new pilots we are getting out now be any criterion, I'm very much afraid flying is only a lost art there now! I came out with No. 32 and so I think I am entitled to pass an opinion on it; my opinion is, sir, that it reached its zenith about September 1916, and it is now a wash-out. Within the last week we have lost three machines, not in service but in *school* flying. Poor old 32!

Since you left us, sir, everything has been one big mix-up. Lieutenant Corbett took over '7888'; he was a game pilot and a gallant gentleman, but inexperienced. Within a week he crashed her. Exit '7888'. I wonder if inanimate objects have feelings; did she miss the master-touch that had controlled her for so long? Who can say? He got another machine, did a few flights in it and went over the line – never to return! Captain Nicholas, Lieutenants Coleman, King and he went on a patrol – King flying a 'B' Flight bus – and encountered a strong Hun patrol. King had bad engine trouble – 'B' Flight again – and was out of the running all the time, and the last that was seen of Lieutenant Corbett was his bus diving hell for leather, with Hun on his tail. I do not know whether he lives yet or not; if not, he is one more good man lost. Captain Henty followed you to hospital very soon, and is 'struck-off'. Lieutenant Hunt took over his place as Flight Commander of 'B' Flight – and lasted a week! He had an arrangement of double guns – two guns instead of one – on his bus, and on his first trip over he failed to return. Isn't war a hellish business?

Mechanics are human beings, *very* human sometimes, and it is awful for them to see these men, good and true gentlemen in the true sense of the word, going off with a 'Cheerio', never to return. My nerve was as steady as a rock until I saw Lieutenant Bentley killed at Vert Galand – I held him down in his death agony – and since then it hasn't been worth a damn. Lieutenant King, Captain Jones and Lieutenant Maremontemboult have all had crashes since you left ('Monty' as he was affectionately called, smashing his sixth bus, and incidentally being struck off, wounded). Just to give you an idea of the type of pilots we are getting; one day this week four pilots in 'A' Flight pulled out a machine and put a new pilot in it. He was perfectly game, although he had never flown a de Havilland before. He did a few circuits and missed the aerodrome twice in landing. He must have lost his head completely then, for he landed *with* the wind, and crashed. 'B' Flight wrecked another today, on the aerodrome. It is sad. Lieutenant Coleman is posted to Home Establishment and left us at the beginning of the week. I believe Captain Nicholas follows suit in a few weeks' time. What will become of us then?

So much for the officers and machines, now a word or two as to the men. Sergeant Saunders went to hospital and I have taken his place in the workshops. One of the flight men went to hospital with some mysterious disease – rumour says 'spotted fever' – anyway, the remainder of the men who slept in his billet, including Jackson and Davidson, were at once isolated. Within a week Jackson and Falconer, the carpenter, followed suit, and are now struck off. I called Davidson to the window of his hut and told him of your letter. He wishes me to thank you for him, and asks if you still have a certain negative which was exposed at Vert Galand. We would dearly like a memento of '7888'. I don't think there is much more to tell, sir; I only hope that I have not wearied you with this rambling epistle. The boys all join me in wishing you the very best of luck, and we will keep our eyes on

the Honours Lists, for you cannot hide your light under a bushel
for ever.
Yours obediently
(Corporal) Chas Wm Dalton

On 26 December 1916, my father's birthday, my elder brother
Edmund, who was a pilot in 24 Squadron, was killed. He had
been with the Army in the Dardanelles and had joined the RFC
later. He was not an experienced pilot when he took on five
two-seaters in his D.H.2. It was a great blow to my whole family.
I don't think my father ever really recovered from his death.

In September I was given the command of an SE5 flight, training
pilots for France and in December I was posted back to France,
as a Flight Commander in 40 Squadron. One of the other Flight
Commanders was Mick Mannock.

I was very conscious how overseas squadrons disliked anyone
coming over to the mainland and starting any bullshit. So I kept
quiet: too quiet. So Mannock nicknamed me 'Noisy'. It wasn't
until Christmas that I made a noise. Mick was very musical and
played the violin. He was of course a hero when I arrived and had
already seventeen Huns to his name. There was a great deal of
Irish in him, that came from his father. But his father – he never
spoke of him. I think Mick was probably very introverted. He
was a slow starter, I think he had to get his guts going. That was
the thing about my flying friends, how much I never knew about
them. I thought I knew them inside out, I did in the air – but
never knew their background.

Mick was often visited by McCudden and they would talk over
tactics; finding new ways. Mick was a brilliant leader of a patrol
and McCudden was particularly marvellous at shooting down
two-seaters.

One flight always remains in my mind because the Huns moved
their circus on to our front. I was to escort six D.H.4s to bomb
an airfield at dawn. I should have had five SE5s, but three of them
never got started, so I was down to three. Well the three of us

wasn't enough, because I didn't know whether the D.H.4s would fight or not. Well, anyway, we were over the lines in good time but it wasn't long before I realised that we were escorted by Huns from below. But fortunately we reached our target and the D.H.4s dropped their bombs and started to climb. The Huns turned and tried to cut us off. They were looking up at us and we were looking down at them. I saw the D.H.4s across the line, then I thought it was a shame that these Huns had had all this flying and nothing to show for it. So I turned back and dived on the leader of their patrol, who was a bright red chap. And, boy, did he get irritated being attacked in front of all his chaps! He didn't like it at all. He came bang back at me – so I attacked him and then he came back at me again. This went on for some time, because neither of us could get a shot in. Then he turned away. By now one of my chums had pulled out and I was keen to join him.

The next thing I knew when I looked around was seeing my number 2, Herbert, fighting this green and white striped fellow. Then this red chap came along too. I was very upset because I thought I had really had enough, but I had to get in and get Herbert out of the mess he was in. I succeeded in doing that. He got some bullets through his aircraft but eventually we got free. It was a very exciting encounter. Like most exciting encounters, there was no result. But I don't know who that red boy was.

Shortly after that I went home on leave and on my return found that the Commanding Officer, Tilney, had been killed, so for three or four days I commanded the squadron. When the RFC became the RAF on 1 April 1918, we had transferred to us from the Royal Naval Air Service, Major Dallas, who'd already had forty victories. Splendid chap, Australian – lots of guts. When we hadn't seen the Hun for a while he went over on his own to one of their aerodromes and dropped an old pair of boots on them with a label attached which said 'Officers, for the use of. You must be wearing out your boots, we haven't seen you in the air, so here's some more boots for you.' To add salt to their wounds, when they came out to pick them up, he dropped bombs on them! He came back laughing. We loved him.

I suppose he was too good for this world, because on 1 June we lost him – shot down while taking on three Triplanes. He was only with us a few weeks, but we got to know each other awfully well.

The Huns lost Richthofen, their ace, in April. He had eighty victories, but in my opinion he had no sense of chivalry, he wasn't attractive, he was just a killer, unlike Boelcke, who got one or two of the chaps from our squadron. He was polite. If he forced them down, he made sure they were all right when they got there.

On 25 July 1918 I heard I had been awarded a DFC and given command of a squadron at the Central Flying School. That great fighting Irishman, George McElroy, told me that he thought my departure was a bad sign. But I was tired, and happy to go home with my thirteen victories and my medal. On my final day we had a farewell lunch and Mick Mannock came over from the Ypres Salient with two of his Flight Commanders, which was a great compliment. At lunch Mick Mannock took McElroy to one side, they were good friends, and said to him, 'I understand, Mac, that you're following the Hun down to the deck. Stop it, don't do it, they will get you.' Six days later Mick was killed by ground fire following down a two-seater which he had hit. They had kept him out too long; he had lost his judgement. He had recorded seventy-four victories. Five days later George McElroy was shot down.

Flight Lieutenant Colin Falconer

I suppose I really got bitten by the RAF – it was the Royal Flying Corps in those days – when we used to go and stay with friends during school holidays in a place called Maybole, near Turnberry, in Scotland. They had a very good tennis court, and some of the RFC officers used to come and play tennis in the afternoon. That was really when I got bitten.

I started off at Cranwell in 1920. We were the first two-year lot of cadets. There were also some midshipmen and sub-lieutenants, who'd transferred over to the RAF, but we were really the first two-year intake. Later I got the first Sword of Honour there. Winston Churchill presented it, and Sir Hugh Trenchard was there.

From Cranwell I was posted to 14 Squadron in Palestine. I was out there with them from 1922 until 1928. First we were at Ramleh, and then we transferred in 1926 to Amman in Trans-Jordan. It was a very interesting place to be. I tried to fly around the Holy Land with a Bible, but got completely lost!

In Ramleh we were using First World War aircraft, Bristol Fighters. At Amman we moved on to D.H.9As. That was a delightful aeroplane, a real old gentleman's aircraft.

It was not an eventful life, for the most part. The only thing that happened of real interest, as far as I was concerned, was that I got wounded in 1924. Ibn Saud and the Wahabis had decided that they didn't like King Abdullah any longer. Ibn Saud sent a raiding party on camels up to Amman, and they were scattered by armoured cars. But there was a shortage of aircraft, and they called on us at Ramleh for a flight to help them out. So we spent the whole afternoon chasing the Wahabis away from Amman. And I got hit! I remember seeing two men up on a camel, and one hanging on by the tail. And one of them was a jolly good shot, because he had a crack at me, and the bullet broke one of the hinges on the elevator, went straight on through my arm, through the cockpit, and out through the engine cowling. My air-gunner produced a very oily handkerchief, which I think he'd been cleaning plugs with, and asked whether he could tie my wound up with that. I said 'no'. We got back safely without crashing, but I was bleeding hard.

In the early days at Ramleh we used to send a flight around various villages and black-tented camps, where the Arabs had their sort of parties. But it was purely a showpiece. So apart from those very few sorties over the villages the RAF didn't do a great deal. We had to go around to inspect landing-grounds, and check up that the petrol hadn't been stolen by the Arabs; and there was a certain amount of co-operation with the Palestine Gendarmerie.

There was some very good flying. Messages were picked up in a most interesting way. The Arab soldiers would stand with their backs to us, holding the message up on their lances while we flew over and plucked them off with the pick-up hook – not always an easy trick.

The Palestine Gendarmerie was spread all over Palestine, a company or so in each place near a landing-ground, and we used to go round to visit them and drop their letters and anything that they wanted. Once I had a fortnight's tour south of Palestine, looking for landing-grounds. That was all on camels, escorted by a nice lot of Palestine Gendarmerie.

We thoroughly enjoyed the life, it was a very nice climate there. We had an Officers' Club in Sarafand. Once a week there was a dance. The families were living in quarters which had been condemned by the Army in 1914. I met my wife when she was four, when her father was posted to Palestine HQ. I knew him quite well. I didn't meet her again until she was an Air Force widow already with a little boy, and within six weeks we were married. My future wife's family had been the first children to arrive, but once they were out there, quite a lot of other families came out as well.

The countryside in Palestine was very beautiful. All around Sarafand there were lovely orange groves and almond groves. It was very hot in the summer. It was very beautiful looking down on this country whilst flying, but you tended to see the scenery once and then you took it for granted.

After Ramleh I was posted to Amman. I was out there for a long time because I kept on volunteering. I had a horse there, though in Amman there was no hunting, just exercising.

We did the first single-engine night flight from Amman to Baghdad. The leader of our three was Flight Lieutenant Wigglesworth, who later went very high in the Air Force.

Once in Amman we were sent to rescue a Spanish fellow who was trying to fly around the world. He was following the track from Baghdad to Ziza, and he ran out of petrol. Instead of sitting by the aeroplane, he went walking. And of course we had to search for a couple of days to find him. He was alive and very angry. He didn't like being found.

Another task the squadron had there was to fly Peake Pasha, the GOC of the Trans-Jordan Army. He was with Lawrence in the Arab uprising, and we used to take him down to places like Aqaba. In fact I took him to one of the railway stations which he'd blown up. He went straight to one place and cleared away some sand, and there was a box of ammunition, which must have been there for ten years. It looked brand new.

I came home in 1928, and did a course at the Central Flying School. From there I was posted to 2 FTS, at Digby, to take over the D.H.9A flight. Later I formed 608 Auxiliary Air Force, North Riding Squadron, North Yorkshire, and was there until 1934.

From there I thought I would have a little rest from instructing for a short time. I put in for overseas, and got posted to No. 1 Armoured Car Company in Iraq. But I wasn't with them very long, because I was made PA to the AOC. He liked flying, so there weren't many places that we didn't land and go and visit. There was nothing much doing in Iraq then, there was no trouble. We had the Royal Exodus Hunt two days a week, that was splendid. You could also go pig-sticking, all of which I enjoyed very much indeed. And it wasn't expensive, because with two horses, a syce to look after them, and fodder, it came to something between ten and fifteen pounds a month on your mess bill. Not too bad at all. It was a very interesting posting. From there I went to No. 5 FTS as chief flying instructor.

I never dreamed there would be another war, not at that time. In 1939 I took over No. 142 Squadron and we landed in France the day before war was declared. In fact we heard Chamberlain declare war on the aircraft wireless set the next day. I served all the way through, though: the Western Desert, Italy and finally finished up AOC, Northern Ireland, taking over from my wife's father. My brother-in-law, Paddy Forsythe, was to fly with Bomber Command, and his son, Dick, commands a helicopter squadron at Middle Wallop.

Sergeant Bob Lucy

I joined the Aircraft Apprentices Wing at Cranwell in 1924 when I was nearly sixteen years old. It was a three-year course and we spent two years at Cranwell in No. 4 Wing and the third year at Halton. 1 Wing and 2 Wing were at Halton and 3 Wing, composed of people who were being trained as wireless operators, electricians and instrument makers, was based at Flowerdown in Hampshire. After two years they closed down the apprentices' wing at Cranwell and moved us to Halton as they had built a new barracks there for No. 4 Wing where I completed the final year of my training.

At the end of my training I was one of six who were finally selected for a cadetship at Cranwell College. I had to go to the Air Ministry for a medical examination before I could qualify for pilot training. I was graded temporarily unfit on the first visit, so I came back to Halton and after a fortnight I went up again; I was temporarily unfit again, and then a third time. The Air Force doctor at Halton said that as far as he was concerned I was fit, so he got four doctors to examine me. They all declared I was fit, so I went up to the medical board again, and of the four doctors there, three agreed I was fit and one was doubtful. I was sent for by the President of the Board, who said he had to turn me down on the grounds that I might crash and cripple myself, and then the Air Force would have to pay me a pension for the rest of my life. They compensated by making me a Corporal.

After a three-month course I passed out and joined the men's service. I went to Henlow, into the Engine Repair Section. Two months later, because I had been trained on the Jupiter VIII engine at Cranwell/Halton, I was made Corporal-in-Charge of a group of officers from the Engineer Officers' course, which trained officers to be engineers who had previously been pilots. I knew the Jupiter VIII inside out, and I had to instruct the officers on it. We had to take it to pieces, overhaul it, clean it, measure it up, and put it back together again.

Afterwards, as some sort of compensation, one of the officers on the engineers' course taught me to fly. So I did learn to fly, but never officially, and that was the end of it!

I was posted to the Cambridge University Air Squadron to assist in some research supercharging of aero-engines but I asked to be excused because I didn't want to be so far away from my girlfriend – now my wife. I put forward the name of a friend of mine who wanted to go. He was accepted and I was excused. Three months later they sent me to India! It was 1928, and I was nineteen. I went over there for five years, until 1933.

I was posted first to Kohat, on the North-West Frontier. I was the fitter for the Station Commander's own special aircraft, a DH9A; I looked after the engine and a Corporal rigger looked after the airframe. After I had been there about three months I asked to become an air-gunner, but I had to be in the squadron to do that. A switch was arranged with another Corporal and I joined 'B' Flight, 60 Squadron as a gunner.

We used to patrol up and down the valleys. The Frontier was really controlled by the Army but I think it had been decided that the Air Force would probably deal with the problems faster, and certainly more cheaply in terms of human life, because the Army had to march all over the place and had to deal with things from the ground whereas we could deal with it from the air.

There were many different tribes and they always seemed to fight a lot amongst themselves. There was always a lot of trouble up on the Frontier. These tribes used to pinch each other's cattle, women, chattels and so on, and a lot of them revolted against the government. About once a year the political agents used to hold a Durbar with all the tribal chiefs and mullahs, trying to spread the gospel and keep the peace. Very often they failed, and then we would wade in and help to separate the tribes. They were threatened with bombing first. The political agents used to go up to their villages and let them know what the position was, and if they didn't obey, they would be warned that on a certain date at a certain time aircraft would come over and bomb their crops. They warned them to get out of the villages and then we bombed the crops.

The pilot was in the front and the air-gunner in the back. The gunner had to lie on the floor, and the bombsight was attached to a bracket in a hole in the floor. You looked at the target through the floor and lined it up with the wires on the bombsight. You gave the directions through a speaking tube to the pilot! It was very crude. To drop a bomb you had a little cable with a ring on the end and you pulled the cable and released the bomb. We would drop them at anything up to ten thousand feet: it seems a fairly safe distance, but we were flying up valleys and these fellows used to get into the hills and fire down on to us sometimes. They very quickly learned the art of deflection; they were firing in front of the aircraft. Several times aircraft came back with bullet holes in them.

The tribesmen used Martini rifles but they'd do anything to get hold of a .303 Lee Enfield rifle which they used to copy. They were very clever like that. They used to get hold of the ammunition as well. On occasion we came under fire, usually just sporadic rifle fire. At one time they had a cannon which they used to fire at the aircraft, but it finally blew up.

I only remember two occasions when we were actively bombing; it might last for a month, die down, and then blow up again, over a period of about three to four months.

There were no casualties as a result of gunfire in our squadron, but we had the odd crashed aircraft. We used to carry what we called a Ransom Chit. That was a chit written in about twelve different dialects and it said that, if you returned this person to the Indian government alive, you would be given 10,000 rupees – a lot of money to them. The tribes had a nasty sort of ritual that entailed cutting off an enemy's testicles and stuffing them in his mouth. That was why we all had to carry these chits. We called them the 'gooley chits'.

Once, when flying, I got taken by tribesmen. Every week at Miranshah, a fort on the border of Afghanistan, a vehicle was sent back to base at Kohat, about 120 miles away, a good long day's journey on those roads. We used to bring back the airmen's pay, the mail, which all came from England by sea, and any spare parts for aircraft that were wanted. Once when I was in charge of the vehicle, we had left Banu and halfway along the road we broke down. Natives came up from the valley, towards us. We didn't quite know what to do, because I'd got about 1,000 rupees on me for airmen's pay. However they were friendly, took us back to the village and sent a runner up to Miranshah to let the Station know what had happened. They gave us bedding and entertainment for the night, too.

I first saw T. E. Lawrence when I was at Cranwell in 1926. My friend Jack Bonner had a motorbike with a side-car which I used to sit in. Every Saturday we used to take it down to Cranwell village to have a cup of tea and a teacake out of the five bob we'd been paid the day before. One day on the way down we were doing a steady 30mph, when an airman on a very, very large motorbicycle came up, rode alongside us, chatted across to Jock, then waved, and off he went. When we got into the café Jock said to me, 'You know who that was, do you?' I said, 'No, I don't'. So he said, 'Well you should, that was Lawrence of Arabia'. I was amazed. Apparently at some point, he'd lived in the same village as Jock. That was the first time I saw him.

When I got to Kohat I heard that Lawrence, or Aircraftsman Shaw as he was then, was at Miranshah. When it was our turn to do a stint up at Miranshah for a couple of months he was there as a storekeeper. He was his own man. Nobody knew him well, he was that sort of fellow. At the time it was said he was engaged in his spare time doing a translation of the *Odyssey*. They gave him dispensation not to sleep in the barrack rooms and put a bunk in the wireless hut for him. The wireless hut was situated away from the domestic quarters and was manned by Corporal Easton. Lawrence used to come to our mess for his meals, but he always went to the wireless hut to carry out his private work and to sleep. Occasionally he came into the barrack rooms, but not very often. He might just wander in of an evening and sit and talk with us, but very seldom.

I remember him telling us how he once got caught when he was sitting somewhere disguised as an Arab: he brushed a fly off his nose and one of the Arabs noticed it. He had to make a very rapid exit because natives never, never brush a fly off their nose. I remember him saying that.

I used to call at the stores now and again when Lawrence was the storekeeper and he was always very civil. Everyone respected him.

Leading Aircraftman Harold Andrews

From 1924 to 1927 I was an Engineering and Aircraft apprentice at the RAF School of Technical Training at Halton. We apprentices were known as 'Trenchard Brats' after Sir Hugh (later Lord) Trenchard who instituted the Aircraft Apprenticeship Scheme. He was enthusiastic about Halton and the Scheme. When the war came, the ground crews were virtually all ex-aircraft apprentices and they were the technical spine of the RAF.

The course I was on was a three-year engineering one with different specialisations such as riggers, electricians, and armourers, and I was an aero-engine fitter. I was in the fourth entry at Halton, each of which comprised six hundred apprentices. As well as the technical training, there was an academic branch to the school. We worked on half-assembled old aircraft and mock-ups to gain practical experience. At Halton aerodrome I experienced my first flight as a passenger in a Bristol Fighter and was pretty sick due to the aerobatics carried out by the pilot. For most of the first six-weeks' training at Halton I was working on a lump of cast-iron with a hammer and chisel. I had, together with the other apprentices, to chisel this into a hexagon and then file it up until it was smooth and absolutely precise. Then we had to make a female hexagon to slide over the male hexagon, in all twelve aspects.

We were only allowed one-thousandth of an inch error. We used to hold it and, if you could see any light between the two, it meant it was over one-thousandth of an inch. This was a very salutary baptism in the use of metal-working tools. The first few days produced many bruised hands and fingers.

We also worked in the workshops learning about internal combustion engines; we even had an engine from an old motorcycle. Here we learned all about petrol engines, four- and two-stroke cycles, and their design, servicing and repairs.

In 1927, at the end of my three years' apprenticeship, I passed out as an Aircraftman First Class (AC1); and was posted as an aero-engine fitter to 56 Fighter Squadron at Biggin Hill. This was a famous squadron that had contained the two First World War VCs, McCudden and Ball. The squadron was equipped with Gloster Grebes, and there was also a night-flying flight containing Vickers Vimys. With others, I used to man the flare path for them, which was cold work.

While I was at Biggin Hill we had a parachute display session given by an instructor from Henlow Parachute School. He attempted the world record delayed opening drop from 6,500 feet. He jumped backwards off the wings of a Vimy and we saw him coming down and down. We said to each other, 'Why doesn't he open his parachute? Why doesn't he open his parachute?' When he got about a hundred feet from the ground it suddenly opened, but it was too late to stop him from crashing on the road, right in front of a poor old chap on a motorbike. He was in a thick canvas Sidcot Suit which kept him together as he was just a lump of jelly inside. We had all volunteered for a parachute drop, but further practice drops were cancelled for the day.

The squadron moved from Biggin Hill to North Weald where

we were re-equipped with Armstrong Whitworth Siskin IIIAs and with supercharged Jaguar engines. I was sent on a supercharger course at Henlow, where I learned about balancing a fan at high speed both dynamically and aero-dynamically. When we had balanced the fan it was taken up to the Sergeant instructor for inspection. One day I went up to him and said, 'OK, Sarge, I think this is near enough.' He said, 'Near enough? It's got to be perfect, go back and get it right.' So I went back and put it right and then went back and said, 'OK, Sarge, it's all right now, it's absolutely perfect.' He said, 'OK, that's good enough.'

While at North Weald in 1929, I was posted to the RAF High Speed Flight. It had been in existence for some while and had gained the Schneider Trophy for Britain, in the 1927 competition in Italy. Flight Lieutenant Webster had come first in that competition in a Supermarine S5 with a 900hp Napier Lion VIIA engine; and Flight Lieutenant Worsley came second also in a Supermarine S5. After this race the High Speed Flight was disbanded but reformed for the 1929 competition when the United Kingdom was the host nation.

The High Speed Flight was made up of the best airframe riggers and aero-engine fitters from each of the fighter squadrons, and so it was quite an honour to be chosen. The race was to be held at Calshot in September 1929. In the original line-up the competitors included the Americans, French and Italians, but one by one they fell by the wayside. Only the Italians and us took part in the competition. We were looking after and servicing the aircraft, washing them down and refuelling them. We had to wear goggles and masks when refuelling with an exotic benzole, methanol and acetone mixture, which used to take all the paint off the floats. The 1929 race was won by Flying Officer Waghorn in a Supermarine S6 with a 1900hp Rolls-Royce 'R' engine; the Italian Warrant Officer, Dal Molin, came second in an Italian Macchi M.52R.

After the race we went back to our home unit, at RAF Marine Aircraft Experimental Station, Felixstowe. We spent the winter and the next year (1930) there. We had about half a dozen practice aircraft including a Fairey Flycatcher and the Gloster IVs. The pilots practised and we kept the planes serviced and prepared. We were conscious, having won the Schneider Trophy twice, that a third victory would lead to the UK holding the trophy permanently.

So in May 1931 we went down to Calshot to prepare for the race, which was to be held on 13 September. There was considerable concern about the financing of the competition. Ramsay MacDonald's government was not prepared to finance the British team and so private sponsorship was required. Lady Houston, the widow of the shipping magnate, Lord Houston, was approached and she agreed to put up the money. The Flight was commanded by Squadron Leader Orlebar with a new team of pilots including Flight Lieutenants Boothman, Long, Stainforth, Brinton and Hope. The total strength of the Flight was now between forty and fifty people. Ultimately the race was something of an anticlimax as no other country arrived to compete with the British team.

Yet there were considerable crowds to watch the British team take its 'fly-over'. The course was similar to the previous race consisting of seven laps of fifty kilometres. I was working on a pontoon used for launching the aircraft at sea and sometimes from the slipways of the Calshot Spit. We had had problems with one of the Rolls-Royce engines of the Supermarine S6B when white metal was found in one of the filters. All the Rolls-Royce engineers in the area for the race were called in and they changed the complete cylinder block of one engine. The white metal was due to piston scuffing on the cylinders.

At Calshot I came across Aircraftman Shaw, also known as Lawrence of Arabia. He was staying aboard Lady Houston's yacht. I met him outside the hangars where the pilots had been changing. He said to me, 'Do you know, Andrews? I've just seen a naked man.' He had a rather wry smile on his face.

I got more experience of flying in the run-up to the 1931 race. It was our practice on the Flight to have another aircraft shadow the main race aircraft. I used to go up with Flight Lieutenant

Long and we did some pretty tight turns. It was common for pilots to black out when going through their practice runs, some of them for considerable periods of time, which was a bit unsettling for their passengers!

The day of the race was like a public holiday. The race itself was a fly-over and Flight Lieutenant Boothman secured the trophy permanently for Britain in a Supermarine S6B by recording a speed of 340.08mph. We had a celebratory dinner for the Flight in Southampton. Two weeks later George Stainforth set a new world speed record at an average speed of 408.0mph. We all felt a considerable sense of team achievement.

1931 was the last year of the Schneider Trophy Races; because having won the trophy three times running it was now permanently Britain's to retain. It can be seen with the actual Supermarine S6B seaplane in the Science Museum in South Kensington, London.

Flight Lieutenant Tony Dudgeon

In the 1930s the RAF was on the North-West Frontier at the request of the Indian government. They wanted peace kept there because the Pathans and the Wazirs and all the people near the Frontier were a bunch of farmers who loved war. Fighting was their hobby. If they weren't fighting each other, they were fighting cousin Charlie. Generally, when the crops were in and they had some money in their pockets they would swoop down on the peaceful towns of the plains to rape, pillage and commit general mayhem to get what they could. They attacked anybody driving down the road, because their pockets were likely also to be filled. The Indian government wanted them kept down, so the RAF came; they were very happy to do it, since it was paid for by, dealt with at the request of, and also audited by the Indian government.

The objective was one which had started in the Sudan. Trenchard began by attacking the tribesmen, bombing and killing them. It was reckoned at that time to be the cheapest war that ever was: two squadrons did what two divisions would have been required to do on the ground. After the Sudan, in about 1921, came Iraq. But it was obvious that it was a bad idea to kill what we now call 'third world' people and so the procedure over the years transformed itself into what they called proscription – keeping the tribesmen off their farmland to touch their pockets. When a tribe was known to have misbehaved – by shooting some political agent, or whatever – we were sent to fly over their rural area with orders to attack anything that moved. Well, we never saw anything move. For four years I flew over there and I never saw anything moving but a donkey which they'd misguidedly allowed to get out of the cave they slept in! So, it touched their pockets because they couldn't work their farms. They could stop this at any moment by coming in and agreeing to behave and pay the fines exacted by the government.

If that didn't work, stage two was that we would be asked to go and knock down a house or a village. Usually the headman's village, because he was the fellow responsible. We would drop leaflets first, to warn them. There's a story about a Fakir who was one of the few people who could read. When the leaflets first came down saying the bombing would start in forty-eight hours, he said, 'Well, they came to bomb but I have turned the bombs to paper.' He got a lot of kudos for that. Then about forty-eight hours later, he said, 'I'm afraid my magic has been exhausted; I can't stop a second bombing.'

Only after the leaflet drop would we go out and bomb. When we bombed the villages, as far as possible, they were empty. I've since learned that perhaps they couldn't get all their flocks out and would leave some of the women behind to look after the flocks and report looters. So there may have been some human beings, but then that is the East: women are chattels.

The only real danger for us was that we might have engine failure, and quite naturally the people down below were fairly stroppy about what was happening to them. They would hand you over to the women. The women would emasculate you and sew what are called the 'family jewels' into the various orifices in your head, so that you were blind and unable to speak and unable to eat. And as you go to Nirvana the way you die, you'd have a rotten old time through all eternity.

Unless, of course, you had red hair. Red-headed people (or people who go to Mecca and are allowed to dye their beards red) are guaranteed a place in heaven. There is an apocryphal story about an air-gunner who was shot down, way back in the Bristol Fighter days, who had red hair and was promptly put to stud! The kudos, the status of a wife who had a red-headed child, would be very high indeed.

We had a wonderful life, apart from the fact, as always, that a junior officer did not get an awful lot of money. We lived in a mess. Being a pukka sahib – white man in other words – I had servants and lived in a bungalow, shared with one other person. I had my own bedroom and sitting-room and bathroom, and I had my Bearer. In the morning, when I went to the bathroom a length of toothpaste had been squeezed out and laid on my toothbrush. When I was dressing he would hold first one shoe out to me and then the other. He would hold my trousers out in front of me so that I could put my feet in. Next, when I was nearly dressed, he would grab my bicycle and dart off up to the mess so that, when I sauntered in about ten minutes later, my scrambled eggs would be on my plate and a chair pulled back for me to sit in. He also had a chokra, a boy who did most of his work. There was another man who washed my clothes and shirts; in the hot weather you didn't put anything on twice, and you had three changes of clothes a day. Then I had a gardener, shared with the chap next to me, and a sweeper who emptied the thunder box and boiled up water for my bath, and a night-watchman to keep the budmarshes or bad men away. So that was six servants to be paid for, some shared, by one pilot officer.

We couldn't afford girls – they were much too expensive. They liked to drink hard drink; we drank beer. We did a lot of swimming and most of us had some kind of hobby. There was a Cavalry unit down the road, and if you would pay for some extra food for remounts then you could have a couple of horses and a syce for next to nothing. So I used to go out riding every morning before dawn. I had my movie camera, and a Leica. I also went shooting, to shoot near-partridge called chikor and duck. We played a lot of games. I kept racing pigeons, and when we played football at another station one of my racing pigeons would bring back the score. We would also go out for picnics in places like the Khyber Pass.

But for me – mad about aeroplanes and flying as I've always been – the flying was absolutely unbelievable! The Frontier itself, where the tribesmen lived, wasn't awfully high: the hills would go up to about 8,000 or 10,000 feet. But when the weather was good, usually in the spring, all around you there was the pure magic of the Himalayas which reach up to over 25,000 feet, topped by mountains like Nanga Parbat and Rakaposhi. We couldn't fly over them because we had no oxygen; we had to fly up the valleys. Of course you never flew up there by yourself. Some of the valleys were fairly steep, going straight down to a foaming torrent at the bottom. From the white, foaming torrent, you could look up the sides of the valleys, through the greens and browns of the lichens and earth and rocks, to the snow line, around 12,000 or 14,000 feet, and then another 10,000 feet on top of that. When the sun shines down on the snow the valleys go a wonderful icy blue, and then, when the sun is pouring through some clouds, the snow can be pink and gold, while above that you have the high altitude sky which is a wonderful dark blue. If the weather closed in you had to come out underneath it down the valley; I have flown down those valleys – with cloud on the top and the two sides going down to a foaming torrent down at the bottom – through a sort of triangular hole in the middle. It was unbelievable, stunningly beautiful and stunningly dangerous. You forgot, practically, that if your engine failed you were dead.

The trips we did far into the mountains from time to time – to inspect landing-grounds – were very much sought after, partly because of the pictures you could get. Drosh, for example, was about 4,000 or 5,000 feet up with a great big cliff face at its end and a fort on the top where the Army lived. We used to take the Army garrison kippers and sausages and other unobtainable goodies, inspect the landing-ground and then come out again. You took off in the opposite direction away from the fort, and climbed like crazy. Once we went as far as we could go without going over the Afghan border, a terrible political crime! Beyond us, 25,000 feet high, was Tirichmir. My Flight Commander allowed me to break off from the flight of four, and take photographs.

Why I didn't kill myself now and again with the asinine things I did I don't know. Life was fairly crazy and junior pilots used to do some pretty stupid things to give themselves a thrill. I found that low flying was the most tremendous fun. One day I took my wings under the branches of a tree and out the other side, and it was great! I loved it and I did this quite a bit. Then another time I found a place with two trees and I flew through the hole in the middle and out the other side with my wheels two or three feet above the ground.

One day a Flying Officer Darbyshire came and said he was bored to bloody tears and wanted to come flying with me. So I said, 'Well, why not? We'll get an aeroplane, and go somewhere.' As we were climbing in, he said, 'Tony, give me a thrill or something, will you?' I came to an irrigation canal and I flew down it with my wheels just above the water and my wing tips just above the banks. Then I saw in front of me two trees on either side of the banks with a hole in the middle, so I went through the hole, wing tips right down on the banks. As I got through the hole, I discovered I was in an avenue and was flying along the canal with my wheels just above the water, trees on either side and branches over the top. So I throttled back as far as I dared and waited. Suddenly I came to a small gap and I pulled hard back on the stick, and BANG! There was a horrible crack, but I was above the trees and still flying. When I got home, the Flight Sergeant said, 'You been chasing birds, Mr Dudgeon? You've got twigs in both your wing tips.' That was the most idiotic thing I ever did in all my born days. Darby just tottered away and never said a word.

In those days we averaged three deaths a year out of 24 flying pilots. That meant the average life of a pilot was something over 1,000 hours flying before he killed himself. It was a dangerous game.

Once I was flying alongside Wally Rowbottom when he had engine failure and finished up on his nose in tribal territory. I watched him go down and whizzed off, but the nearest landing-ground was several miles outside the nearest Army camp. I landed on their polo pitch inside the camp. A polo pitch is only 300 yards long. So I came over trees at one end and just got her down in the 300 yards – it pleased me a lot. The Army sent troops out and picked up Wally. The Army CO wrote to my CO a little while later. Could he ask his pilots not to land on their polo pitch because the mark of the tail skid made a great gouge across it and grass was difficult enough to grow in this country? Moreover, there was a landing-ground only a few miles down the road, could they please use that? My Squadron Commander wrote back and said he was awfully sorry but it had been an emergency, a matter of life and death. Believe it or not, the Army chap then asked if we could please give them adequate warning of an emergency so they could prepare the polo-ground to land on!

One of our jobs was to reinforce Singapore or Egypt if a war came along. So each year we used to do a practice flight to Singapore, or to Egypt. I did both. Singapore was 3,400 miles; a long way in those days. We flew there with landings at Ambala, Cawnpore, Gaya, Calcutta, Chittagong, Rangoon, Mergui, Victoria Point, Alor Star, Taiping, Singapore. All our own pilot-navigation. We had no radio, no radar; map-reading all the way. You flew it and did the calculations yourself. Your passenger was either a fitter, or a rigger, or an NCO. Flying over the Malayan jungles was a different kind of danger. From above they look like giant cow-parsley gone mad. If you crashed you just went through the 200-foot-high trees and down to the ground beneath. That was the end of that. Or you could jump out in your parachute and starve to death caught up high in the branches. Nobody ever talked to us about jungle survival or anything useful like that. We just flew.

When we reached Singapore we had been flying for a week, doing 500 miles a day. You got up in the morning before dawn, packed up your bedroll, went down to the airfield, put your bedroll in the containers under the wings, did your daily inspection, got into the aeroplane, and flew off, probably at 8.00 a.m. You flew for about two-and-a-half hours to your next airfield, where you landed, parked your aeroplane, filled it up from a dozen four-gallon cans and did a check on your aeroplane; got back in, flew another two-and-a-half hours, and landed the other end. You then did any maintenance necessary on your machine, refuelled it again, put the covers on to protect it from rain and anchored it down with ropes tied to three enormous steel corkscrews, screwed down into the ground. You took your bedroll out of the aeroplane, went up to the resthouse at the top, unpacked your bedroll, and had some kind of dinner. Then, of course, the local expatriates would come round and want you to drink with them. They would be terribly charming: they probably hadn't seen a strange face for about a year. You'd get to bed about 9.30 to 10.00 – to be up before dawn next day. When we got down to Singapore we were asked out to dinner, and somewhere around the soup course, I am told, I put my head down on the table and went sound asleep! Everybody thought I was pissed. I was actually out, completely and utterly out. I was only twenty years old.

Leading Aircraftman Harry Ward

As a young man I wanted to be an artist but when, in 1921, I left the Bradford School of Art my family couldn't send me to the Slade or the Royal Academy School because we were too poor. But I had a friend who'd joined the Royal Naval Air Service at the age of sixteen, and he was enjoying it. They were plugging the RAF about that time – since it had only been formed in 1918 – and they'd brought out this new blue uniform which looked so glamorous. I decided I'd have a go. I joined on my eighteenth birthday.

I went to the recruiting office in Leeds, from there to Uxbridge to be kitted out, and then was posted to the School of Technical Training at Manston, where I was trained as a carpenter rigger. I was there till 1923, and was then posted to Northolt.

I was settled in at Northolt within a month. Our CO there was a famous First World War flyer, Squadron Leader Collishaw. Collishaw was a legend; when he came on a posh parade he seemed to be flying left wing low with all his medals. He'd got everything but the VC. There were two squadrons at Northolt, 41 Fighter and 24 Army Co-op, as well as the Inland Area Communication Flight which I was in. I did a hell of a lot of flying there in all sorts of kites. Flight Lieutenant Leslie Hollinghurst taught me to fly his Bristol Fighter. Aircraft in those days were wooden with fabric-covered wings, and it was my job to look after the airframe of his plane.

Hollinghurst belonged to Air Defence of Great Britain Headquarters, and he used to take me on his flights to visit RAF exercise camps. The aircraft was dual control and he'd let me take over and fly from the rear cockpit till he took over to land. On occasion he put me in the front seat of the Bristol.

Early in 1925, two officers, Soden and Pierce, were sent to the States to take a look at the Irving parachute. When they came back they formed part of a travelling parachute section, based at Northolt, which was set up by Flight Lieutenant Soden. It had a couple of engine fitters, two riggers and Sergeant Woods to fly the aircraft. Corporal East taught me to pack chutes.

One day Soden came in to where I was packing up the chutes. I wasn't too concerned. I thought he was checking me out. He watched as I stowed the lines and then the canopy, and when I had closed the pack and was jamming the rip-cord pins home, he suddenly asked, 'Would you jump with that?' 'Of course,' I said. I thought he was testing my competence. 'Come on then,' he said. 'Let's do it.'

What a mug! There was no way out. I had committed myself. But I wasn't going to duck out and be thought a chicken. I found myself with Corporal East helping me into a Sidcot flying suit and checking the buckles and rip-cord ring. Everyone was grinning around me.

Soon the word got around the camp: 'Harry is going to jump' ... All the 'erks' were running down to the airfield to watch. 'You must be barmy!' That's what they were saying, as East put me on this tiny platform which had been added to the lower wing of the Vimy.

Sergeant Woods, the pilot, grinned and said, 'Don't let go, not until I tell you.' As if I would!

The engines roared away and the whole kite was shaking as it taxied across the field ... I was terrified, terrified. Then it took off. I tell you I clung to that strut like a lover. It seemed an age to climb 2,000 feet. Then I could see Corporal East signalling from the cockpit for me to turn around. Hugging that strut as hard as I could I inched round until I felt the full blast of the wind in my face. I clutched hold of the ring in one hand, then East lowered his hand and I pulled the ring. For a second nothing happened, then the chute opened and pulled me off, and I found myself looking through my legs at the Vimy disappearing in the distance. Then the chute was above me. It was the most beautiful thing I'd ever seen. I floated to the ground, and just lay there, laughing. That was April 1926.

Then in 1927 East was killed on a long-delay drop and I was asked to be a member of the team, although I had only made the one jump. We travelled from station to station demonstrating the parachute, which wasn't at all popular among RAF pilots in those days. Everybody thought them dangerous!

We were trying to demonstrate to pilots that the parachute was a safe thing to wear, because they thought they were inviting trouble by wearing these and they didn't fancy the idea of jumping out and abandoning their plane. So we used to go round to all different squadrons trying to convince them to wear chutes.

We used to do free falls then, from the rear cockpit – from the old Vimy. I carried on doing this until about the end of September 1927, at which time they decided they'd do away with the touring team and station us permanently at Henlow. But rather than stay at that damn awful place I put in for a posting to Hendon.

I went to 601 Squadron, which was an auxiliary squadron, at my old trade – carpenter rigger. Promotion was slow and the future looked bleak. So I left the RAF in 1929.

I got a job driving a London bus. Solid tyre jobs. A few of us got together and formed the Busmen's Flying Club. We used to meet in a pub in Camden Town and we got the LGOC – the London General Omnibus Company, as it was then – to agree to deduct sixpence a week from all the members of the LGOC sports club so that we could buy a plane. We bought a Redwing, and went to Herts and Essex Flying Club at Broxbourne. I finally took my official pilot's licence in 1932, flying a Cirrus Moth. I was also doing a few jumps here and there. An American parachute company had opened up at a place in Stoke Newington. Their chute was called the Lobe. It was a good chute, and I went over there to see if there was any chance of jumping for them. John Tranum, the famous Danish parachutist, was their regular demonstrator. I did a few jumps standing in for him.

In 1933 I left the buses and joined Cobham's Air Circus fulltime. I got £15 a week and £2 per jump. We did 180 towns a year. I generally jumped twice a day. Straight out of the cockpit, all free falls. Cobham was a very hard taskmaster: he wanted the best and he saw that he got it. If you weren't any good you were out.

I left Cobham at the end of 1933 and joined 'The British Hospitals Air Pageant' in 1934 and stayed with them. It was the same kind of thing only under a different name and I was with them up until the end of 1937. We toured the whole of the British

Isles including the Irish Free State. I was jumping from an old Avro 504 biplane. The kite would come over at only 1,000 feet, because the public wanted to see you clambering over the sides and dropping off. Then you delayed for a couple of hundred feet or so before you ripped. The idea was to land bang in front of the crowd. One season I did double jumps – 'parachute races' – with a chap named Bill Hire.

In 1934 I did a tour of India, and when I returned I joined the same old crew under the new name 'Jubilee Air Pageant'. We went on much as before: I made a couple of mistakes and jumped with broken ribs and even with my foot in a cast. For a while I also jumped with a pair of what looked like bat wings from 6,000 feet!

But by 1937 people were getting blasé about air shows. I got a few jobs in films, at £50 a jump, £6 a day standing by. But in 1937 the whole business folded up. I only got sixpence in the pound from what was owed me. So I joined Imperial Airways as a mechanic and then, in 1938, went into the RAF as a civilian instructor at Cosford.

When war broke out in 1939, I put in for a commission and got it. In 1940, I went down to the Air Ministry and there was my old friend Leslie Hollinghurst. He had just been made a Group Captain, and he told me they were opening a parachute school at Ringway, Manchester. Within a month I was there. I met up with some of my old Air Circus friends: Louis Strange was our CO, and our chief pilot on the Air Show, E. B. Fielding, was in charge of flying. Bruce Williams and Bill Hire, who used to parachute with me, completed the team. So there were five of us, all from civil aviation. Nobody else knew anything about parachuting, and we didn't know much about the military. We were to train Army volunteers, who were sent in batches, and we had to do it from three old Whitley bombers, which weren't ideal for the purpose!

When I arrived, it had just started, and I took over as Chief Parachute Instructor. Just before Christmas 1940 I was sent down to Cardington to try out a balloon of the type that had been used for parachuting displays by Major Spencer before the First World War. We got the balloon up to Ringway in March 1941, but we had to do over two hundred jumps from it before the Army would permit their people to train from it. We had balloons made specially, of 60,000 cubic feet. We used to put them up to 500 feet for jumping.

The trainees' first drops were done from a Whitley until we got the balloon. They would have a bit of ground training first, jumping through mock-ups, and then a bit of air experience – we would take them to Tatton Park and let them see some jumps. Then we'd take them up and put them out in singles, and we had a few casualties.

We trained X troop of 11th SAS Battalion (later 1st Parachute Battalion) for the first operational drop by British airborne forces in February 1941. It was to be a night drop; that was all we knew. Night parachuting is doubly difficult, as visibility can be a problem, and the ground would be hard. We lost one of the trainees when he was blown off course and through the ice of a pond.

In February they went off to their secret assignments to blow up the aqueduct at Tragino in Italy. The operation was a success but all thirty-eight men were captured.

PART TWO

THE SECOND WORLD WAR 1939–1945

2

THE FALL OF FRANCE AND THE BATTLE OF BRITAIN

The RAF, which had 1,911 combat-ready aircraft to oppose Germany's 3,609, began offensive operations the day war was declared, 3 September 1939. Gallant, but usually ineffectual daylight operations against German naval harbours demonstrated above all that bombers could not protect themselves against fighters – of 22 Wellingtons raiding Wilhelmshaven on 18 December 1939, twelve were shot down and three more crashed on return. Winter night-raids with leaflets or puny bomb-loads exposed the problems of navigating and finding targets, and the dangers of aircraft icing.

France, Belgium, Holland, 1940
The RAF's Advanced Air Striking Force in France (eight squadrons of vulnerable Fairey Battles, two of Blenheims, three of Hurricanes) and the British Expeditionary Force's Air Component (five squadrons of Lysanders, four of Blenheims, four of Hurricanes) fought desperately against the Blitzkrieg of May 1940.

The Battles and Blenheims were virtually annihilated attacking advancing German columns, though in quality, if not in numbers, the Hurricanes held their own. Eventually the equivalent of sixteen Hurricane squadrons fought from France. Spitfires, conserved for home defence, first fought in strength over the Dunkirk evacuation. In the six-weeks battle of France, the RAF (and Fleet Air Arm) lost over 900 aircraft, including 450 fighters.

The Battle of Britain, 1940

A German invasion of Britain depended upon the Luftwaffe defeating the RAF and then neutralising the Royal Navy which was otherwise strong enough to defeat any German fleet. German air attacks on coastal towns and shipping began in July 1940. By August, 52 RAF fighter squadrons (660 aircraft, 1,300 pilots) faced three German 'Air Fleets' of 2,600 aircraft. The destruction of RAF Fighter Command was the Luftwaffe's objective and the all-out assault began on 13 August. Despite the effectiveness of radar, systematic ground control of the squadrons, the 'Ultra' translations of the Luftwaffe's secret radio codes, the RAF faced crisis by early September with over 400 fighter aircraft lost, 230 pilots killed and wounded, and front line airfields and radar sites devastated. The shortage of pilots was the most serious deficiency, for the vital airfields were saved when Hitler switched the offensive to bombing London in retaliation for weak RAF night raids on Berlin. Far from drawing the battered RAF squadrons into a final battle, the onslaught on London gave Fighter Command a vital respite. The airfields were patched up, and the casualties replaced. It was enough. The Germans failed to achieve daylight air superiority over south-east England; their invasion fleet was relentlessly bombed in the Channel ports by night and, on 17 September, Hitler abandoned the invasion plan though air fighting continued throughout October and the German night bombing 'Blitz' continued until spring 1941. RAF Fighter Command lost about 1,000 aircraft; the Germans 1,733. Britain's survival in 1940, at a cost of over 510 fighter pilots killed, was decisive to the outcome of the war.

Aircraftwoman Elsie Bartlett

All types turned up at Hallam Street to enlist: short, fat, thin, small, dowdy, glamorous; typists and shop-girls, married and single, from all walks of life. They were fussy about who they took at the beginning, and I hadn't a lot going for me – what with spinal curvature and bad eyes. However, I slipped in as a C3 and, by that evening, was in Harrogate with the King's shilling and a sore arm from injections.

The Grand Hotel must have been grand once, but when we arrived there was no heating or lifts. We marched round the gardens opposite, all wearing a strange collection of garments. I had on my camel coat, brown hat and brown suede high-heeled shoes. Marching in that lot was awful, but we were given our uniforms soon afterwards.

Just before Christmas, we were sent to an empty boys' school called Pannal Ash. It was so cold our toilet bags froze solid. And it snowed and snowed and snowed – so much that we couldn't even get down to the station. I don't know why, but everyone else was sent off in twos and threes, except for me. I was always sent off alone. When I got my posting, I opened it and read 'RAF Dunkirk'. Well, I nearly had heart failure! My God, I thought, things must be dodgy.

My Dunkirk turned out to be a village in Kent. So there I was, a small WAAF weighed down in a heavy greatcoat, hat pulled down tight, carrying a gas mask, a tin hat, a case, a kitbag almost as big as me, and clutching my orders and a packet of Spam sandwiches. Off I staggered to Kent.

The camp stood well hidden in the middle of a wood. All the staff worked at the Radio Location (RL) camp which was much further up the hill. I shared my hut with Corporal Beet, a medical orderly; Marie, a batwoman; Dixie and Dot, who were kitchen bods; and Rose from the office. It was like Alaska in that hut. Draughts swept through it like miniature blizzards, and I quickly perfected the art of getting dressed under the blankets. I didn't get to know many other people there as RL was very hush-hush, although the Special Police would bring us dogsbodies a cup of tea with our early morning call, which was nice. We were all kept very busy by our Flight Sergeant – once I was sent to scrub the fire buckets, inside and out! I think she was something to do with the First World War. She was very fierce, with an Eton crop, and a face which would have scared even a German. In fact, I often wondered why she wasn't on their side.

I started off scrubbing floors and walking our officer's dog. Then, after a while, I was sent to the kitchens to work for the LACW there, a real bully called Joan. She can't have been fond of soap and water, because there was always a great tide-mark around her neck, and her overalls concealed drab, grey underwear. However, she was friendly with one of the gunners, and as they always met in the dark I suppose he never noticed! Still, I'm sure Joan smirked as she watched me try to tackle the big iron pots we used for porridge. It took two WAAFS even to lift them. When I had the chance of going into Canterbury to get rations with the Catering Sergeant, I jumped at it.

The Catering Sergeant persuaded me to go on a course as a catering clerk – which meant that I got all the dirty work on the books while she swanned around doing nowt! I'd never been good at figures, and this entailed working out how many sausages we'd need to feed hundreds of airmen . . . I could see myself getting into real trouble.

Halfway through the course, which was held at Melksham in Wiltshire, a pal and I got forty-eight-hour passes and decided to go home. We got stuck for a lift on the way back, and when we phoned the camp from Reading station we were told to stay put, we'd be collected the next morning. We were pretty fed-up about this, and when an Army tender drew up, offering us a lift, we accepted. He dropped us right outside our guardroom. Now this was the time when spies were supposed to be dropping out of the sky dressed as nuns, so extra soldiers were walking around, all with their fingers on the triggers. Suddenly, as we were making our way in the pitch black dark, a voice bellowed, 'Advance and be recognised!' A rifle bolt clicked back. We were petrified. To cap it all, our hut had been changed round over the weekend, and all our gear shifted. We stumbled around, banging into things, and being cursed soundly. What a night! The sound of that rifle put years on me.

Our exam came round the next week. The menu was brown stew and jam pudding, and if the exam bods could put a knife into the pudding you passed! Now I was allowed to wear a white apron and a turban, but I still hated cooking, so I asked to be re-mustered back. At least scrubbing floors and dog-walking had variety!

Soon I was off again, travelling north with a fellow WAAF to Cardington. It was a fraught train journey, sitting wedged between a morose sailor and a tipsy Highlander, and being sat on by a fat Army ATS. We arrived at an immense place, full of great big girls, all very brawny and striding about in battledress with knives stuck in their belts. A red-faced Sergeant collared us at once: 'Stand up straight, you dozy pair! Wait here!' My friend and I looked at one another, and as soon as the Sergeant went into the office, we picked up our gear and hitched a lift on a tender to the balloon site in Rotherham.

Flight Lieutenant Frank Carey

I was a fully-trained pilot when war broke out. I had joined the RAF in 1927, and had four years' flying experience and even one year on Hurricanes before anything started. In November 1939 I was sent to a North Sea station from Tangmere with 43 Squadron.

It was a very, very cold winter. We were in a sort of hutted camp in Acklington, which is not the warmest place at the best of times! Our first important task there was to find a way to cope with the Germans who used to come over with an individual Heinkel 111 when the cloud base was at about 1,000 feet. They'd pick out small fishing boats and coastal shipping and bomb and strafe them. Our job was really to clobber these chaps. This was very difficult because, if they spotted us, they went up in cloud and hid for a while and came back down again, for as long as they had fuel. I don't know how we thought of it, but one day the idea came that we should keep right on the deck – because you can't be seen nearly as well if you're skating across the sea at nought feet. The moment we did that we started to have success. We hit them before they could clamber up and get away. It made all the difference.

Then we went from Acklington up to Wick in Scotland. By that time the weather was getting a little warmer; it was March. We thought that we would be even further away from the action, but suddenly we had a raid on Scapa Flow. So we even had fun up there.

I was then commissioned, and went straight to France with 3 Squadron from Kenley. We patrolled the front line, wherever it happened to be at the time. The Hun aircraft were all over the place – you just took off and there they were. If you flew anywhere in the Pas de Calais or east over Belgium, there were lashings of them, absolutely asking for it. And they had very few fighters about at that time. Over the first four days after my arrival, I must have had about twenty engagements. I shot down what I think was about fourteen aircraft in that period. I didn't get out of my clothes because we had nowhere except the floor to sleep. We had nowhere to eat. We used to ask the ground crew to get bits and pieces from the local village and bring it out to us. On my fourth day there, I was finally given a billet. So I picked up my kit – which was still on a big pile at the edge of the airfield – and took it to this place. I was on the dawn shift the next morning, so I couldn't sleep there, and I thought – tomorrow night I'll have a bath and I'll have a sleep. And then I was shot down.

I was attacking a Dornier 17 and it did a snap half-roll – which was an extraordinary thing for a kite of that size to do. I did the same and followed it closely down. It was nearly vertical; in fact, the pilot was dead, I think, because it just went straight on in. But before I'd realised that, the rear-gunner fired and hit me well and truly. Stupidly, perhaps, I'd been following it rather close – because it was such a fast aircraft and I knew it could get away from me. If I'd known the pilot was dead, of course, I wouldn't have bothered. Then I was busy getting down myself. First of all, I was on fire. So I thought, right, I must get out. I thought what

I had to do in my mind, pulled the thing up into nearly a stall, and stood up. Of course with a 100mph draught over me I got thrown back, and my parachute pack got caught up in the hood. Well, of course the aircraft slowly got itself into a dive, and the faster it went, the harder it was for me to get out. Eventually, I climbed up on to my own legs to get back into the cockpit. Then of course my ticker was going at a fairly fast rate; but at least the fire seemed to have gone out and I was able to select a big ploughed field and had no difficulty in getting it down. When I stood up in the cockpit I heard a little clink – it was the core of an armour-piercing bullet which had come straight through the engine and finished up in my parachute! I knew I'd been hit in the leg, but didn't know how lucky I'd been till I examined the bullet holes in my trousers: I could have finished up with a very different category of voice! I was very lucky because I was in what they would have called, in the First World War, No-Man's-Land. The British ground forces had retired to a river a few miles back just the night before.

Being ignorant of the changed circumstances on the ground I started walking due east, which was quite the wrong way. I'd gone quite a distance when I heard two motorcycles coming. I pulled out my revolver to sell myself dearly and greeted these two chaps by shouting at them to halt. I didn't know who they were. When they started to talk it was even more confusing because they were Belgian motorcyclists who had been on a morning patrol and had met some German tanks up the road. They'd seen me come down and they jolly bravely went across a lot of ploughed fields to where I was – and they were greeted by a revolver! I got on the back of one of these motorbikes and they rushed me back. But all the time, of course, they were pretty worried about being caught themselves. They left me with four or five British sappers who were blowing up a bridge we had just come over, which saved me a swim across the river.

I then took up walking with the refugees along the roads; we were regularly strafed by Heinkel 111s. Then a British Army truck came along and took me to a village somewhere south of Brussels.

I had a slight leg wound, and they said there was an Army Medical Officer in one of the houses. I went along to see him, and he gave me some brandy and cleaned up my leg quite painlessly.

Then I was put on another truck for a while and joined up with a bloke who had the best part of a Blenheim front end in his eyes, and his bomb-aimer, who had only one hand. They'd been shot down a few miles from where I was. They were strafing one of the German columns and ran into a solid block of anti-aircraft guns, which threw an awful lot of stuff at them. It blew the nose off a long-nosed Blenheim straight into his face and took a hand off the front bomb-aimer. Of course, the pilot only had very imperfect sight through all the bits of perspex in his face and eyes; he crash-landed it with what little he could see plus the directions of the one-armed bomb-aimer. They'd done their best to bury the rear-gunner who had been killed outright, and collected the contents of his pockets for his next of kin. They not only brought back their parachutes, they'd disconnected the gun and brought it with them, too. And they'd crossed a river with that lot! I thought they were fantastic. It sort of pulls you back and makes you think how proud you are of them. There was I, limping along, thinking I was badly wounded! It took all the limp away from me, I can tell you.

We then got into a 1914 Crossley ambulance, where they asked us if we would hold down a poor chap who was badly shattered in the pelvis with a bit of shrapnel. We were taken to a casualty clearance station which was just over the French border. That took an hour or two and it was a very bumpy trip; the poor devil was screaming his head off. On arrival, I sat on a bench in a tented camp with a lot of other people, delighted to sit down stationary at last. Then I don't remember any more, and they said that, by the time it was my turn to be dealt with, I was fast asleep. Well, I'd had four nights with almost no sleep and no clean clothes – I must have smelt to high heaven. They dressed my wounds – they didn't bother about any anaesthetic, put me into a bed, and I woke up late the following day.

I was taken out of this casualty clearing station to a Dieppe hospital; I finished up in a ward where there were only four of us. There was the Blenheim pilot, a chap with meningitis, me and the Duke of Norfolk – a very nice fellow, very shamefaced because he was in with gout! We played Rummy for two or three days. But the Hun was moving along fast and getting closer, and eventually the commander of the hospital decided to evacuate everybody. He arranged for a hospital train, and we had just settled into our seats when a couple of dozen Heinkels came and unloaded everything they had on us. They hit the train. That was when the boat *Maid of Kent* was sunk in Dieppe harbour: it was alongside the train. The interesting thing was that, when the bombing started, there was I with the leg, limping again, and His Grace with gout, and it was touch and go who was beating whom! We did about a hundred yards in four seconds! Then we felt rather sheepish because we could see all the fire and damage behind us, so we sort of tottered back and did what we could to save the seriously wounded and move them into the part of the train that wasn't burning. The walking wounded then disconnected the burning part of the train. The French driver had already unhooked his engine and disappeared. Then we pushed the train out. It was very flat there, and once we got it moving it was all right to keep it going. We pushed it out of the danger area – probably about a mile or so. Those that were able to just leaned against it. It staggered me that we were able to do it, but we did. We were left with a very limited number of medical supplies and no Medical Officer that I could remember seeing; but several medical orderlies did a wonderful job. We also got our driver and engine back once the bombs had stopped. After two or three days we finished up in La Baule, a well-known resort town right on the Atlantic coast. There the Hermitage, an immensely posh hotel, was the officers' hospital.

Suddenly it was impossible to believe that there was any war going on at all. All lights were on, we had strawberries and cream – we were in totally new surroundings! And very thankful we were for it, too. The next thing was that they were going to evacuate that hospital back to England. Much to our disgust, the chap with the damaged eyes and I were discharged back to the nearest Royal Air Force unit, which was an aircraft stores depot not too far away from Nantes. I was still in the same uniform; it was full of bullet holes, but at least the shirt had been washed. There we joined up with two similar RAF derelicts. None of us knew where our units were, so we were stuck.

In the second week of June we got a message that there was a British aircraft on an adjacent airfield that somebody had left several days previously. It was a Bristol Bombay – a bright yellow transport plane. We checked it over and filled it up with some petrol we got from a small French Air Force contingent there. The next morning at dawn we left, all four of us. They put me in the back at the rear-gun, as I was the only one who had fired a gun. All the way back I was trying to find out how to work the thing! We felt very naked, I can tell you – a bright yellow plane, clear blue sky and doing about 120mph! We were not sure where the front line was: the whole place was a mass of rumours. Even the Forces broadcasts didn't seem to know where anybody was. We had to take our chance. We didn't see a thing until we got just off the English coast, where the British fighters intercepted us. There were all sorts of funny-looking aircraft coming from the Continent over those days; nobody took a pot at us. Everybody knew what we were – bright yellow, 120mph – complete lunatics! They could have hit us with rocks.

We landed at Hendon, and then I had to find out where my unit was. It turned out that my squadron had left France only two days after I was shot down! They had nothing much left, so they were sent up to Wick to relieve 43 Squadron, who came back to Tangmere. Well, 43 was my old squadron, and I wanted to get back into action. I asked Air Ministry if I might rejoin them. They said they'd have a word with the CO, Squadron Leader George Lott. Two days before, he had taken twelve aircraft on a Dunkirk patrol, and arrived back with just two. One Flight

Commander and himself. They didn't all get killed – some of them were shot down over the water and were picked up by boat. Others fell on land the other side and scrambled out; they were coming back in broken condition for quite a few weeks. So I was very lucky because the CO was dying to get some pilots, and I started flying again with 43 in late June.

I had arrived back ready for the Battle of Britain with lots of experience. In the Battle of Britain sometimes, you would see enormous formations of Germans – a terrific stretch of them. Once we were taking off from Tangmere to look after a convoy called, I think, 'Peewit'. It got badly battered from the Dover Straits right down; it was almost eliminated. And we were taking over to do our stint. There were six of us on this patrol. As we arrived, we could see planes stretched out in great lumps all the way from the Isle of Wight to Cherbourg. At the bottom, Ju87 dive-bombers; above those, Me109s in great big oval sweeps covering the distance; and above them, Me110s. The Flight Commander had told three of us to do the fighter protection at the back, and we got up into them. The situation was absolutely ludicrous – three of us to take on that mob! The others went straight into the dive-bombers. Within seconds we were split up all over the place. The only advantage was that it was a hundred-to-one against hitting your own side; you could fire at anything.

I took a tremendous amount of damage that day. In the odd way that air fighting has, one minute you're in a mass, and you do three or four turns, and everything had disappeared. Where the devil have they all gone? And they can return just as fast. After this first kerfuffle I looked around for my two and I saw a formation and went to join them. And of course they were Me109s, but they hadn't seen me. They were in a very curious long echelon line. I got hooked on to the tail of the last and started firing away quite merrily. Then I had an awful wallop: it was an Me110 with his four cannons sitting just behind me. I got one in the port block of guns and ammunition; there was a big bang, and there, in the wing, was a hole a man could have crawled through. It threw me over on my back and, by the time I'd straightened up again, I thought I'd better find someone friendlier to join. I had a slight wound from one of their explosive bullets. They used to explode almost into powder. Suddenly my arm was perforated just as though someone had stuck a lot of pins in it all the way down. For a few seconds an immense amount of blood came out and I thought, God, my arm's coming off: but it was all right.

By that time I was nearly in Cherbourg. As I was on my way back I came up behind some more 109s who hadn't seen me. And again a 110 was looking after the 109s and it blew off the whole of my rudder, one whole elevator on one side and a lot of the canvas skin covering the other elevator. Really, I shouldn't have been able to control the aircraft, and I thought I'd better get back to Tangmere. When I arrived in the circuit the ack-ack opened up on me! The little bit of rudder and tail I had looked very peculiar, I suppose. I'd no idea of the extent of the damage at the back end! A rudder didn't matter so much, but the elevators were very important, particularly at the lower speeds. But somehow it flew. It was a great tribute to the Hurricane.

On another attack I was ably assisted by an Me109. Going in to attack some Ju88s one day, we could see the fighters above, but we thought we would get a nice burst in before they got near us. I got behind this Ju88 and pressed the button, and to my utter amazement bits flew off and the damage was astonishing! Our .303 guns weren't heavy enough to do so much damage. Then I saw fire over my head. There was a 109 trying to hit *me* but shooting high and we were both knocking the hell out of this poor old Ju88! It went down. Really I shouldn't claim that one, I should have given it to the 109!

The trouble with the .303 on the Hurricane was that one had to learn to conserve one's ammunition: we only had fifteen seconds of fire and then you were finished. Chaps used to put on long bursts, and then they would only have half a burst left and that was it. An unarmed fighter is pretty useless. It was always a worry, that shortage of ammunition. I don't think the Spitfire was much better. Altogether I did about a hundred sorties in the Battle of Britain – from early July until 18 August. The most I did was six sorties in a day; roughly about an hour to an hour-and-a-half each one. On 18 August I was shot down again.

I crash-landed at Pulborough. I don't know what shot me down. I was leading the squadron for the first time and we had just refuelled and taken off in a bit of a hurry and gone in to attack a mixed bunch of fighters and Ju87s. The fur was flying everywhere. Suddenly I was stitched right across the cockpit. I handed over the squadron to the no. 2, called base, and said I was going to return because I'd been hit – I could make it there, I thought.

They said, 'Don't come back here, they're just about to bomb us!' I slowly eased my way north over the downs, did a circle, losing a bit of height all the time, and asked again. They said, 'No, no, they're still all around us!' So I dropped into a field which didn't look as though it had any anti-invasion holes or poles. I got cocky and stupidly put the wheels down, which I should never have done, and just as I settled the plane down I said to myself, 'God, Carey, you're a wonderful pilot!' I was suddenly thrown forward as the plane flipped over. I thought, that's it. The next thing I knew I was laid out in the field looking up at the blue sky and two women were slitting my trouser legs, looking for bullet holes. One said, 'I can't find any more of them.' She seemed quite disappointed. It turned out that the locals had dug a trench and covered it over with grass. Of course I really mucked up the trap. I was very lucky because a Hurricane flipping over like that at almost flying speed nearly always killed the bloke by breaking his neck. The other lucky thing was it didn't catch fire as it took the rescuers quite a time to get me out.

Chaps used to get out of their aircraft far too quickly. New pilots especially. Once over the Sussex coast I spotted a Hurricane flying along quite perfectly upside down without a pilot. I went right up to it and looked at it and it seemed to be totally undamaged; I knew who the pilot was from the marking on it – it was a Sergeant Buck who had been flying it. It turned out he had a bad wound in the leg and he baled out a few miles off the coast of Bognor. But by the time they picked him up he had drowned even though he was a strong swimmer. If he'd stayed in the aircraft he'd have got to land.

I nursed another plane back from out in the Channel one day. The pilot got a glycol (coolant) leak – it comes out in little white puffs that get more and more frequent. I flew alongside and said, 'You stay there as long as that thing will take you back to land. Don't worry, it's all right.' I don't know what he was suffering in the cockpit, mind you. His cockpit was open and it must have been pretty hot. When it was no longer a puff but a regular little stream, he couldn't stand it any longer and got out. I followed him down and spotted him in the sea. I circled and radioed for help until I ran out of fuel. He was never picked up. I can only suppose he got tangled up and pulled down by the parachute. When he went into the sea he was only about a mile-and-a-half off Selsey Bill.

We didn't have any air-sea rescue then. The Germans did. They used to fly rescue seaplanes even right along the English coast.

Air fighting is a very detached sort of warfare being fought, as it were, between machines with the human factor very much submerged in a 'tin box'. Once in a while for a few fleeting seconds when someone bales out, one can suddenly be aware that humans are actually involved but, as the parachute descends, machines quickly regain the centre of the stage once more.

On one particular sortie from Wick, however, the human angle predominated for quite a while. The formation in which I was flying came upon a rather lonely Heinkel 111 way out in the North Sea which we naturally proceeded to deal with. After a few shots, a fire was seen to start in the fuselage and the Flight Commander immediately ordered us to stop attacking it. The enemy aircraft turned back towards Wick and we escorted it on its way with me in close formation on its port side where the fire was. Being only a few feet away from the Heinkel it was all too easy to become sympathetically associated with the crew's frantic efforts to control the fire and I even began to wish that I could jump across and help them. Thus was I suddenly converted from an anxious desire to destroy them to an even greater anxiety that they survive. We had got within a few miles of the coast and had really begun to hope that they would make it, when we were all outraged to see a Hurricane from another squadron sweep in from behind and without a single thought about us all around, poured a long burst of fire into the Heinkel which more or less blew up in our faces and crashed into the sea without any survivors.

It was all I could do to prevent myself from spinning round and having a crack at the Hurricane in response to its action. I felt a sense of personal loss as I stared at the wreckage on the water – what dramatic changes of attitude in such a short space of time.

Squadron Leader 'Henry' Szczesny

As a boy at school flying was my dream; flying was all I wanted to do because it lifts you up – you become like a bird. That is why, as soon as I could, I joined the Polish Air Force. I joined as a cadet and became a Pilot Officer in 1933.

I then taught pilots as an instructor. I emphasised the fighting skills of British pilots, most of all Mannock, from the 1914–18 war. I told them he was the best English fighter pilot. I got a photograph of him through the embassy. I put his picture up and he looked at me like 'Sailor' Malan did later. I told the student pilots about how he would fly and shoot, how he was always on the spot, and not afraid of anything. But I also talked to them about the tactics of Richthofen and of Polish pilots who had served with the Russian and German Air Forces.

In 1939 I was transferred to the east Polish border teaching advanced flying in PZL7s. We knew the war was coming, so we were preparing. Poland was the first to be invaded, on 1 September

1939. I was posted to a bomber station with six Polish cadets to fly defence for our bombers. Fortunately I was lucky and shot down two Dorniers and damaged a couple more of them, but I was wounded. Then, as we were being beaten back, I flew to Rumania and to Bucharest. There I had an operation on my leg because gangrene had set in. When I recovered, I made my way to Malta and then to France. I finally arrived in London on a foggy day and for the first time I had a lovely English breakfast of bacon and eggs. But outside I couldn't see anything. It was fog, fog, fog.

All the Polish aircrew were sent up to Blackpool, we just gathered together. The RAF sorted us out and I was sent to Aston Down for Spitfire training. It was very difficult for me because the Spitfire has the undercarriage down, flaps down, everything different! In Poland you pull back the throttle, with the Spitfire it was the reverse. I think the Spitfire was flying me!

On 5 August 1940 at RAF Hornchurch I joined 'Sailor' Malan's 74 Squadron. He was famous even then. He was South African and younger than me. He seemed to like me even though my English was nil. I was learning slowly, it was a very difficult language. But I wanted to fly so I had to learn. Malan and all the pilots helped me. They were really very good. There were South Africans, New Zealanders, Australians, all sorts. They talked to me slowly, and I had a dictionary. And the mechanics, they helped me very much. There were two of us Poles in the squadron but no-one could say our names so they called Brzezina 'Breezy', and me 'Sneezy', and sometimes just Henry the Pole.

I remember first thing on 13 August we were told that bandits were coming from the Belgium area very low, without fighter escort. This was the day the Germans called 'Eagle Day'. So Malan, he says 'Tally Ho!' And we saw about twelve of them; they had come to bomb Eastchurch where I knew there was a Polish settlement. I got one, I shot him down. But he also got me. My undercarriage was down so I took off to West Malling and landed on one wheel and crashed, but I was OK.

Every day we were always fighting and flying and shooting but I couldn't say whether we shot anything down. But Malan always seemed to do so. He used to say, 'Henry, keep my tail, don't miss it.' So I flew on his tail all the time. I learned so much from him. He was a very great fighter. He had good eyesight. If he saw somebody they were dead.

He taught us many lessons. He had 'ten commandments':

First: wait until you see the whites of their eyes before you fire. Then fire short bursts of about one or two seconds, but only when your sights are on.

Second: think of nothing else while you are shooting – concentrate your whole body.

Third: even when attacking keep a sharp look-out, especially after a breakaway. Don't watch your 'flamer' go down except out of the corner of your eye.

Fourth: if you have the advantage of height you have the initiative.

Fifth: always turn to face the attack. If you are attacked from above, wait until they are committed to their dive and within 1,500 feet of you, then turn suddenly towards him.

Sixth: make your decisions promptly and smartly.

Seventh: never fly straight and level for more than thirty seconds while in combat area or at any time when enemy aircraft are likely to be near.

Eighth: when diving to attack always leave a part of your formation above to act as top guard.

Ninth: initiative; aggression; discipline in the air; team work; all mean something in combat.

Tenth, and finally: get in quickly, punch hard, get out smartly.

I remember once in the middle of a battle watching hard to see if I had got one, when Sailor came up in my ears and said, 'Henry, don't think numbers, kill!' He was right.

The money, my goodness! I got twelve pounds something a month. It lasted only for three or four days. I didn't want to keep it because I never thought for a moment I would stay alive. Every day someone was missing – so always I thought one day it will be me. So I used to get my money and spend it. We then lived on King and Country, the mess bill.

Always, though, I thought I might return to a free Poland.

Wing Commander Al Deere

I came to Britain from New Zealand to join the Air Force in 1937. The Air Force had started to expand, and they advertised in the national press in the then Dominions for young men. I applied and was one of the first eighteen to be selected.

Twelve of us went to White Waltham near Maidenhead, where we learned to fly. I flew a Tiger Moth. I went from the initial training to No. 6 Flying Training School at Netheravon to train on Hawker Harts and Furies. I was always keen to be a fighter pilot and kept saying so. Eventually I was posted to 54 Squadron at Hornchurch, which was equipped with Gladiators. I did a year in 1938 in 54 Gladiator Squadron, but thank God we didn't have to fight in the Gladiator! It was a lovely aircraft, but it was so outdated. We were disappointed then, but fortunately Munich kept the war off for about a year, and by that time we'd gone on to Spitfires.

The three squadrons at Hornchurch – 54, 65 and 74 – were the first Spitfire squadrons to be sent over to Dunkirk to try and protect the evacuation. I was then operational on Spitfires. Not all the squadron were but we had a hard core of experienced pilots. Unfortunately, we lost most of them at Dunkirk. There were seventeen pilots in the squadron and twelve aircraft at Dunkirk – I crashed, one or two chaps baled out and got back, but we lost quite a few.

The first time that we knew that we were going to be involved on the Continent was when the Station Commander, 'Boy' Bouchier, assembled all the pilots in the billiard room in the officers' mess to tell us we had been assigned to take part in the protection of British troops over Dunkirk. For fourteen days we went non-stop:

I did something like 37 hours in ten days. We just kept flying. We had no reserve pilots.

For the first week or so we went across and cruised around in an old 'Vic' formation which was already outdated. We didn't see anything and thought this was a piece of cake. One morning 74 Squadron's CO, Drogo White, got shot down and crash-landed at Calais/Marck airfield, which was still in French hands. It was decided that our CO would fly a Master – a twin-seat training aircraft – to pick him up, and I and a chap named Johnny Allen went along to protect the Master. That's when I got into the first dogfight with an Me109; the battle was observed by the CO, who was on the ground hiding in a ditch. That was my first combat. Johnny Allen, my no. 2, was above the cloud, and he shouted when the 109 arrived. It came through the cloud right in front of me. It was a sitting duck. I wasn't all that good a shot, but I was close to him. I turned behind him and he saw me and pulled up, which was the worst thing he could have done, because he slowed his plane and I shot him, and down he went. Johnny Allen got one too. We got three altogether. The Master picked up Drogo and brought him back.

That afternoon we went out again and were jumped by some 109s. I shot a lot of ammunition not in the right direction. Then I got behind one and in range, had a couple of bursts, and then ran out of ammunition. I thought I would stay with this guy; in retrospect it was a bit stupid, but I did it; and I found that I could stay with him in every manoeuvre except when he dived. When I got back, I made my report to the powers-that-be that I'd flown with this chap and was convinced that the Spitfire could do anything the 109 could do and in some cases better: it could turn better, it could climb better, but it couldn't dive quite so well. They laughed at me and said that didn't match up with their figures. But they hadn't accounted for the fact that 54 Squadron was equipped with the Rotol constant speed propeller. All other Spitfires were two-speed. It gave me a lot of confidence.

The next time I went up I got tangled with an Me110. A few

days later I was coming back and I saw two strange aircraft and wondered what the hell they were. They were 110s. They didn't see me – it was cloudy – and I managed to shoot one down. I had no difficulty because it didn't know what to do. The other one pulled into cloud.

On 31 May No. 54 Squadron flew one last patrol before 41 Squadron came to relieve us. I was leading the squadron, and just as we arrived over Dunkirk, a Dornier 17 came flying up the coast. We went after it and, being the leader, I was first there. I was lining up behind to shoot it when the rear-gunner fired; he hit my engine and the glycol header tank, which is the cooling system. I had to break off; I crash-landed north of Dunkirk. The tide was out and I got down on the beach, but I knocked myself out on the edge of the windscreen. When I came to I got out and was looked after by a girl who stitched me up with an ordinary needle and put a plaster on me. Then I headed for Dunkirk, where I knew the British Expeditionary Force (BEF) was intending to evacuate. We had been reading in the British newspapers that the British Army was retreating 'according to plan'. Somewhere en route to Dunkirk, I went into a small café where I saw two Tommies. I asked, 'Am I heading for Dunkirk? I understand the British Army are going to be evacuated.' They looked at me and said something to the effect of 'What British Army? There's no retreat, chum, there's bloody chaos.' Dunkirk was a complete shambles – burning buildings, abandoned vehicles, falling masonry. On the beach were thousands and thousands of troops. They were swimming out to the boats.

I could see a destroyer coming in. I think it was the last destroyer to go into Dunkirk harbour. I managed to force my way on to this against the wishes of the Army: the troops were all down the side of the pier for protection from the bombing, but I ran along the top, and a Major jumped up at me and said, 'Get down there!' And I said, 'Not bloody likely.' Anyhow, I got on a destroyer and the Army aboard weren't very impressed at all – where the hell had the RAF been? All I could say was, we've been over here: I wouldn't be here if we hadn't been over here. They weren't friendly at all. We were bombed quite badly, and about halfway across the Channel a harassed Army Captain came to me and asked if I'd come up on deck because they didn't recognise the aircraft and didn't know which to shoot at. So I finished up on deck identifying aircraft for the gunners.

When we got to Dover they had an orderly disembarkation. Again, I wasn't going to be held up, so I climbed up one of the mooring ropes and got off that way. I went to Dover Station and on to the train. I was looking a bit of a mess by this time: I was bleeding, dirty and unshaven, and had a filthy bandage wrapped around my head. I got into a carriage with an Army General. The ticket chap came round, and I said, 'I haven't got a ticket; I've just come back from Dunkirk, and I'm going back to my base in Essex, and you'll have to charge it up to His Majesty the King or something because I haven't got any money. We don't carry money.' He wanted me to get off the train, but the General stood up for me. I went through to London, took the tube and got all the way back without a ticket. I walked into the mess at Horn-church, much to everyone's surprise.

My squadron had moved north to Catterick to re-equip and refurbish. I went up to rejoin them. It was only when I arrived there that I realised what losses we'd had. I think we were down to eight or ten aircraft. We'd lost a lot of pilots, a lot of friends. We lost two Flight Commanders. I became a Flight Commander because of that. We had lost the experienced ones. That's always the way: they were leading. I'd gone out to fight full of excitement, but after a few days of that I realised war wasn't all that much fun.

I got five enemy aircraft in that time over Dunkirk. It was very intense, comparatively speaking it was more intense than the Battle of Britain. The Battle of Britain went on longer, but we were operating over our own territory. We felt a bit safer. At Dunkirk we were a long way away.

*

The squadron came back to Hornchurch about mid-June. At that stage the Germans were bombing the convoys going up the Channel. So we were doing convoy patrols most of the time. They were sending progressively more aircraft intruding over England, trying to get us up in the air so they could knock us down. July was a very hectic month: they were building up into a crescendo bombing the convoys.

Then they started bombing the airfields. 54 Squadron's forward base was Manston, in Kent, which was the most forward airfield in England – we could see Calais from Manston. We operated from there. We used to go off from Hornchurch about half an hour before first light, land at Manston, and stay there all day. We did sometimes four sorties a day, sometimes five, not always making combat, but being shot at and shot down. We very rarely arrived back with the number of chaps we went out with. One morning, after we'd had a bit of a fight over a convoy, we were sent off to intercept a raid coming across the Channel at 3,000–4,000 feet. We went off south of Manston, and found some 109s at between 3,000 and 5,000 feet. And down in the water I could see a seaplane. I didn't know it at the time, but it was a German air-sea rescue plane, which had come in to try and pick up one of their pilots. I told Johnny Allen, who was in my sub-section, to go down and get the seaplane, and I'd look after the 109s. Just at that moment the 109s saw us. They started to turn around just as we did, and I found myself in a circle going head-on towards a 109 coming from the opposite direction. I pressed my gun-button more in hope than anything else, and I think we must have done the same thing. I felt the bullets hit, and the next thing I knew we had collided. It was all very quick. I hit underneath him. My engine seized straight away, and the cockpit filled with smoke. When I tried to open the hood, it was jammed. I was trapped.

I had some control of the plane but no engine. I kept it gliding for as long as I could and just kept on going until I hit the ground in an open area where they had put a lot of anti-invasion posts against enemy gliders. Of course I ploughed through these, and finally came to a halt. By this time I was on fire. I managed to break my way out of the cockpit. We had a little thing inside, a little jemmy thing, and I managed to smash my way out with that and my bare hands, and got clear of the aircraft. I was pretty shaken, I was burned, my hair and eyebrows singed from the flames in the cockpit, and my knees were badly bruised, but I was in one piece. The aircraft burned and all my unused ammunition went off.

A woman came out from a house nearby, and asked if I'd like a cup of tea. All I remember saying was, did she have anything stronger? She rang Manston and within a fairly quick time the ambulance was up, and took me back. Of course when I got back, inevitably the whole squadron had gone back to Rochford. I was all right for flying the next day. I'd have preferred to take a breather, but we were just too short of pilots.

A few weeks later, on 15 August, when the Battle of Britain was going strong, I did a stupid thing and was shot down again. We intercepted some 109s over Dover who were escorting some Junkers 87s. They were dive-bombing Dover. I'd already got one down when I got on to the tail of another. When he turned for home I followed him, shooting. I realised in the end that he was getting too far out to sea and I was getting too far away. As I turned I ran into some more 109s. They set about me and shot me up rather badly. By the time I got back to the coast my aircraft was smoking badly and it was clearly going to burn. I jumped out and I landed in a field not very far from Dover, where by this time it was dusk. It was my fifth sortie of the day and I was pretty tired: I'd hit my wrist badly trying to bale out and was in terrible pain. It happened that an RAF ambulance came by the field I landed in, and they picked me up and said they'd take me to Kenley. Well, they got lost in the blackout. We went around and around and around. They finally dropped me at East Grinstead hospital at midnight, with my wrist throbbing like hell.

We started to complain about operating from Manston because it was so far forward that, in order to get to the height of the

Germans – some 20,000 feet – we had to climb inland. As well as that, we had been bombed on the ground. We'd had a hell of a time. I think it was a morale thing: Churchill had apparently said we mustn't give up any piece of land. It was an expensive way of gaining the moral victory: in the end we were losing chaps taking off and landing. Eventually the powers-that-be gave in and we went back to Hornchurch, which was much more comfortable because we climbed straight up to height. But by this time it was into August and the Germans were getting further and further inland. They started bombing the London perimeter airfields, of which Hornchurch was one.

The third time I was shot down was by a Spitfire. I was pumping away at a 109 when the Spitfire jumped me from behind. I was filled full of holes, but I was still flying. I headed for home, but I could see I wouldn't be able to keep airborne: the engine was rough, I couldn't move the controls properly, and I couldn't see what was wrong behind. So I decided to bale out.

At this time I was somewhere near Hawkinge airfield, on the way back to Hornchurch. I'd had a rough experience getting out the previous time, because I had hit the tail. I tell you it takes a lot of guts to turn your Spitfire upside down, knowing your harness is undone. So this time I put it on an even course and went over the side. I landed in a field, five or ten miles from Detling. It so happened that the raid we had intercepted had bombed Detling airfield. I arrived at Detling to find that they had had quite a few casualties and the place was chaos. But there was an Anson there, on the airfield, and a chap called Desmond Garvin, a fellow pre-war RAF rugger player, who was commanding the Defiant Squadron and had been shot down in the same do. We were flown back to Hornchurch together: he to discover that his Defiant Squadron was no longer, the Germans having massacred the lot of them in two sorties; and I to find that we'd had pretty severe losses again. Once again I thought I might get a break. But I was told it was impossible, we had no-one else who could lead.

You never knew if you were going to be bombed on the ground

or not. I finished my Battle of Britain on 31 August by being blown up by a bomb when taking off from Hornchurch. Radar picture got a bit confused and they buggered around sending us off. Eventually they told us to get off as quickly as possible.

I was leading the squadron at this time. We had a new pilot in the squadron named Sergeant Davies. By this time we had practically all new pilots, for only five of us were left of the old guard. This young chap was my no. 2 and in the excitement he taxied out to take off and, not knowing where to position himself, he stopped in the middle of the airfield right in front of me. The other nine aircraft went off. He eventually realised and moved, but before we got off the bombs came down and blew the three of us out of the sky. I went up in the air and on to my back. That was a nasty experience. The terrifying part was that I was upside down in the cockpit, embedded in the ground. I could hardly see daylight and I could smell petrol. And I knew that I was likely to go up in flames at any moment. I heard this voice say, 'Are you there?' And it was Eric Edsall, later killed in the war, who was my no. 3. He had had his wing blown off, and he'd got out of his cockpit, saw me, and had crawled across to the aircraft.

The Spitfire has a little side door which drops down. Eric managed to lever this open, and I got my straps undone, and my parachute undone, and managed to squeeze out of this little door. To find that he couldn't walk. His hip was dislocated. So I got him up and carried him to the safety of the hangars just as some 109s came down to strafe us. I was scalped and concussed – I had gone along upside down for about a hundred yards. As for the no. 2 he was blown outside the airfield perimeter still strapped in his cockpit, his Spitfire being dumped in a nearby creek. Miraculously, he was unhurt. The next day the squadron was moved to Catterick. For me the Battle of Britain was over.

When I went to Catterick, I think it was on 2 September, I was knackered. I was running on overdrive. I don't think I realised till I got up there what sort of state I was in. I really was pretty exhausted. And so too were James Leathart, who had been taken off earlier; and his replacement Donald Finlay, the famous Olympic hurdler, who had lasted only two sorties. On his second sortie he was flying no. 2 to me to get experience, and I had told him that at height it was very difficult to keep position, and if he got behind he'd had it. Well, he got behind, was shot down by a 109, and had a great chunk shot out of his bum. James Leathart, who had been released for a rest, had to come back. After a few days he took the squadron up to Catterick, and then went off for a rest. By that time there was himself, Colin Gray, George Gribble, and myself, we were the lot left out of the original 54 Squadron.

There was a tremendous amount of fatigue. It was difficult to judge who was pulling their weight and who wasn't. I had a chap on my flight, and he came up to me one morning – he'd been flying pretty intensively – and said he wasn't well and couldn't go on. I said, 'Well, I'm not well either. But I've got to go on, you've got to go on, chum.' He looked a bit pale, but I thought he'd be all right. That afternoon, he said again that he wasn't feeling well. So I said he'd better go and see the doctor. Well, he had malaria. But I'd thought he'd gone yellow. The thing was, we were all frightened and the urge was to preserve yourself, and it was bloody difficult at times.

At Catterick, the squadron was broken up and we began to train pilots. I was in a mock dogfight with a trainee pilot one day when we had a mid-air collision. As a matter of fact he hit me, he chopped my tail off. I was at about 10,000 feet, and I jumped out. My parachute didn't open properly, and I was in the horizontal position when I hit. I landed in a farmer's cess pool, which cushioned the blow and probably saved my life, apart from the fact that I very nearly drowned swallowing the stuff. I hurt my back rather badly, an injury that's still with me, and after that I found my nerves were all to hell. I was made Squadron Leader, taken off flying, and became a Controller in Station Operations.

After a few months, I was posted to 602 Squadron as Flight Commander and went to Ayr. On patrol one day I had engine trouble and made a forced landing in a potato field. Once again the plane flipped over and I was on my head. This time I had no help extricating myself, and it wasn't easy.

In July we moved south to Kenley where we were assigned to bomber escort. Bomber escort was an unpleasant assignment for a fighter, because under attack your first priority must be to stick with the bombers. In August I was made Squadron Leader of 602 Squadron. I was hit again while escorting bombers over Lille, and somehow managed to keep the aircraft up until I was back over England. I landed safely at Manston airfield.

In May 1942, after six weeks in the United States lecturing the Army Air Force on fighter tactics, I returned to England as Leader of 403 (Canadian) Squadron, based at Rochford. Eventually I was made Wing Commander at Biggin Hill. I was there when Biggin Hill recorded its 1,000th aircraft destroyed. The intensity of operations at Biggin Hill put us all under stress and squadrons had to be withdrawn from the front line periodically. I felt again that instinct for self-preservation overriding the sense of duty.

We were doing withdrawal cover escort. The American bombers would pick them up just by Paris, and we'd fly with the wing over 8/8ths cloud, unable to see the ground, and with no way of getting back other than the master bomber. And the temptation was not to fly your allotted time to get there, knowing it was pretty rough reckoning anyway. If you didn't see the B-17s, if they hadn't arrived and you didn't know how long to go on, the temptation was to turn tail and to get out of there. You had to keep saying, well, I've jolly well got to go on. There was a lot of that happening, and I don't think it was a question of one chap being braver than the other. It was a question of just screwing up just a little extra courage at the time. We were all frightened to hell, we were all tired. When you actually got into combat, you forgot about that, but it was those moments before, the waiting and climbing up, which were really frightening.

The fear increased as the war went on. One would have thought it would get less. It's a funny thing, this. I did four tours of operations: at Dunkirk and in the Battle of Britain I was frightened but somehow not over-frightened. The next tour I did, I was less happy; the third tour I was bloody unhappy. I'd had one or two narrow escapes and I was frightened. But the fourth tour, when I was leading the Biggin Hill Wing, I somehow felt that I wasn't going to be shot down. Not because I'd had enough, I just had a feeling that I was going to be there at the end. And I was. In fact I flew right up until I collapsed in briefing.

I had become a bit tired and got something called 'Sone Dysentery'. I'd been flying with it, knowing I wasn't well, but not knowing I was so ill. I was taken into East Grinstead Hospital. I was on the DI (Dangerously Ill) list. I remember the specialist who saw me happened to be a fellow countryman, and he said I had acute enteritis. Had I kept going for another forty-eight hours I'd have died.

So that was the end of my operations. But I had had a good innings. You had to have luck, and I, I guess, had had more than my share.

Pilot Officer Bob Doe

I fell in love with the Spitfire the first time I saw it. We had been flying Blenheims and Battles with a Bomber Squadron at Leconfield when a Spitfire landed. This marvellous thing taxied over to our hangar and we swarmed around it. It was an early model; the wings had a coating on them, so the rivets were flush. It was absolutely smooth, almost hand-made. We walked around it, we sat in it, we stroked it, oh it was so beautiful. It really was beautiful.

The next day fifteen more turned up, which was a dream we never thought would happen. When you closed the cockpit of the Spitfire, you just felt part of it. You were out of the world, you were on your own. You were your own boss, you were everything you wanted to be. The first time I took off in a Spitfire was, I think, the greatest joy I have known. The joy of this thing that rocketed up into the air and was so easy to fly, so smooth to fly! And in spite of its looks how easy it was to land!

By June 1940 the war had begun in earnest and we were moved to St Eval in Cornwall as 234 Fighter Squadron and assigned to convoy patrols. I know of nothing more boring in life than convoy patrols! You take off and meet a convoy, you circle that convoy for an hour, and then come back. The most boring thing I have ever done. We also had to do night patrols over Plymouth. There were only four of us that were deemed night operational, so we had to do all of the night patrols, as well as the day patrols.

In Cornwall you get odd weather conditions where the weather will suddenly clamp without any notice at all. Once when I'd gone on patrol down off the Plymouth area somewhere the weather clamped. I was entirely on my own, and I found that there was a gap in the cloud cover around the coast between the top of the cliffs and the sea. So I went from Plymouth right the way round the coast. I hadn't realised how far it was until I got back to St Eval – I had been up two hours and twenty minutes, which is more than maximum endurance of a Spitfire. In that time, the rest of the squadron had started to auction my gear; they had sold quite a lot of it. I had trouble getting it back.

I suppose we were developing a callous sharpness – it was our way of dealing with death.

On 15 August 1940 we were ordered up to Middle Wallop. We flew up there but I was feeling very strange in the sense that everything was distant; we hadn't been involved, it wasn't real. We landed on the grass airfield, were put into a lorry, and halfway up to the mess, they bombed the airfield. One of the hangars was hit, and a WAAF was killed in a trench. Up to that moment we had been seeing war from a spectator's point of view.

A bit later that day we were scrambled over Swanage. I really had the worst inferiority complex at that time. I felt I was the worst pilot in the squadron, and I was convinced I would not survive that trip.

We took off and formed up into four Vics of three in sections astern, which is the stupidest formation you could possibly fly in. There's only one person looking round, everyone else is formating. And we patrolled up and down the sun, which, again, is a stupid way of flying. At one point, we turned back down sun to find we were only nine strong. We had lost three; our rear section had disappeared, one killed and the other two shot down. Then, all of a sudden, we found ourselves in the middle of a gaggle of Messerschmitt 110s and 109s. God knows how we got there; we just landed in the middle of them. I was flying at no. 2 to Pat Hughes, who turned off after a 110, gave him a quick squirt, then turned on his side, and pulled away. But it didn't look quite right to me, so I formed on the 110, got quite close to it, and kept on firing until he went down into the sea. This was the second time I'd used my guns, the first was into the sea to try them out. I thought, this is something! I'm not dead and I've done something! That feeling was really fantastic. I followed him down, pulled up from the sea, and another 110 overshot me from behind. I just closed on him and shot him down.

I shot two down without really knowing anything. I realised on the way home that I'd been so lucky it was ridiculous. So I started to do some thinking. In fact, I went to bed early that night, and I stayed in bed just thinking. I realised that you're usually shot down from behind. So what do you do if you see bullets coming past you from behind? I worked out that, whatever I did, I must go down, straight down, because if you tried to roll or anything you stayed in the bullet path for longer, and if you pulled up you were a sitting target. So I drilled it into my head that if I saw anything coming past me from behind, I would just hit the stick. I wouldn't think, just hit it.

I then started thinking about why we had found ourselves in the middle of a gaggle of the enemy. I realised that I had to see them before they saw me. And I couldn't be in formation if I was going to see them: I had to get away on my own.

The following day we met a load of 109s high up over the Isle of Wight, and I found one on his own. I settled down on him.

Now, although I'd shot two down the day before, I was not certain about shooting. I couldn't trust my judgement and distance, and I couldn't trust my shooting. So I aimed above him first, then below and eventually, I shot him down. But I had been so involved that I hadn't seen another 109 behind me. Fortunately Pat Hughes had spotted it and shot it off my tail. I was dead lucky.

I followed the plane I'd been concentrating on down and saw him plunge into the sea. I circled the crash, and found someone shooting at me. It was a Dornier Do18, a flying boat, out there looking for survivors. He put a bullet slap into the middle of my spinner, but didn't do any damage so I had a go at him. That was the first time I was hit. After that, almost every time I was in action I got hit, so I always knew I'd been close to it somewhere.

On 18 August we were scrambled again. They sent a very formidable force over the Southampton area. We had three sorties that day. I got one on the first, one on the second, and damaged one on the third.

We were so confident at that time. There was no doubt in our minds. We knew we weren't going to lose. It never, ever, entered our minds that we could lose. I suppose, in retrospect, we were bloody stupid, but it never entered our minds that we could possibly lose this war.

Then we had a new CO posted in, and he decided to come as my no. 2 on a scramble. We found a lone Ju88 over Winchester. Well, I had a go at it; he had a go at it; no effect. So I got behind it, got as close as I could, and filled it with bullets. He hit me through the mainspar, then stopped firing and went into the ground. When we landed back at base, the new CO, very keen, wanted to go and have a look for the Ju88; it had crashed in a field very close to Middle Wallop. I'm now very sorry I went to see it, because someone informed me that every aircrew helmet had bullet holes in it, and that brought everything home to me.

I had to fly the Spitfire down to Hamble for repair. It was a lovely, warm day, with interceptions going on overhead all the time. The foreman of the place invited me home to lunch, and his wife started talking to me and suddenly, for the first time, I realised that ordinary people in the street knew what we were doing, and that they admired us. She was saying things that made me blush. It really was quite something. I hadn't been aware of it; it hadn't entered my mind. People could see what was happening.

I don't know how many I'd shot down by then, but I was getting very confident. I had very good eyesight. I'd learned an awful lot about seeing aeroplanes; and was very good at spotting them. You never see an aeroplane if you are looking straight at it. You see it ten degrees off to the side. You might see movement, at one o'clock, two o'clock, and then that's it, you've got it. This became apparent to me very quickly, and probably saved my life on a few occasions. In general, I saw them before they saw me, and that is important, because you can then position yourself for your own attack. I also found that the really effective way to attack was to go straight in. Don't muck about. They never expected you to go straight in, and they scattered like wildfire when you did.

Then, too, at first I tended to be very much on my own, because our squadron never went in formation at all after that first occasion. But I found that, if you're on your own, you spent an awful lot of time looking round. After that, Sergeant 'Budge' Harker and I started flying a couple of hundred yards abreast. That way you can each see anyone on the other's tail. This was the start of Finger Four flying, although the Germans had it ages before that. If we'd had any Intelligence in the Air Force at that time we would have known about it, and we wouldn't have lost a lot of the people we did lose.

Once on patrol I found myself above a big bunch of 109s. If you were on your own above 109s they tended to ignore you. So, I sort of rolled over and came down to try and take one out and, as I hit him, I hit his slipstream. Well, at that time, the carburettor in a Spitfire didn't operate under negative 'G' conditions. So my engine cut dead, and there I was with a bunch of 109s getting interested. I went into a dive and headed downwards. When I was clear I pulled up, my engine started, and I caught up the bloke I'd hit and finished him off.

We continued patrolling from base, Portland or Kenley, and on 3 September over Tangmere we came across this massive circle of Me110s. I dived across it, had two separate squirts of two seconds at 250 yards which destroyed two of them. On my way back along the coast I was feeling pleased with myself when I saw another 110, which I got, but I had to share that one with a Hurricane.

The first London raid, they say, was on 7 September 1940, but in fact it was 5 September. That was the first one I saw, anyway. I was there when this mass of bombers dropped their bombs on the docks. This stays very clearly in my mind – it was the first real attack on London. I saw the whole docks area erupt. It was a fantastic sight, flames and smoke. I was gawping at it so much, I nearly got shot down. It was a hell of an experience, seeing it. It made me extremely angry. But they had masses of 109s there, and every time I turned there was a 109 shooting at me. I was turning like mad, and not firing my guns, so eventually I decided that, if I went down to Dover at about 10,000 feet, they'd be going home, and I should pick up one, or even a brace. I headed for Dover with Budge Harker, and because we were flying so that we could see each other's tail he got a yellow-nosed 109 that was right behind me. That was the first time we used that technique of flying.

The next day, 6 September, we did the same thing and met fourteen Do17s, and a lone 109 which I destroyed. I then had a go at the Dorniers and stopped three of their rear-gunners shooting back. I then ran out of ammunition, got intercepted, and decided to go home. You could get away in a Spitfire by turning. If you went into a turn and stayed there, you were safe.

On 7 September – which is the day that they always say that the bombardment of London started – there were 350 bombers over London. I got one Heinkel, and then a 109 who came into my sights and left a piece of his wing behind him. By then I suppose I had ten or eleven confirmed, but the cost to our squadron had been considerable. Of the 21 who landed at Middle Wallop on 14 August only three pilots remained. We were all very tired and were sent back to St Eval to rest, re-train, and get new pilots. I was out of the action for nearly three weeks.

On 28 September I was posted to Chilbolton and given a flight with a Hurricane squadron, 238 Squadron. I had two half-hour trips in the Hurricane, learning to fly it, and went into action on the 29th.

It was a bit of a come-down, a Hurricane. There was much more room in it, it was far more manoeuvrable than a Spitfire, and it was a very good gun platform. But it was crude in comparison. I was in a Hurricane the day I did a head-on attack on a formation of Heinkels and got one. But I got a bullet through the wooden bladed prop which split it from tip to base. There was about a quarter-inch gap, and the weirdest noise, flying home. I was surprised it didn't come to bits.

The last major daylight raid of the 'Blitz' was on 7 October, which was when they headed towards Bristol. We had five aeroplanes, I think, that day. I somehow managed to get into the middle of the bombers, and damaged a Ju88. He started to drop out, so I dropped out as well, and did a quarter attack on him from the beam. His tail suddenly blew up, which seemed incredible. Apparently, they stored all their oxygen in containers just in front of the tail. Three came out, but the last one pulled his rip-cord too soon and his parachute started burning. I watched him going all the way down with his parachute burning. One of the crew who survived wrote to me years later. Anyway, that was the last trip of the Blitz, and when I got back I found I had eleven holes in the plane. So, I was very lucky.

Then I got shot down. On 10 October we were scrambled, Hurricanes against high-flying 109s, on a day when there was solid cloud from about 4,000 up to 20,000 feet. Once in the cloud, I lost everyone. As I broke the cloud, I was hit from behind and in front. The first thing I knew, a spark came over my right shoulder into the dashboard. Then I heard a thump underneath my bottom, and a cannon shell hit my right foot and cut the Achilles tendon. I was hit in my left shoulder, which was like a blow from a sledgehammer and I was also hit in the hand. I thought I was going to die. All sorts of thoughts flashed through my mind – I was to be married in two months and I regretted not having the chance to get married. However, I had worked out before what to do if I was attacked from behind, and I hit the stick and bunted back into the cloud.

Then I realised I was still alive and that I ought to get out quickly. I'd pulled the pin which holds the Sutton harness together, but due to negative 'G' the straps would not release. In sheer panic I tore at the harness, which must have pulled the straps free and I popped out like a cork from a bottle. I've no idea how I got the hood back, all I remember was the joy of floating down in the air. It was a most wonderful feeling. I looked around quite calmly for a parachute handle, found it and pulled it. I felt an almighty jerk and, still in cloud floating downwards, started looking round me to see what the damage was. I could see a load of blood everywhere; I couldn't use my left arm or my right leg. Apart from that everything seemed quite reasonable. I was just floating down. Eventually, I came out the cloud over a blue lagoon. It was beautiful. A lagoon in England! Blue, with an island in the middle of it that I was drifting towards. Poole harbour!

I then realised I was coming down rather fast because the cannon shell which had hit my armour-plated seat had destroyed quite a bit of my parachute canopy. I began to shout which was a stupid thing to do as there was no-one around. Because I was minus a leg and an arm I didn't land properly – landed on my bottom and was knocked out. When I came to, I was in the middle of a quagmire on Brownsea Island with an Irishman standing over me with an iron bar saying 'What are you?' So I used my basic English to tell him exactly what I was. He then kindly carried me about half a mile to the jetty, where a naval boat had been sent across, and they took me into a hospital.

For me the Battle of Britain was over. I was twenty years old and had 14 confirmed kills to my credit. On 7 December I got married. Twenty-seven days later I was to crash at Warmwell in a Hurricane.

Squadron Leader Myles Duke-Woolley

I was Flight Commander of 'A' Flight, 253 Squadron, Kenley, and early one morning in October the Controller called to tell me he had an enemy singleton on the radar screen just over Dieppe. I went up with my no. 2, Guy Marsland. We flew our Hurricanes at 500 feet, over the railway line running south from Redhill, and started climbing at 1,500 feet per minute. As the boost pressure started to fall with altitude I maintained 'plus four' as long as I could, opening the throttle all the way. Ten minutes after starting we levelled off at 16,000 feet with Beachy Head below at one o'clock ahead. The sun was coming over the south-east horizon above low cloud.

I saw the bandit almost immediately, a black speck 2,000 feet above us, nearly ten miles away, flying north-north-west. I steered to the left of him, letting the spot move slowly across my windscreen to my right. I waggled my wings to Guy to close formation and, when he had done so, pointed forwards and waved him out again. He opened out to fifty yards or so and thirty seconds later I saw his thumbs-up signal. As the spot became a blob I knew that we were closing, but I was aiming to cut off his retreat by getting south of him. He was turning gently westward. I continued west-south-west.

Two minutes later we were within five miles of him, and his silhouette was beginning to look like a Heinkel 111, the workhorse bomber with considerably less speed than the Junkers 88 or Dornier 17 which I had expected. A lone Heinkel 111 made no sense. I quartered the sky and the sea, but I couldn't see that he had anyone with him. We closed to within a mile, with him north-west of and still apparently unaware of our presence. Brighton was square to port and the Heinkel was doomed. Which meant I could afford to break RT silence. I called Control that we'd made the sighting.

I edged towards the Heinkel, keeping his image steady at the side of my windscreen at about two o'clock. Thirty seconds later the Heinkel turned sharply left and started a gentle dive. I turned inside him, closing quite fast. It seemed possible he still hadn't seen me, because the dorsal gunner had not yet opened fire. When they saw a fighter bearing down air-gunners would immediately open fire, as this encouraged an attacking pilot to fire back, often at an excessive range. I checked our speed to prolong the time it would take to reach our best killing range – 250 yards. If the gunner had seen me, I thought he must surely have opened fire. I closed to 600 yards.

To my astonishment, the Heinkel suddenly jettisoned his bomb load. No reconnaissance aircraft was ever burdened with bombs! That was unheard-of. There was also the size of the bomb and the way it fell. The Heinkel 111's usual load was four 250-kilogram bombs stored vertically behind the cockpit and – unusually – nose-up. I had seen them drop, they came tail first and wobbled around before assuming a normal falling curve. This bomb was vastly bigger and fell away horizontally at first. Our Intelligence had reported provision for the external carriage of one or two 500kg bombs, but to me this looked like 1,000kg. Tangmere was away to Kenley's west and almost on the coast, and I wondered if that had been his intended target.

My target was the Heinkel's port engine. In my very first encounter with a Heinkel 111 I had learned that a steel mono-coque fuselage could take a great deal of punishment. The liquid-cooled engines were much more vulnerable. Flying trials of a captured Heinkel had revealed that it flew better on its port engine alone than on its starboard, because of the off-set prop-wash caused by the rotation of the airscrews. So I was lining up my aim on the port engine in relation to the nose of the fuselage. When the two were in line, the angle was almost precisely fifteen degrees. The radius of the circle surrounding the central dot of my position gave an angle of twenty degrees. When the same tip was in line with the dorsal gun I aimed for a 20°-shot at 250 yards. The gunsight allowed precisely for a target crossing speed of 100mph at correct firing range. I had to guess at his air-speed, but in a gentle dive, and doubtless in a hurry, I thought it near 300mph. So I needed a deflection of one radius of my sight-ring. With it bisecting the port engine, and with the engine pointing straight at the central dot, I needed only to be flying with no skid or slip – otherwise there would be some sideways wind across my gun muzzles. I took a check on my turn-and-slip instrument, low down on the left of my blind-flying panel, and it showed the top needle vertical. I squeezed off a full one-and-a-half-seconds burst at killing range.

Halfway through the burst, white smoke spurted from the target engine and became a thin stream trailing for 200 yards astern. He'd got a serious coolant leak, and if he didn't shut down that engine it would quickly overheat and seize up. Sure enough, the port airscrew stopped and I could see that the blades had been feathered.

I throttled sharply back as the Heinkel's speed dropped, and came up abreast of his port wing. From perhaps fifty yards I looked across at the pilot, a thick-set man in pale brown overalls and a dark brown flying helmet. He looked back at me, and for ten seconds or so we gazed into each other's eyes. Then I stabbed my finger downwards three or four times and made landing motions with my arm. When there was no response, I pulled back the hood and repeated my gestures. For a few seconds he looked at me and then, to my relief, he raised a hand in acknowledgement. I closed my hood and followed the Heinkel in his slow starboard turn.

I waggled my wings to Guy to rejoin formation. We circled and watched as the enemy bomber landed. It seemed intact. The crew of four climbed out and huddled together on the ground.

We flew back a short distance to a main road and spotted a police car, which stopped. A figure gazed up at us, hooding his eyes with his hands. We flew a half-mile west, turned and then came over him on a direct line for the Heinkel as I waggled my wings. We circled again and watched the car continue a short way and stop. Two figures got out and went into the field next to our prize.

As I flew back low over the Heinkel, I was surprised – and rather touched – to see the Captain line up his crew and then salute me. On impulse, I fished out my half-smoked packet of Players cigarettes, wrapped one of my rubber earpieces from my flying helmet around it, and tied them up in a not-terribly-clean handkerchief, opened the roof, came in on a slow low run and threw them out. They fell close to the group. As I circled round I could see him handing them out to his men.

I called Guy into close formation for a final fly-past. We came in low and, as we neared them, they came smartly together to salute, and held it as we thundered past. I climbed away towards Kenley looking back at them. I have often wondered who the Captain was, but I never found out.

A few days later, 253 Squadron was scrambled to intercept a 'twenty-plus', believed hostile, near Selsey, height (as usual) vague. Cloud was 10/10 at around 4,000 to 7,000 feet and that raised a doubt in my mind, 'but theirs not to reason why!' We climbed to 20,000 feet and fairly soon were intercepted by around forty Me109s, a dozen of which were carrying bombs which I saw being jettisoned. So there we were, high and dry, with the opposition having the height on us. I deployed the squadron into a long line astern and defensive circle. Graves was no. 12 in the line and was nibbled at by an Me109, before I blew it away, which caused them to pause for thought.

I asked Controller if they thought any 'big babies' were around as the sky seemed to be full only of 'snappers'.

We orbited and I scanned around, waiting for news. Now and then a snapper made a frustrated dart. I got tired of this stalemate and led the squadron for cloud cover, dipped into it, and asked them to reform below as I steered south-west, intending to climb up into the sun and try again. I saw a green-and-brown camou-flage wing near to my tail, but thought nothing of it. My error – a 109 camouflaged with our colours. Suddenly it was snowing in the cockpit, there was an almighty bang on my left foot and rudder pedal, and a powerful smell of cordite and petrol in the air.

An odd phenomenon which I experienced in moments of danger was that time seemed to slow down. Perhaps because my adrena-lin-boosted brain went into overdrive. And time is relative anyway. Snow in the cockpit was the sign of tracer. I couldn't pull away to either side because of my flanking no. 2 and no. 3. So I slammed on starboard aileron and slid under my no. 2, and discovered that my rudder controls had been shot away. The 109 broke away to port, and my Polish no. 2 clobbered him. I had petrol sloshing about, so it was time to 'take silk'. I had always hated the thought of getting burned. I had seen men I knew well become unrecognis-able through burns. I snapped my goggles down over my eyes, unclipped the oxygen tube (the RT plug pulled out easily; but the oxygen had a bayonet-fitting like a light bulb into its terminal); unpinned the Sutton harness; trimmed the aircraft nose-heavy and got ready to leave as soon as the hood was open.

I slammed the hood back, and immediately the vortex of air behind the windscreen sucked the petrol out of the leaking tank all over me. As I crouched on the seat holding the stick I could feel it splattering on the front of my overalls and trickling down my face and neck. I took a glance all round. All I had to do was give the stick a good kick and the Hurricane would go down whilst I went forward.

At that precise moment the engine stopped. The gravity tank, which I'd been flying on for thirty minutes, was empty. I suddenly felt a right Charlie, half-standing in the seat with my head and shoulders outside the cockpit. The danger of bursting into flames had passed, and we were not so flush with Hurricanes that one could afford to throw any away unnecessarily. So I sat down again, throttled back and switched on the main tanks. The engine picked up immediately, so I decided to fly it back to Kenley. I felt sure I could fiddle the landing somehow without the benefit of rudder, but checked for brake and differential-braking which all registered. No sweat. Kenley here I come. At least I can taxi under control. So I turned off to go home, and found I had no radio. No worry, I knew where I was, and my faithful no. 2 was back in formation. By dumb crambo I indicated no RT and my intention to return and land. He nodded and gave a thumbs up. In a routine sort of way I then flicked the contents switch to starboard to confirm that the main tank was full. It wasn't. It was barely two-thirds full, and the port tank was the same. Squinting backwards on either side I could see a faint haze tail behind each mainplane, and decided the main tanks were both leaking fast. The question was, how fast?

I timed a five-minute run after reducing revs to minimum and leaving throttle well open – a good formula for max-range flying. After five minutes I calculated ground covered, ground to go and re-checked my fuel. About one-third full on each side. It would be a dead heat between arrival at Kenley and fuel exhaustion. Say five minutes left, check again after three. Airfield just about in sight, with Homer's wireless masts dead ahead. Exchange 500 feet for more speed – leaves 20,000 feet still for baling out.

The sensible thing to do was leap out after all. But that would really give the Luftwaffe one more victory. I thought, dear old Hurribubble, can't desert you now! I signalled to my no. 2 a straight in approach, the die was cast, the speed cut down, the undercarriage lowered and, as late as possible, the flaps. I throttled right back to reduce to a minimum the swing caused by change of torque from different power setting and resultant yaw, and lined the aircraft up with the runway using aileron and elevator. Got it straight and set it down. Rolled off on to the grass as the speed dropped to around 40mph and steered towards dispersal. Eighty yards short the engine coughed apologetically and stopped and we drifted to a halt with fifty yards or so to push.

It was a triumph for mental arithmetic and stupidity. I asked my Flight Sergeant, always on the spot, to check the aircraft over; longed for a cigarette but decided that smoking was much too dangerous; and cantered off to the mess reeking of 100-octane. Long hot shower and total change of clothing, and back to dispersal. My Flight Sergeant met me with a slow, wry smile, and passed the strange request from my ground crew that I get back into the cockpit, 'to see their handiwork'. I was mystified but I climbed on to the wing and saw what they had been up to. My rigger explained that they had been threading strings through the holes in the tail to the holes in front. There were about twenty of them. When I sat down there was no position I could find that didn't cause me to bend at least three of their strings. The Flight Sergeant asked me if I had discovered any holes in myself during my shower – which the grinning faces all round seemed to find absolutely hilarious!

I went on trying, with the seat up and down, but it was no good. Three bent strings was my lowest possible score. How could that have happened – don't know. Not, that is, if you discount some powerful outside agency. I never did, though. Fools and drunkards traditionally are His wards, and some traditions I totally accept.

I lost many friends during the battle but none more courageous than Squadron Leader 'Spike' O'Brien. Spike and I had our first combats on the night of 6 June 1940, and Spike's saga started then.

It was a gin-clear night with a full moon, and Spike took a new pilot up with him in a Blenheim I to show him the Sector that night. After take-off he was diverted to, and intercepted, an He111 that was returning after bombing Birmingham. In the gun-fight the Heinkel went down and Spike's Blenheim went out of control in a spin. At that time no pilot ever had got out of a spinning Blenheim alive, because the only way out was through the top sliding hatch and you then fell through the airscrew. The new boy probably didn't know that but nevertheless he froze, and Spike had to get him out. He undid his seat belt, unplugged his oxygen, and threw him bodily out of the top hatch while holding his parachute rip-cord. He told me afterwards that he felt sick when the lad fell through the airscrew. Spike then had to get out himself. He grasped the wireless aerial behind the hatch, pulled himself up it and then turned round so that his feet were on the side of the fuselage. Then he kicked outwards as hard as he could. He felt the tip of an airscrew blade 'pat' him on the earpiece of his helmet.

He landed on the outskirts of a village and went to the nearest pub to ring base and ask for transport home. He got himself a pint and sat down at a table to chat with another chap who was sitting there in uniform. After some time, thinking the chap's dress was a bit unusual, Spike asked him if he was a Pole or Czech.

'Oh, no,' said his companion in impeccable English, 'I'm a German pilot actually. Just been shot down by one of your blokes.'

At this, Spike sprang to his feet and said, 'I arrest you in the name of the King. And anyway, where did you learn English?'

The German said, 'That's all right. I won't try to get away. In fact I studied at Cambridge for three years, just down the way.' Then he said, 'I shall be out of here anyway in a week or two's time, you know.'

'Like bloody hell you will!' said Spike.

'Let's agree to disagree,' said the German. 'My shout, what's yours?'

Said Spike, 'Hey, you can't go buying me a drink.'

'Why not?' said the German. 'I've got plenty of English money and it's no more your pub than mine.'

So that's what they did, sat and had a drink.

A few days later Spike was posted for a rest to a Controller's course in the West Country. One morning, when strolling along the tarmac of the airfield, he was surprised to see a Do17 overhead at 2,000 feet. Alongside the perimeter track was a visiting Spitfire. Spike leapt in, started up, and took off in pursuit. No helmet, no parachute. He caught the Dornier and shot it down. When the

AOC 10 Group heard the story he was immediately promoted to command a Spitfire squadron at Middle Wallop.

In late August his squadron reinforced 11 Group on one sortie against a raid by Me110s on Hawker's Weybridge factory. Spike was seen to be engaging an Me110, believed destroyed, whilst being himself attacked by another. Some fifteen minutes later he appeared in the circuit at Biggin Hill. He lowered the undercarriage and flaps and was turning on to finals at around 600 feet when his aircraft caught fire. Probably an incendiary bullet had lodged in his petrol tanks, and then sparked off the petrol vapour above the fuel when its level fell. He was seen to bale out, but his parachute was not fully deployed when he hit the ground and he was dead when the ambulance reached him.

I spoke later to the doctor who was in the ambulance. When he examined Spike's body, he found that his left arm had been shot off at the shoulder, and his left eye shot out of his head. Yet he had flown that Spit right down to approach for a normal landing! It was almost unbelievable that he had done that with one arm. Throttle control, airscrew pitch, control column, undercarriage control, flap control, elevator trim – that's what you needed to juggle. Opening the roof is one-handed – if you let go of the stick – but then to have climbed out with those injuries and pulling the rip-cord – must have required almost superhuman will-power and guts.

But then that was Spike.

Flight Lieutenant Peter Brothers

I learned to fly as a schoolboy, but my father hoped I would settle down and join his business. As soon as I was seventeen-and-a-half, however, I pissed off and got a short service commission in the Air Force. That was in January 1936, and I was sent to Uxbridge first, for ground training, getting kitted out and so on.

At Uxbridge there was this splendid First World War pilot, Ira Taffy Jones, who stuttered terribly. One day he stood up and said,

'There is going to be a b-b-bloody wa-wa-war and you ch-chaps are going to be in it. I'll give you one piece of advice – wh-wh-when you fir-first get into a co-combat, you will be fu-fu-fucking fr-frightened. Ne-never forget the ch-chap in the other cock-cockpit is tw-twice as fu-fucking fr-frightened as you are.' I reckon he saved my life with that piece of advice. In my first combat over France, I suddenly thought, My God, the chap in that other cockpit must be having hysterics, and shot him down. But I give all credit to Taffy.

I was posted to Biggin Hill in the autumn, and I operated there, flying Gloster Gauntlets and doing practice interceptions on civil aircraft. We were the first station to have an ops room. It was all chalk on blackboards in those days, and one aircraft had a clock on the transmitter which transmitted for fifteen seconds every minute, so that the radio stations could get a DF (Direction Finding) bearing on you. Meanwhile, the radar were also checking on that, so we had a dual-fixing situation. The idea was to see how close the interception worked out on the incoming aircraft. The radar would plot incoming aircraft to Croydon, for example, and we'd go off to intercept them somewhere over the Channel or East Kent. We'd just fly past and report how close we'd been and when we first sighted them. That was very interesting and amusing, because the Station Commander would give you a course to steer, vector so-and-so, and off you went. Then you'd hear him over the radio, saying, 'Vector . . . How the hell can I see the blackboard with your fat bottom in the way?'

The Gloster Gauntlets were biplanes, single-engine, single-seater aircraft. Very cold, with an open cockpit. In 1938 we converted to Hurricanes, and carried on doing the same sort of thing, plus gunnery practice. I never really bothered to think that we'd actually face an enemy. It was like being in a glorious, but expert flying club.

During 1938 Winston Churchill used occasionally to come into the mess at Biggin Hill, on his way home to Chartwell. The door would open just before six o'clock, and he'd come in. We'd say,

'Good evening, sir,' and he'd say, 'Would you mind turning on the radio, so that I can hear the six o'clock news?' Sometimes he'd have a glass of sherry, and then he'd ask us about our Supermarine Hurricane aircraft, whether we were content with them, and that sort of thing. He'd spend a few minutes with us, then he'd get on his way home. But we never reminded him that we were actually flying Hawker Hurricanes.

The first hint of war came into my life with the Munich crisis, when I began to think, yes, this is deadly serious. Then came the so-called 'phoney war', convoy patrols and constant scrambles, but you never saw the enemy. When we went into action for the first time, on 10 May 1940, we were told to ground-strafe an airfield in Holland which had been captured by the Germans. I was leading the squadron because the Commanding Officer was new, and flying no. 2 to me. We left 'A' flight up above to protect us whilst we went down to ground-strafe, but to my surprise the airfield was covered with Junkers 52s, troop transport aircraft. They were all burned out in the middle, but the nose, tail and wing tips were still there. We thought this was very odd, so we didn't fire at them because it was a waste of time. Then we found one undamaged aircraft parked between some hangars. We set that on fire and came back to base. It was some months later before we discovered that the Dutch had recaptured the airfield just before our arrival. They'd destroyed those aircraft on the ground, leaving one in which to escape to England. And that was the one we'd set on fire.

We then started doing the usual thing, going to France for the day. We started in Belgium, at a place called Mooresele. It was only a little flying club airfield, and when we arrived, the chaps there, 615 Squadron, were rather jumpy because refugees were streaming down the road, and that morning one of their Sergeant pilots had been found with a knife in his chest. We operated from there during the day, but it was all very chaotic. We received no instructions, and not only did we have to refuel the aircraft ourselves, but we also had to hand-start them. We'd start mine, then

I'd get out and wind somebody else's, and so on, until we'd got them all started. We received no assistance whatsoever from the French. In fact, on one occasion, we were refuelling when a Dornier 17 flew over us at about 8,000 feet. We thought he was going to bomb us on the ground, but he carried on his way. Meanwhile, there was a French fighter aircraft doing aerobatics over the airfield. When we shouted to the Colonel and pointed to the aircraft, he said, 'Oh, today he is only authorised for aerobatics, not combat'.

It was a very tiring business, because we were getting up at about three o'clock in the morning, having breakfast, getting airborne in the dark, flying inland across the French coast and arriving at first light. We'd spend the day operating there with no assistance, begging food from a local farmer or something, then come out at Le Havre and back across the Channel, reaching Biggin Hill at nine-thirty or ten at night, having a meal and going to bed. Then being called up in the morning again. Very wearing. It all seemed rather pointless too, because we didn't feel we were achieving very much. We had several engagements in France but not enough, I would have said, to justify our presence there.

The bombing of UK ports started next, as well as attacks on our airfield at Biggin Hill. I had got married in 1939, and one night I went to see my wife, in Westerham, and discovered that she'd been sitting at her dressing-table one evening, and a bomb splinter had come through the open window and smashed her mirror while she'd been sitting there. I decided these people needed to be taught a sharp lesson.

Prior to the evacuation of Dunkirk in 1940, we had several combats while we were operating in places like Merville. The first chap we lost was my great chum, Johnny Milner. He baled out and became a prisoner-of-war. Interestingly, all the fatal casualties were new boys. Chaps got shot down, they got burned and were wounded, but they survived. The only ones who were killed were the replacements coming in. Of course, most of the chaps had been in the squadron for a couple of years, so they knew the aircraft, they knew the tactics. They knew what they were doing.

Taking on the enemy was a game to start off with. It was great fun and you didn't wish to hurt anybody. You wanted to shoot an aircraft down, but when you'd actually hit a cockpit . . . well, it was a bit sick-making to see that you'd killed a chap. That was only in the early days. Later on, you couldn't give a damn whether you'd killed someone or not – you thought, So much the better! I vividly remember shooting a 109 down and seeing him crash in Kent. He went straight into the ground, and I flew over it, thinking, Jolly good, that's one. Now, where are the rest? The object really was to shoot the bombers down as the fighters weren't doing any damage to anybody, apart from ourselves. The trouble was that, when you attacked the bombers, you got jumped by their fighter escort. That often used to happen to me, probably because I was Flight Commander leading 'B' Flight. 'A' Flight would go in after the bombers first, followed by us, by which time the fighter escort was coming down, and so we'd be the ones who'd break away to fight them off. Bringing down a bomber was really satisfying, particularly if you got it before it dropped its bombs. Getting them when they were on their way home was better than nothing, but if you caught them before they'd made their drop, it was a real success. You usually went for the engines, but one of the best ways to attack them was head-on. The Heinkel 111, for example, had a glazed nose, and they could see you coming, but they'd got no protection head-on; all their guns were firing backwards. Our machine-guns were arranged to fire a pattern at 250 yards, although some of us decided to have our guns turned in to concentrate at a point. Usually, we tried to get much closer than 250 yards. In head-on attacks the question was whether you went over the top of the aircraft or underneath it after firing. I always used to go down, because I thought the bomber would probably pull up instinctively.

I was hit once in those early operations. I got shot up and the controls were broken, shot away. I was halfway out of the cockpit before I realised the aircraft was still controllable, and climbed back in again.

Stukas were pretty easy meat because you could shoot straight into the top of them as they pulled out of their dive and they were slower than we were. That awful screaming sound they made had been built into them to terrify people. Once they had started the dive, you could follow them down, and hit them if you were lucky. If you were too close, of course, you'd overtake.

Before the battle I realised that if the Luftwaffe gained air superiority then, of course, the whole country was open to them. However, one didn't have time to consider the background; you were worrying about your own chaps, your own aircraft, and your own ground crew. It was day to day, minute to minute. I realised that they were going to come in greater masses. The going then got heavier, as I think everybody realised, and one was tired, inevitably. I am a fairly equable person but occasionally used to lose my temper. Having got engaged one day I pressed the gun button and nothing happened at all, because the guns hadn't been reloaded. On landing back, I had the armourer in the office, drew my pistol, and said, 'I'll shoot you if you ever do that again.' But I was tired.

Our tactics didn't change, apart from the fact that we'd thrown away the idea of Fighter Command Attack no. 1, no. 2, no. 3, different formations and so on, because they didn't fit in with what the enemy was doing. We were often compelled to attack from the stern, because we were usually scrambled late in the day. The Controllers, quite rightly, didn't wish to launch us off too soon and find that it was a spoof raid. Then we'd have to turn back to base and refuel and be caught on the ground. So, inevitably, they would delay as long as possible before sending us off.

The result was that we'd be struggling for height to try and get up, not only to the height of the raiding bombers, at about 18,000 feet, but above them to launch our own attack. I mean, ideally you wanted to be up-sun, but it rarely worked out like that. You just had to keep away until you'd got the height, otherwise they flew over the top of your head, and you were cat's-meat for their escorting fighters. It was quite impressive, meeting this black cloud of aircraft, all piled up like – as somebody described it – 'the moving staircase at Piccadilly Circus'. They would be up in their hundreds, with the bottom squadron leading. They'd be stacked up behind, as well, with the fighters sitting up on top. One thing I remember from those early heavy raids, was the density of the rear-gunners' fire. They'd put up a sort of barrage that you had to go through if you wanted to get in close – to about fifty or a hundred yards – which was vital. The aim was to get that rear-gunner out of the way. There was nothing you could do to avoid it – you'd collect a few holes and just hope for the best.

Once, I'd made my attack and broken away, when suddenly the sky around me was empty. Everybody seemed to have vanished. I looked around and saw five 109s in a 'V' formation, heading for home all on their own. I thought, Well, this is splendid. I'll just climb up behind them and start picking them off, one by one. The chap on the far right of the formation had obviously seen me coming and he eased away to the right, so I thought, Oh, I'll be content with this chap today, and not bother about the others. An almost fatal mistake. As I was about to open fire, he opened the throttle wide and started climbing rapidly. I pulled the stick back to follow him, and at that moment all hell broke loose. The other four came in behind and they all had a go at me, and filled me full of holes. I was so angry with myself for being so stupid! I was chattering with rage and frightened, I shot off fairly quickly and they all whizzed past, firing at me, and then they were gone. I didn't get anything other than a severe fright, but I never did that again. In fact, I used to warn chaps about it. I also used to warn them that, if we were jumped by escorting fighters and you saw tracer passing on your left, 'turn into it, not away'. Instinctively you want to turn away, but the enemy, having seen he was firing to the left of you, was then correcting his aim to fire to the right. Well, if you turned left you threw his aim completely; you went through some of his fire, and took your chance on that.

It was all fairly intense, but the waiting around at base was the hardest part. We'd either sleep, play mahjong or read. When we were 'scrambled', one of our chaps would run to his aircraft, be violently sick, and then jump into his aircraft and be off. Your adrenalin really got going once that bell went. We all swore we'd never have a telephone at home after the war; because as soon as the telephone rang you'd all automatically be at the ready. Then you'd hear, 'No, Corporal so-and-so has just gone to get his lunch' and you'd all relax again. It would either be that or, '32 Squadron scramble 18,000 feet over Ashford' and off you'd go.

After we returned from an operation, the Intelligence Officer would want all the details. We weren't all that interested, it was over, finished. But he needed the information. We'd give him the information and then perhaps we'd be off again. We could be scrambled in the middle of telling him something. During one of the raids on Dover, I'd shot down a Stuka and then gone into Hawkinge to refuel and rearm. I didn't even get out of the aircraft. They were rearming the aircraft and there was a chap standing on the wing in front of me, pumping fuel into the tank. The battle was still going on up above and, as we watched, a Spitfire shot down a 109, and the pilot baled out. The airman who was refuelling me said, 'Got him!' And then, when the pilot's parachute opened, he turned to me with a look of utter disgust on his face and said, 'Oh, the jammy bastard!' As soon as they'd finished I was off again, back into the battle. But it was rather amusing. I got a 109 later on that day.

The hardest day was 15 August. That was a very big raid. There was a change of tactics and it took us by surprise. Quite a few aircraft were caught on the ground. They were bombing Biggin Hill from high-level, a raid against which I was involved, but they also ran a low-level raid at Kenley, which was next door to Biggin Hill.

Wilhelm Raab was on the Kenley raid, and his squadron suffered tremendous losses. His gunner was wounded, and he landed at the first base he reached in France to off-load the wounded crew. In fact, I shot him down later, on 15 September. His unit lost most of its aircraft on that low-level raid. Meanwhile, we were unaware of the low-level raid at Kenley. The Germans threw everything they had at us. We did three sorties that day, all around midday, one of them was fifty minutes long, one was an hour, and the other was an hour and a bit. I got a 109 and a Dornier 17 at high-level. The Germans lost 75 aircraft that day. Although they attacked all four fighter groups, their bombers caused some damage, but no great success. They never came again in such numbers.

The raid on 15 September was a tough one as well, and when we went up we thought it was going to be one of those days, a hard day. By then I was with 257 Squadron, and we made only two sorties that day: one of an hour and ten minutes and one of forty minutes. I got a Dornier 17, and a Ju88.

After that September raid things abated slightly. On 19 and 20 September we ran defensive and convoy patrols, but we saw no action. The general feeling was that we'd seen them off. On 28 September we did two patrols, a 'Big Wing' with 73 and 17 Squadrons. We were flying in and out of cloud, when suddenly we were jumped by some 109s. I saw one going past, attacking 17 Squadron, who were below and in front of us, leading. This 109 knocked off a Hurricane before anybody could do anything. Suddenly we realised that there were several of them about, and of course, the Wing broke up and everybody got involved, but without any great success.

The sporadic raids went on into December, then they reverted to 109s carrying bombs. 257 Squadron had moved from Martlesham Heath to North Weald, and one day, when I'd gone over to the mess for tea, suddenly the scramble sounded. We were raided by 109s dropping bombs, and I dived under the table. They dropped a bomb right outside, where I'd parked my old open Red Label Bentley. It was filled with soil, but fortunately not damaged.

The winter was coming and clearly there was not going to be an invasion. The Battle of Britain had been won.

First Officer Diana Barnato Walker, ATA

When I was a girl, you had nannies and governesses and chaperons and you weren't allowed off the leash at all. I thought if I learned to fly I could escape all the supervision. That was the basic thing.

I went to Brooklands, which was the snob flying club, where I had been as a kid to watch my father race his Bentleys. It was very expensive, £3 an hour. The Civil Air Guard had already been started by Harold Balfour, where you could learn to fly for 7s. 6d. an hour, but I was far too much of a snob to mix with the 'hoi polloi'. I learned in a Tiger Moth, and went solo after six hours. I had no idea what I was doing! I really didn't! I've never forgotten that first solo – as I was taxi-ing out, a little man came running up to the aeroplane, and put his hands on the side of the Tiger's cockpit. They were all gnarled and burned, and so was his face. He said, 'Oh Miss Barnato, Miss Barnato! Don't fly! Don't fly! Look what it's done to me!' It was frightening, but my solo went off all right.

Shortly after that I ran out of pocket money. I'd done ten hours. My parents were parted and both had remarried. They weren't going to give me any more money because, first, they didn't want me off the chaperon's leash, and second, they thought I'd break my neck. So that was the end of the flying for two-and-a-half years.

When the war started, I joined the Red Cross, but I had some friends in the Air Transport Auxiliary (ATA) at the time, who told me I should join them. They needed pilots. So they were out to get anybody suitable. But, of course, I would have to do a flying test, and I hadn't flown for years. So I took my Bentley out, and I went along the bypass watching the grass verge, at forty, at sixty, at eighty, reminding myself of all the Tiger's take-off and landing speeds. I had an RAF admirer, and we sat on the sofa pretending we were in a Tiger and went through exactly what you do for circuits and bumps. Then we went out and we went riding and, as if by chance, we met the Chief Flying Instructor. He rode an old cob that was rather scruffy, and there was I on a beautiful mare and perfectly turned out.

Well, he fell for the idea and made a date for the test. Apparently, when the test day came I turned up in a leopard skin coat! I can't remember it, but that's what I've been told. Imagine getting into a dirty old Tiger in a leopard skin coat! That is the sort of life we led. It horrifies me now how irresponsible I was.

While waiting for the result, I went up to hunt in Leicestershire. The hunt was rained off, and while we were riding I had a bad accident. So when my acceptance came in from the ATA, I couldn't go because I was in hospital.

That six months was a life-saver, because during that time the ATA training was set up. If I had gone in with only ten hours I wouldn't be here now, because I couldn't have coped with the small amount of flying instruction that was given in the early days.

The ATA trained in their own way: they categorised the aircraft into six classes and you learned one in each class. Then you could fly anything in that class. We flew dual control, then solo, and had classroom lessons of course, and even a little engineering, although we never actually did any engineering work on the planes. We also had to learn about weather and balloons and the airfields we'd be flying into around the country. Then we had a handy loose-leaf notebook, which had every aircraft we were likely to fly in it, one aircraft to a page, and if you couldn't remember, you mugged it up before take-off and in the circuit before landing.

I wasn't the least bit frightened because the training was so gradual, and one progressed so slowly that I always longed to do the next thing. Once you'd trained on twins you were sometimes a taxi pilot and sometimes a delivery pilot. A taxi pilot fetched and carried everybody to and from the beginnings or ends or link-ups of their jobs. During the first part of my training, I was six weeks at Hamble padding my hours, getting a bit more general flying experience.

I didn't fly four-engined aircraft because at Hamble, an all-woman ferry pool, they had enough four-engined pilots, and also by the time I was ready to be converted they had ex-RAF chaps seconded to us who couldn't fight any more, but were perfectly capable of ferrying.

When we arrived, in the morning, our chits were set out on the table. We'd rush and grab ours. Then we went and got our chutes out, went to Met and checked the forecast for the route that we were going to fly, checked maps and signals in case anything nasty had happened or been put up in the way, checked the balloons as well, and then the taxi Anson would be called and we'd rush out to our first drop and off we went. Some of the jobs were there-and-backs and some were link-ups; often, of course, the middle one went wrong, but for some you were just picked up in the Anson from somewhere at the end.

The idea was to get back at night, but you didn't always because something went unserviceable or the weather was stinking and you couldn't get back. We weren't expected to fly at night, we had to land twenty minutes before dusk. We would get as far as we could and then put down. We didn't fly with radio, and we couldn't fly on instruments if the weather was bad, because they didn't teach us to fly on instruments. We didn't have radio because the enemy might have heard the transmissions, and also the RAF needed all the air time that they could get. So we used to get stuck out on an average one night a week.

I delivered many different aircraft. But I flew more Spitfires than any other type. They weren't all the same mark, of course; the Spitfire went right through the war to the end, and it grew and changed and got progressively longer and bigger and more powerful.

I had flown 260 different Spitfires by the time I was twenty-two, as well as many other types of aircraft. We were an extraordinarily mixed bunch. We had one-armed pilots and one-eyed pilots, and lame pilots and First War pilots, and all sorts of people who couldn't get into the RAF. We had twenty-nine different nations flying with us who came from all over the world, including foreign women. For instance, we had a Chilean girl at Hamble. We called her 'Chile' – she was beautiful and a marvellous pilot. She had flown in the Chilean Air Force. They told her she couldn't fly until she learned English. At the end of the day when we'd been sitting warmly in our classrooms, Chile would come in covered in oil. But after three months all she'd learned was the swear words, because the engineers thought it frightfully funny to teach this sweet little girl to swear.

We also had twenty-five American girls brought over by Jacqueline Cochrane.

Of course, I fell in love with an RAF chap. It happened during my training days, when I was flying a Magister – an open mono-plane – on a cold day that was really too windy and rough for a Maggie. I shouldn't really have taken off, and I shouldn't have landed either, but I wanted to keep my breakfast. So I put down at Debden and a couple of pilots I knew introduced me to a man called Humphrey Gilbert, who was a Squadron Leader. Humph-rey was a shock-headed dark fellow whose hair wouldn't stay down. We all went out together that night and next day I went down to my aeroplane and it wouldn't start. The ground crew came to look at it, and there was general conversation. Later an RAF crew who had force-landed there after a raid took me up for a little trip in a Havoc. It was the first time I had been in a warplane and I suddenly realised this was it. What I was doing was important. The next day my plane still wasn't fixed. Of course, by this time I'd fallen for Humphrey and he had made a pass at me – in the nicest, sweetest, gentlest possible way, because one didn't make direct passes in those days.

The next day the aircraft still wouldn't start. By this time my CO in Training Pool was getting rather growly, because he wanted his Maggie for other people to fly. So Humphrey got on the phone and explained that it really wouldn't start, that they were work-ing on it. So we had another evening of happiness and fun. The romance began.

The next day the aircraft started and off I went. Then

Humphrey came to fetch me from White Waltham at the end of every flying day and brought me back for the night to Debden and the next morning he flew me back and dropped me. And when he couldn't do it himself he sent Bob Sarll to do it. Bob always got lost, so I had to do the flying. I wasn't very good either, but at least I didn't get lost. So the romance continued.

One day we went to London and danced in the 400 Club. Then we decided to get married. He was going to come up and meet me in my flat and we were going to discuss marriage plans. And he never turned up. I thought I'd been stood up. I was very disappointed. I rang the station – nobody would tell me anything about him. I didn't know what had happened, I thought he didn't want to talk to me. The next morning I went to the telephone box and was finally put on to Group Captain John Peel who told me he'd been bumped off. I assumed it had happened on ops because he had already been flying for more than one tour of ops.

I came out of the telephone booth, and there was a one-armed pilot furious because he wanted to get on the phone. He saw I was crying, and he put his one arm around me and tried to comfort me. Then I went into the common room and the hatch opened and the CO, Captain Pickup, called me. He took a little pair of wings out and (usually you had a ceremony, to be presented with wings) he slapped them down and said, 'Here, Miss Barnato, are your wings, but, Miss Barnato, because you have your wings does not necessarily mean you can fly.' He then slammed the hatch down. He was still annoyed with me for having stayed away with his aeroplane for four days, and wasn't going to forgive me very easily. It was an intense little romance really, and very short – a month, six weeks – very intense. Of course it was. I went to the funeral and it was very emotional.

The war went on, and I got posted to Hamble. Then, three years later, Tony Bartley, the pilot who'd introduced us at Debden, asked me to go out to dinner with him one night, but that day I got stuck out, I couldn't get back to base. You always got back if you could when you had a date – you flew through much worse weather to get home for a date than you otherwise would. But I couldn't get home. The next day when I got back to Hamble, one of the hangar fellows told me Tony had been there looking for me. He asked me if he wasn't the fellow who'd taken a WAAF up on his lap in a Spitfire. Well, he was, I had heard the story when Humphrey and Tony were laughing about it one day. Stupid thing to do, but he'd got away with it. I said, 'So?' This fellow said, 'Well, he got away with it, but it had a very unfortunate sequence.' I said, 'Oh?' He said, 'Yes, his CO was killed the same way.' His CO, of course, was Humphrey Gilbert. And it turned out he had not taken just a little WAAF up on his lap, but a large flying Controller fellow. And of course, they hadn't got off the ground. They broke the aeroplane and broke their necks and that was that. But I didn't know. They didn't tell me, it was all hushed up.

The day I'd learned he was dead, I was given a Hart to fly, and one of the turning-points was Debden. I thought I was given Debden to see if I was trustworthy enough not to land there. Because, of course, everybody knew about Humphrey. I'd circled the aerodrome at Debden, looking for Humphrey's Spitfire, and I couldn't find it, so I thought he had been killed on ops. But he hadn't, he'd been killed doing this silly thing. They'd been talking and laughing about Tony's exploit, and guts and youth and exuberance and everything else just took over. It was a terrible waste.

Everything was so serious and sad, because people were getting killed – friends and admirers of all sorts – and we realised the fragility of life. Most people were there and then not there any more. I never thought it would happen to me, though. I wasn't the slightest bit frightened. None of my friends were mutilated or burned, that would have been the worst. I always remembered the little man who'd been burned and called out to me. That was always in my mind. So when I got into tight places and had a problem, I always thought of Max Aitken saying, 'Fly level and think.' That was the one thing – think! Relax!

I got that lesson just in time, really. One night I was out in London and finished up in the 400 with Max Aitken and Billy

Clyde. Billy had taken off his boots and waltzed with me in his socks. Max and Billy were horrified to discover that I hadn't been taught to fly on instruments. Not only hadn't been taught, but didn't even know how the instruments worked! Apart from the airspeed indicator and the altimeter. They thought it was unbelievable. So they sat down and gave me a lesson on instruments.

They drew the instruments, in ink, on the pink tablecloth in the 400. They described it all to me and Max said that, when you get into a cloud, you will probably hit it sideways, and you have to straighten up and think, watch your spot heights, climb up above your safety height, turn round on a rate one turn – I didn't know what a rate one turn was – let down gradually, as shallowly as you can, and leave your throttle setting where it is if it's a fighter, and before you start your descent decide what your break-off height is going to be, so you don't fly into the ground. All these things I didn't know!

The next day, having just come off leave, I was a bit late getting back, and I was in my best uniform, which had a skirt. I didn't have time to take it off and put on my trousers, I just rushed out as I was and got into my aircraft, a Spitfire. I was going north over the Cotswolds over Little Rissington. It was a lovely sunny day, then suddenly I was in cloud. And except for the previous night's lesson, I hadn't been taught instruments! Well, I did everything that Max had told me: I turned round on my reciprocal and I let down in a series of unequal stages, and decided my break-off height was going to be 650 feet, because I thought I was coming back past Little Rissington, which was 600 feet. Imagine only leaving fifty feet as a break off! Barmy! But I didn't know.

I contemplated jumping, but I felt I couldn't jump because I had my skirt on! It was crazy! I was so vain! Coming down on a parachute with wartime stockings and panties made out of parachute silk, I thought, was going to look silly and also going to hurt! I couldn't jump out, so I had to get down! Well, I went down and suddenly I looked at the altimeter and saw I was at 600 feet! I should have been at 650 feet, and I was just about to go up again when I saw some trees and at the same moment I saw the wing of a parked aeroplane, through a little hole in the swirling cloud. It should have been Little Rissington, because I'd gone up that way and I was coming back that way on my reciprocal. So I did a circuit just above the trees in and out of cloud. But it wasn't Little Rissington, it was a little plain patch of grass. I saw a Nissen hut there, and an aeroplane, but the whole of this little grass patch was covered in water, because it was pouring with rain. Well, if you landed a Spit in a puddle, chances were you'd tip up, because it was nose-heavy. But I had to land there. So I landed. It was very boggy and I made it without going on my nose and parked near the Nissen hut. I got out into pouring rain, and I hadn't got a coat, and I was in my best uniform, and I was drenched in no time. When I got on to the wing my knees collapsed from reaction. I couldn't walk.

Meanwhile, out of this Nissen hut came a very tall friendly giant in RAF uniform with a camouflage cape above his head, keeping him dry. He came to the wing and he held the cape over me. I swivelled round and pretended to be scrabbling for my maps because I didn't want him to see that I'd been frightened. I wasn't frightened at all when I was flying because I was too busy doing everything, but obviously I had used up all my adrenalin and suddenly my knees wouldn't work. Then I recovered and got down off the Spit, and we walked in under the cape to this Nissen hut and there was an enormous sign in RAF blue reading 'RAF Windrush – Blind Flying Establishment'! And this chap said that I must be good on instruments. When I said, 'No, I can't blind fly' he roared with laughter because he thought I was making a joke. So someone then put me in the Link trainer and gave me my first hours of blind-flying training, and I 'fell out upside down'. It was amazing that I'd got down in one piece.

Another fright I had in the air happened when I was flying a Mitchell. With heavy aircraft you needed a flight engineer, and my flight engineer this day was a chap called Brown, who was an old man of about thirty(!), with a round face and watery blue eyes and fair hair. We took the Mitchell off Hamble towards the Southampton balloon barrage and it was fine. In a heavy plane, when you have a flight engineer the pilot opens up, takes off, then the flight engineer puts the wheels up. The pilot then throttles back to climbing and the flight engineer evens up the revs when you get to cruising height. We were flying up past the Wrekin, a high hill near Shrewsbury. There is a tradition among pilots that you tip your hat to the Wrekin. That day we were cruising along happily, but it was very misty, and visibility wasn't very good. Suddenly there was an enormous bang, and all our instruments went out – and I mean all! I instinctively throttled back, but the engines were still purring away happily, so I opened up again. We weren't going to fall out of the sky, but we hadn't got any engine instruments – no rev counters, no boost gauges – nothing! Flight Engineer Brown and I fiddled around and got the engines evened up, but we didn't know what power we had on either boost or revs. We decided to fly on to our destination at Hawarden rather than land somewhere closer. We got into the circuit at Hawarden, and as luck would have it they were landing on the short runway! So there we were – only the short runway on to Hawarden, no airspeed indicator, no engine instruments, no altimeter, no anything. So we did a circuit and I came down to what I thought was between 800 feet and 1,000 feet and came in to land.

On the approach I realised I couldn't make it on the short runway because I was far too high. So I opened up and told Flight Engineer Brown to put the wheels up. I saw him wiggle in his seat, and I thought, poor Brown, he's got the wind up – well, I didn't blame him! But he said, 'It will be all right next time.' I came round very nicely, very low, we got away with a good landing. But even before the nose-wheel dropped, Flight Engineer Brown leaned over and scrabbled between my breasts and undid my harness and banged me in the chest to undo my parachute. I thought he'd gone mad. He said, 'Quick, Diana, quick, brake!' There was nothing wrong with the landing but I quickly braked, whereupon he switched off, took me by the hand, yanked me

spirit and we laughed so much together. We married on a sunlit day in May 1944. Eighteen months later, he was killed flying a Mustang.

Derek, November 1945
by Diana Barnato Walker

I saw you glistening in the sky
Like gleaming vapour flashing by,
I saw you next upon a marble shelf
A scorched grotesqueness of yourself.
The house you hit was still a smouldering shell
That storm we had has turned my life to hell.

I went along to see
What could be done –
The smell of singeing flesh
And jagged, ugly hunks of metal
Still remained.
The wheels were there, and bricks
And burnt-up privet hedges,
A single yellow rose
Was blooming on a blackened stem.
I stood and looked and wept
My heart cried out to Him.

And as I stood, a little man
Came up and watched as well
'Your house, Ma'am? And your garden, Ma'am?
It will all grow again . . .'
But when I turned and looked at him
Just then he understood.
He picked the rose and gave it me
'I'm sorry, very sorry, Ma'am,
I didn't know,' he said.
'Someone I love,' I cried,
'My heart sighs out for him.'

The years have passed,
My searing pains remained,
I went along again to look
And there, as in a dream,
A house of Phoenix stood,
Agleam and clean, with bright blue paint.
(The yellow rose was there)
And underneath the hedge of privet lay a puppy
And a battered teddybear, and close by
Stood a pram.
'Life for a life,' I cried,
And wept for freedom from my Calvary.

Commander Margot Gore, ATA

Gabrielle Patterson was a very good flying instructor; the first woman, I think, in the country to do this. She started the National Women's Air Reserve and we got very cheap flying, at about 15s. per hour. She thought I had potential, and I took my 'A' licence quite quickly. You didn't need very many hours in those days – about fifteen. Then I went on to an Assistant Flying Instructor's course at weekends, for which you had to do one hundred hours' flying.

To enable me to go down from Liverpool Street in the evenings, I got a typing job in Smithfield Market. I started at 5.30 in the morning and finished at 12 noon, earning about 32s. 6d. a week. So I took my Assistant Flying Instructor's endorsement, and by then the Civil Air Guard had started. I was just beginning to instruct the Civil Air Guard boys – there were no girls at that stage – when the war came. We were shut down overnight.

I got a job in MI5 for a time, running up and down stairs with files, but Mrs Patterson had said to me, 'Don't get yourself involved. Don't join the WAAFs or WAACs.' She was one of the first to be called into the Air Transport Auxiliary (ATA) in 1940 and I think she put my name forward. In 1940 I was asked to go for a test at Hatfield. Pauline Gower took me for a couple of circuits in a Tiger Moth and asked if I could join. I said I could. So I joined the ATA almost immediately. We had no uniform, just slacks, a blazer, and a sweater of our own. They issued us with a flying suit, boots and helmet, and all the rest of it.

So we started flying Tiger Moths all over the place from Hatfield where they were being made. Naturally going from a Gipsy to a Spitfire was a little difficult. You had to convert on to a Master before you flew a Spitfire. In August 1940 they started sending us to Central Flying School, where we converted on to a Master and then on to an Oxford. I did about three hours on the Master and was sent solo, terrified. Then I was sent solo after three hours and twenty minutes on the Oxford, which was a twin. Of course, I'd never even sat in the seat of a twin before, and again I was terrified.

We flew quite a lot of Masters and Oxfords over the next year, and then, quite suddenly one day, we were told a Hurricane was coming over for us to do circuits. And the senior ones – Margie Fairweather, Winnie Crossley, Joan Hughes and I – all went up. By this time the De Havilland workforce had heard the rumour – these wretched girls having a flight on a Hurricane! – and they all rushed out. They were not, I think, confident or hopeful that we would crash it, but were probably *expecting* us to crash it. I'm glad to say nobody put it on its nose. It was a frightfully easy aeroplane to fly. Then of course we got just Hurricanes on our books from then on. And Spitfires quite soon afterwards.

By this stage I was a First Officer. We wore BOAC ranking, Cadet, Third Officer, Second Officer, First Officer, Flight Captain, Captain, Commander and Senior Commander. In fact there was quite a funny story about our uniforms. Eventually Philippa Bennett and I were sent to be measured. All the well-to-do had had their uniforms done specially, but we went off to the BOAC tailors as First Officer Gore and First Officer Bennett. We were ushered in, and there was a most ghastly silence! They were expecting two men! They didn't know what to do with us at all. Two tubby little men then met us and we were sent into a changing-room and one stayed outside and one came in with the inch tape. He sort of threw the inch tape round our top half, averted his gaze, and then they whispered the measurement through the door: and so on with the waist and arms. But, of course, when it came to the slacks, the inside leg was beyond him. With averted gaze he did it. And when the suit finally came, the crutch was down at the knees somewhere and we had to have it completely altered.

Quite soon after that it was decided that the ATA were to move from Hatfield: we were getting a bit too big for it. Towards the end of August 1940 Pauline Gower, our Commanding Officer, sent for me to say that we were going to have to divide up. There had been rumours that we were to be posted all round to male pools; but she had prevailed upon headquarters to let us take over a pool at Hamble where there were six or eight men. She asked if I would command it. I said I would have a go. I was to choose eight people from the pool to go with me. Philippa and I went over to White Waltham, where they had their own school, and were converted on to Blenheims. We still ferried Spitfires, Hurricanes, Oxfords and Walruses as well, but we had to be converted on to the more advanced twin. We went straight down then to Hamble. We shared the mess at Air Service Training, where they were not used to women on the aerodrome at all. I think we had one toilet, because they had some typists. But eventually we had our own pool build-ing built with a canteen and all the rest of it. In the end I had about fifty pilots and an engineering section composed of men. When we went on to four-engines we had two women flight engineers and a male flight engineer as well. We had an RAF Met. Officer posted to us with all the gadgets for forecasting too. There were very few difficulties, it was a lovely place to be. I don't think I ever had to discipline a pilot, because they all wanted to fly. Sometimes, of course, you had to tick them off lightly, but I never, ever, had to take disciplinary action. They wanted to fly and they knew that if they erred they wouldn't.

We were bombed continuously for ninety nights. Every night it was a red alert, because they were bombing Eastleigh and Hamble for Spitfires. I didn't lose any of the girls in the bombing though one or two of them crashed. At Hatfield, of course, we lost Amy Johnson (who in 1930 made her historic solo flight to Australia). It cast a gloom, because we didn't understand what had happened – nobody ever has. It's a mystery; and she was a mystery herself. We knew her husband, Jim Mollison, very well – he was one of the funniest men you could ever meet, and used to make you absolutely die with laughter.

I did not have all that number of casualties; we had a little under the average ten per cent death rate. Very surprising really, because the weather was often very peculiar, and we had no navigational aids whatsoever: we only had a compass, but no radio, although we did have a radio with the four-engine planes. The authorities were frightened of things falling into the hands of enemy agents. So we had to fly by contact, and we had to have certain minimum weather conditions – a cloud base and a visibility which they increased for faster aircraft. But still, if the weather was bad and you were under an 800-foot cloud base, you didn't see very far. So it was surprising, really, that we didn't fly into more hillsides.

I was fortunate: I never had an engine quit on me, I never had to put it down anywhere. It was all luck, of course. I mean, when you consider it: Air Service Training were given a contract for repairing Spitfires, and their workforce was the mechanics from London Passenger Transport Board! They'd never seen an aeroplane in their lives before. Marvellous, really. I mean, they had just come straight off a bus. After all, it didn't matter if it stopped again after they'd repaired it!

So we cleared all the factories such as Eastleigh and a place called Marwell, where we had a rather unpleasant little east/west strip. Eventually we took Halifaxes out of it, which was a bit alarming but it was quite narrow and you went through a gap in the trees. At Chattis Hill there was an old racecourse, and you took off up a hill which was part of the gallops.

The most exciting thing I experienced happened there: one day I went into the operations and found on our books a page-and-a-half of Spitfires marked P1W – Priority One aircraft were urgent; you moved them before everything else. And 'W' was even worse, because it meant you had to go and sit there, wherever the plane was, and wait till you got it to wherever it was supposed to go. Of course, this coincided with the most ghastly spell of weather! The cloud was absolutely on the deck. There was no way you could take off. So we dutifully went over by car to Chattis Hill, where they were, and sat there. Then they rang up and said, 'Haven't you moved those Spitfires yet?' I said, 'Have you looked out of your window?' – 'We haven't got any windows!' they said. This was 41 Group at Andover. I said, 'Well, I have got a window, and I can't even see the far side of the aerodrome, which isn't very far away.' – 'Well, they are absolutely vital! You must get them off!' I said, 'We cannot get them off!' But I went over, my aircraft happened to be the one tied down on the tarmac. I said, 'I think the cloud is lifting. Quick! Quick! Run it up!' and I leapt into it. They said, 'I don't think it is, dear.' I said, 'Yes, yes, I think I can see a little bit of a rise. We'll go off a bit lower than the proper height.' And I ran it up and took off straight into a cloud! So I fell out of the sky again as quickly as I could back on to the aerodrome. There was no way.

It took about four days before we could get them away. We eventually got a letter from Churchill thanking us for the part that we had played in the delivery of these marvellous machines. They got to Malta just in time, I gather; they were down to about two Swordfish by the time they got there.

We had seen the Battle of Britain happening above our own heads, so we knew exactly how important these aircraft were.

It is difficult to assess the effect produced by constant, exacting and routine flights (as opposed to occasional light hearted trips in Moths) on a man's make-up. Undoubtedly it does something, even to the toughest. One has only to see how in every gathering the flying men gravitate together to talk the most engrossing shop in the world, to know that their calling takes them, with a certain arrogance, perhaps, with great simplicity, apart . . .

Fear, fatigue and exaltation combined, perhaps, to produce a friction sufficient to burn away the clutter of inessential things which cumber most of our lives and strip the main fabric bare. I think that it did something of the sort of John, heightening his perceptions, his capacity for suffering and joy, giving him a delight in absurdity and riot, in such contrasting things as the roaring company of his friends in smoke-hazed bars, the jigging figures of a film cartoon, the quiet safety of nights in his own home which held off the loneliness known by the men who fly constantly through darkness and in danger, a loneliness at which we others who wait for their return can only guess.

That loneliness went with him always. So he could write 'Sometimes when I can't sleep and it's cold and black and I feel afraid to die, I think to myself: "Soon she'll be by my side, I shall put out my hand and touch her, and there would be an end of loneliness".'

And yet in other moods: 'so it is that even in love we live apart, shut into our own lives . . . we shall be as two pilots flying wing-tip to wing-tip, who, for all their nearness and understanding, each of the other, can only communicate by clumsy and laborious effort.'

JANE OLIVER (Mrs John Llewellyn Rhys)
from her Preface to *England is my Village* (1941)
by John Llewellyn Rhys, killed in action, August 1940

3

THE MIDDLE EAST AND MEDITERRANEAN

Libya and East Africa, 1940–41
Italy entered the war on 10 June 1940, opening new fronts in North and East Africa. The RAF had 29 squadrons of out-dated aircraft to cope with whatever was needed in four-and-a-half million square miles of Egypt, Sudan, Palestine, Trans-Jordan, East Africa, Aden, Somaliland, Iraq, Cyprus, Turkey, the Balkans, the Red Sea, the Mediterranean and the Persian Gulf. Fortunately, the Italian Air Force was similarly out-moded and RAF biplane fighters clashed with Italian biplanes until increasing numbers of Hurricanes, Blenheims and Wellingtons completely outclassed the Italians. In Libya, in early 1941, the RAF ably supported the Army's advance and the capture of Benghazi, crippling the Italian Air Force for negligible losses. In East Africa, squadrons of out-dated RAF and South African aircraft supported the Army's eventual victory against some spirited Italian resistance.

Greece, 1941
When Italy invaded Greece in October 1940, Britain honoured a defence pact and nine RAF squadrons from the Middle East Air Force were sent to Greece (mostly Blenheims and Gladiators). The Italians were held but the Germans intervened with massive airpower in April 1941. Greek resistance was overwhelmed and the British evacuated what forces they could. In the retreat the RAF lost 209 aircraft in combat, or destroyed and abandoned, plus 150 aircrew.

Iraq, 1941

The RAF had maintained two bases in Iraq since the Anglo-Iraqi treaty of 1930. But in May 1941 a new, pro-German, Iraqi prime minister launched his army against the RAF flying training school at Habbaniya. Its defence, relying on a motley collection of old training aircraft, was a minor epic of the wartime RAF. The gallant success preserved British dominance in Iraq. The Iraqi regime was overthrown and a pro-British Iraqi government declared war on the Axis powers in January 1943.

The Western Desert Air Force

German forces arrived in North Africa in March 1941 to prop up the Italians and promptly pushed the British back to Egypt. After the Greek fiasco the new, initially weak, German Air Force was opposed by just four RAF squadrons.

The Army needed close air support from the much reinforced Desert Air Force, but the ranging battles of May and June 1941 ended in mutual recriminations with the RAF on the use of air power. For the 'Crusader' offensive to relieve Tobruk in November 1941, 27 RAF squadrons supported the ground forces, testing new joint methods of controlling air support. In the confused fighting Tobruk was relieved and Benghazi recaptured, but then the British were thrown back in another long desert retreat. The RAF lost some 450 aircraft in fighting almost as intensive as the Battle of Britain. From Egypt, four Wellington squadrons resumed the almost nightly bombing of Benghazi.

The Germans attacked again in May 1942, driving the Army deep into Egypt. The Western Desert Air Force was outnumbered and its fighters were inferior to the German Me109F. As the Army retreated and airfields were abandoned, ground attacks on the German advance and its long supply lines were hard and costly. The Germans were eventually stopped at El Alamein in July. The RAF had lost 200 fighter aircraft in six weeks, but the Luftwaffe was temporarily exhausted, its serviceable aircraft virtually spent. The arrival of General Montgomery to command 8th Army brought total emphasis on effective Army-RAF co-operation.

At Alam Halfa, in September, the Afrika Korps was driven back, harried now by overwhelming Allied air power. In the Alamein battle of October/November 1942, which brought victory in the desert, the RAF flew 10,405 sorties and lost 77 aircraft. At one stage in the German retreat two Hurricane squadrons were even operated from far behind the German front lines.

The Allies invaded Sicily on 10 July 1943 and Italy in September, when she surrendered. Despite almost total Allied air superiority – increasingly American – the German Army stubbornly resisted in Italy until 1945.

Malta

German convoys supplying the Afrika Korps ran the gauntlet of British aircraft, warships and submarines based in Malta. Massive enemy retribution came from German and Italian air forces in Sicily and Italy in 1941 and 1942. There was desperate, outnumbered air fighting for the new RAF fighters based on the island. The famous three Sea-Gladiators were replaced by Hurricanes flown off HMS *Argus* in August and November 1941 (a flight of six Hurricanes disappeared into the sea). Thirty-one Spitfires were flown into the island from HMS *Eagle* in March 1942. (The *Eagle* was sunk on another Malta convoy in August 1942.) On 20 April 1942, the USS *Wasp* got 47 Spitfires into Malta. The enemy retaliated, and after forty-eight hours only seven remained serviceable. However, by May, more aircraft had been delivered and the tide had been turned with *Wasp* making a second run, this time with *Eagle*.

Sergeant George Allen

I had been with 8 Squadron of Middle East Command at Khormaksar in Aden since the summer of 1938. Basically we had been policing the North Aden and Somaliland Protectorates, keeping the tribesmen from being troublesome. We used to fly around in lovely old Vickers Vincents which had a top speed of 90 knots.

In the summer of 1939 the squadron was re-equipped with Blenheims. When I first sat in the cockpit, I saw on the control column 'your vital actions'. One read, 'slow down to 130 before selecting the undercarriage down'. That made my day. It was a lovely aircraft, one that you could trim to fly hands and feet off.

On 9 June 1940 I was sent for by the CO. He wanted me to fly to the Kamaran Island, a communications post in the Red Sea, and collect some documents. As I had to fly close to one of the Italian airfields at Assab, he told me that I had to return that night, because the following day the Italians were going to declare war.

The next morning Mussolini threw in his lot with the Germans, so we were on a war posting straightaway, but we had been ready for quite some time. We were briefed that the Italians had two hundred aircraft just across the water in Ethiopia; we had twenty. 'That's fair,' said the chap next door to me, but he was ground crew!

We had two false starts and each time it was a 3.00 a.m. briefing for a dawn raid which meant getting up at 2.30 a.m. and having greasy fried eggs on fried bread. I'm sure the egg had been there since midnight. The third time we were briefed for a dawn, high-level bombing raid on Assab airfield. A young Pilot Officer called Jaeger came over and shook hands with me and wished me luck. It made me feel really good. Sadly he was killed on his first sortie.

We took off on that first sortie and I was climbing up to gain position in formation. I got butterflies in my stomach; it was like I felt waiting for the starter's gun in races at school. But as soon as I got into formation I didn't have time to think about anything else. It was just concentrating on close formation. We bombed the airfield, but were heavily attacked by fighters on the way out. My gunner, who was an LAC, as was my navigator, kept saying, 'For Christ's sake, get down, George, get down. They keep coming up underneath and I can't get at them.' I couldn't say to him, 'Look, I have to keep in tight formation.' I got my exhaust cowling blown off by flak. I don't know what the result was, but a few days later we found out how ill-prepared for war the Italians were.

A recce aircraft discovered that at a satellite airfield near Assab all their aircraft were lined up on both sides of the runway so off we went for a low-level bombing raid on them. There were all these beautiful aeroplanes lined up, wing tip to wing tip, just like the Hendon air display. Soon afterwards we dive-bombed the hangars at Assab airfield. So by the end of those three operations I had experienced all the three different bombing attacks – and lived.

Sometime later I was sitting in the mess with two others drinking a lime and lemon, prior to doing another trip the next morning, when one of my colleagues called 'Happy' Gay, a Sergeant pilot, came back from an outing. He said, 'Well, chaps, you're looking at somebody who is not coming back tomorrow.' This was the first time that I had met anybody who knew he wasn't coming back. I was a bit startled. I jumped up and said, 'Look, Happy, we don't want any of that nonsense, go to bed.' He was quite sober and normally there might have been fisticuffs for a short time or prolonged argument, but he just got up and went to bed. The next morning I got up and knocked on his cabin door. He said, 'I'm in no rush because as I told you last night, I'm not coming back.' I said, 'Don't be so silly. It could be any of us.' We walked down together to the airfield, and sure enough he was shot down in flames. But he survived as a POW.

There seemed to be a lot of luck involved in operational flying. When my own crew flew with someone else for the first time, they were shot down and taken prisoner by the Italians in Ethiopia, and they survived. But another Blenheim crew died the death of a thousand cuts at the hands of tribesmen.

As the campaign went on more and more chums were going for a burton and being replaced. After I'd done about thirty operations someone said to the CO that George Allen must be the best pilot in the squadron. The CO replied, 'Allen is an excellent operational pilot, because he has no bloody imagination.'

We continued operations, attacking Italian infantry moving in columns from Ethiopia to Somaliland, and their artillery. It was the first time I had attacked moving targets. We dive-bombed these columns and when the enemy saw us coming they ran off into whatever cover they could find. Of course their fighters attacked because they had fighter cover.

I suggested to my Flight Commander that the best attack we could do on the vehicles would be to hit them low level with incendiary bombs and burn the lot out. But I didn't think anyone would take any notice of that. I never felt anything personal in attacking soldiers on the ground, it was completely impersonal. Either I got them or they got me.

I'd flown about forty sorties so the CO decided I should have a rest – a week's rest in the hills. So I went to the Mukeiras cabin; a stone-built place, not very comfortable but at least it was healthy. One day it was arranged for us to go by mule to the edge of the mountains. When you looked down there was a sheer drop for thousands of feet. It was spectacular. We turned round and started back and we were going through a narrow ravine in a line astern of mules. The mule behind mine bit my mule's backside and the blasted mule I was on turned its head round and grabbed the first thing it could see which was my leg! He got it firmly jammed between his teeth. The caravan boss had to hammer and almost knock its head off before it let go. I thought, here I am supposed to be on holiday, and I'm going to die an excruciatingly painful death from all these germs in my leg. By the time I got back and washed it the only thing to put on it was iodine. I carried the scar of the teethmarks for many years.

Flying was a damn sight safer than donkey rides so I was very pleased to return to base. A recce plane again had shown that the Italians never learned. They had what was left of their aircraft, a very large number of them, on a satellite airfield outside Diredawa, in Ethiopia, stashed away in scrub for cover. The scrub was tinder dry. My Flight Commander called one of my friends, Claude Young, and me into a meeting and said we were going to Diredawa that night. He then said, 'You'll be very pleased to know, Allen, that you're going to fly up one side of this scrubland with incendiary bombs and set it all on fire.'

Young took off fifteen minutes before me. As I approached the area, from a long way out, I could see it was burning beautifully. So I just homed in on that. All one side of the landing strip was on fire. We dropped more incendiary bombs on the other side, turned round and watched it all burn. Then all the aircraft started to explode – terrific explosions. It looked good, it really was. That was a spectacular night-time attack.

Then Somaliland and Ethiopia and Eritrea were taken by the British and South African forces and it was the end of the campaign.

Squadron Leader Tony Dudgeon

By the beginning of 1940 I had done five or six years abroad, so in June 1940 I was sent back to England by boat. I only got as far as Egypt, however, when Mussolini declared war. So I went to command 55 Squadron and started flying a Blenheim over the Western Desert.

In the Western Desert I flew for Raymond Collishaw, who was the AOC out there. He was a Canadian World War I ace, a terrific chap. The only problem I had was that he rather worked on the basis that, if you were sent out on a raid, it was like going over the top in World War I. You went out and either succeeded and came back – or got yourself killed. I was rather a believer in the proposition that 'he who fights and runs away lives to fight another day.'

We used to do a raid nearly every day. It was very bow-and-arrow stuff because there were no beacons, no radar, and we had to observe radio silence. Collishaw would ring up and tell me to bomb, say, Tobruk at eleven o'clock the next day. So then I would make up my ops plan as to how I was going to get there. How about the weather? And would we come from the north, or the south? We always liked to come downwind because it was faster and therefore we spent less time at risk. We also liked to go towards the sea because the fighters didn't like flying over the water for any length of time. If it was a squadron raid, I always led, because in those days it was the Squadron Commander's job. Later on, Squadron Commanders were forbidden always to lead because too many were being lost. If the raid was for three aircraft, I would select which flight was going to do it, and the Flight Commander would select his crews. Either way, I would brief them in the evening about six o'clock and that would be that.

The Blenheim had no under-gun and you were at risk from the Italian CR32s and CR42s, which were very manoeuvrable biplanes. They could sit underneath and just squirt at the belly of the aeroplane until they got you. We had no self-sealing tanks, so if you didn't run away somehow or another you were dead. I didn't want to be dead, nor did I want my people dead, so I used to roll the plane on its back, stand it on its nose, go straight down and pull out at the last possible moment. When the fighter couldn't get underneath you your gunner could fire at him, so he would fly away.

We invented in the squadron a wonderful device. We got a 20lb bomb, took the front end off, screwed it on to the business end of a parachute flare, and hung it on the small bomb-racks when we went out. If we got picked up by a CR42 we would drop off one of these things, the parachute would open, and it would hang there for four seconds. Well, when you're scared and in a Blenheim doing about 220mph that means about one hundred yards per second and the ideal firing range for a fighter from behind a bomber is 400 yards. So four seconds later the parachute flare would fire off a 20lb bomb; there would be a bloody great boom, clouds of smoke and the fighter would quickly decide he didn't like it, and shove off.

My policy was to give strict instructions but, if my crews felt they were unattainable, they should come back and tell me about it. Our day-bombing force was pitifully small, three squadrons only, and I wanted my crews alive today to fly for me tomorrow. I'd much prefer to miss one target and hit three later than hit one and not have another chance to do it again. That was unlike Collishaw.

I was very lucky because I only lost three crews in six months and we had completed about 150 raids: to lose one person in fifty raids was really pulling the odds.

I lost one crew because a bomb came off on take-off and blew them up. Another pilot I lost was Peter Blignaut, a South African. We had been told to go out and cut the road, down which the Italians were escaping, in as many places as possible. We went off with nine aeroplanes, separated them, and we came in to arrive at the road at nine places at the same time. But Peter Blignaut's aircraft never came back. I think he was picked off by some fighters.

I, personally, only killed two people during the war. I got one of them on that raid. I was starting my bombing run along the road and saw a lorry packed with Italians racing towards me. I gave a squirt from my front-gun, and a chap sitting on the bonnet of the lorry sprang off. The lorry ran him over.

The third crew I lost was captained by a nineteen-year-old called 'Milly' Singleton. Millward was a quiet, gentle Old Harrovian. Collishaw had sent us to bomb Bardia four days in a row, each time one hour earlier than the day before. We were setting up a pattern the enemy could recognise, so I spoke to him about it. He said, 'Haven't you got the guts to carry out my instructions, Dudgeon?' So we went out again. Nearing the target I said to my gunner, 'There are twenty CR42s coming in ahead of us', and he said, 'There are thirty coming in behind, and that makes fifty, sir.' We had nine aeroplanes: three managed to force-land on our side of the lines; Potter lost one engine because a bullet struck one blade of the propeller and it shook the whole prop off the engine. A Blenheim normally wouldn't fly on one engine: you couldn't feather the prop and the drag would make one gradually lose height. But, having no prop on the dead engine Potter got it all the way home. We lost Milly, shot down in flames, and three had force-landed behind the enemy lines. My navigator had watched them go down and pin-pointed them, and as my aeroplane was undamaged, we went back, landed on the desert, picked them up and brought them in.

The second time I personally killed a man was after a bombing raid on Tobruk. There was a 50mph wind hiding the desert with blowing sand, so we had to come in upwind from the sea. I didn't like it at all so I took three aeroplanes and led the raid myself. We got over El Adem and my observer saw the sand plumes of the fighters taking off, and it was a question of whether they got to us before, or after, we dropped our bombs. I hoped we'd get them after, because before you drop you're flying straight and level and you're a sitting duck. We all dropped our bombs just before they got into range and I swung us round going lickety-split for the sea and a row of clouds, almost flat out with the fighters coming behind. I waved my other two away because if you're by yourself you can go a little faster and, as there were only three fighters, we wouldn't have more than one each. I was going as hard as I could go, nose well down, and just as my pursuer was getting within range I popped into a cloud. I swung round and came out the side of it, and there he was on top of the cloud looking for me. He came down behind me again and just as he was getting too close I popped into another cloud. All the time I was edging further and further out to sea with a 50mph wind behind me.

This went on for quite a time till he suddenly realised what was happening. He turned and went for home. I turned too and followed him about 5,000 feet above, watching. He was right down on the water to get as far as possible out of the wind. I'd plenty of fuel so I wasn't worried. I thought, you bastard, this'll teach you: if you want to play with the big boys, you play big boys' games. I was aged twenty-four, thought that I was an old man and, having 3,000 hours' flying behind me, felt I knew it all! At 5,000 feet I could see the coastline in front of us, when suddenly his propeller slowed up. He was out of fuel, being a fighter, and he went down. The CR42 had a fixed undercarriage and he flipped over on his back. I told the gunner, 'Get the dinghy out and we'll drop it to him', and I went down and circled. But he never appeared. His machine just stayed upside down, and no little head bobbed up alongside.

I flew around for about five minutes while the aeroplane was gradually sinking and there was no chap there. So I pushed off home. I have never felt such a shit in all my life: to trick a man into committing suicide. He never got a shot in. I didn't shoot him down, I drowned him. I felt awful. When I got back I rang up Collishaw, as I always did. I said we'd dropped the bombs and that I'd got one man. 'Bloody good show, well done, well done!' he said, slapping his leg as he always did. 'Killed somebody, bloody good.'

Wing Commander Fred Rosier

I was twenty-five when I took my squadron to the Western Desert in June 1941. In the six years since joining the RAF as an Acting Pilot Officer I had spent three happy, carefree years at Tangmere, near Chichester, flying Hawker Furies and Hurricanes; had become a married man; commanded a flight in a Blenheim night-fighter squadron; taken a flight of Hurricanes to France; had been hit in a fight with Me109s, badly burned, but escaped by para-chute; four months later had regained my medical flying category and been posted to command my old squadron, No. 229, at Northolt. The Battle of Britain was still on. We were at Speke enjoying a rest from operations when I was told I was to take the squadron to the desert.

Life in the Western Desert was tough and demanding. We had to put up with the extremes of heat and cold; the sandstorms which got worse and even more depressing as time went on; the flies, particularly where the Italians had been; the shortage of water; the monotony of the daily diet of bully beef and hard biscuits; and the fear – that feeling in the pit of the stomach before going on operations.

But there were compensations. I was fascinated by the desert; the beauty and vastness of the night sky; the sunrises; the seemingly limitless horizons; its blossoming after the rains; or was it the silence? For a time I had a violin and sometimes in the late evenings when the mood took me I would scrape away at it under that night sky and the sounds would come back to me transformed. There was the uplift that came with the arrival of the beer ration; the squadron parties; the occasional dip in the sea; the rare weekend in Cairo or Alexandria; and the marvellous spirit that prevailed amongst the Australian, South African and RAF squadrons.

The start of the desert interlude came when we set off from the Clyde in the aircraft carrier HMS *Furious*. My ground crews had already left on their long voyage round the Cape. On arrival at Gibraltar we went to stay in comfort at the Rock Hotel whilst the Navy went off to chase the *Bismarck*.

When the ships returned preparations went ahead to take us to a point in the Mediterranean from where we would take off for Malta. But there was one uncomfortable moment. At a briefing shortly before we left we were told that we were scheduled to take off in darkness. I refused. So did the COs of the two other squadrons. None of us had ever taken off from a carrier. The timing was then changed, somewhat reluctantly I thought, to first light. For the flight to Malta strict radio silence was enforced. Our aircraft had been fitted with extra fuel tanks at the expense of guns and ammunition. The last thing we wanted was to give away our position and be intercepted en route by enemy fighters. In the event there were no problems and we arrived safely in Malta.

That evening – I had been invited to dinner by Air Vice-Marshal Lloyd, the AOC – he tried to get me to agree to stay in Malta but I argued out of that one. The next day we flew to Mersa Matruh and then on to Abusacur in the Canal Zone. After a few days' sightseeing in Cairo my pilots left on attachment to other squadrons. Some went to Palestine, the rest to the Western Desert. I was left with nothing to do and, feeling frustrated, I protested strongly and rather boldly to the powers-that-be in HQ, Middle East.

The following month, July, I not only got my squadron back again but was given an extra flight from 73 Squadron which had recently come out of Tobruk. We were based on one of a clutch of landing-grounds at Sidi Haneish, a hundred-odd miles back from the forward area. In certain operations we would use the LGs at Sidi Barrani. One of the most trying and disliked operations was the escorting of lighters, slow-moving ships, taking supplies and reinforcements to Tobruk. They aimed to get to Tobruk at last light. Consequently they would be very close to the main German LGs at Gambut in the late afternoons. And this was when they could expect attacks from Stukas with their escorts of Me109s and 110s. There would be no warning and the aircraft would make their approach out of the sun. It put us at a great disadvantage, and the sun was blinding.

In September I left my squadron and was attached to Air HQ Western Desert. One day, having heard that some Italian Air Force Stukas had force-landed in the forward area, a Wing Commander Bowman and I got permission from the AOC, Air Vice-Marshal 'Mary' Coningham, to go and investigate and if possible bring one back. Taking an Italian Stuka pilot prisoner with us, we flew up to Sidi Barrani from where we started an air search. We soon gave that up because our ancient Wapiti aircraft was a 'sitting duck' for enemy fighters. We also decided to do without the Italian. He was too frightened to help. I think he was afraid of being captured by his own side and accused of helping the enemy.

The next morning a Hussar regiment – I think it was the 'cherry pickers' – provided us with transport and an armed escort and the search was on. After a few hours of nothing but sand we met a patrol, a very efficient lot. Not only had they seen a Stuka which appeared intact but they had left a guard with it. Pointed in the right direction we soon found it. Whilst the Wing Commander was organising the refuelling I was in the cockpit fiddling about with the switches. Suddenly there was a shout and everyone ran like mad. I had jettisoned the bombs. But there was no danger, for the bombs had to fall a long way before they became armed.

We were keen to get away. It was getting late and we were worried about Italian fighters, CR42s. Two of them flew right over us. And in any case we wanted to get back in daylight. After several attempts we got the engine started. Then, waving farewell to our escort and with the Wing Commander at the controls, we took off.

All went well for about twenty minutes and then the engine spluttered and stopped. We had to land on a bad piece of desert, damaging the undercarriage. The outlook was bleak. We were far away from any established routes. That night we slept in the folds of our parachutes. At dawn, after leaving a message in stones, we started walking due north.

For hours we saw nothing, on land or in the air. And then in the afternoon we saw some trucks in the distance. They had to be friendly. So we unfolded a parachute we were carrying and tried to stream it in the wind. To our great relief it was seen and we were picked up. The Stuka was repaired soon afterwards and was flown back by the same Wing Commander.

Soon after my return I was put in command of a newly formed fighter wing, No. 262, and given the acting rank of Wing Commander. Together with the established 258 Wing commanded by Group Captain 'Bing' Cross, we would be responsible for the operational control of the desert fighter squadrons. It was a marvellous posting.

It was the time when preparations were in hand for a new offensive, Operation Crusader. The fighter force moved forward to new LGs at Maddelena and the operation started on 18 November 1941. Four days later I was ordered to go to Tobruk to organise the operation of fighters from there. I set off that afternoon in a Hurricane in which I had put all my worldly goods.

Two squadrons of Tomahawks, No. 112 and No. 3 (Australian) escorted me. We were well on our way when we were intercepted by 109s and the fight started. When I saw a Tomahawk diving down streaming white smoke and then landing, I decided to try to rescue him. I went down and landed close to him; he ran across and sat in my cockpit. I discarded my parachute, sat on top of him, opened the throttle and then disaster. As we started moving a tyre burst, the wheel dug into the sand, and we came to a full stop. For the second time in two months I faced the prospect of a long walk. This time it would be through hostile territory; and I would be with an Australian pilot, Sergeant Burney.

My first thought was to avoid capture for I had noticed several trucks not far away. Quickly we removed my possessions from the Hurricane and hid them under some brushwood. Then we ran to a nearby wadi where we hid behind rocks. Soon some trucks arrived full of Italians. They spread out to search and soon found all my stuff which included my wife's picture and a silver tankard, given to me by the CO of No. 73 Squadron in memory of 73/229. It must have been the fading light that saved us. They came to within yards of where we were hiding.

I decided it would be safer to walk towards the east rather than try the shorter route to Tobruk. We started later that night using the North Pole star for navigation. In the early hours of the third day we began to see odd shapes around us. They were enemy tanks and trucks. There was nothing else we could do other than to continue as silently as possible. Once we thought we had been spotted, for some lights came on and we heard shouts in German. We lay motionless and soon the lights went out and there was silence. We were making little progress. It would soon be dawn and I was worried. But once again the fates were with us. We saw a ring of brushwood ahead. It was around a dried-up abandoned well and we hid there.

Later that morning – I think we had been sleeping – we heard gunfire and the sound of shells passing over us. We could see the guns and thought we could hear shouting in English. Anyway, we decided to make for them. We were pretty exhausted and Sergeant Burney's feet were in a terrible state but we just ran and ran. At last we were safe. At first the gunners were suspicious, but then we were taken to a Guards unit who passed us on to a Brigade HQ. We were then driven back to Maddalena to find we had been given up for lost. Sergeant Burney went back to his squadron. I returned to the wing.

Operation Crusader was successful in pushing the enemy back to the bottom end of the Gulf of Sirte. But satisfaction was short-lived. Rommel attacked. The day before, I had returned to our most forward landing-ground (LG) at Antellat. The rains had come and thick mud had prevented flying. Then came the attack. We were in danger of being overrun and losing the fighters. But by tremendous efforts each aircraft was manhandled to the only possible take-off position and they all got away safely.

The Army was ill-prepared to counter Rommel's offensive and back we went to the Gazala line. Early one morning, as we were shaving, Group Captain Cross remarked, 'You know, Fred, shaving every morning makes all the difference between an orderly withdrawal and a disorderly rout.'

I based my wing HQ at El Adem, a radar mast was deployed at Gazala and a 'Y' service unit, which listened to German and Italian Air Force radio transmissions, was close to my HQ. We were in a very good state to control operations by the fighter force based further back at Gambut.

One day I made good use of the 'Y' service and the Gazala radar. There had been heavy rain and our LGs were seas of mud. Our fighters were bogged down. All was quiet. Then 'Y' reported signs of activity at Martuba, an enemy air base north-west of Gazala. More reports followed: Italian Air Force Stukas are airborne; German 109s are taking off; they will escort the Stukas; Tobruk is the most likely target. A little later Gazala radar reported plots to the north-west moving east.

It was then that I decided to try to interfere with their bombing mission. I would make use of the enemy's 'Y' service. I would scramble imaginary fighters and pretend to carry out an interception.

Firstly Gazala radar was told to respond to all instructions to the so-called fighters with the single word 'roger', meaning message received. This would make it almost impossible for the enemy to pin-point the source of the reply. I then scrambled these imaginary fighters and started giving them instructions for the interception. It wasn't long before 'Y' reported that the enemy formation had been warned by their 'Y' that our fighters were on the way to intercept.

It was when the enemy raid was getting close to Tobruk and had been told our fighters were closing in that I thought that I had failed. Then came an excited voice from 'Y'. The Stukas had jettisoned their bombs and turned back. The leader of the German fighters was saying what he thought of them.

I was awarded the OBE a few months later. Perhaps this dummy interception had something to do with it.

However, the squadrons were still suffering from the losses sustained in Crusader. They had fought with great courage but their Hurricanes and Tomahawks were no match for the 109s. They needed time to build up their strength and they needed better fighters, Spitfires and Kittyhawks. They got the first, but the second were slow to come.

During one of the slack periods I flew to Cairo for a short break. One morning in my hotel I was contacted by a South African Major. He said he had something important to show me. We met and he presented me with the silver tankard I had last seen being taken away by Italian soldiers. He told me that he had been the CO of a South African armoured car unit which had shot up a convoy somewhere near Benghazi. One of his men had found the tankard in one of the trucks. He also said that it was by sheer chance that he had found out I was in Cairo and staying at the Continental Hotel.

Rommel's next offensive resulted in the fall of Bir Hacheim, the capture of Tobruk and the retreat to the Alamein line. Throughout this time I was second-in-command of the newly formed 211 Fighter Group. It meant very little to my daily routine. I was still involved in the employment and control of the fighter force. My CO was Group Captain Guy Carter, a man much admired and respected. On occasions he would say to me, 'Let's go off and see what's happening.' We would then take a couple of Hurricanes from a local squadron and off we would fly. Naturally the deeper we flew into enemy territory the greater the risks of being intercepted, but this never appeared to worry him.

When Montgomery arrived he achieved wonders in a very short time in raising the morale of 8th Army. He made it clear that he and the Air Force would work closely together. He believed that Army and Air staffs should not be remote from each other. He believed in the joint planning of air and ground action. He was putting into action what Air Vice-Marshal Coningham had long advocated.

In the Battle of Alam Halfa, when Rommel attempted his final push into Egypt, the results of this joint action were clearly seen. I accept that, by then, the capability of the Desert Air Force had increased greatly. We had been joined by squadrons of the United States Army Air Corps and more Spitfires and Kittyhawks had arrived. The really important factor, however, was that no longer was the ground situation allowed to become so confused that air support became limited. We knew where the enemy were and were able to attack them in relays with light bombers and fighter bombers. The attacks even continued at night with Navy Albacores dropping flares to help the night bombers. Rommel was defeated. Joint action had paid off. It all helped the outcome of the next battle, Alamein.

I left the Desert Air Force when we got to Tripoli. Although delighted to be returning to the UK where I was to command a Spitfire station, I was sad to leave some of the finest men it had been my privilege to serve with.

Sergeant Dudley Egles

Our Wellington squadron, No. 148, was based at Kabrit and we were regularly bombing Benghazi, because that was the main supply port for Rommel. Flak there was solid. I was shot down twice. The first time was a ditching. The system out there laid down that, when a new crew came out from the mainland, on their first op they would have an experienced navigator (or 'nav') with them. At this time I was due to go on leave, so I'd had a few extra jugs, to celebrate. The next morning, the nav leader, who was going to go with the new crew, got dysentery and I was next on the list. So I had to scrub my leave and go flying. At the briefing with these bods, I was confident: 'It's a piece of cake,' I said. 'If this is Benghazi, there's a groove through the sky, because we go there night after night.'

We bombed the target, and then we got hit by flak and lost an engine. The navigator was hit on the head and knocked out, so we stuck him back on the bed, and I took over the navigation. The pilot had already been given his course, because this was done before going into the target in case the navigator was incapacitated. I asked, 'How's it going on one engine?' He said it would be OK. I advised him to keep to the coast so that we had some beach if we had to prang.

When we got near Tobruk, I knew our own chaps would shoot at us, because they shot at anything; the Jerries had captured several of our aircraft, so even if you came in at three feet they'd shoot at you. We fired colours of the day, we even went on plain-language radio, but they still shot at us, so we had to jink out to sea a bit. Halfway across a bay, our other engine packed up. The pilot called, 'Ditch, ditch, ditch!' We all got ready for the impact, hanging on. Just as we were coming down, the bloke who was unconscious on the bed came to and sat up at the moment we hit. On impact, everything took off, including the Elsan at the back of the aircraft. WHAM! it went – hit him on the back of the neck and knocked him out again! The pilot made a good landing, though, doing a tail sliding and straight in. The plane had flotation gear in but it didn't work; it must have had flak in it, so we all got out, pulling the unconscious man with us, and got into the dinghy.

There were six of us in the dinghy. Before we ditched, I said to the pilot, 'I'll take the Very cartridges, and you bring the pistol for signalling.' So there we were, sitting around, at one o'clock in the morning. It was like the inside of a cow; you couldn't see anything. We had a paddle with a couple of Roman candles at each end, a couple of water bottles, some Horlicks tablets, some chocolate – 'only to be opened in the presence of an officer' – cigarettes, a hot-water bottle full of brandy and a small first-aid kit. And I'd taken my hand mirror, which I had in my navbag. Nobody was cut except the other navigator, so we put a field dressing on him.

The dinghy was OK to start with, but then it began to go down, so we had to pump it up; the pump broke. So then we had a semi-inflated dinghy. We also had shark repellent, a dye which creates a great yellow patch all around you, so we put this out in case anyone was looking for us. It was getting light and we could see the coast, so we thought, If the worst comes to the worst, we can swim. Only two of us couldn't swim. I said, 'Before long, the Photo Reconnaissance aircraft will be along. So, I'll give it a signal.' Then I found that when the pilot dived out he'd lost the pistol. But we had the two signal distress flares, and just as it was getting light along came a Hurricane, and so we let the signal off: WUMPF! Nothing. The plane disappeared. I said, 'He'll be back in quarter of an hour; we'll try again.' He came back; WUMPF! Nothing; it didn't work either!

By now, it was getting light, and I was signalling with my hand mirror to the shore, SOS, SOS. In no time at all, we got a message flashed back: 'Cheer up, blokes, help is coming.' Next thing we know, a Wimpy (Wellington) appeared in the sky, obviously coming to look for us. He started doing a square search, but seemed to be getting further and further away. We were waving like mad, and he eventually located us, and beat us up with his trailing aerial out, which must have been about ten feet away – if it had hit us, it would have cut us in two. Anyway, he circled us and we signalled that we needed another dinghy, so he went up about a thousand feet and dropped masses of bundles of things which all sank, except the dinghy, which was an old triangular one. We swam out for it, and then tried to pump it up but this too had a broken pump. Eventually we had two semi-inflated dinghies, which was better than one, and masses of yellow dye.

This type then disappeared, so we thought he'd send somebody to help us. Not very long after, we heard a single-engine aircraft coming from the north, which we realised must be a Jerry. There was nothing we could do. Suddenly, WUMPF! Hurricanes appeared, escorting a Walrus. Marvellous! The Walrus, an amphibian, circled round and dropped a smoke float to get a wind. That nearly hit us! The Walrus landed on the water and taxied round. Our Aussie skipper stood up, got hit in the back of the neck by the float of the Walrus, and was knocked out cold! Anyhow, it was getting rough, but we all managed to get into the Walrus. It had a crew of three, and so with the six of us it was a bit crowded. The pilot said, 'I don't know if I'll be able to take off with you lot, but I can't leave you here, so I'll do what I can.' Under a lot of strain, he pointed south, and taxied to reach the beach, where he landed, much to the amazement of the local Army, who were all standing there.

It turned out to be twelve miles, this distance we had thought we could swim, but we were safe with the South African Army. They stuck us in a tent, and a doctor came round and looked at our bodies, patched people up. Then in came steak, chips and brandy, exactly what I'd asked for – as a joke – when we beached. They'd shot a desert buck that morning and made a steak out of it for us. They had yam, from which they made chips, and they always had masses of brandy. So we were feeling a little bit better, and we said we'd like to see the fellow who had signalled to us. 'Come over and we'll show you,' they said. The heliograph was an enormous thing; we'd thought it was a little tiny hand-held thing like we had, which explained why we got the wrong impression of distance. Anyway, they got us to bed; by then it was early the next day.

The next thing I heard was WUMPF! WUMPF! Jerry was shelling us from just down the road, so we spent the rest of the night in a slit trench. Then they wheeled us up to Sidi Barrani the next day, and we radioed back to base, and got picked up. Everything had gone wrong, but we'd survived.

Squadron Leader Tony Dudgeon

The most frightening thing that happened to me in the war was to become involved in an RAF epic. A bunch of unseasoned British pilots fought a horrendous battle, doomed to failure – and won.

The top men, both government and military, made a major series of errors in their judgement of Iraq between the wars. Our ambassador in Iraq didn't believe that the Iraqis posed any particular kind of danger: Iraq was our political ally. Wavell and Longmore, the Army and Air Force commanders-in-chief in Cairo, reckoned that any problems with the Anglo-Iraq treaty of 1930 would be political, and therefore a matter for negotiation and they transferred responsibility for Iraq to the India Command. That was the atmosphere and attitude even after the military coup d'état in 1941.

As early as 1933, however, the Germans were deeply involved in Iraq, and fostering unrest. They were co-operating with a powerful figure, Rashid Ali al Gailani. He hated the British. The Germans also gave the Iraqis medical training and education, they poured money into the press, making several papers pro-German. This continued even after the start of the war. Although the German legation was closed, the Italian legation was not, so the Germans still had a marvellous line through to Rashid Ali. Both the Germans and Rashid Ali hoped to trigger off a jihad and cause the whole Arab world to rise up and throw the British out of the Middle East, lock, stock and barrel. On 2 April 1941, the pro-British Iraqi Regent fled, abandoning the boy-king Feisal. The next day, Rashid Ali, then prime minister, executed a coup, and declared himself President and Chief of the National Defence government. Ribbentrop in Germany reckoned this was the right time to move, and on 8 April sent Rashid Ali a written promise of German financial and military aid if the Arabs got into a war with Britain for their freedom. At the same time the Egyptians, and in particular the Egyptian Army, were also fed up with the British occupation. They wanted to attack the British from within Egypt, and were waiting only for Rashid Ali to move in Iraq.

I had been sent for a break after many operations in the Western Desert to Habbaniya Flying Training School, some fifty miles from Baghdad. It was soon clear to me and others that we ought to make preparations in case of an uprising. I suggested that we modify our training aeroplanes, which consisted of Audaxes and Oxfords, and a few Gladiators, to make them capable of carrying live bombs and ammunition. Air Vice-Marshal Reggie Smart, who was the AOC in Habbaniya, answered that it was not in the regulations and so therefore we were not allowed to do it. Against orders I fitted up some of the Audaxes to carry 250lb bombs instead of 20lb bombs. I also made a set of modifications so that the Oxfords could carry 20lb bombs, instead of practice bombs. We ran out of bomb-racks and machine-guns, but even so our illegal modifications doubled the number of aircraft we could use offensively, and doubled the total bomb-load we could carry.

The AOC was in a difficult position. He was woefully deficient in military strength. However, when he asked for aircraft and troops, Wavell and Longmore, with the backing of the Air Ministry and the Foreign Office in London, turned him down. They foresaw no problem of a military nature in Iraq. In fact, when the ambassador left at the beginning of April, he said there was no need to worry much about Rashid Ali.

India, however, responded. Four hundred troops were sent to

Habbaniya. Rashid Ali went to see the British ambassador, Cornwallis, and said that the treaty of 1930 did not allow us to station more people in the country. Cornwallis gave him no satisfaction. So Rashid Ali signalled to Germany to say that the British had committed an act of war against Iraq, and that he would move against the British in about ten days' time. He requested the troops and money which he had been promised. Hitler dragged his heels because of the impending attack on Russia and so nothing happened. About 23 April, Rashid Ali repeated his request, saying he expected to engage the British on the 28th.

On the 28th he sent an absolutely overwhelming force to settle on a plateau above the airfield at Habbaniya. According to the British archives, it had light tanks, light ack-ack, twenty-eight guns, armoured cars, and 5,000 armed Iraqi soldiers. Behind them Rashid Ali had an Air Force of seventy modern operational aeroplanes.

Against that, Smart had the School's 64 hastily armed training aircraft, the 400 King's Own Royal Rifles' troops from India, and about 1,200 Assyrian Iraqis who might or might not fight their blood brothers. But on the whole the Assyrians hated the Iraqis more than they hated the British, so we could only hope! We only had machine-guns, one or two mortars, and six World War I type armoured cars which had civilian Rolls-Royce chassis, with some thin armour-plate fitted. Smart decided that, if we were going to mount an attack, we had to start in the morning and carry on throughout the day, because if we started in the middle of the day they might come in at night and, with their tanks, we had no hope whatever of stopping them. Five o'clock in the morning of 2 May was the start time.

The School was divided up into three squadrons. One squadron of nine Audaxes, carrying two 250lb bombs each. A second squadron was of twelve Audaxes, with eight 20lb bombs each. They had something like fifteen machine-guns between them. These two squadrons were commanded by two Wing Commanders: Paul Holder, the Chief Administrative Officer out of headquarters, and an Engineer Officer who could fly, called John Hawtrey. Larry Ling, who was the Chief Flying Instructor, was to run that outfit. They were on a landing-ground that had been built in the middle of the camp by bulldozing together the golf course and the polo pitch.

The airfield, which was outside the perimeter fence and encircled by the Iraqis, was left for the other squadron which had 41 aeroplanes – 27 Oxfords, a few target-towing biplanes, and some Gladiators. That squadron came under me.

So on the first day, 2 May, we took off when it was still dark and flew over the plateau. It was terrifying because the plateau wasn't very big. We only had thirty-nine pilots, but that meant thirty-nine aeroplanes flying around over an area the size of an eighteen-hole golf course, peering down to see if we could see a target in the half light. We also had ten Wellingtons from Basra on that first raid. We started bombing at five. Within seconds we could see the flashes of guns firing from the plateau, and the flashes of shells landing in the camp. The first attack was over fairly quickly, and everybody poured down on to the airfields to reload. We would land on the airfield, nip round the corner behind the hangars to hide from the Iraqi guns, then off again and down again, and off again and down again. We took off along one edge of the airfield, swinging away from the plateau, and landed back by the other edge of the airfield. We just went on and on. We had an Oxford shot down in flames, and we had a lot of aircraft damaged, but you just took another aeroplane and went on. At the end of the day, about seven o'clock in the evening, we took stock. We had flown 193 sorties. Of our 64 irreplaceable aircraft we had twenty-two shot down or unflyable – one-third. Of our 39 pilots we had ten either dead or in hospital – a quarter. All this in just fourteen hours. And the question was what to do? And the only answer was, we must do the same again tomorrow. What else was there?

The Iraqis shelled the camp all that night. There was nothing we could do about it – we had no guns with which to fire back.

Two hundred shells landed between midnight and 3.00 a.m. Nevertheless, the troops worked tremendously during the night, and patched up a lot of the damaged aeroplanes. Mostly they just took a bit of fabric, doped it and slapped it over the bullet hole, and if it hadn't gone through anything vital like an oil pipe the plane went on flying. So we managed to have about fifty of our original 64 aeroplanes going the next day.

The Wellingtons had lost one aeroplane, it was damaged and had to force-land on the airfield, where it was hit with a shell and blew up when its bombs went off. Of course the debris had to stay where it was, nobody could go out, day or night, to move it. So that was another hazard. When the other nine Wellingtons returned to Basra, they were all damaged, and we never saw them over Habbaniya again.

The next day the same again, we flew and flew and flew. John Hawtrey by that time was the only Wing Commander standing on his feet. So we divided the remaining aircraft between the two of us. We put all the Gladiators and the Audaxes on to the polo pitch as one squadron under him. The Oxfords and the Gordons, which were bomber aircraft, were under me on the airfield.

One of our most immediate tasks was to stop the Iraqis shelling us at night. The only possible answer was to fly at night. But, in front of the Iraqi guns, we couldn't use a flare path. John Hawtrey said that, with the moon shining during the first half of the night, he thought he could get the Audaxes off the polo pitch and down again by moonlight. But the second half of the night there was no moon, and he couldn't bring them down in the black on a polo pitch surrounded by trees. The Oxfords had landing lights, but they could only work off the main airfield. I counted up a bit, and there were three people – a Warrant Officer, a Flying Officer and me – who had flown at night in anger before. I thought we could cover from midnight until morning. My plan was to go off on three two-hour trips, and drop a bomb every fifteen minutes on the plateau to cut down the shelling.

Taking off and landing in total darkness was interesting! I

started the aeroplane up behind the hangars, and then was guided
out to a gate in the fence by a chap with a shielded torch. Then
I taxied on a compass course between the edge of the hangars
and the crashed Wellington at the bottom. You couldn't see anything of course, it was pitch black. My bomb-aimer down below
me, Sergeant Prickett, timed me for about three minutes of taxi-
ing at fast tick-over which should have taken me down near the
end of the airfield but not far enough to drop us into the ditch at
the far end. Then I would turn on to a new compass course
parallel to the hangars, open the throttles and go, keeping straight
on the instruments. I'd pull her up into the air as soon as we'd
got enough speed on board and hope I didn't hit the ten-foot
earth bank at the end of the airfield. So off we went, and flew
around at about 1,000 feet for two hours, dropping bombs inter-
mittently. Although there was no moon, by starlight you could
see the waters of the Euphrates River. It was a different colour,
slightly blacker than the desert. Then, after two hours we'd follow
the Euphrates to a particular bend, throttle back, and come down
at 500 feet per minute in a steady rate one turn to the right. And
when I'd done a half circle, facing the opposite direction (if my
instrument flying was accurate) I ought to be at about 50–100
feet above the plateau, with the airfield below and in front. So,
no choice but to throttle back and wait until I got down to 50
feet; that is, 50 feet above the airfield, but below the level of the
plateau. I would know I was past the plateau if I hadn't hit it. Then,
flip on the landing-lights and, when I saw the ditch and road under
me on the near side of the airfield, drop her down on the other side
– flip the landing-light off again so as not to be seen, keep her
straight on the instruments, put the brakes on and hope that we
didn't run into the crashed Wellington. On coming to a standstill
I'd sit, take a deep breath and then look across towards where the
hangar had to be, and where there was a chap with a shaded torch.
Taxi towards him, and he'd take me through the gates again.

The next chap off was the Flying Officer. The poor sod did
exactly the same thing and, when he got down, said, 'I'll never

do that again as long as I bloody well live!' Who could blame him? And the third chap went off, and he did all right. He landed in the dawn's light, of course.

The third day was the same as the previous two. The third night I again did the first sortie. The Warrant Officer started the second but hit the bank at the far side and somersaulted into the marshes beyond, and that was the end of him – and his crew. It really wasn't at all nice. Although the second and third times weren't as bad as the first time, on the last sortie I frankly chickened out, hanging up there till I could land in daylight.

We kept this up for the second, third, fourth, and fifth days. We weren't bombing all the time, because at the same time we were sending aeroplanes to go and attack the Iraqi Air Force. The Iraqis were using Audaxes and Italian Savoias to bomb us. On the third day we got three fighter Blenheims in from Egypt. One of them was up when two Iraqi Audaxes came in. The Blenheim shot one down into the river, and was so low that the water from the splash went over the Blenheim's windscreen.

It was the same rule all round; if the aeroplane would fly you flew it. If a man could fly, he flew. A part-time air-gunner, Wad Taylor, is an example. He was called Wad because he always used to take a large sandwich up with him. He was up in a Gordon during the battle, and a bullet came from below, went through his eyebrow, scarred his forehead, into his leather helmet and went out through its top. His eye was full of blood so he covered it with one hand, and went on firing his gun with the other one. He didn't tell his pilot because, he said, he thought it would worry him. Down on the ground again they rushed him off to the hospital. He was back from there about an hour and a half later, stitched up with his head all wrapped in bandages looking like a white onion on top of his shoulders, and he flew the whole of the rest of the time. He could see, and he could walk, and his hands were OK, so he bloody well flew. That was the measure of the day.

After five days and nights of constant battle, on 6 May the Iraqi Army ran away and we followed them down the road. They met reinforcements coming in from the other direction, and they stupidly stopped nose to nose – just when every remaining Audax, Gordon, Gladiator and Oxford fell upon them. It was mayhem. Having been nervously husbanding our ever-diminishing resources for the last two days, we went back to flat-out effort – bomb and fire in minimum time. It was race home, don't stop engines, reload, bomb, race back. We made 139 sorties in two hours and left the road a sea of flames. Everything exploding, cars, lorries burning by the dozen. We lost one Audax shot down.

During those five days the Training School had flown 647 sorties, dropped three thousand 20lb bombs, 2,250 one-pounders and fired 116,000 rounds of ammunition. We had lost 13 killed and 21 badly wounded, plus four pilots grounded through nervous strain. But the plateau was clear and the Iraqi Army morale was broken.

About that time Churchill sent a signal to Wavell saying, in effect, 'Get cracking and send help to Habbaniya. The situation can still be saved.' Five days after our battle, the hastily assembled column started out. It arrived at Habbaniya on 18 May, and they had not fired one shot in anger on the whole way along.

After our battle we got some RAF reinforcements and went over to the offensive against their Air Force. We took out the airfields, destroyed their parked aircraft and burned their fuel dumps. Within ten days we had reduced them to powerlessness.

On 15 May we learned, to our horror, that a German special Kommando had arrived in Iraq. They had flown in via Athens, Rhodes and Syria to Mosul. Their brief was to help the Iraqis capture Habbaniya. They had modern bombers and fighters to pit against our pre-war trainers. Nonetheless we attacked them. Unluckily for the Germans horrific and magnified tales from the soldiers who had run away from our intensive day and night bombing had filtered back to the rest of the Iraqi Army, and the Kommando got no help at all! Also, as Hitler was not disposed to send good money after bad, we were able to reduce them to powerlessness as well before the end of the month.

Our Army column stayed around Habbaniya until the 27th, when they moved off towards Baghdad. They took the surrender of the Iraqis in Baghdad on the 31st. Rashid Ali was arrested just north of Baghdad, with the pay of the troops in his suitcase.

Rashid Ali had had the capacity to take Habbaniya with no problem at all, if he had moved. He was waiting, I think, for the Germans to come but they took too long. And we, the Air Force, had by then cut him off at the knees before the Germans even started, on 6 May. But he could easily have taken Habbaniya and welcomed them there.

The official German archivists wrote: 'The war in Iraq was won by the RAF. First, they mopped up the Iraqi Army. Next, they mopped up the Iraqi Air Force. Finally, they mopped up the German forces as well. Hitler threw away the chance of a substantial victory.'

Indeed Hitler missed the boat. With Rommel in the Western Desert beating towards us, and more Germans welcomed and sitting comfortably on all our Iraqi oil to the east, our Middle East base would have been split two ways. And with Egypt in a state of revolt as well, there would have been no way to produce the massive build-up of force needed to make the Battle of Alamein possible.

Those youngsters of the Flying Training School fought a hundred hours of hell. They won a crucially important victory. Without it, the whole course of the war would have been changed.

Flight Lieutenant Jerry Harrison

When I'd finished my training at Tern Hill, I applied to go to the Middle East, because I'd wanted to go there since I was a child. I thought I'd join a Blenheim squadron, so I asked for light bombers, but I found myself at 33 Squadron at Helwan, in Egypt, with Gladiators. They did have a light bomber flight up in Palestine; they were still flying Audaxes.

Helwan is about twenty miles south of Cairo. In those days all the squadrons had three flights, 'A', 'B' and 'C'. We had two flights at our base, and one up in Palestine. It was April 1939 when I arrived in Egypt, so the war hadn't started.

It was considered too hot to fly in the afternoons, so you started work about six, went through until about midday, had lunch and then went and had one or two hours' sleep. There was no night-flying initially, although we did a bit occasionally later, when we had a bit more experience in the aircraft. The Gladiator was not only a pretty aircraft but a real delight to fly. Very manoeuvrable and a marvellous acrobatic aircraft. Unfortunately its speed and armament were no match for the monoplane fighters such as the Me109.

It was a very relaxed, comfortable way of life: you had your own servant to attend to your room and your clothes, and all that sort of thing. I had to do my tour as Squadron Adjutant for a month, and then I was posted to the station, as Assistant Station Adjutant, away from the squadron for some months. I stayed there until about February 1940, screaming to get back to flying. Eventually I got it: I joined 112 Squadron, which had come out to Egypt not long before, at Ismailya. This was still with Gladiators. I stayed with them and we went up to the desert. The war had started in England by then, but it didn't really affect us. Nothing much happened until mid-summer, I suppose, when the Italians declared war, because, of course, the Italians, who ran Libya in those days, were in Tripoli. We then found ourselves in the Western Desert, from the Egyptian–Libyan border out to Algiers, flying Gladiators, doing offensive patrols.

We were flying over the Italian forts – protecting the Navy, which had a very large presence in the Middle East. They used to steam up the coast, westwards, bombarding these Italian forts, and they'd get attacked by Italian Air Force. We weren't that popular with the Navy, because they would detect the Italians coming in before *we* saw them; and before we knew there were any enemy aircraft about, we were being shot at by the Navy. They didn't care a damn. And then, by the time we'd seen these

Italian bombers, nine times out of ten it was too late, because they were much faster than we were. That went on for some months.

We were flying every day, until about January 1941, when we were suddenly told we were going to convert on to Hurricanes. Everybody was tremendously excited. But then, as with many of these rumours, nothing came of it, so we continued with our Gladiators, and in January 1941 we were off to Greece, to a place called Yannina. It was near the north-west coast, but a bit inland, about as far north as you can get towards the Albanian border. We were flying patrols, escorting bombers, Blenheims, mainly 211 Squadron, bombing ports in Albania.

Conditions were terrible; we were freezing cold in the Gladiators, so we flew with our pyjamas under our uniforms, and leather gloves and flying boots. And of course the maps were pretty useless for that area, so it was extremely difficult meeting the bombers; we often didn't know where we were. We also didn't have the range, in most cases, to follow them to the target. We would stay with them for part of the way, then they would go on and do the bombing, and we would hover about and meet them on the way home.

Then, as time went on, rumour had it that there were Me109s in the area, and so we were sent to find out if this was true. And we did find them, but of course there was nothing we in Gladiators could do about 109s. We would see them in the distance, but I don't remember ever getting that close to them. They attacked us, but their speed was such that we couldn't reply.

Another problem was that the airstrips were just soggy grass, and when the Germans really started kicking us out, they bombed our airfields and left them full of potholes. So then it was a question of taking off in a zigzag pattern, trying to get around the bomb craters, coming back the same way, trying to land without sticking the aircraft on its nose. It was all a bit primitive. And of course, in those days, the radio communications in the aircraft were really quite useless; there was so much traffic on the radio that you could really do very little. And ground-to-air communications were pretty much nil; you soon got out of range, so you were very much on your own.

The Germans really started making a nuisance of themselves about April. The Messerschmitts were strafing our troops, and our job then was to try and protect them. We got a very bad name there, because trying to find Army battalions, dug in on the mountain slopes, was practically impossible. One mountain slope looks very much like another. So they thought, Where the hell are the RAF? Feelings ran fairly high.

Eventually the retreat started in earnest, we had to give up our airfield, and we flew back to Athens. Our airfields were very close to the capital, so we could see what was going on in the air battles there. Hurricanes flew, but we were forbidden to; I think they wanted to save the aircraft and get them back to Egypt.

There was one epic air battle on 22 April, when 'Pat' Pattle was killed. He was probably the highest-scoring pilot in the Air Force, but being in the Middle East, he wasn't really in the news. He was on 33 Squadron, but we used to fly, as a wing, with 33 Squadron. Pat was a marvellous leader, a ruthless chap in combat, but otherwise a gentle sort of man. He had a hell of a lot of kills because he took time to study enemy bombers and their gun positions. He was also a very good shot.

We often went on patrols with him and he would spot the enemy long before anybody else did. When he was shot down, some people just couldn't believe he had gone. There were a number of chaps killed on that day, and he was amongst them which was a very great blow. I think he was shot down by a Messerschmitt; he had been flying four or five patrols a day, and he had a very bad case of 'flu, and really shouldn't have been in the air at all.

It wasn't very long after that, in late April, that we were told to pack up and get out, with no warning at all; we lost everything we had. Greece, I think, was a fiasco. I don't think we should have gone to Greece in Gladiators. But then Churchill had promised them that we would go, so we went. All told the campaign cost us 209 aircraft, 72 lost in combat and over 150 aircrew. We jumped in our aeroplanes and flew to Heraklion, in Crete. When we arrived there we did a few defensive patrols, because nothing much was going on.

I was one Flight Commander then, and Homer Cochrane was the other, so Middle East HQ said that one flight could be relieved because we had all had a pretty tough time. Homer tossed a coin, and my flight won the toss – or lost it, whichever way you look at it – and we were told to go to Egypt. So we left our aircraft there, and they sent a Lodestar over, with some more pilots from the Middle East, who took over the aircraft that we left. I remember standing out at the end of the runway at Heraklion and this Lodestar came in, taxied to a stop, and these chaps piled out. We shook them by the hand and wished them the best of luck, then jumped into our aircraft and, at about twenty feet above the waves, flew back to the Western Desert.

On 20 May the Germans invaded Crete using paratroops and so of course many of those chaps that we left behind were either killed or captured. It was such a waste, because if we had had two or three Hurricane squadrons, then the story would have been entirely different.

Flight Lieutenant Thomas Cullen

I joined the Air Force in June 1940, having trained as a doctor at Middlesex Hospital in London. They didn't give us any additional medical training in the Air Force, but we did some military training of a minor nature at Halton.

I was first sent as a doctor to Manston, but I wasn't there long before I was sent to be on a medical board in London, examining candidates for aircrew. Some of the people we examined were Polish airmen. I reckon they had flown thousands and thousands of hours, but from a medical point of view they were hardly fit to fly. They were interesting people.

The next move after that was to the Middle East, in November 1940. I travelled out on a convoy, round the Cape, and up through the Suez Canal to Alexandria. I went first to the Middle East Headquarters in Cairo. We'd been told that we were wanted out in the Middle East as soon as we could get there, and that they were short of medical officers. But when we got there they said they had more medical officers than they knew what to do with. So I was sent to Heliopolis and got a bit of a holiday there.

Then I went to El Shallûfa, at the bottom end of the Suez Canal, near Port Taufiq where there were a couple of Wellington squadrons. I wasn't there long before I was posted to 30 Squadron, and sent to Greece. That was my first posting to a squadron.

I went in a convoy by sea on a ship that used to carry pilgrims to Mecca. On the way, we ran into one hell of a storm, and our ship got separated from all the rest of the convoy. The ship was tossed about very violently, and that's the only time I have ever been sea-sick. Eventually we weathered the storm and reached Piraeus. I got pleurisy, so I was in hospital for three days or so, then went to Eleusis. I wasn't there long before Greece fell.

We were ordered to Crete and arrived in mid-April 1941, at Maleme, which was more or less just an airstrip defended by New Zealanders. There were other chaps there already, mainly from the Fleet Air Arm off *Illustrious*. They had a few Swordfish planes. We had our Blenheims with us but I didn't really know why the squadron was in Crete, or what the point of defending Crete was, and I still don't – there wasn't much there, except a few olive trees. Most of the people who were defending Crete had been evacuated from Greece – the New Zealanders, and 30 Squadron. After a short time 30 Squadron was withdrawn, and was supposed to be relieved by 33 Squadron. When 33 Squadron came, they didn't bring a Medical Officer with them. So I had to stay.

33 Squadron, commanded by Squadron Leader Howell, who was later severely wounded, had a few Hurricanes which they flew around for a bit, and shot down one or two German planes. By this time, the beginning of May, the Germans were over us all

the time, bombed us quite a lot, and shot down anything that flew in the air. There were so many of them that it was just impossible for any Air Force to exist at Maleme. This must have been pretty obvious to everyone who was there. It was clear there was not much point in having any planes there, because they were all being shot up, on the ground even, before they could get into the air. And nobody thought of blowing up the airfield. God knows why – we couldn't use it. If they had, it might have made all the difference later.

It was a depressing situation, because we knew by then that we were going to be attacked. We anticipated an airborne attack, it was fairly freely talked about. And we had a pretty shrewd idea of when it was coming. On 21 May, or thereabouts, we expected it, and that's when it came. I don't know how this information got around, but it did.

In spite of the German bombing and strafing the number of casualties we had before the invasion was very low, since we were in the slit trenches most of the time. There was much more trouble with dysentery and that sort of thing. I kept hoping that someone would come along and say another doctor had arrived and that I could go back to my old squadron.

We just messed about and waited. I don't think that there was any way of getting us off this island. The odd Sunderland went, and got some people away. They didn't take us. The nurses at the British General in Khania were evacuated.

Morale was reasonably high because we didn't think that an invasion could be successful. We had the aerodrome defended by New Zealanders, and we thought that they could defend the place without any trouble at all. But they had lost a lot of their equipment, though they were very brave chaps. Most of the RAF people there were not trained for fighting especially against experienced airborne troops.

Then the day came, 20 May, and the sky was full of strange parachutes and gliders. It was a most spectacular sight. Of course a great many of the German parachutists and people in the gliders were killed before they landed. Anybody that had a gun was shooting at the parachutists. Our fitters and others fought valiantly. I didn't have a gun but I think I would have used it if I had. The Germans landed around the airfield, and at various places on the island. Once they got on the ground, they spread out Swastika flags so that equipment and food could be dropped to them. It seemed to take a long time. There were a lot of them being scattered around. All the time we had the German fighter planes flying around about us, shooting at everybody, except where the Germans had got their flags out. So there we were, with all hell let loose.

My medical orderly, Norman Darch – who was later awarded a Military Medal – and I decided to get back a bit from the aerodrome which was under heavy fire, and join up with the medical officer of the New Zealand battalion just over the brow of the hill. We picked up a few wounded, and began looking for them. Then we were overrun by the paratroops. We found a sort of cave on the side of the hill, and had a bit of protection there for one or two wounded chaps. We really expected, I suppose, that the New Zealanders would come rushing down past us and mop these paratroops up. But that didn't happen, so we thought that we had better try to get back to the New Zealand position, but we didn't succeed.

There were two or three wounded chaps lying around me – we were all lying flat on the ground by this time. They threw some grenades at us, but fortunately none of us got hurt. They rushed up to us. I had a Red Cross band on my sleeve, and said that I was a doctor. The Germans were pretty frightened, too, and they ordered us to go back to where they'd come from, towards the Tavronitis River. So, taking the wounded chaps with us, that's what we did. Darch managed to get to the New Zealand trenches.

Eventually, during the day, I got taken with the wounded to a little village on the western side of the Tavronitis River. We were put in a kind of barn and told to look after the wounded. The Germans set up a casualty clearing place of their own on the other side of the road, but they didn't look after any of our wounded. As I was there, and a doctor, they thought that I could do it. Not that I knew how to do it, really, I simply had to. I was dealing with all sorts of wounds – head, chest, abdominal, leg, the lot. We had a table we could use as an operating table, and some chloroform. The chloroform was effective, it knocked people out quickly. What I had to do was knock them out myself with some chloroform, and then hand over to other people who were willing to have a go. I would get them to drop some chloroform on the mask every so often while I did whatever was necessary to the patient. I had some very primitive equipment which I think the Germans gave us. But it was adequate to operate with.

The Germans really thought that they had lost the battle the first night. In fact some of them said they expected our people to come in the next day. They were expecting a counter-attack, they really thought that they had lost. So they had, if the counter-attack had ever come, but it never did. So the Germans were able to land troop carriers the next day. The Germans had involved 22,000 troops in the capture of Crete of which over 6,500 were killed and over half those killed were airborne troops. These were devastating losses so you could see why some of them felt they had lost. As the fighting grew more intense, more and more people kept pouring in. I was on my own for two or three days, the only doctor.

Once I had treated people they just sort of lay about all over the place. Some were walking wounded rather than stretcher cases. There were one or two amputees, partly because the damage to their legs was so severe, and because there was a danger of gangrene. I think perhaps we were over-anxious about gangrene. I hadn't been qualified very long and to me it seemed a real danger. Sometimes there seemed to be some evidence of it developing, and we didn't know how long we were going to be there. I had never done an amputation before Crete, but I had to just get on with it. I got very tired, I had dysentery myself and wasn't very well. I kept falling asleep for short periods, almost while I was standing up, then waking up again and trying to do something.

We couldn't do anything for the severe intestinal or chest wounds, nothing at all. All we could do was stick a dressing on and hope for the best. Any open wounds we tried to close up in some way, or at least to dress. The serious wounds we just put dressings on.

A day or two later, the Germans began to evacuate some of our more serious casualties to Greece by air. They were fairly civilised about it, they did their best in a way. I don't think too many died. People were pretty fit, and could and did withstand a lot. It was all very hazy, and all continuous. After a while Dr Longmore joined me, and another New Zealand Medical Officer, Captain Stewart, was pulled in, which made things a bit easier. We just went on and eventually the wounded were removed and sent over to Greece, the less seriously injured by sea. Our casualties went to a prisoner-of-war hospital in Athens. For so many the Battle of Crete was over. It had been very costly. The RAF had fought hard alongside the Army and lost 71 men.

Eventually I was taken over to a POW hospital at Kokinia, near Athens, with some casualties, and continued to work as a doctor. The hospital had been established since the fall of Greece, and it was fairly well equipped, because the equipment of the British hospitals was left behind when Greece was evacuated. We also had quite a lot of doctors. The officer commanding the hospital was Major Brooke Moore, an Australian. Half the staff from the hospital were members of 5 Australian General Hospital, which had been captured in Greece.

Although it was all under German supervision, of course, they left us to get on with it ourselves. We had a completely free hand with the treatment of the casualties that were in the hospital. Most of the casualties had had their definitive treatment and were recovering from their injuries. It was possible to carry out proper surgical treatment at that stage.

Most people with abdominal injuries died. The chest cases survived if the bullet went right through the other side. But it wasn't very easy to do much with them. There were some facial and head injuries, quite severe – bullets that had gone into the brain. Nothing very much was done for those, except to remove some bone to relieve pressure. This wasn't done by me, but by the others who were more experienced surgeons than myself.

Most of us were young. I had minimum experience, others had a bit more, but not that much more. We were all helping each other, trying to do our best in so far as we knew what to do. It just had to be done in some circumstances. We were really doing the best we could. Over the next six months people were gradually getting better. As they were able to walk about, and fit to go to an ordinary prisoner-of-war camp, they were transferred to Germany.

I went with some casualties, who were pretty much better, on an Italian hospital ship, from Piraeus to Salonica, not long before Christmas. Then we were in a transit camp in Salonica for three or four weeks. That was dreadful! It wasn't a good place at all, it was an old, big barracks. It was absolutely alive with bed bugs, no hot water or anything of that sort. We were all pretty unhappy.

After Salonica I was moved up to a prisoner-of-war camp in Poland, north of Warsaw, where I was held for three years. In fact, as far as I know, I was the only RAF doctor held prisoner-of-war by the Germans – that was until I escaped to Sweden with the help of some immensely brave Poles and a coal-ship.

Squadron Leader 'Laddie' Lucas

It is only a small island, the size of the Isle of Wight, but from its strategic position anyone could see that if we lost Malta in the spring of 1942, then the effect, not only on the Western Desert, but also on the landings in north-west Africa, was going to be serious.

The Royal Navy's submariners, based at Lazaretto, were a bloody marvellous lot, sinking Rommel's stuff right, left and centre on its way from Europe to Libya. And the strike aeroplanes from Luqa, the torpedo Beauforts and earlier the Blenheims, combined splendidly with the submarines to knock a real hole in

Rommel's side. I know from a very good German friend, Eduard Neumann, who was commanding Jagdgeschwader 27 in the Western Desert, in support of Rommel, what he considered the real impact of Malta to have been on the Desert campaign and on the Afrika Korps. He told me, unequivocally, that Malta was the key. Because, as he explained, at El Alamein, Rommel was fatally overstretched. He had a great logistical problem; he had really been weakened far beyond what he had expected, simply because the Axis had had to stop bombing Malta for a short time, allowing the island to recuperate as an offensive base. The strike aeroplanes and the submarines had then been knocking Rommel's convoys going across. Neumann told me his squadrons were down to between fifty per cent and sixty per cent serviceability, which was critical. And that, really, was the key to the impact that Malta had on the Mediterranean and North African campaign.

It is also absolutely clear that Hitler, in February 1942, was agreeing that 'Herkules', the invasion of Malta, should go ahead. The German and Italian General Staffs wanted it, and Field Marshal Albert Kesselring, C-in-C South, in command of the Axis Air Force in Sicily, got this undertaking from the Führer that the invasion order would go ahead. But Hitler got cold feet; he had lost a lot of people invading Crete, and thought he was going to lose a lot more in Malta. He was very doubtful of the ability of the Italian Navy to take on the British Navy, and he was probably quite right over that. So basically, he fluffed it. As a result, the Germans then decided that they would saturate Malta, the three airfields, Grand Harbour and the rest, just try to starve it out, and bomb it out.

The moment the Germans had to shift some elements of the Air Force from Sicily to the Eastern front, on to Crete and to the Western Desert, Malta got a respite and the recuperative powers of the island were such that they could establish strike squadrons again. This was the key. If the Germans had invaded Malta, then the course of the North Africa campaign would have been radically different. Kesselring made this quite clear after the war.

From the Allies' point of view, of course, in order to be able to hold Malta we had to win the fighter battle. If we didn't win the fighter battle then all the rest of it would simply go for nought. And in the Hurricane period, before the Spitfires arrived, the pilots put up a marvellous show. They were out-performed by the more powerful Messerschmitt 109Fs, but never out-flown, because our fellows were so good. Most of them were peacetime pilots, who had been in France and the Battle of Britain. When we went out to the island in February 1942, in a Sunderland flying boat, we had been told that the Spitfires were going to be there. We'd all been Spitfire pilots in Fighter Command. And the first bloody thing we saw, when we got off this flying boat at dawn on a lovely spring morning, was an incoming raid. And then we saw these five, clapped-out Hurricanes struggling for height. You could almost feel the ground vibrating, the aeroplanes were so old and cannibalised. Our Squadron Leader, the Canadian, Stan Turner, a marvellous chap, had come out with us. His remit was to turn the flying in Malta upside down, and modernise it. We saw these old Hurricanes going up and then a whole lot of 109s came sweeping in over the top, going like the clappers in their wide-open, line abreast formation, always beautifully flown. Turner looked up, took his pipe out of his mouth and just said, 'Good God.' I've never forgotten it.

We had a month of that, and as a matter of fact I'm glad we did, because it enabled us to understand what those chaps had been enduring with the Hurricanes. The question was, how could we get enough Spitfires into the island? We had HMS *Eagle*, but to begin with we could only fly fifteen or sixteen aeroplanes off that carrier, but as soon as they got in to Malta, due to unserviceability or numbers lost in the air or on the ground, this simply was not enough. So in the end Churchill, in a deal with Roosevelt, got the use of the massive American carrier, USS *Wasp*. This turned the battle, there's no doubt about it. The first fly-off from the *Wasp* involved two squadrons, 601 and 603. They were loaded on to the carrier up in Greenock on the Clyde, with their forty-eight aeroplanes. One of them was cannibalised for spares and they flew forty-seven off on 20 April 1942. After going through the Straits of Gibraltar to a point roughly three hundred miles out and about seven hundred miles west of Malta, they flew them off and forty-six landed on the island. One, flown by an American, deserted. Of course the Germans, under Kesselring, had monitored these aeroplanes all the way down the Med; they were ready for them when they came in and landed. The turn-around arrangements on the island were then very poor, mainly because there had been too much secrecy and not enough detailed preparation. So within forty-eight hours we had only seven serviceable Spitfires left, out of the forty-six that had landed. This was the most terrible thing, the absolute nadir of our fortunes.

Somehow or other Churchill persuaded Roosevelt to let the *Wasp* have another go, and she went back up to Greenock and loaded up with forty-eight more aeroplanes and, this time, first-class pilots. Mostly they came from No. 11 Group in Fighter Command, whereas most of the others from 601 and 603 had really not had much operational experience. Five of us, all experienced Malta pilots, were sent back to Gibraltar, to lead these aeroplanes in. USS *Wasp* and HMS *Eagle* joined up together at Gib, sailed east down the Med for about three hundred miles, to a point fifty miles north of Algiers, and some 650 miles west of Malta. From there they flew off together, and got sixty-four aeroplanes in. *Eagle* turned round at once, came back to Gib, and loaded up again with another seventeen aeroplanes. I led that lot off so, in a matter of twelve days, we flew in nearly eighty aeroplanes. After that, it was 'never glad confident morning again' for the Luftwaffe. That was the turning-point of the battle for Malta. From then on, although there were some really fearsome battles right up to October 1942, the Germans never had the ascendancy that they had enjoyed before. That was really when the Battle of Malta was won.

Then of course Montgomery defeated Rommel at the battles

command of 249 Squadron in Malta. It became the top-scoring squadron in the British Commonwealth Air Forces. 249 was lucky, because, from the Battle of Britain onwards, it was always in the right place at the right time, and a lot was owed to that. When I commanded it, the two Flight Commanders were both English. One was Raoul Daddo-Langlois, who was first-class, and the other was Norman Lee, also highly competent. The rest of the squadron was an entire Commonwealth and United States mix. If anything, the UK people were in a minority; we had Canadians, Australians, New Zealanders, South Africans, Rhodesians and Americans. The spirit in that squadron was absolutely without parallel. It was one of the things that made me go into the House of Commons after the war: I felt that, having had that experience with those guys from all around the world, I had built up lessons which ought to be imparted, used for the benefit of others.

During the battle for Malta I believe the Germans' Intelligence was very poor, while ours was brilliant. With Ultra and its advance posts in Malta and in Cairo, there's no doubt that the information which the Allies were getting on the sailing of the convoys going across to Rommel was vital. The codebreaking, achieved by the Ultra people at Bletchley Park in the UK, was absolutely invaluable, and we also had the 'Y' service – teams of men and women working underground on Malta, monitoring Axis transmissions round the clock. Obviously it was essential for the Germans never to think that we were actually busting their Enigma cyphers and picking up this vital information, so the commanders had to be extremely careful not to act in a way which might alert them. It was brilliant, really: we had this tremendous advantage, knowing much of what Kesselring was doing. We thought that there would quite possibly be an invasion around March, April or May 1942, and the Governor of Malta, and the AOC, Hugh Pughe Lloyd, were sending signals back to London saying that it was absolutely imperative to get more fighter aeroplanes out to the island; but in fact the Chiefs of Staff knew, via Ultra, that Kesselring was moving squadrons away to the desert, preparatory to Rommel's advance there, and also to the Eastern Front. The fact that the Germans never discovered that we were going to reinforce Malta in such strength with the *Wasp* and the *Eagle* in April and May shows how poor their Intelligence was by comparison with ours.

Only a handful of senior officers ever knew the full extent of our Intelligence operations, and I can remember when I was commanding 249 in June, we had just got down to Takali about five o'clock one morning, for dawn readiness. I was putting on a Mae West and the operations telephone rang in our dispersal hut. The Controller at the other end, a first-class chap called Bill Farnes, said, 'Look here, Laddie, the "Y" service says there is some activity south-east of Malta, about fifty or sixty miles out, and it's probably worthwhile sending a section of four aircraft out for about twenty-five minutes at 1,000 feet to have a look. If you don't see anything, come back. Don't get annoyed if you don't see anything, but we think it's worthwhile going out.' So I said OK, and I took three more of my guys, all Canadians, and we went out on a heading of 130° for twenty-five minutes. We were just coming up to the end of the run, when my no. 2, Frank Jones, called out: 'Tiger Leader two Junkers 88s at eleven o'clock right down on the water flying east.' And there were these two aircraft; they had seen us against the lightening sky, but Jonesy had also seen them with his good eyes. By that time they had got into line-abreast, quite close so that they could get protection from their crossfire. I said to Jonesy, 'OK, you and I will take the port aircraft, and Lint and Mickey (Linton and Butler, my nos. 3 and 4) will take the one to the starboard. We'll do beam-into-quarter attacks concurrently.'

And so we got on either side of these two aircraft and turned into them. The two tail-gunners didn't half have a go at us. We did two fast attacks from each side, and that was that. Each aircraft terraplaned and then went straight in. We circled for about four or five minutes over the spot, but there were no survivors. I really felt very sorry because they had put up a hell of a show, and one didn't want to see people with guts like that lost. And all that was due to the 'Y' service operators; there was nothing on the Ops table, no radar plots, or anything. It was all due to these buggers who used to sit there with their earphones on, down in the bowels of Valetta, in the most bloody awful conditions; the 'Ditch' we called it. Christ knows how they stuck that awful heat and damp and mugginess.

In addition to this, of course, we had our own radar. Malta was the first place they had radar outside the United Kingdom, before the war. And our radar picked up the Germans when they were beginning to build up over Sicily sixty miles away, so we were always ready. The Senior Operations Controller, Group Captain A. B. Woodall, was marvellous. He was a World War I pilot, and he understood all about tactics. He'd been at Duxford in the Battle of Britain and he'd commanded the sector at Tangmere when Douglas Bader was leading the wing there. He had a genius for reading these raids, predicting what they were going to do, and putting us in the right position. And because we were usually out-numbered by anything from eight, ten, fifteen and twenty to one, the fact that we were always put in the right position, probably 5,000 or 6,000 feet above and up-sun of the enemy, ready simply to steam into these raids with bags of speed, was responsible for a great part of the fighter victory. I think Woodie was *the* outstanding Controller in the Royal Air Force during the war; he was brilliant, absolutely brilliant.

When we shot the Germans and Italians down, we used to go and see them in hospital, at Imtarfa. One of them was a fellow called Kurt Lauinger, a southern German, who could speak English quite well. We used to go and talk to him, funnily enough not to try and get information out of him, but just because we were interested, rather like fishermen comparing notes and telling a whole host of lies about what had gone on in the day. When we were talking to Lauinger, one day, we told him his squadron commander, Hermann Neuhoff, had been shot down. 'Oh,' he said, 'Neuhoff. No-one can shoot down Neuhoff.' So I told him to write out a message to Neuhoff and I would see that it was taken to him in hospital over on the east side of the island. A message would be brought back. So he wrote a note which was taken over to Neuhoff. Neuhoff apparently laughed and wrote out a reply which was brought back to Lauinger. Kurt read it and he couldn't believe it. 'And the things Neuhoff used to say to me about my flying,' he said, 'and now both of us have been shot down!' It was extraordinary, really, this sort of chivalry and comradeship. I couldn't feel any hate for the other side. It was just entertaining, really, like two teams sitting down for a meal after a hard game of rugby football.

But one day I stopped the squadron from doing it. It was at the beginning of July, and I was nearing the end of my time with the squadron. There was a raid, and Woodall was controlling it. He'd talked this raid through, giving us a brilliant running commentary. There were three Italian bombers in a tight V-formation, with a great beehive of fighter escorts, about eighty-plus, Me109s and Macchi 202s, and the whole idea was that the bombers were decoys. There were ten of us, I had a four, Raoul Daddo-Langlois had a four, and the New Zealander, Jack Rae, was leading his pair of two. We were flying in line-abreast as we always did. Woodall had got us into this marvellous position, up-sun and at about 26,000 feet; and I had pushed the thing up another two thousand because you never lost anything by having excess height. Bader always had this piece of doggerel that he used to recite: 'He who has the sun creates surprise. He who has the height controls the battle. He who gets in close shoots them down.'

We were now about 5,000 or 6,000 feet above these fellows. So I said to my guys, 'Look, we've got bags of height, we've got the sun, but there are a lot of 109s about, so we'll go straight through the lot of them, and have a go at the three bombers. After that go straight down to the deck.' We went steaming into these bloody things. I had a go at the bomber on the left, and saw it disintegrate, going down in flames. I saw Raoul's go falling away, and then Jack came through and knocked out the bomber in the middle.

All three of them went down in flames. Then I said, 'Now roll on to your backs, fellers, and go down to the deck. There are far too many 109s about to stay and mix it.' So we went down and landed at Takali.

The next day, I took two or three of the fellows who had been flying that day, plus one of the chaps from headquarters who could speak Italian, to the hospital where all the Italians who had baled out were in bed. I walked across to the bed on the left of the ward and there was this good-looking young Italian with his arm all bandaged up. The interpreter said to him, 'This is the CO of the squadron which shot your aeroplanes down, and these are some of the rest of the squadron.' And this young Italian, who couldn't speak English, held up his hand and said, through the interpreter, 'I have lost my hand.' It made me feel terrible. Then the interpreter asked him, 'What did you do in peacetime?' and the boy just said, 'I was a professional violinist.' I said to my chaps, 'I'm going to go out now,' and I waited for them until they had finished talking to the Italians; then I said to them, 'Look here, we are never going to visit these wounded prisoners in hospital again when there is an emotive injury or wound. It is so terrible and bad for morale. I can't stand it.' For weeks after, long after I'd come back from Malta, I used to wake up in the middle of the night thinking about it. It was a dreadful thing, because I had no feeling of hate for these people.

Another problem was tiredness. When you flew in Malta it was usually up and down – just short trips; there weren't any long flights. Most interceptions lasted probably forty or fifty minutes. But the pressures were continuous. If you chased things back to Sicily, you might be up for an hour or so. No more. We also had unpleasant illnesses, made worse without antibiotics in those days. We had 'Malta Dog', a horrible sort of dysentery, with sickness and diarrhoea. Another was sandfly fever, which was foul too. I had that for about seven or eight days once. I felt bloody awful with a perpetual headache. And we were always hungry. It's an extraordinary thing about hunger: you can get used to it, provided you know that there is nothing more that can be done about it. If you're hungry and you think that the admin isn't right, and you're not getting enough food for the squadron, that's quite a different thing. We all ate the same food, pilots, ground crew, everyone. It was all bully beef and hard biscuits, and stew, the same thing every day, day after day. We knew exactly what we were going to have. The fellows in the kitchens tried to fry up and make the things look different, but it was really always the same.

Another problem was keeping morale, team spirit, going. I had this brilliant Canadian in my squadron, 'Screwball' Beurling, and he was the most outstanding individual fighter pilot that I personally saw in World War II. I'd been warned that, on sweeps at home, he was always buggering off over France and coming back by himself saying he'd shot one down; going off on his own, which you were never supposed to do. But I thought he was just the sort of chap that we might be able to use in Malta, so I said to Beurling, 'I want you to come and have a talk with me after tea.' So we sat down, and I said, 'Now look here, you've come out here with quite a strange reputation, but you start here with an absolutely clean sheet. I'm told that you fly well, I'm told you can shoot, but I'm also told that you go off on your own. Well, you can't bloody well do that here, because if you do, a) you'll get shot down, and b) you'll leave the other guy you are flying with to get shot down. We all play things together here in 249.' So he said, 'Yes, boss'. He never called me 'sir', always 'boss'; he was a Sergeant pilot.

When I got command of the squadron, Raoul took over my flight and became responsible for Beurling. So I told him to watch this Canadian, saying that he had marvellous eyesight, had excellent positioning, and that he would go in like a rugby centre three-quarter going through the middle. He'd go in fast, he'd get in close and fire short bursts. There was no doubt he had exceptional ability. Well, after about a week or so, Raoul told me Beurling was certainly pretty good, but that he was always pissing off on his own. I sent for him and said, 'Now look here, Screwball, if you go on doing this, I give you fair warning, you'll be on the next aeroplane into the Middle East.' And he looked at me with those Scandinavian eyes, bright piercing blue eyes, and said, 'OK, boss, I'll play it your way.' And he never gave us another bit of difficulty. He was exceptional and I think he shot twenty-eight aircraft down. Malta was made for him, because it was an individual's theatre, and we gave him his head, and he had the ability. He survived the war, but soon after was killed ferrying aeroplanes out to Israel.

The last vital element that should be mentioned about Malta is that the island obviously depended, for its supplies, on what the convoys could bring in. And because everyone was always hungry, this spectre of starvation was always there. And in my time, from February to the end of July 1942, the Navy tried to run through four seaborne convoys. The February convoy from Alexandria had to turn back as it was going through Bomb Alley, between Crete and the Libyan coast; the Narrows there were the most terrible place. The Germans were bombing it from Crete and Libya. In March, the convoy with *Breconshire*, *Pampas* and *Talabot* came from Alexandria. As it approached Malta, there was very low cloud, a mistral really, with wind and rain, and it was absolutely made for the Germans to go darting in and out as they attacked the ships. *Pampas* and *Talabot* made Grand Harbour, but as soon as they were in they got bombed, and that was that. *Breconshire* had to be towed in and beached. Then she was bombed. They got a certain amount of stuff off the ships, probably about 5,000 or 6,000 tons before they were sunk, but not much more. So that was the March convoy.

We were getting pretty low; food really was beginning to get short, morale was beginning to fall, and the civilians were having their belts pulled in by the fortnight. The next attempt was in June. There were two convoys. They had this idea that if they ran two convoys in together, one from Gibraltar and the other from Alexandria, it would divide the Germans' and the Italians' attacking strength. The one from the east, from Alexandria, when it was going through Bomb Alley, spotted the Italian fleet coming down from the north-east, so they were forced to turn round and go back. That was awful. The one from Gibraltar had started out with six merchant ships, and in the end only two got into Grand Harbour; it was the most terrible fight. We could see a third, the US oiler, *Kentucky*, which we so badly wanted, sunk as it approached the final run in. Of the two which reached Grand Harbour quite a lot of stuff was unloaded, enough to keep us going until August when the 'Santa Maria' or 'Pedestal' convoy fought its way through. I had gone home by then, but I can remember that June convoy. When these two merchant vessels had about a hundred miles still to go, Woodall rang me on the Ops line at Takali and asked 249 to organise cover for four Fleet Air Arm Albacores which, he said, would be attacking two Italian warships lying off to the south of the incoming convoy. And I can remember seeing these bloody biplanes, tight down on the water, flying at 90 knots, when we were about 5,000 feet above, and saying to myself, 'Thank God I can see them.' Then I saw a long-range fighter, a Junkers 88, coming in to attack them. We couldn't give chase, because we hadn't got the fuel, but it turned away as the pilot saw us. Then we saw two Italian warships shining like silver paper on this beautiful, sunny June day. When the Albacores got to within about five or six miles, the warships began to open fire. But on the aircraft flew until one, obviously hit, pulled away to the left; but he had let his torpedo go. The other three also let their torpedoes go as they pressed their attack; two torpedoes missed, but one struck the leading warship, fair and square, amidships. It didn't sink the vessel but immobilised it sufficiently to allow the Royal Navy later to deliver the coup de grâce. I saw a lot of the Royal Air Force doing these terrible shipping attacks in 1941 off the Dutch coast, but never had I seen anything braver than these Albacore crews; it was absolutely fantastic. Those Fleet Air Arm guys we served with in Malta really were a super lot. They had these awful aeroplanes to fly,

high-wing loading characteristics which were most unusual for an aircraft of those days. It was very heavily armoured, and carried a 4,000lb bomb-load, as a medium bomber. They lost a lot of these aircraft in training because of these high-wing loading, high-speed landing and take-off characteristics. So it got the name of the Widow Maker, because a lot of crews were killed early on. The RAF only equipped two squadrons and five South African squadrons with them. No Commonwealth units flew Marauders from the UK, only the Americans. They took part in D-Day.

I was an air-gunner, and sat up on the top turret, which was cramped, not much more than shoulder width. We operated with two .5 machine-guns. There was complete rotation of the turret. You could fire right up and round, and down to a certain extent. You sat on an armour-plated seat which you pulled up beneath you. In operations, whenever you were a box leader, the top-gunner took over the control of the box, because you saw where the flak was bursting and told the skipper hopefully how to avoid it. And you thus controlled the other aircraft in that box, since they immediately followed you. So you had to know what you were about.

On finishing OTU we were immediately sent into the Desert Air Force campaign, which was at the time being carried forward from North Africa to Italy, and went straight into operations. I flew my first operations when I was eighteen and nine months; none of the crew was much older. We took part in the Italian campaign, mainly up the Adriatic Coast. I was sent to 21 Squadron, South African Air Force. At times we operated over Yugoslavia. On one or two of our missions we were carrying what we called 'extraneous bods' with us. We weren't allowed to speak to them, we didn't know who they were, but we had to kick them out at various places over Yugoslavia. We found out afterwards that they were people going out to assist the partisans, SOE people. We did bombing missions there, too, but mainly we were operating in the area over northern Italy and southern Austria. A lot of our work was interdiction, cutting supply routes, close support work for the Army, and attacking factories and shipping.

In that part of Italy, also, single aircraft were tasked to go out and attack anti-aircraft guns, in support of main formations. You did low-level, and carried 4,000lb of 20lb fragmentation-bombs on those raids, low-level meaning 400 or 500 feet. We went right down over the guns. In general, in every one of the attacks that we made we managed to clobber the guns. The fact that the guns stopped firing at us proved the point. On some of the raids from Italy into Yugoslavia against targets like railway bridges, we were reporting misses because we couldn't confirm that we had actually hit them. But the Intelligence came back afterwards and showed that they were hit. So we felt that something had been achieved.

My first raid was to Yugoslavia. It was interdiction. The briefing was that we were to fly from our base at Iesi, northern Italy, and wipe out the rail bridges at Zidani Most. There were reports of German concentrations moving down through Yugoslavia, to the north of Zagreb. That was one of those that we reported a miss on, but in fact it turned out that we had actually succeeded. That was our first raid; it happened to be quite a light one in that there was very little opposition, and we got away to a fool's paradise. The next one we went on was the raid on Udine marshalling yards in northern Italy, in which we were clobbered.

We were up against the Panzers, and they were very heavily equipped with heavy artillery. It was Christmas 1944. Unknown to us there were two or three trains of German heavy ack-ack guns in the area. We ran into a massive hail of flak, and one of the chaps I joined up with, Johnny Hipwell, was flying in an aircraft about a box away from me. I saw his aircraft take a direct hit, and he was blown out of the sky. It took the two wing aircraft with it. There wasn't a single aircraft came back from that particular mission that wasn't holed. We came back with an aircraft more like a colander, but not one of us was hit! I was in the upper turret of the Marauder, which was a very heavily armoured plane, with the steel armour-plate beneath the gunner's seat. I felt a thump under my seat, and didn't think anything of it, because we were anxious to get the hell out of this as quickly as possible. But we also carried our parachute underneath our seat, and after we landed I took my parachute out, and there was a hole right through it. So I was thinking to myself that the fates were with us, because if I'd had to get out and jump, I'd have just gone straight down. I have a piece of that parachute still, in fact my wife wore a piece of it on her wedding dress. Our wing lost three aircraft – eighteen crew members. I'll never forget it though at the time I didn't allow it to upset me. But immediately afterwards there was a very severe winter in northern Italy, and we had a week or two when we couldn't fly. Then there was time to reflect on the loss of one's friends and you started to wonder what the hell you were doing there.

It was two or three weeks before we could fly again. But it was still icy conditions. Once we were just getting ready to take off, and had been scraping the ice off the wings. One of the 30 Squadron aircraft crashed on take-off and plunged into a taxi strip, where there were three other aircraft, and they all blew up. I was blown off the wing of my aircraft. Twenty-two people were lost, eighteen aircrew and four ground crew as well.

Because I'd been blown off the wing I was a wee bit shocked, but that afternoon they put us up into the air to do a raid right away. So we didn't generally have time to reflect on the happenings of the time. But when I look back on it, I wonder how on earth the losses weren't greater than they were, when you consider the conditions of the airfields from which we were operating and the weather conditions. The ground crews did magnificent work in servicing the aircraft, especially as the Marauder was such an intricate aircraft that the slightest thing would put it off. And with the high take-off and landing speeds you had no room for error.

In the raid that followed the accident, we went to a place called Malcontenta, in northern Italy. Our target that day was a huge ammunition dump. And we hit it. We hit it from 10,000 feet, and the explosions and the flames were going up 15,000 feet. Our aircraft were rocked all over the sky with the force of it. It was a real good hit. There were four squadrons of us. The dump was spread over quite an area, we blanketed it, and had direct hits on it and took it out. It must have severely affected the enemy troop supplies.

On another raid, when we were flying in a formation of twelve, I suddenly saw eleven aircraft going away above me. In fact, it was us falling, we had been hit in the starboard engine, and we were losing height very rapidly. The Marauder was electric powered, including the guns, and of course the skipper said we weren't to use anything. We had to conserve all the power we'd got. We were afraid of being attacked, but suddenly we saw two aircraft coming up beside us, and thankfully they were Spitfires coming to escort us back. We were losing height all the way, and were getting a lot of light fire on the way down. Then we were hit in the port engine, which was the good engine. We were just off the coast, just south of Venice, and we were getting ready to ditch in the sea, when we saw a landing strip. We didn't know where we were. The skipper decided to put down there, but we didn't know whether it was behind enemy lines or not. Well, we got in, and by good luck we made the runway and scrambled out of the aircraft just before it blew up. And we found we'd landed at an advance Allied airstrip in northern Italy which had only been captured a few days before.

Another raid was on a seaport called Montfalconi, in northern Italy, we lost an aircraft on that. The crew baled out and four of them were back in the squadron the next day! The Italian partisans picked them up, and had got them to the Allies. But we lost two of the chaps in the sea. I remember that because we couldn't believe it when we saw these two guys coming back. The usual pattern was, when a crew was lost, all the equipment was put together and raffled amongst the other boys, so that all the proceeds could be sent to relatives. We were doing this when the boys walked in.

Eventually, towards the end of the campaign in Italy, in the early part of 1945, we were involved with work which we all liked to do, if you can like to do anything in wartime, and that was close support work for the Army. We had some pretty interesting experiences especially in the light of today's 'friendly fire' controversy: on one or two of our missions we were recalled, because of the rapid advance of the Army, when we were just about ready to bomb.

We followed the advance of the British troops all the time, we did a lot of support work, they were moving their transport up all the time. We were only a few hundred yards ahead of them at times.

We sometimes attacked the German troops on the ground. We got a whole lot of them at one stage, on an early morning flight, when we were after flak guns at Treviso, northern Italy. They were on the parade ground and we went down and machine-gunned them. We carried cannons, two .5s in the tail, two on the top, there was a .5 in the front in the nose, which the navigator operated. And there were four fixed guns, two on the side of the aircraft, and two on each wing.

We could see the troops parading, and then they scattered. It was just a chance we took: we wouldn't have seen them if we were higher, but we were at 500 feet because we were going for guns.

Perhaps it's good there's a mental safeguard, because even when dropping bombs you were divorced from the impact at the other end. In most cases they were shooting at you, too. So it was a situation where you didn't have feelings of remorse or guilt, or anything else. It was a job to be done and you got on with it. If there were enemy troops and you managed to knock them out you were saving some of our guys from them.

The Germans were brilliant; when you knocked down their bridges they re-built the bridge under the water. They concreted it, they raised the level of the bed, they were absolutely marvellous at the speed with which they could do things. We would clobber the marshalling yards, and have to keep going back to them, because they were repaired so quickly. This was where interdiction was so important, because you had to stop the supplies coming down. And they managed to hold up the Allies in Italy for a long, long time. A thing that I think is not appreciated is that, if the Allies hadn't done what they did in Italy, all those German troops and materiel would have been free for Normandy. The campaign contained them, and kept them back.

Once we did a bit of an interchange with the Army during what they called a slackish period. They sent some of us up to the front lines with the troops, to see how things worked. And they sent some of the troops back to the squadron to fly. We both came back from our respective efforts saying, I wouldn't do your job for anything! To see the conditions that those fellows were operating in, on the front line! That was an interesting experience.

I was actually in the Italian campaign for a year. It was the last year, and a year of fairly non-stop flying, apart from that few weeks during the horrendous winter. We spent most of our time there digging out of the snow. We were living under very, very crude conditions, in tents. We had no beds, I slept for three months on a couple of blankets on top of a sheet of corrugated iron, we were dug into the ground and were getting the odd sporadic attack. Operating in those theatres was different, and I think this is a thing that is not often said. I'm not taking one little bit away from the marvellous things that were done in the UK, but chaps who came back from raids could go into a pub and mix with other people. We had none of that, we were in it the whole time, twenty-four hours a day. We had no leave breaks or anything, you just couldn't. We had to just keep going without a break. I was on my second tour before I was twenty. One just went straight from one tour on to another. And out of the forty chaps that went out thirteen of us came back to the UK, they were all eighteen- or nineteen-year-olds. Some were transferred to Liberators, and they took part in the drops in Warsaw, where they lost heavily.

At the end of the war some of us got to Dachau which wasn't very pleasant. The place was so silent, not a bird singing or anything else, a complete air of doom. It is very hard to explain it. We saw where they were digging the big mass graves. The bodies weren't all incinerated. A lot of them were just in the graves. You just didn't take it in, really, it was horrible, repulsive, you knew it was, but it didn't make you react. You were immune, you had had an injection, you were immunised. Even now it's impossible to recall the full horror of it.

In retrospect, what was unique about the Italian campaign was the many different forces that were there working together. We were a mixture of Indians, Brazilians, New Zealanders, Goums from North Africa, the Americans, Jewish battalions, and all the Eighth Army brigade, it was amazing. On our squadron the ground crew were South African, both native and white South Africans. We had no problems. It was a wonderful experience to have had in life. You don't know what life is going to hold for you, but I feel to have had this mix with all these different nationalities, to mix with Afrikaners, and Blacks as well as Australians and New Zealanders gives one an appreciation of life. A lot of the chaps I knew are buried in the Commonwealth Cemetery at Udine. It is a great eye-opener for people to go there and see the last resting place of nineteen- and twenty-year-olds, South Africans, Brazilians, Indians, British and so many others, all side by side. All for one cause. It makes you wonder where we go wrong now and again.

War is a horrible thing, there is no doubt about that. It debases people, but it also brings out the best in people. And I think that I was fortunate in that for everybody I knew it brought out the best.

4

ON THE OFFENSIVE, 1941–1945

The Battle of Britain won, RAF Fighter Command began its long offensive against the Luftwaffe on 10 January 1941 when nine fighter squadrons ranged over the Pas de Calais while a single light-bomber squadron attacked German gun positions. From then until D-Day, Fighter Command and the light, day bombers of No. 2 Group, Bomber Command, took the war to the enemy. It had a language of its own. 'Circuses' were fighter-escorted bombing attacks on short-range targets intended to draw German fighters into combat; low-level 'Rhubarbs' were usually flown when there was cloud cover, small groups of fighters and fighter-bombers marauding over enemy territory and attacking opportunity targets. 'Ramrods' were like Circuses, but the destruction of the bombers' target was the prime objective. 'Rangers' were strong fighter sweeps over enemy territory hunting German fighters. 'Rodeos' were a variety of Ranger. 'Roadsteads' were attacks on enemy shipping, at sea or in harbour, which often involved fighter-bombers or escorts for Coastal Command aircraft.

The offensive was maintained despite the Spitfire Mk V being out-classed by the Luftwaffe's Focke-Wulf 190 which appeared on the Channel front in May 1941. Fighter Command countered with the Spitfire Mk IX and the new Hawker Typhoon, a superb ground-attack weapon once its engine and structural problems were overcome.

The massive, day-long air battle over the Dieppe landings on 19 August 1942, involved 70 RAF squadrons, 61 of fighters. The RAF, at least, claimed a victory in stopping the Luftwaffe adding to the bloody shambles on the beaches.

From 1942 the United States Army Air Force began its increasingly mighty daylight precision bombing offensive over Europe. While the RAF Spitfires and Typhoons lacked the range to escort the US bombers deep into Europe, the superb P-51 Mustang gave the Americans a fighter which outclassed the Luftwaffe's best and had the range of a bomber. From December 1943 the crucial attrition of the Luftwaffe day-fighter force was increasingly achieved by USAAF Mustangs fighting far beyond the range of RAF single-seat fighters.

The Luftwaffe's offensive against Britain faded to sporadic daylight 'tip and run' attacks by fighter-bombers while at night a dwindling number of enemy bombers braved the RAF night fighters. From June 1944, however, a new German weapon, the V1, demanded massive efforts from the RAF, both fighters and bombers, to intercept the flying-bombs and attack their launching sites.

In preparation for the D-Day invasion, 2nd Tactical Air Force was created in June 1943. (Army Co-Operation Command then ceased to exist.) It drew on the tactical lessons of the Western Desert Air Force as the Spitfires and Typhoons and the day-bombers – Bostons, Mitchells, Mosquitoes – prepared for the Allied armies' fight back into Europe.

Flight Sergeant Charles Cox

Before the war I used to repair the neighbours' radios. I got a reputation as a repair man, even though I was a cinema projectionist then.

After I'd done my training as a Radar Mechanic I was posted close to my home in north Norfolk, but I was eventually sent down to Hartland Point where we used to track the Germans coming up to bomb Liverpool.

I was there for quite a while, but then a call came through, telling me to report to the Air Ministry. When I got to Whitehall, I reported, told them who I was. They said, 'Hang on a minute, there's another chap here.' And he was called Corporal Smith; we both waited and then were sent up to Air Commodore Tait.

He looked up from his desk, where he was writing, and he said, 'You two men have, I gather, volunteered for a dangerous job.' So this bloke Smith said, 'Yes, sir.' And I said, 'No, sir.' 'Oh,' he said, 'well now you're here, would you volunteer?' 'Well,' I said, 'what's the job, sir?' He said, 'There's a war on, and people get killed in wars, but I promise you you have a pretty fair chance of survival.' So I said, 'All right, sir, I'll volunteer.' What else could I do? Especially since I had just been promoted to Flight Sergeant, a bribe!

Anyway, while I was there I did some parachute training at Ringway aerodrome. It was my first time in an aeroplane; we did two balloon jumps, which was bloody frightening. I didn't like that at all, because you come straight down. Then we joined the Whitley aircraft and had to jump out of the hole in the floor. We all got round this hole, and I said, 'Where's Smithy?' They said, 'Oh, there's something wrong with his 'chute and he's had to go back.' So I did the jump, and went to find Smith. 'Oh,' he said, 'I couldn't stand it.' 'What do you mean, you couldn't stand it?' I asked. He said, 'I couldn't stand that bloody aircraft.' So I was on my own.

I did about three or four more jumps. First singles, then doubles. Then an officer said, 'He hasn't done a night jump.' So off we all went to Tatton Park: the balloon crew, the doctor, the ambulance, just for my one night jump! I did it, and it was the worst of the lot.

And then they sent me down to Tilshead, on Salisbury Plain. I had no idea what I was going to do! But I knew it was something hairy because there were a whole lot of parachutists. There were also a couple of Sappers and a Signals bloke. That was the first time I met Captain Vernon who was with the Parachute Field Engineers. He was a charming man. We examined all this British radar equipment. Of course I knew what it was, without being told. Vernon asked the questions because he wasn't conversant with radar. So I had to tell him what each part was, and what it did.

Then one night, 27 February 1942, we all got together and went down to the aerodrome on Salisbury Plain and had cups of cocoa. We donned these parachutes, which were different from the others we had been using. They'd been black and white, and these were camouflaged. And we got this cocoa down us, which I'm sorry to say we later regretted doing, and then got into the aircraft. We hadn't got the foggiest idea where we were going until just before we embarked, when they said, 'You're going to a place on the north coast of France called Bruneval, to dismantle an enemy radar dish and bring as much of it as possible back to England.'

The plane took off. We could hear twelve aircraft, and I was to jump no. 6 in the sixth aircraft. We had a little singsong. I sang 'Rose of Tralee', and 'Because'. It's difficult to sing in an aeroplane, because of the noise, but it went down well. Major John Frost, who was commanding the raid, nodded approvingly down the line to me. I had a revolver strapped to my inside, and I was wearing my Air Force uniform with a proper tin airborne helmet. The powers-that-be would not let me go in Army uniform, which was strange because, if we had all been captured, I would have stood out like a sore thumb in my Air Force get-up. My tool kit wasn't with me; that was dropped later in the containers after we had jumped.

As we got closer to the target, Bruneval, the hole in the floor was unblocked, and I could see the sea beneath. Then we flew across the coast and the flak started coming up which was a bit worrying. We then got the red light so I sat on the edge and then the green light came on. Then we went out one, two, three, four, five, six and out I went.

I got on the ground and I looked up and could see the aircraft going off in the distance, with a flame coming out of its exhaust. And then, of course, we had to answer the call of nature, because we'd had that cocoa. We had our first pee in France and of course were very vulnerable at that time. If Jerry had known we were there he could have knocked us all off, but he didn't.

We were about two hundred yards from our objective. Major Frost got us all together. Then Captain Vernon said, 'Flight Sergeant, I'll go ahead and recce.' So he went ahead. I couldn't see what he was doing, because it was that dark, but I could hear firing down in the village, and more firing from the Presbytère, which was a copse of trees. I went up to Captain Vernon, and he said, 'This is it.' So we looked at the radar dish and there was a curtain on the back. He lifted it and I looked at it. It seemed very simple, so we started taking the boxes out. There was one big box at the top which I subsequently learned was the transmitter/receiver, and our screwdrivers, despite being very long ones, wouldn't reach the screws. So Captain Vernon said, 'Let's give it the old one-two.' He hung on to one handle and I hung on the other, and we gave it one, two, three, and it came away, with the equipment and aerial. This was very good, because there was only one aerial, and the system had to be sorted out on the way down. I didn't know, and still don't know to this day, whether this was the first equipment and aerial. But all the boffins were very pleased with it.

All this time, of course, there was enemy fire whizzing past my ear. It didn't worry me at all, because I was too busy. Captain Vernon was helping me; I was telling him what we wanted, and he was carrying the necessaries. Then Major Frost got a bit worried, because he could see lights from the road. He thought perhaps the Germans were coming from Le Havre, so he said, 'Come on, we'll go.' So we started to go with all the equipment, carrying it on our shoulders. One or two of the Engineers gave us a hand. Some of it was very heavy. We started coming down a sort of slope, down to the sea.

It was quite a distance, and when we got down there, the Germans started firing at us from the other side of this dip. Of course we tried to make ourselves non-existent, very small, but I think another lot of parachutists had come up behind us and taken the pillbox. So that was OK. And then someone from the beach said, 'Come on, the beach is clear,' so we went down. We slid down on our bums, still carrying the stuff. Nothing was dropped, although the aerial had a bullet hole through it, and I had a crease through the boot – it was very close. Sergeant-Major Strachan got two in his stomach, unfortunately. They had to give him some morphine. He was lucky to be alive.

Anyway, when I got down to the beach there was one of these parachutists, and there was a German, with his hands up and his back to the blockhouse. And the parachutist had his gun trained on him. We went on to the beach and sat under the cliffs, with all this gear we'd pinched.

This Welshman who was with me got very morbid. He said, 'We're going to be captured.' So I said, 'Nah, don't be silly, the Navy will come in.' And of course you lose track of the time. But we seemed to be there a very long time.

Major Frost was walking up and down the beach, firing Very lights. And then suddenly we heard motors and in came the Navy. Landing-craft came in, right on the correct spot. So we rushed for them, carrying the things we'd pinched. I was carrying mine above my head, but of course it was winter, February, and so I was all right until the ice-cold water reached my unmentionables and then COOOORR!! Anyway, we climbed aboard the landing-craft, and there was a boffin. He was a brave man, because he had no need to be there. He said, 'Hello, Flight Sergeant, what have you got?' I said, 'I think I've got everything you want, sir.' He said, 'Jolly good show.' And we went to the ships.

I think they were gunboats, these ships, and I went down to the Captain's cabin and he said, 'Now, I want to know everything about what you saw.' I said, 'Excuse me, sir, I want to be sick. I've never been to sea before.' He said, 'Give an account of everything you saw and your impression of it and then you can be sick.' So I did, I gave him everything I saw and how it had all appeared to me. And he said, 'All right, Flight Sergeant, now be sick.' I was. Then I lay down on the Captain's bunk and had a cup of hot cocoa, fell asleep immediately, and woke up as we were coming up the Solent.

When I came on to deck, I saw Spitfires come over, heard boats honking, and the music over their loudspeakers, playing 'Land of Hope and Glory'. It was a great moment. Spitfires overhead tipping their wings made us feel very proud. Then of course, we had all the aircrew come on and all the people connected with the raid came on, and we had a big meal.

After the dinner, we went to Tilshead. And of course as we went in through the gates there was a crowd of the airborne forces, on either side and they gave us three cheers as we came in. Then they laid on booze for us, but no sooner had I got a pint of something in front of me than they said, 'They want you in the office.' So I went, and they said, 'They want you at the Air Ministry.' So they put me on the train, and off I went to the Air Ministry. Once I got there, I marched into Air Commodore Tait's office and I saw the German radar gear lying on the floor. He said, 'Good show, Flight Sergeant.' Then he said, 'What do we do with you now?' I said I'd like to go on leave for a couple of days. 'We'll send you for a week,' he said.

They gave me a train warrant and some money, and I got on a train to Wisbech, where my wife was living. I walked in about eleven o'clock at night; my mother and father were there with my wife and baby daughter. I said to our family, 'I'm a bloody hero.'

I had an Uncle Harry, and he had a Military Medal from the First World War: I think he captured about a dozen Germans, all on his own. So when I got mine we had two in the family.

Flying Officer Robert Barckley

In 1913 No. 3 Squadron was the first RFC aeroplane squadron. That's why our motto is 'Tertius Primus Erit'. The squadron in 1941–42 was operating as both night and day fighters. At night we flew jet black Hurricane IICs. We were doing night readiness and scrambles – for old-fashioned night fighting, co-operating with searchlights and before the advent of radar. Our bread-and-butter work was dawn and dusk patrols over the North Sea and convoys.

We used to pick up the convoys round about Harwich and fly north with them, No. 3 Squadron doing the night element of the dawn and dusk patrols. We used to take off just before nightfall and relieve Spitfires who had been patrolling the convoy by day. Usually when we got to the convoy we were greeted by flak. We didn't hold it against them as they were, naturally, edgy. We used to waggle our wings and flash the code letter of the day to show our credentials.

I suppose the first time I engaged my guns in anger was on the Dieppe raid on 19 August 1942. We knew in advance that a Combined-operation raid was planned as, in May, we had been moved to a forward base, Shoreham, for the operation. After a few days' waiting it was called off and we returned to Hunsdon. It was re-activated for mid-August and we returned to Shoreham. Our first task was to take off before first light and strafe heavy guns on the west cliff at Dieppe. The trouble was, we arrived at Dieppe too early; it was still dark, we couldn't see a thing. So we flew around in a great big circle back over the Channel again. By the time we did go in, the Germans were thoroughly stirred up and there was a fair amount of flak flying. We went in and strafed the gun positions in two passes. We lost one pilot on this sortie.

When I got back to Shoreham I was told by the Controller that there were German aircraft in the area. So I flew down the coast, though by this stage I hadn't any ammunition left, and at Brighton I saw a lone Spitfire at 2,000 feet and a Me109 above it at 5,000 feet. The Spit suddenly pulled up – he must have seen the Me109 – in an almost vertical climb, and the Me109 dived. The two aircraft just crashed into each other; they locked together and the wreckage went into the sea.

Our next sortie that day was attacking E-boats off Boulogne, who were attacking the flotilla. We hit two E-boats. They were operating behind a French fishing fleet. On our third sortie we weren't so lucky. This time we were strafing the gun positions at the Casino on the promenade. We had a Spit squadron giving us top cover, but Focke-Wulf 190s came straight through them and the first I saw of them was one virtually formating on me. It picked off our CO, Squadron Leader Berry, a New Zealander. He just went straight into the ground on fire.

That was the first one of our pilots I'd seen shot down from the air. I was upset, but there was nothing you could do about it. You particularly don't like losing the CO. Of course you don't like losing anybody, but losing the CO does something to the squadron.

Dieppe was a shambles. I vividly recall seeing a tank trying to get up on to the promenade; it was standing right up on its end. One or two troops may have got up on to the promenade, but the poor devils didn't live to tell the tale. We could see scores of bodies lying on the shoreline.

Our last sortie was covering the withdrawal. The Channel was full of landing-craft. Spits were also providing cover over the Channel. I don't think many landing-craft were strafed on the way back.

The purpose of the operation was to discover if it was possible to make a head-on attack on a defended post. The answer was No. That's why we had to take our own port with us on D-Day – the Mulberry harbour.

After Dieppe we went back to Hunsdon. We carried on with our night-intruder operations, and the dawn and dusk patrols and night fighting. I think we were then the only single-seat night-fighter squadron to be fitted with radar – it was an experiment. I flew with it several times. I'm afraid we gave it the thumbs down; it was too much for one person to do. It was all right for aircraft with a two-man crew but in our case we were expected to fly the aircraft, operate the radio, fire the guns, do the navigation and also operate the radar! A particularly disconcerting aspect was that, when you got close to another aircraft, first you got a blip then, as you got closer, it developed wings. On a black night you suddenly found yourself flying on the wings of that aircraft as if it were an artificial horizon. So the experiment was cancelled. Shortly after that we were re-equipped with Typhoons. That was at the end of 1942.

At that point I was commissioned which, in the Air Force at that time, unlike the Army, was a very casual affair. The Adjutant came up to you one morning and said, 'Your commission is through.' Previously, you had been up to headquarters and had an interview with the Air Officer Commanding. You were commissioned in the field, as it were. The RAF were very laid-back about doing things. This matched the casualness of being awarded one's wings. It has always amused me. We had a lot of pilots in the squadron who were trained in America and Canada. For those trained in America especially the Wings Day was a tremendous event. The band was out, the families were invited, everybody stepped up smartly and their wings were pinned on them. I remember at Kidlington when I got my wings. Up to that time we still had tunics with buttons; on passing out one was issued with battledress. I went to the stores to draw my battledress and I asked the WAAF serving over the counter where one got one's wings. 'I think you might find a pair in the pocket,' she said. And that was all the ceremony attached to getting our pilot's brevet.

So we became a Typhoon fighter-bomber squadron and went operational in April 1943. The war was beginning to turn. Things were going well in North Africa, and were turning nasty for the Germans. The Germans had got to about their furthest advance in Russia – right up to Stalingrad.

We started our operational activities with low-level and dive-bombing sorties over the occupied countries. We had a very nasty experience on about the fifth or sixth trip. I wasn't flying on it, I'm glad to say. We were dive-bombing the German airfield at Poix in northern France and, of the eight Typhoons deployed, five were shot down. I lost my best friend, Pilot Officer Bob Inwood, DFC, who was one of our night-intruder aces.

We had a very simple dive-bombing technique in Typhoons; we

came over the target at 12,000 feet, rolled on our back, pulled the stick back and just went straight down. We hadn't any sophisticated bombsights, we used the reflector gunsights. We were going extremely fast – about 540mph – at the bottom of the dive. We would dive through flak at about 4,000 feet, and drop the bombs. We would go down vertically, yank back on the stick, then just completely black out and come to at about 10,000 feet, still climbing.

One blacked out doing steep turns in any fighter aircraft. It's most peculiar; it comes on in stages. First of all, as you're in a tight turn, you feel a great weight on your head pushing you into your seat, next you feel your eyes dropping down on your cheeks, then things go grey, and then, if you keep pulling, you black out completely. Usually when you black out like that you unconsciously push the stick forward and then you come to again. It was just part of flying; a normal thing that happened when you were doing steep turns or pulling out of dives.

In May 1943 the squadron had moved from Hunsdon to West Malling where the Station Commander was Peter Townsend. One of our operational activities at that time was code-named 'Rhubarbs'. These were done with just two aircraft in bad weather conditions – the cloud base had to be 1,000 feet or lower over the Continent – and they were against targets of opportunity. My Rhubarb operation was approved for 2 June 1943. I took as my no. 2 a Canadian, Pilot Officer Ricky Purdon. We crossed the French coast in cloud, let down again, and the first target I attacked was a locomotive on the line between Poperinge and Ypres. I flew low over it, buzzing the engine to give the engine-driver time to get away. Then I went in and blew it up with a very satisfying explosion. We then found some barges on a canal and my no. 2 attacked those. The weather started getting too good; the cloud base had gone up to about 4,000 feet. But we still had our bombs. I decided to drop them on an advanced German airfield on the coast near Dunkirk. As I was approaching that area there was a sudden terrific burst of flak close to us. My aircraft was thrown on its side, and I must have been hit some-where because I could smell burning though I couldn't see any smoke. My radio had gone completely. I looked down, and in the town of Bergues there was a very long goods train pulling out of the yards towards Dunkirk, with tarpaulins covering what looked like guns and vehicles. It appeared a better target than the airfield, so I waggled my wings to my no. 2 to form up. I had to go in very low because it was pulling out of the yard and there were houses around. I fired my cannon along the length of the train and dropped my bombs from a low height.

Then I found myself unfortunately going towards a flak tower in the yard that was firing at me. I yanked back on the stick as hard as I possibly could, stood on my tail and went straight up – to over 1,000 feet I suppose. I shoved the stick forward to get down to ground level again where it was safer. I then experienced a terrific crash under the aircraft and my control column went completely limp. No control at all. I then saw the end of my starboard wing splinter and come off. I went straight down through a wood, hit the ground with a huge crash and shot about sixty feet up into the air again. Fortunately the plane kept reasonable equilibrium and came down in a field, the right way up. No matter how tightly you're strapped in you always seem to hit your head in a crash. I hit mine on the reflector gunsight, cut my scalp and was knocked out. When I came to there was smoke coming out from behind the cockpit, and a German vehicle coming down the road.

That galvanised me into action. I got out of the aircraft and started running. I didn't know why, but I kept falling over. The Germans were shouting, and one started firing at me. I thought I would distract the German's attention by drawing my revolver and firing off a few shots at him; and after that he kept his head down.

I was bleeding and, although I kept getting blood in my eyes, I ran on. At times I saw German patrols on the road, so I kept to the fields, always making my way south. Once I came to a railway line and saw a German patrol at the level-crossing. I waited in the ditch until I saw them occupied, then ran up the embankment, over the railway line, lost my footing and rolled down into a drainage ditch and dislocated my shoulder.

I kept going; across fields, through woods, for, I would say, twenty-five miles. At one stage a German aircraft, a Fieseler Storch, was searching for me. I heard it coming and dived into a spinney until it flew off. By now I was feeling very weak and I thought I should get some help. After a while I found a little village church. I knocked on the door of the Presbytery and the priest's housekeeper answered. She looked rather horrified and said, roughly, 'Go away, go away. Come back after seven o'clock this evening.'

I went back into the fields and kept the church under observation. After about an hour I saw the priest leave on a bicycle. I went back again at seven and she took me into a shed at the bottom of the garden, and then brought me a bowl of bread and milk. I was to have quite a lot of bread and milk in the next couple of weeks. After a while a doctor came, set my shoulder, bandaged my head and said somebody would come for me. I lay there very apprehensive.

At 2300 a French farmer appeared on a bicycle and I was told to follow him to a farm which turned out to be about three miles away. After about three days there a Resistance man came down from Dunkirk and interviewed me and gave me some civilian clothes. I exchanged my Smith & Wesson .38 for a rather nice 7.6mm Beretta automatic, was kitted out and taken into St Omer – where the headquarters were of the German Luftwaffe in the west. I had to have a photograph taken for my identity papers – a nerve-racking experience because the town was absolutely crawling with Germans! I went into the studio and I hadn't been in there for more than ten seconds when I was hauled out because a couple of German Luftwaffe officers had come in to have their photographs taken. I sheepishly hung about whilst they – very smart in their no. 1 uniforms – were photographed. Of course at those times you felt that every German you passed was looking at you and saying 'he looks like a RAF pilot!' In fact, before having my photograph taken, I was told to shave off my moustache as they said I looked too British.

From there I went to another active Resistance group in the Pas de Calais and did some work with them. From there I went to Arras, then Paris, then Nantes, and down the west coast to Bordeaux, to Saint Jean de Luz, over the Pyrenees and into Spain to San Sebastian. A car from the British embassy picked me up and took me to Madrid. I had to wait there until a British ship put in to a Spanish port. After some days I was provided with false British seaman's papers and driven down to Seville where I had to pretend to having been found drunk in a brothel, and was hustled on board the British ship just as the gangplank was pulled up. Then down the Guadalquivir to the sea and thence to Gibraltar. I was flown back to England on 18 August. I'd been away for just under three months. I was debriefed by Special Operations Executive at Baker Street, and was back on my squadron within six days.

Until I'd arrived in Madrid my parents thought I was dead because when my no. 2 came in to attack about twenty seconds after me, he saw my bombs explode – he said trucks were actually airborne and there was a terrible mess – he lost sight of me and thought I'd flown into the ground. He was shot down three weeks afterwards in Dunkirk harbour attacking shipping. So I never saw him again.

The squadron in the meantime had moved from West Malling to Manston and I decided to go down to see them. The officers' mess was in Westgate, about three miles from the base. I phoned the squadron dispersal from there and asked to speak to the CO, who was a Belgian, Squadron Leader De Soomer. I said, 'Hello, sir, this is Bob Barckley.' 'Who?' he asked. 'Bob Barckley,' I said again. 'No,' he said, 'that's not right, he was shot down; he was killed.' So I said, 'No, I assure you that I'm very much alive.' My God, he was so excited. He said, 'Where are you?' He must have driven at about 90mph – without a uniform – down to the officers' mess, to pick me up. It was tremendous! I was the only pilot on No. 3 Squadron to be shot down and to make it back to England.

From then on I was back on the squadron, doing the same sort of thing as before – fighter sweeps, Rhubarb operations, attacks on shipping, airfields and the like. In March 1944 we were the first squadron to get the Tempest V fighter.

Then the squadron moved to Newchurch on Romney Marsh in preparation for D-Day. The landing was an amazing sight – a tremendous armada. As far as the eye could see, there were ships. The fact that I'd been with the Resistance made me feel it very deeply.

We patrolled the beachhead, shooting down a number of German fighters. We also escorted American bombers. They obliterated whole towns – places like Caen and Saint Lô – with B-26 Marauders and B-25 Mitchells.

It was just after D-Day that the flying-bomb attacks started. We were supposed to be based in Normandy on D-plus-four but were kept back because of the flying-bombs. I had surprisingly already attacked a flying-bomb on 8 May 1944. I was on a night-intruder operation, flying the Tempest from Newchurch. South of Paris I suddenly saw a bright light in the sky. I thought some idiot had left his navigation light on! So I positioned myself behind it.

Now, you never attack anything with throttle fully open at night, because it's impossible to judge distance. You gradually open up with more and more speed until you can see outlines of things. I did that, but I didn't seem to be making any sort of progress. When I got beyond Le Havre I fired a long burst and it immediately went down. In my log book I wrote 'Chased airborne light from Evreux to Le Havre. Fired three bursts, went down in sea. Jet ship?'

Nobody knew what it was. Some of the chaps on the squadron suggested I was seeing things – because another one of our pilots had also seen odd lights one night that no-one could explain. All

I could say was it looked like what a jet ship might look like. Rather precognitive of me! A month later one of these 'jet ships' flew right over our airfield at Newchurch and we all realised then what it had been. This was the VI. Over the next three months we were engaged in shooting them down; the squadron shot down 305 of them, and our Tempest wing 705.

VIs would fly at about 400mph and at about 1,000 feet. You had to get above and dive on them to attack from astern. Then you'd get within two hundred yards and open fire. Sometimes the warhead exploded and you'd have a nasty experience avoiding the debris. Sometimes you'd shoot a wing off. Anything could happen, but probably half of them exploded in the air.

It wasn't impossible to tip them up, but quite difficult. I only did it once – on 14 July. On that particular patrol I'd already shot down two. I'd used up my ammunition when this one came in over Eastbourne. I called up on the RT to get some assistance, but nobody appeared. The thing was flying towards London. I thought I'd better do something, so I decided to tip it over. I had to formate on it in the first place. I found that every time I put my wing underneath its starboard wing, it just skidded away; I had upset the airflow. So it was well off its course. In the end I thought, I've had enough of this! and decided to modify my technique. On the next try I slipped my wing under and immediately flipped my stick over to the right, and that tipped its wing right over and it just catapulted into the ground: I saw it hit a wood, well clear of Sevenoaks. That's the only one I ever attempted to tip. Later we heard that the Germans were putting detonators on the wings, so not many pilots tried it.

At the end of September 1944 the squadron moved to Brussels a few days after it was liberated. This was a great time, but too good to last. By 1 October we had moved into the corridor leading to Arnhem. Our airfield at Volkel had been bombed a few days before when it was a Luftwaffe base and over 900 bomb craters were counted there, and no buildings were standing.

Our main task was combating the Me262 which, although we

were the fastest Allied fighter, was around 100mph faster. They bombed our airfield quite regularly with anti-personnel bombs, killing a number of our ground crews. One of our pilots, Pilot Officer Bob Cole, shot the first one down on 13 October and we destroyed and damaged many others in attacks on their bases at Münster and Osnabrück. I collected a 'blighty one' whilst attacking one of the German airfields, and it was hospital in the UK for me and then an operational rest. I took it on secondment to the Fleet Air Arm on test pilot duties.

Flight Lieutenant Johnny Bentley

I went to 264 Squadron at Church Fenton in March 1944, flying Mosquitoes. On 18 March 1945, I was taken by a Flight Lieutenant Brooke in an Oxford and delivered to an airfield in Holland. The two of us, along with Flight Lieutenant Moss, were to fly three Dutch officers into occupied Holland and parts of Germany, so that they could communicate by radio with the local resistance, and bring back vital information. This operation was named Blackmail.

I don't know why I was picked, all I can say is that I got to Gilze-Rijen on 18 March, did an air test on the 19th, an exercise on the 20th, and on the 22nd did my first operation.

In the Mosquito there was only myself and a Dutch officer in the cockpit. We sat alongside each other. The Dutch had all their own radio stuff, and we had our normal VHF. They were speaking to the Resistance on the ground, but we hardly ever discussed it between ourselves. We'd just come back to the operations room in Tilburg, and report, and then Tactical Air Force headquarters assessed the information gathered at local level and deployed aircraft to bomb the target. The information was so good and so specific, that on several occasions Typhoons were able to pin-point individual houses. In many cases the information was acted upon very quickly and I can recall listening to the BBC Radio at 9.00 p.m. and hearing that Typhoons had attacked a particular area, an area which we had flown over that morning. That was brilliant and rewarding. Most of the flights lasted little more than an hour, but sometimes we would go as far as the Ruhr which would take over two hours.

There were three Dutch officers, Jaap Ludolph, Leo Fleskins and Hilda Bergsma. We would spend time with them on the ground and they were good company. But it was important that we knew little of what they were doing in case we were shot down and captured.

On their uniform they wore a cloth badge with three witches. I think our guns were still in the Mosquito, but we had no ammunition. It was thought rather desirable that the aircraft were as light as possible in case we had to escape from any of their fighters, but in fact I never saw one, because they weren't coming up at that stage of the war, but it was good to know that you could go a bit faster. We used to manage nearly 300 knots. I was flying these tasks from 18 March to 14 April. We flew most days – it wasn't particularly hard work. Once we got over the target area the officer would only need fifteen minutes or so, and I'd just circle around. I never felt vulnerable because we were jolly high, at about 20,000–25,000 feet.

I did one night flight, with a Captain Macmillan, so there must have been some British involvement. He was transmitting as well, doing the same job as them. I flew Hilda Bergsma only once. She was older than us, about twenty-eight, and rather nice-looking. She just did her job, and we came straight back. She flew more often with Flight Lieutenant Moss or Brooke.

It was an interesting month, one of the best bits of the war really. One was on one's own and it was quite fun. However, it was only after the war that we saw and realised the terrible suffering of the Dutch under the Germans.

Flight Lieutenant Alec Blythe

I had recently married and was living in Ashton Keynes, a tiny Gloucester village. A week before D-Day, I rode my bicycle at a leisurely pace through the quiet and peaceful countryside, past little places like Cerney Wick, to the airfield at Down Ampney, where I was stationed with 48 Squadron. There I was to prepare for what, I supposed, was to be the largest military operation ever.

I had met the Royal Engineers, whom I was to drop on D-Day, and they seemed jolly nice chaps. However, when they came up to the Dakota on the night of the operation with blackened faces they looked a fearsome lot. One pulled out his dagger and said that it was going to find a German that night.

Pathfinders are supposed to set up a piece of radar beacon, called Eureka, which would guide us to the dropping zone (DZ). Unfortunately very few Pathfinders dropped accurately, so most of us found there was no Eureka beacon to track to and we had to fall back on our own navigational equipment. My DZ was one-and-a-half minutes' flying time from crossing the French coast to dropping. The briefing therefore had to be tremendously detailed. Accurate models of the Normandy coast and hinterland were constructed. From these models cine films were made of the tracks to each of the dropping zones. So we were prepared with a mental picture of what we could expect to see as we flew in. The films were made in daylight, whereas we would be dropping at night.

As we crossed the coast, my navigator reported two large houses which we expected to see before a line of trees came out of the murk. I was getting ready to drop my troops south of the road to Caen. There was a fair amount of moonlight and I could see that the Germans had flooded the area south of the road where we were supposed to drop. I didn't have much time to think, but decided I had better drop to the north of the road rather than in the water. The red light was on and the Engineers were standing ready. There was some flak but I hadn't had to take evasive action. I was intent on making as steady a run as possible when suddenly the aircraft banked almost 45 degrees. In a flash of light from the ground I saw a Stirling passing in front of us. Clearly we had been caught in his slipstream which threw us off course. I had therefore to bring the wings level and regain heading as quickly as possible. The paratroops in the back no doubt were hurled about and were probably cursing me for taking violent evasive action. I never saw them again to explain the reason for their discomfort. Unfortunately the accuracy of the drops on D-Day wasn't as high as one would have hoped. I would like to think that my Engineers were accurately dropped especially as the two bridges assigned to them were blown up.

The following evening we resupplied 6th Airborne Division in the same area. The Royal Navy apparently hadn't been told about this because a couple of ships started to shoot at us. I could see the tracer criss-crossing in the evening sky. Fortunately they were not very good shots and we were not hit. When I got back to Down Ampney and had been debriefed, I quietly cycled home.

Flying Officer Tom Rennie

Prior to the formation of the RAF Regiment in 1942 defence of airfields had been the responsibility of the Army.

In the early days the Regiment consisted of three types of squadrons: Rifle, Light Armoured, and Mobile Anti-Aircraft. My appointment to an Anti-Aircraft squadron was due to my interest in ballistics.

After being commissioned in 1942 my first posting was to a squadron on Grimsetter airfield in Orkney. After about twelve months the squadron was posted to Tangmere and thence to the airfields on the Romney Marshes in Kent. Our main priority was the protection of the airfield installations and against low-flying enemy attacks in which the Regiment was very successful. We then moved to Manston airfield and, in December 1943, to

Inveraray for a Combined Operations course in preparation for eventual landing in Europe.

Boarding freighter ships in the loch at night on scrambling nets from small 'drifters' – where we would plan our beach landing for dawn – formed one part of our exercise. Once 'safely' ashore we would advance inland and consolidate before returning to base to iron out any landing problems.

In the spring of 1944 we moved to Salisbury Plain where we carried out further training. It was here we were informed that our squadron would land on D-Day at 'H' Hour plus 12. We were, naturally, a little apprehensive as this was our first intimation that we were to be the first of the Regiment to land on the beaches.

All vehicles were then prepared so that they could be driven through water. The exhausts were fixed vertically – like periscopes – and the engines and guns cocooned (covered with waterproof material). 'Tentage' was prepared; food, stores, fuel and ammunition loaded; and on 31 May 1944 we moved down to Felixstowe harbour under cover of darkness on the right-hand side of the road so that our drivers could become accustomed to Continental driving.

Arriving at dawn we found masses of Landing Ship Tanks (LSTs) alongside the harbour. We located our ship and, with our vehicles and guns, queued to go on board fully aware of our destination because we had already been issued with a 'ration' of French francs. Our men thought that the south of France might be rather nice!

We lay off Felixstowe harbour for five days but communication with the shore was absolutely forbidden and any letters we wrote were retained and posted after we had sailed. On the morning of 4 June – when we were due to sail – a message came through that there were heavy storms and Operation Overlord would be postponed. However, much to our relief, at eight o'clock the following morning, 5 June, we set sail for Normandy. We were the first British convoy out of Felixstowe and I stood on deck watching friends on the other ships waving and wishing us luck.

We cruised down the coast very slowly and nothing appeared to be happening. As we were passing through the Channel, however, at about midnight there was an awful explosion and everything stopped. The last ship in the convoy had brought up an acoustic mine.

Eventually we sailed on and by dawn the next morning we were off the Isle of Wight, looking at an incredible scene. It was almost impossible to see water for ships – vessels of all shapes and sizes and just masses of them!

We arrived off the beaches of Normandy close to a village called Le Hamel. Guns were firing at us and we were all very apprehensive indeed. HMS *Warspite* was laying well out and then she got a 'lead' on the guns on the Arromanches headland. The first salvo appeared to drop behind them, and the second probably landed on the beaches but, eventually, the lights stopped flashing. Then we had to get ashore but the sea was very rough. The Navy brought pontoons alongside – great motorised platforms called Rhinos. Our ship dropped its ramp and the first 'DUKW' rolled down on to the Rhino, tipped over and went straight into the 'drink'. We pulled back and remained just off the beaches where we were bombed.

The next day half of our squadron landed on a receding tide. First the vehicles came off – the three-tonners towing the guns – then moved up the beach. It was a chaotic situation: fires burning everywhere, self-propelled guns overturned, and many LCAs destroyed in the sea. The Germans had driven triangular steel tripods into the beaches with mines on top. At high tide the sea covered the mines but as the tide receded they became visible with the result that we lost a lot of men. The noise was indescribable, guns firing left, right, and centre with flashes of smoke and fire everywhere. Amid all this I saw a wounded pilot lying on the beach smoking a cigarette while waiting to be taken home to Blighty.

As soon as our convoy was ashore, I instructed our men to prepare the guns for action. Passing minefields, already taped for safety by the Royal Engineers, we made our way about three miles inland to our landmark, which was close to the village of Crépon. The rest of our squadron came ashore the following day, when I was instructed to return to the coast accompanied by a Corporal, to guide the men across country. While we were waiting at a crossroads a jeep came along with General Montgomery who acknowledged my salute. At that moment an Army Sergeant came out of the woods and said, 'We're getting sniped at down there.' I told my Corporal to keep me covered and took out my pistol. As I was going into the woods, out came five Germans and gave themselves up. Fortunately a Provost-Marshal came along at that very moment and took them off my hands. The countryside was littered with Germans giving themselves up and being taken down to the POW cages further south. Our chaps were saying, 'I got ten prisoners today,' and others were saying, 'Well, I got twenty!'

The severe storms meant that hardly anything else managed to come ashore for two days, but at dawn on the third day, I heard the rumble of vehicles and tanks. The all-important supplies were arriving once more.

When the first landing airstrip, B1, was built at Crépon, on steel tracking, our fighters started arriving from Tangmere at dawn – flying back home at dusk. While all this was happening around us our guns were in constant action and we were frequently being shelled from the German lines. The nights were the worst. While I was on duty one night the Intelligence Officer came on the field telephone and said that we were to hold fire at 2130 hours as friendly heavies would be passing over the area, heading for Target 'X', which was Caen. As daylight was fading, the sky spreading from England became black with aircraft. I counted 600 Lancaster and Halifax bombers as they passed overhead. That was just the first wave. Half-an-hour later along came another wave to continue the bombing of Caen. We could feel the ground vibrating as we were only a few miles away. We saw a number of our aircraft being brought down in flames while others were limping home.

We carried mobile Bofors guns – twelve per squadron, six per flight – each mobile gun having a crew of seven or eight. They could be taken out of action in three or four minutes and ready for action again in three. They were sighted for aircraft flying up to about 10,000 feet and the barrels elevated to not less than 45°. Shells were fused to explode in seven seconds. At 45° they either exploded on impact with their target or before they hit the ground.

In the meantime, I had been detached from my squadron to join 83 Group Control Centre, as one of three ack-ack liaison officers on 24-hour duty. Group Control Centre would radio news of incoming aircraft, approximate numbers and height. We, in turn, would pass instructions to our gunners on the airfields so that they would be lined up ready for action.

When the bridgehead breakout started we moved rapidly across country roads where there was devastation everywhere: poor innocent horses and cattle blown to pieces, and trees stripped of life. We crossed the Seine at Vernon, on a pontoon bridge, and continued on to Beauvais, eventually arriving in Brussels for the liberation where we received a terrific reception; the population was ecstatic at their new-found freedom after over four years of occupation.

When the news came through of the collapse at Arnhem I was instructed to rejoin my squadron which, by then, had reached Brussels and we moved swiftly via Eindhoven to an airfield at Volkel, near Nijmegen, in Holland.

It was there that we had our most hectic day. It was, in fact, New Year's Day 1945. The Germans thought that, being British, we would all be celebrating New Year's Eve and probably 'under the influence'. The following day, therefore, would be the perfect opportunity to have a go at us. I reckon they must have put every single aircraft in the air that could still fly and they all attacked us at deck level. My younger brother, George, a Signals officer, was on the other side of the airfield and his vehicle was turned completely around by the blast from their guns. Fortunately none of his crew was injured. One German aircraft came right down, flying at 100 feet off the ground. Our fighters shot him down. I think we fired more rounds that morning than throughout the rest of the whole campaign.

The winter in Holland was long and extremely cold. I woke up one morning in my billet, such as it was, with my eyebrows literally frozen! When we arrived, of course, the rains were starting. Outside the perimeter of the airfield the land was waterlogged which meant that our vehicles could hardly plough their way through the mud. After the rains, came the frost and then the snow.

We remained at Volkel until the spring of 1945, then we crossed the Rhine into Germany, heading for Lüneburg Heath. On the way there we came to Belsen Camp. The Army had arrived there first but we took in any spare supplies that we had and left them with the Military. The hutments were absolutely appalling. The inmates were lying in indescribably filthy bunks and it was difficult to say whether they were men, women, or children. One dear old soul who was lying there like a skeleton, whispered, 'Hôpital, hôpital.' I tried to assure her that she would soon be in hospital. Everywhere the smell was terrible. There were open graves, each with approximately a thousand bodies and mountains of boots and shoes from the dead prisoners. The uniformed guards were all well-fed, yet there were hundreds of dead emaciated bodies lying all over the place.

The typhus cases had all been isolated behind barbed wire. They just stood there staring at us – gaunt faces in uniforms of striped pyjamas. It was terrible. When we left the camp I sent a driver to nearby farms to collect all the beds he could find and take them to the camp. Those sights will remain with me for ever.

A week or two later the ceasefire was signed on Lüneberg Heath and with that our job of airfield defence had ended.

My next move was across the Kiel Canal to join a squadron going into Jutland in order to take over the Danish airfields and clear them of the enemy. Other Regiment squadrons were despatched to the island of Odense and to Copenhagen for the same purpose.

The RAF Regiment had, therefore, seen action in five countries since leaving England – France, Belgium, Holland, Germany and Denmark – but the best one of all was England in 1946!

Flight Lieutenant Alec Blythe

After D-Day 48 Squadron transported supplies to Europe and brought casualties back. We were alerted for a number of airborne operations which were cancelled because of the rapid advance of the ground forces. Eventually in September the assault on Arnhem was launched and most of us were to tow gliders. As it was a long way to do this we were fitted with long-range tanks in the fuselage of the Dakotas. There were no fuel gauges with these tanks and we had been briefed that the tanks would get us to the Dutch coast, where we should switch on to main tanks for the remainder of the flight. Somebody had miscalculated, because most of us ran out of fuel about mid-Channel! So there you were, towing a glider with twenty troops on board, suddenly losing power. Fortunately, almost to a man, the pilots immediately switched to the main tanks. We had a hand pump to force the fuel through and those lovely Pratt and Whitney engines immediately sprang to life. One wretched pilot's immediate reaction when his engines spluttered and started to stop was to pull the 'glider release'. I could see this unfortunate glider spiralling down until it landed on the sea. Meanwhile the pilot of the Dakota had restarted his engines and returned home. By some miracle the men in the glider were picked up by an air-sea rescue launch almost before their feet were wet.

The enormous train of tug aircraft and their gliders was most impressive. You were stimulated by a certain amount of fear, a certain amount of excitement at the very size of the force, and of course your adrenalin level was raised when you were attacked by ground fire. Whenever that happened a couple of Mustangs immediately appeared from nowhere and silenced the enemy on the ground. Despite the excellent support of these ground-attacking Mustangs, we had casualties. I watched a Stirling alongside catch fire, which from a small trail of smoke gradually grew until the aircraft was engulfed before crashing into the ground. Nobody got out.

On the first day the opposition was comparatively slight and the glider landing was successful, despite collisions on the landing zones.

A second lift of gliders was flown in the next day, but I was not involved. On the third day we were briefed to resupply 1st Airborne Division. It had been assumed that the Airborne Division would form a perimeter within the environs of Arnhem. In the course of the briefing we were told to drop at a particular DZ. Then as the briefing progressed the DZ was changed. Just before we took off we were told to drop as originally briefed!

Three Royal Army Service Corps despatchers pushed the panniers along rollers to the side door. When I went out to my aeroplane the despatchers were waiting. I said, 'Do you know where we are going?' They replied, 'No, sir.' I told them we were going to Arnhem in Holland, which brought the response, 'That will be nice.' I replied, 'Well, it might be dangerous. We're liable to be fired at, you know.' They just smiled. We used to speak of 'ten-tenths flak', meaning that the sky was just full of exploding shells. Well, as you approached Arnhem you got the impression that there wasn't wing-span room between flak bursts, not to mention the small-arms fire! To my right a Dakota, I think flown by Flight Lieutenant Lord, caught fire. One of the despatchers was desperately trying to get out but he couldn't get through the door. Unknown to us the DZ was in the hands of the Germans. Whatever our troops may have done to attract our attention we probably wouldn't have seen. And, after the briefing change, we would have ignored any ground signals as decoys.

Having dropped our load, we banked and weaved as violently as possible to avoid fire from the ground and headed home. When we got back to base my three despatchers were full of the joys and said, 'Well, sir, we thoroughly enjoyed all that weaving and turning on the way back!' Ignorance is bliss.

The resupply continued for a further six days and losses were severe but I never ceased to be amazed at the damage the Dakota could sustain and continue to fly. One came back with a hole in the fuselage large enough to push a chair through. Many flew all the way back on one engine. Others with lesser damage were repaired by the ever-willing and untiring ground crews to be ready for the next day.

Arnhem was a disaster. We could have flown the 1st Airborne Division there in one day. It would have meant some of us flying two sorties in the day. In Burma we flew as many as three sorties a day. Had we delivered the division more quickly they would have had a better chance to form a firm perimeter and secure the bridge. Our resupply would then have been successful instead of so much gallantry being wasted in sending supplies down to the Germans.

Commander Margot Gore, ATA

After D-Day our lives in the Air Transport Auxiliary got busier. I was flying four-engined aircraft by then. We had converted on to the Halifax at Marston Moor in 1943. Cheshire was the Commanding Officer there at the time. He was having a rest from his first hundred sorties.

Converting to the four-engines wasn't hard. Well, we were much more experienced and really and truly they weren't difficult. They were huge of course. I only had one Stirling; I didn't like it because it had this tremendous side surface and it used to swing. The Lancaster, though, was a very easy aircraft; a beautiful aircraft. But of course one has to remember, we had no bombs, nor a full load of petrol.

On the four-engines we flew with a flight engineer, who had to control the fuel cocks which you couldn't reach, and you needed somebody to check the other controls with you. Also, after you opened the four throttles you had to have two hands on the stick. So you opened the throttles yourself, and then you said 'Hold!' and the flight engineer held them and you pulled off. Then you brought the throttles back and when you were coming in you reduced your throttles, and of course he did all the things at your request for flaps and undercarriage and all the rest of it. And then at the last minute you said 'Cut!' and the flight engineer cut the throttles while you pulled the stick back. The planes weren't really heavy. I was quite strong, of course.

That sometimes surprised people. Once I was landing a Halifax at Marston Moor, and had to call up for permission to come in. When I had landed I went to Flying Control to report in. At the top of the steps in the Flying Control I met a rather infuriated-looking Air Vice-Marshal. He looked at me and said, 'Were you flying that Halifax?' I said, 'Yes, sir.' 'Good God!' he said. 'Now I've bloody well seen everything!' and he stormed down the steps. I didn't know whether it was compliment or what, and I never will. I said to the man at the desk, 'My goodness, he seems a bit cross!' 'Oh,' he said, 'he can't believe that any woman can do it.'

I had taken another Halifax one day when there was quite a nasty crosswind. I landed and went up to the Flying Control to report in. I suddenly heard a tremendous commotion going on behind me: everybody was belting out of the place. I looked out of the window and I saw a Halifax heading for a ditch which had been dug across the front of the Flying Control. So I took off – there was no thought of women and children first! And as I went I fell over the lead of a spaniel which was being led up the stairs by its owner, Gus Walker, who was the CO of the station and had only one arm. He wasn't half giving them stick for running away! Afterwards, in the mess, the poor young pilot who had done this swing off the runway, said to me, 'You brought one in before me, didn't you?' and I said, 'Yes.' He said, 'I suppose you ran at it straight,' and I said, 'Well, of course, the wind wasn't so strong when I came in.' Poor little brute.

By the time of the Battle of the Ardennes we were beginning to slow down. The Air Force tended to pick up more of their own planes, and they weren't being utilised anything like so much as they were before. The urgency was off. So, after five years, we closed the pool in August 1945. But they had been remarkable years. The ATA had started in 1939 with thirty men, all British. By the time we disbanded we had aircrew from twenty-two countries. The number of flying personnel reached its peak in the summer of 1944 when we had 551 men and 108 women pilots, and were flying 99 different types of aircraft. In all, we had 154 ATA personnel killed on duty, but we had ferried over 309,000 aircraft.

Squadron Leader 'Pinky' Stark

The Typhoon was bigger, heavier and twice as powerful as the Hurricane. The latter was a delightful aeroplane to fly and the first aircraft with which I felt able to take liberties. The Typhoon took a little more getting used to but I didn't really have any problems with it. I quickly came to like it and against the Me109s and Fw190s we coped fairly well.

When I joined 609 Squadron, our tasks were largely defensive. We were based at Manston and then later at Lympne and my first 88 operations were all standing patrols around the coast to intercept 'tip and run' raiders which were mainly 190s and 109s.

The training we got on Hurricanes at OTU was extremely good and if one followed the tactical principles one had learned there and applied them to Typhoon operations, they were very successful.

Roly Beamont was my CO in 609 Squadron. He was the sort of chap who led from the front and had had a lot of previous experience in France and the Battle of Britain, mainly on Hurricanes. I learned a lot from his advice and his example.

On defensive patrols we operated in pairs and flew back and forth off the coast between North Foreland and Dungeness looking out to sea and hoping to see the enemy coming in. Of course we had radar controllers directing us on to any 'bogies'.

On 12 March 1943 I was patrolling as no. 2 to Flight Sergeant Leslie when we were directed on to a number of 'bogies' somewhere between Dunkirk and Mardyke. We came upon a couple of Fw190s and in the ensuing dogfight, I managed to hit one sufficiently to produce a lot of black smoke but was hit in the oil tank by the second one who climbed away into the sun. I got back to Manston by going flat out at sea level. Neither Leslie nor I saw the Fw190 go down so I claimed a 'probable' but two days later our Intelligence Officer, Frank Ziegler, told me that he'd had word that it had crashed. So I was then credited with a 'destroyed'.

It was six months before I met the enemy again. By October the patrols had ceased as far as we were concerned: we were then based at Lympne, and we were doing Rangers and Rhubarbs. We were out looking for enemy aircraft and anything else to shoot at, on the ground or in the air. My next engagement was on 5 October when I and my no. 2 got through to the Paris area where I successfully destroyed a Junkers 88. That turned out to be 609 Squadron's 200th enemy aircraft destroyed, and I got a prize when I got back. Curiously, the last Junkers 88 that 609 had destroyed was their 100th kill. We hadn't seen another Junkers 88 since then. Then, on the same day, one of our Belgian pilots came back about an hour-and-a-half after me saying he'd just got the squadron's 200th. And the one he got was also a Junkers 88! We got another Junkers 88 in November.

We had to go and look for these fellows, they weren't coming over to the UK except at night. We normally got them over France, as far south as Paris. We'd go down, say, the east side of Paris and sweep round the south, then come back up the west side. They weren't flying offensively, they were probably training or doing air tests.

We did a bit of night-intruder work. The problem was we had to do it on moonlight nights, and hope that we saw something. I never did. We were doing night-intruder work more or less down at deck level. Roly Beamont was a bit of an expert on this type of work, he knew the schedules of the railway trains that took men on leave. I think he shot up more railway trains than anybody else.

At this time we didn't have rockets, we were using cannon. We attacked the odd convoy off the Dutch coast. The attack technique really depended on the circumstances. The important thing was the element of surprise. So we might attack from the stern, the beam, or head-on, it varied. These attacks were mostly carried out at dawn. It was unlikely that cannon would sink a ship, unless of course it hit a vital part and set it on fire. Very often one had to assume the amount of damage one had done.

In January 1944, I got a half. I shared a Dornier 217 over Holland with one of our Belgian pilots. We had a lot of Belgian pilots including Detal, Van Lierde and Lallemant (all aces) but the top-scoring Typhoon pilot was Johnny Baldwin. He was on 609 with us before he went to 198 as CO. He was way ahead of the rest of us with fifteen kills. He was a very good shot.

Later on in January 1944 I got two more. Near Brussels a Caudron Goeland, a light transport aircraft, just happened to get in the way. And then right at the end of January I got another Fw190 down near Paris. That was quite a trip because we were flying in support of 198 Squadron, and we got three Fw190s and 198 got nine – in one trip. My tally was then five-and-a-half.

Partway through February, I was posted to 263 Squadron as a Flight Commander. The squadron had recently converted from Whirlwinds to Typhoons, but they didn't much like them. The Napier engine, at this stage, didn't have a good reputation; it was inclined to stop occasionally. Their morale was not high when I joined them, inasmuch as they'd just lost their Commanding Officer and two other chaps in one trip. I like to think that I helped them regain some morale. I fought to get them into some offensive operations, and that was important.

They were a splendid bunch and they just needed a bit of confidence. It took about a month, and then we were on our way. We did a trip round the Paris area in the middle of April and one of the Flight Sergeants, who had never actually crossed the enemy coast before, destroyed a Messerschmitt 110; three other chaps shared a Dornier 217; two others shot up a Heinkel 111 on the ground; and various other things like staff cars and Army trucks were damaged. So that was very worthwhile. The chaps came back cock-a-hoop.

We started the air-to-ground stuff at the end of April when they slapped 500lb bombs on our aircraft. We were dive-bombing, mainly on coastal shipping, the odd destroyer and escort vessels, around the coast of the Brest Peninsula. By now we had moved down to the West Country to Harrowbeer, near Plymouth, and we were sent out to search for targets across the Channel.

We got a new Squadron Commander called Michael Gonay, a Belgian, a splendid leader with quite a lot of experience. We went on through May 1944 on targets like anti-shipping roadsteads, against all kinds of shipping. We were using mainly 500lb bombs and dive-bombing. In fighter-bombers you can either drop at low-level or dive-bomb, and I always reckoned I was more likely to hit them when dive-bombing. And you were less likely to be hit yourself. We would dive from about 8,000 feet and release the bombs at about 2,000 feet. It was a bit hit-and-miss, but we had some success. We had the gunsight in the cockpit and used that in a modified way. Later on the gunsight was slightly modified for use with rockets. Lots of other squadrons, in 2nd Tactical Air Force, had been using rockets before 6 June 1944.

On 4 June, I flew from Harrowbeer to Manston and from there back to Thorney Island. On 5 June I flew back from Thorney Island to Harrowbeer. By the time I arrived back I was quite convinced that something was going to happen, because you could have walked across from the mainland to the Isle of Wight on the backs of the ships! Every harbour along the south coast was packed with shipping. It was an incredible sight. We went off at the crack of dawn that morning, 6 June, chasing some ships off the Brest Peninsula, and we didn't even know it was D-Day until we got back to base!

We still didn't belong to 2nd Tactical Air Force. We belonged to the Air Defence of Great Britain, i.e., Fighter Command, right through June. We were still doing Ramrods and Roadsteads across the Channel. Sometimes attacking gun positions and sometimes ships, sometimes with bombs, sometimes with rockets. Some of our aircraft had rocket rails and some had bomb-racks, so you could switch for whatever sort of target you were attacking. By the end of June we'd moved from Harrowbeer to Bolt Head, in Devon, which was a grass aerodrome right on the edge of the cliff, so that when you took off you had to become airborne or you fell into the Channel!

On 3 July, I got a 40mm shell right through the engine. I thought I would keep it running as long as I could, but eventually I saw it was beginning to get a bit hot and there were flames appearing at the bottom of the cockpit, so I baled out. I lost a shoe: I should have been wearing flying boots but that morning I had put my flying boots in to be re-soled. Fortunately, I had also changed my parachute just that morning. I'm sure the previous parachute was soaking wet, we had a terrible tendency to leave it in the cockpit and it was bound to get damp. I came down right in the middle of the Brest Peninsula and when I got there, there was nobody there but a French boy scout. He found me some civilian clothes and boots, and took my uniform away. He then took me down into a forest and introduced me to a man whose photograph I still have, but one never knew anybody's name. This man led me to a huge great arms dump in the forest and left me in charge of it with a .38 revolver. I was petrified. Later that day the Maquis arrived and after six days with them I managed to get back to Devonport with some help from the Royal Navy.

If you had been shot down in enemy territory then you did not go straight back to the squadron. Somebody in the Air Ministry decided that I was due for a rest anyhow. I had been flying on operations from January 1943 to July 1944.

I eventually went back to operations in early March 1945. I then joined, for the first time, 2nd Tactical Air Force. I was posted to 123 Wing – which was based at Gilze Rijen in Holland – as

Flight Commander in 164 Squadron. 123 Wing consisted of 4 Typhoon squadrons, including 609. I was posted to 164 Squadron, and I was there for only four days, whereupon I was promoted to Squadron Leader to command 609 Squadron on 16 March. I was delighted to be back with 609. There were a number of chaps still on the squadron whom I had known previously; I had left just over a year before. I stayed with 609 until the end of the war.

We were now using rockets almost exclusively. We were after tanks and anything that you could shoot at in support of the ground forces. One of our major operations was on 24 March – the Rhine Crossing – and on that day our job was to silence the ack-ack guns just on the other side of the Rhine, using rockets. First of all you had to find out where the guns were and the only way you did that was by seeing the flak coming up. Then the trick was to whip round and attack them as quickly as you could with cannon and rockets. The rockets had 60lb explosive heads and we fired either pairs or salvo. Occasionally, if we were attacking a large, heavily armed establishment like an Army headquarters, we would fire twelve in salvo. Sometimes we attacked buildings, Army positions on roads, or headquarters in the middle of the villages. I broke off one attack one day. We were taking out a bridge in Holland, while the Germans retreating across it were using horse-drawn vehicles. I didn't want to kill horses.

On 3 May, when the war was in effect finished, during an armed recce we found a three-funnel liner with two other smaller ships anchored in Lübeck Bay. I did see a 1,500-ton motor vessel sneaking quietly out of the Bay in a north-easterly direction, so we fired some rockets at that and stopped it. It didn't sink, but at least it stopped. I came back to base and told at debriefing about these larger ships lying at anchor. I said, 'Look, they're not going anywhere, and any minute now the war is finished and we're going to need a lot of shipping.' I was appalled, later on, to find out that three or four squadrons had been sent out and had sunk the lot. The occupants of these ships were political refugees and they were all killed. I was most upset about it. I had said that there was no point in sinking these ships, they'd be useful, but somebody, somewhere, had decided to take them out. It was a sad business.

Six months later we flew back to Lasham to disband. I had flown 578 hours on Typhoons.

Flight Sergeant Allen Billam

I joined 609 Squadron, in West Riding, in June 1944. It was one of the original auxiliary squadrons, and I was one of the few Yorkshiremen in it. We had all sorts: Belgians, New Zealanders, Canadians, Australians, Argentinians, Germans, Mauritians. By the time I actually went on operations, I'd amassed six hours on Typhoons.

On the first few trips I did, the aeroplane flew me, I didn't fly it. They were big aeroplanes, and they'd a lot of nasty tricks. I had flown Hurricanes before, Defiants, Lysanders, and one or two other odds and sods, but the only operational flying I did was with 609 Squadron. All the other aeroplanes were, in effect, training aeroplanes, and I'd done about six hundred hours on these, so I was a 'virgin' only on Typhoons.

We went over France about three weeks after D-Day and were based about four miles from Caen. The thing I remember most about Normandy was the dust – it was everywhere. In fact the Sabre was a sleeve-valve engine and it used to suck the dust into the air intake; it was like emery paper on those sleeves. But then somebody came along with a modification. It also used to get up, on the bottom side of the wings, where there were openings for the cartridge cases from the guns to come out, and it used to jam up the guns. In fact once I fired my guns, and found both starboard guns stopped, so I'd only two on the port side. This meant that every time I fired we skidded round the corner with the force. But again somebody came up with modifications: they stuck a piece of toilet paper over the openings on take-off, and the weight of the shells coming out tore it.

The Typhoons were pigs to start, and one night I couldn't get mine started. They were fired by a Koffman starter, like a shotgun cartridge which used to fire into cordite in a cylinder which then used to explode and kick the engine over. You had about six of these to fire and then you'd had it – you had to reload. I was trying to get the plane started, when suddenly I saw a figure winging away through the grass in his pyjamas; it was the flight mechanic of my aeroplane. He came racing across, jumped on the wing, put his head in the cockpit, fiddled around, pressed the starter and away I went. This was typical of the spirit. He was in bed asleep when he heard me trying to get started, and over he came. It was about half past nine at night, and we flew to attack some tank concentration south-west of Caen. I haven't much recollection of it; I dived when the others dived, fired my rockets when the others fired, and that was about it. This was how the first few trips went: I did what the others did until I got to know the ins and outs. And then I started hitting things.

By the time the Falaise Gap came round, I'd done about twenty operations, or more. I knew what I was doing. If you can imagine the M25 packed with tanks and horse-drawn vehicles, ambulances and you name it, it was like that, except of course they were on little narrow roads, with a lot of trees, and the Germans were very adept at hiding things. But once you'd spotted something, you set it on fire, the smoke went up, and then we came in like vultures. At one period, I think we went out on a wing strike, about four squadrons, and we were allowed about five minutes each to attack, because we were queuing up to attack the transport; it really was fantastic. There was none of this 'You mustn't shoot the enemy, you mustn't say it's like a turkey shoot, you'll offend the enemy', that sort of thing; you went there and you killed as many as you could. This happened over a period of about a week, maybe a bit less. Forty miles away from where we were, once you'd got operational height, you could see the fires.

The size of the Falaise Gap is difficult to explain: there were a lot of roads, valleys leading up to the exit to the gap, which they got closed, eventually. Every little country lane, like the little roads on the Yorkshire Dales, was full of petrol lorries, tanks and all sorts of supply vehicles. They had made their attack, and got blunted. The Americans came round from the south, and the British, Canadian, Polish, came round from the north, and started nipping. The Germans just weren't allowed to retreat at first, and when they were allowed to retreat, it was too late. During daylight hours, nothing moved, because if it moved it got shot at. But at night, they could move.

So this was when we really saw the tremendous effect of rocket power, although the 20mm cannon was very effective, too. We used to carry a warload of two high-explosive and two armour-piercing incendiaries. Soft-skinned vehicles almost disintegrated. A cannon shell would go through an engine block; it could penetrate a tank!

Primarily, though, we attacked vehicles, trains, barges, that sort of target. The only time I can ever remember attacking troops, as troops, I was flying with an Argentinian, just the two of us, and we came round the top of this hill, and they were digging a tank in. Pancho, who was leading, went down and blew it up – he set it on fire. And of course the troops who were digging the tanks in ran across the field to get into the hedgerows just as I was coming in to attack. And the effect of four cannon can be imagined: all you had left was strawberry jam.

The Germans certainly fought their own corner during the week of the Falaise Gap. They believed in concentrated flak, whereas the British convoy would stretch over two miles, and have the regulation fifty yards between each vehicle. The Germans believed in putting them close together, and having flak all the way round them, and in the middle of them. I was hit once or twice with flak, and once I nearly got hit by debris from my own rockets. This was leading up to Falaise. I was elated, I could see this truck under the tree, and I went down on him like a ton of bricks. And of course you forget that with an aeroplane that weighs seven tons, when you pull the stick back, while the nose comes up, the aeroplane doesn't start climbing straightaway, it keeps going down. And of course I was that keen to get at the stick, I pulled it back too late. I thought, I'm not going to do it, but I did of course; this was the sort of thing you only do once.

We never sensed during our attacks that we would not defeat the Germans; as far as we were concerned it was simply a matter of when, not if. All they were doing was fighting a rearguard action. Everything joined in the attack on the Falaise Gap: Spitfires, Mustangs, Thunderbolts, you name it, they were in. But because we had the rockets and the 20mm cannon, we were doing the damage, certainly against the armoured fighters.

The Basra Road in the Gulf War brought it all back to me. When the Americans said it was like a turkey shoot, there were people on the box saying that they shouldn't say things like that, because it was men they were killing. To me this is so strange. As far as I'm concerned they're the enemy and they're there to be killed. There's no two ways about it; you don't shoot the guns out of their hands, you try and kill them.

Throughout the whole time in Normandy the general feeling was one of excitement. The morale was fantastic. If we were going with eight aircraft, we always took nine, and the spare aircraft flew as far as the bomb line, in case any had to turn back. And the spare aircraft used to be up to all sorts of tricks, for if they once got across the bomb line they became operational, so they might as well carry on.

I continued until February 1945, then I got sent on rest, for two months. I was able to rejoin the squadron afterwards for the final push into Germany. Of course it was all over very shortly after that. It was a totally different experience, because before, when we landed, we were among friends. Now we were in Germany and it was a matter of watching your back. Not that we had any unpleasant experiences – the Germans were thoroughly beaten – but you could never relax like you could in France and Holland. We actually finished up, when peace was declared, at a little German strip, at Plantlunne. And the squadron finally finished up at Wunstorf, near Hanover.

Mentally, you get into an odd state during wars. Subconsciously, you'd got yourself written off. Consciously you didn't, because when everyone took off, the CO would say, 'Well, I'm sorry, some of you probably won't come back,' and you'd look round and think, I'm sorry for these other blokes, I'm coming back. But subconsciously it's less clear-cut: for instance, the CO came up to me in Holland, and said, 'I don't want any arguments, final decision, you're going on rest.' And I thought to myself, I'm going to live. It was a ridiculous thought, because consciously, I'd never thought I was going to get killed; yet subconsciously we must all have written ourselves off as soon as we joined the squadron. When I joined the squadron, an operational tour was thirty trips, on plain fighters; on ours, it was about two hundred hours or something ridiculous. But when we were dive-bombing with rockets, because of the casualties, they reckoned thirty trips was enough. Of course they couldn't afford to send us on rest, and so they kept extending and extending and extending, and I got ninety-nine trips, eventually, and some of the chaps I joined with got more trips than that. They just carried on going until the end.

We organised a little fiddle for home leave. We sent somebody off in a passenger aircraft, and we used to fly a Typhoon across the Channel, land, and he'd bring it back; we used to go and have a forty-eight-hour leave. Then someone would bring it back, and so it went on. There were all sorts of other fiddles: food was at a premium on the Continent, of course, and coffee was gold. So people with empty long-range tanks on, filled them with coffee beans. Certainly when the aircraft came back from England it used to be packed with bread and anything other than biscuits and bully beef!

At the end of the war, I was shattered. There's nothing quite so tiring as doing an hour's operational flying, because it's concentrated, ninety per cent boredom, five per cent terror, and five per cent elation.

When the war was over, I moved on to Spits, on to a photographic reconnaissance unit. It sounds like a line, but once the shooting had stopped the fun went out of flying. That time in Normandy was the most exciting of my life, and I would not have missed it for the world.

Flying Officer Ken Adam

I was born in Berlin. We were Jewish, but had a very liberal upbringing, so until Hitler came to power, I never even realised I was Jewish. My family had been in Germany for five hundred years or so. My father considered himself one thousand per cent Prussian, and had been a much-decorated cavalry officer. A much older brother of mine, who had been studying in France in 1932, saw what was happening in Germany, and advised my mother that she should send her children away. So we left Berlin and went to Scotland, then to London.

My father, who was wealthy, had many friends in exploration and aviation. Roald Amundsen used to come to the house and my father sponsored the first German fliers who went east to west across the Atlantic. I remember clearly the enormous reception he gave for them in Berlin. So flying was very much in my blood. I had to learn English when I first came to London and did enough to pass the Common Entrance into St Paul's. I was studying architecture at University College, and I was articled to a Gower Street firm. All this time, in my late teens, in 1938 and 1939, I was trying to volunteer for the University Air Squadron or the Civil Air Guard. Obviously, I was always turned down, because I couldn't become a British subject until I was twenty-one. Also, we were worried because of the practice, once war broke out, of interning 'enemy aliens'.

One morning, while I was living in my mother's house in Hampstead, the police called on us, and said that my younger brother and I would have to be ready in two hours' time, with all our things packed, to be interned. My elder brother, who was eight years older than we were, was already naturalised British, and in the Army. Now I was actually working unofficially for the War

Office, doing drawings in my architect's office of the retooling of the Bofors. My mother said, 'Why don't you ring up your boss and tell him they are going to lock you up?' He rang up Scotland Yard and I was not interned. But my younger brother was on the Isle of Man for three months before I got him out.

I joined the Auxiliary Military Pioneer Corps, because the RAF wouldn't have me, meanwhile firing off application after application to join the RAF. And much to everybody's surprise, including my own, one day I got a transfer.

So I made it into the Royal Air Force. First I went to Perth in Scotland for a sort of pre-elementary flying. There, my instructors found I was a natural pilot, and sent me on to Canada, but I managed to wangle a posting to America. There I was trained, under what was known as the Arnold Scheme, for about a year.

I finished training and joined 609 Squadron on 1 October 1943, stationed at Lympne. In the meantime, I had changed my Christian name from Klaus Hugo to Keith Howard, but everyone usually called me Heinie! I went straight on to Typhoons. Our job was basically to escort American bombers.

On my first operation, I nearly ran out of fuel because my Typhoon wasn't fitted with long-range tanks. We were flying medium-level escort over France, and my engine had cut on main tanks, so I switched over to reserve, but I thought I had better call up the CO. He gave me a terrible bollocking: 'Reduce your revs, and try and glide back to England.' Then, as I was turning, I saw planes being attacked right and left of me. There were no enemy aircraft around, but there was a high-level escort of American fighters who had never seen a Typhoon, and they thought we were Focke-Wulf 190s, and so they just took a dive at us. And our Squadron Commander was shot down, along with a couple of others, and an American pilot in 609, a famous ice-hockey player, Artie Ross, was also hit, though he managed to get back and force-land somewhere on a beach. Then they sent Artie Ross to all the American fighter stations to show them a Typhoon, and

I believe some pilots were later court-martialled. It was a terrible thing to happen, especially on your first operation.

The plain fighter stuff which I think 609 Squadron had pioneered was 'Rangers and Rhubarb'. They were operations, involving only two aircraft, rarely more, where you took off in overcast conditions from Manston, or wherever, to fly over the French or Dutch coast and find military targets, troop concentrations, locomotives, German transport, and attack them with 20mm cannons. They would scramble two or three squadrons of Me 109s, but we just went into cloud cover, and came straight back. These were very successful operations, but the whole success of it depended on the fact that we were only a couple of aircraft, and they had to scramble a whole squadron to try and get us.

Then they decided to equip us with this new secret weapon, eight rockets, four under each wing, each rocket with a 60lb warhead, more or less the same explosive as the six-inch naval gun shell, a very powerful weapon. On top of that we had our four 20mm cannons. We were probably the most powerful support weapon in the RAF. But we had no electronic aid, no way, except physical aiming, to aim the whole plane, through your gunsight, so we had to allow for angle of dive, and wind direction. And in those dives, we used to get up to 550mph. You released your rockets at about 800 feet, because you needed to pull out quickly. The Typhoon had a nasty habit, if you pulled out too suddenly, of going into a high-speed stall. A number of our pilots lost their lives that way. So you had to pull out gradually, and so many of us were hit not only by the flak, but by our own explosions.

First of all they used us for silly things like attacking German V1 sites, but rockets were no use at all against reinforced concrete. We had enormous losses.

They finally found our most effective use was to attack German tank concentrations, and special targets – like Gestapo headquarters. It was either my squadron or 198 that attacked Rommel. He was blown up in his staff car. Typhoons did that. Plus we attacked shipping, 105mm and 88mm gun concentrations, and since we were attached to the Army, we advanced with the Army.

A few days after D-Day, we were stationed on these airstrips in France. There we invented the system called 'cab rank'. This involved four Typhoons, at the end of the airstrip, sitting in readiness for take-off. On a signal you used to circle up to an operational height – 8,000 feet – then an Army Controller took over in a tank or armoured car in the front line and would tell you to proceed to a grid reference, and attack when we saw yellow, blue or red smoke. We would then dive-bomb either Tiger or Panther tanks, then return to the airfield. The moment you took off, another section of four Typhoons took your place like a taxi rank, so there was continuous air support for the Army.

But we had suffered losses, too, because we were so vulnerable. With that enormous in-line twenty-four-cylinder engine, you only had to get a revolver bullet in your radiator, and you had a glycol leak, and the engine seized up within a few seconds. The extra load of the rockets also made the aircraft much less manoeuvrable, and there were complaints about this at that time. If you were going to engage in any air combat you had immediately to jettison all eight rockets, but even then you were not as manoeuvrable because you had rocket rails stuck under the wings.

After Falaise Gap, we managed to get some leave and we went to the area. The first thing you noticed was the smell, mainly of dead animals. It was incredible; all the horses or cattle were completely rigid. Then we started seeing the bodies of the Germans we had killed. In fact I managed to win a German Volkswagen, one of these staff cars, but I didn't have the courage to get the two bodies out of the car; I left that to a New Zealander to do. So we had a German VW with our flight for seven or eight months, but we could never get rid of the smell – the sweet smell of death. To see all these dead bodies, and dead animals, was terrifying. Their tanks in their retreat had driven across anything in their path. It was grotesque, ghastly. It was the first time I had come into contact with the enemy and the dead. In a plane you might see someone running, but this was the first time I had come into such direct contact, and it was a profound, awful experience, and I've never forgotten it. It was terrible. It was similar to the carnage on the Basra Road in the Gulf War – it was vast.

We had two doctors, Doc Bell and Doc Edgar, at this time, and their job, apart from looking after our bodies, was really to keep the morale of the pilots up, to discover when a pilot became dangerous because of fatigue, nerves or whatever. They were incredible. We had many accidents on the airstrips, our lovely Flight Commander Woody had a burst tyre, turned over, and broke his neck. We immediately all ran out, and we became livid with Doc Bell because we insisted he do something. Woody had half his head missing, but there was still movement of the hands and so on. So we said, 'He's still alive, you've got to do something about it.' But Doc Bell said, 'There's nothing I can do about it, forget it.' That was a very emotional moment, but he was well dead.

But war is a very emotional time. Since I was always artistic and had a lot of imagination, I was usually shit-scared. I never made a secret of it. But at the same time, I seemed to outlast many other pilots, perhaps because of this sensitivity, or resilience? People from Australia, or the backwoods in Canada, where they are physically very tough, fit people, were the first ones to crack up. I always found that interesting.

Even in wartime we used to have arguments about fear. It used to annoy me when someone used to say, 'Well, I've never been afraid.' I would say, 'You must be lying'. One man I knew well, a very close Australian friend of mine called Norman Merrit, used to say he didn't fear death at all. In the air, he always used to volunteer for almost suicidal missions, and nobody could understand it. Once, just prior to Falaise, the whole squadron was supposed to get some German 88mm guns inside Caen. In those days we, the Tactical Air Force, were so close to the German lines that you had to climb up above your airstrip to 8,000 feet, because you were being fired on all the time by German anti-aircraft, and they were very good. So most of us never got to Caen; we were all hit, including myself. But Norman carried on by himself, though he was hit, destroyed the German 88mm guns, and just managed to limp back at ground level and crash-land.

The other thing which I found interesting at the time, and unbelievably touching, was how some people died, being fully aware that they were going to die. There was a Canadian pilot, called Piwi Williams, and we were flying on a normal operation over France. I could see his aircraft gradually losing height, and I called on my radio, 'Piwi, what are you doing?' And he called back and said that he was hit, and paralysed, and so he was literally going down for several minutes or so, straight into the ground. And I think his last words were, 'Order me a late tea.'

The RAF was incredible, Fighter Command, and the whole thing about it. Because it was all treated like playing rugby, a game. We all became part of that, and we all started to talk alike: 'Woody went down in flames, hard luck', things like that. I suppose it was a defence mechanism to hide my real emotions. When you were flying with great friends, people you'd been together with for two years, sharing a tent or whatever, and suddenly one of them was shot down in flames, or crashed, or was hit by flak, your first reaction was always, 'Oh, thank God it wasn't me.' Once you landed, the other reactions took over, and you realised he wasn't there any longer, but the first reaction was always one of self-preservation. The grief came later.

I was never brought up in any religion, I didn't believe, but I had to create my own superstition, or fetish. I remember that I had a gold signet ring, made up of the wedding ring of my mother and father. Before I went on an op I would turn this ring three times. On one particular occasion, we had to attack a Gestapo headquarters in the middle of Dunkirk; we were already in France, but Dunkirk was still in German hands. And as I started my engine I went to turn my ring, but it wasn't there. I must have dislodged it when I was grabbing my parachute. So I said to myself, 'Well, this is it.' I started looking for any possible reason to abort the mission. But the plane was behaving perfectly. I took off, and it was a very nasty attack. We lost the Squadron Commander, plus two or three other pilots. I was hit several times, but managed to get back. As I climbed out the fitters were walking towards me, grins on their faces, holding my ring.

Another interesting thing was what fear did to people. You would jump into your aircraft, and across the way one of your pals would be vomiting against the tail plane. But you would pretend not to notice it. Because nobody wanted ever to admit to fear.

I myself never felt that I didn't want to get back in the aircraft, even when we had these big losses. I didn't expect to finish the war alive, so that's maybe the reason why I was able to get back into the cockpit. I had made up my mind that I wasn't going to live. So I lived from one forty-eight-hours to the next.

Flight Lieutenant George Bell

I had been the Medical Officer on a training squadron at Kidlington when I got this posting to join 609 Squadron at Manston. There I was in a training unit, which isn't the war really, and suddenly I was pitched into Manston to 609, one of the heroic squadrons. I stepped into another world; from one where young men were being trained to fly, to the front line.

That was the turning-point in the war for me – having to deal with these young men with decorations on their chests like fruit salad. Here I was with blokes both younger than me and my age, with DSOs and bars and DFCs, talking in the language which, when you hear it on the television now, you don't believe. They were learning to fire rockets. I was learning the technique of transporting sick quarters under canvas in lorries.

Manston was a tremendous place: you had a Medical Officer permanently on 'Crash Duty'. The bell would ring, you would jump into a wagon and go. There were some appalling things; you learned to live with death as part of war very quickly; and you learned to turn the impersonal screw higher up just to go on with life.

During our time in Normandy we were based at B7 in a little French village. The beachhead was a small strip of land crammed with people where nobody knew what was happening. You just lived from day to day. Where we were, just off Sword Beach, there was little or no movement for several weeks. Then came the Falaise Gap, there was tremendous activity, and the casualties started mounting. Blokes would come to the squadron and I wouldn't get to know them. They were there for a moment – some of them didn't get a proving flight – that was the rate of casualties. I would be sitting up at dispersal and counting the Typhoons coming in and if there was one missing, that wasn't a bad day. They were rough times.

At Falaise we had the Germans encircled in a pocket and it was like shooting fish in a barrel. The boys were destroying tanks, lorries, petrol dumps. They would come back elated with their efforts. This was the first time they were defeating the enemy. There was this air of excitement about it, albeit some of them didn't come back. The excitement was there. It's odd nowadays to think that people felt such enormous excitement about war.

We had a Belgian called Manu Geerts who was much older than anyone else, probably forty-odd. He had incredible flying experience in the Belgian Air Force and he could fly anything. He eventually took command of the squadron while we were in Normandy. I had been looking at him and I could see he was getting to the end. I said to the Wing Commander, 'Sir, he's at the end of his tour, he'll need to come off.' Whenever the MO said that, that was it; they didn't send them back up. Manu was furious with me and he cursed me up and down. And I, being much younger, tried to explain why I did it. But Manu wouldn't listen and he left. I felt saddened by this whilst at the same time saying to myself, 'Good God! I saved your life, you were getting to the stage where you may have misjudged things.' Forty years later, I met a young Belgian who visited him regularly, and he said, 'When Manu talks about you, he says – Doc Bell saved my life.' And I felt a great feeling of relief.

The feeling of nervous fatigue amongst the pilots was terribly intense. Here was a group of young men who went out and faced danger day by day. I'm sure that many of them will tell you that they had to fight the fear to go up and do this, to drag themselves into the cockpit. They weren't going to let anyone else see that they were afraid. People talk about the fearless young men, it wasn't particularly true, except that they conquered that fear and that took great courage. There was never anyone who came to me with a lack of moral fibre. There was one pilot, Ken Adam, who was a German Jew. He had the incredible courage to fly over Germany with the chance of being knocked out of the sky. He once had to turn back with engine failure, and one of the engineer officers suggested to me that there may be a hint of lack of moral fibre. I did my nut. I told him that Adam was flying with twice the risk of anyone else, because if he baled out and survived the crash, he most certainly wouldn't be taken as an ordinary POW. To me he had incredible courage to climb into that plane day after day. I was young and I could get quite angry and emotional with these people who couldn't see his side of it.

Don Inches was hit and his plane went on fire and he baled out between enemy lines. His legs were badly burned and what saved him was that he paddled in a stream. I knew that he was missing and I went into the mess in the evening, and there he was rejoicing with everybody buying him drinks. I said to him, 'Before you drink any more, come with me – the drill is: if you're shot down, you have to have a medical examination immediately. So we'll get it done and then get back to some serious drinking.' I had no idea he'd been burned. I took him over to sick quarters, got him to undress and he had the most appalling second- and third-degree burns on both legs. I said to him, 'You're crazy! You'll have to go to hospital.' And he cried that he didn't want to go. He didn't want to leave the squadron. I sent him off and that was it. If he had left it to the following day, he would have had infected burns and anything could have happened.

The Typhoon had a nasty habit on take-off, especially on the

Sommerfeld tracking. If a little bit of the wire got broken and turned up – it could burst a tyre. The Typhoon would then flip over on its back, and one or two blokes sustained broken necks that way. This happened to Tom Annear, a New Zealander, a big burly fellow. I realised from the position he was in that he must have damaged his spine, so I went through the usual drill and got him on to a stretcher. I never saw him again but I heard he had a fractured spine. He telephoned me years later, in 1990, and said, 'You know, when you sent me off in that ambulance, you sent me off to the loneliest period of my life.' He was away from the squadron, from the intense camaraderie, from the adrenalin, to a world of hospitals, and he was out of the war.

We were called down to support the Army in the American sector at the Ardennes, and got there in the middle of a night of dreadful fog and frost. I got there first and set up the sick quarters and waited for the squadron. The weather was dreadful. The squadron came down the next day. Somebody would do a weather recce and come back and say, 'Nothing doing, cloud too dense.' This went on for a few days and eventually, Walter Dring, who was Wing Commander Flying, said, 'Look, I think the weather's reasonable, I'll do a weather recce myself.' He went up, came in, did an approach where he slid across the runway and was going to straighten out and come in. But when his wheels touched down, he was still on this sideways movement and he just slid straight across and hit a pile of snow that we had cleared on the edge of the runway, tipped over, and broke his neck. Now the Wing Commander Flying dying a needless death had a tremendous effect. I went into the mess that night, and there was almost total silence. After we finished dinner we went to the bar and started drinking, it became a night of vandalism. People who had never been drunk in their lives got drunk that night. When things got like that, I had to leave them, because they had to get rid of the tension. I came up the next morning early for breakfast and the place was about three inches deep in glass, they had smashed everything. It was just simply anger and frustration.

You'd find a bloke who would come into the mess at night and order a pint. Then a few days later you'd discover that this bloke would have four or five pints. And you thought – well, maybe that's a one-off. The next night he'd have four or five pints, and that would ring warning bells. The opposite could happen, the bloke who usually had four or five pints would suddenly just have a half-pint or orange juice. So you looked for those things. You would get some information from the other pilots. Perhaps in the heat of a debriefing he'd shout, 'You stupid clot, what did you do that for?' If you got this once or twice, you'd think, I'd better take him aside. You would never confront them. Never ask them to sick quarters, rather, you would quietly sit with them in the mess, and that's when they would unload and tell you things weren't all that well. There were many physical symptoms to indicate fear.

I remember the tremendous camaraderie in the squadron and the tremendous rivalry between 198 Squadron and us. They were interchangeable, one day in 609, the next day a Flight Commander in 198. That was so evident in any games in the mess. They used to get up to the usual horseplay. There was always a rugby game of sorts. But inevitably at some point or another there was the feet on the ceiling – it was a death-defying thing. They would pile chairs up on tables – it was terribly unsafe – but you had to climb up and get your foot blackened with soot and stick it on the ceiling. Then somebody passed up a pen and you wrote your name after it. It would stay there until somebody painted it out when we moved on.

There was a New Zealander, a big lad, not with our squadron. He was just finishing lunch as I sat down, so we were together about five minutes, and he left with the usual, 'See you tonight, Doc.' About twenty minutes later, when I was having coffee word came down to the mess, 'Crash on the 'drome'. I got to the crash and there was the New Zealander under this Typhoon, with his head totally flattened. The last words from this vibrant young man, 'See you tonight, Doc,' and then you go and fish him out, and put him in the back of the wagon and he's dead. You curse the war. That was it, someone else taken away from you.

The other crashes you saw were the impersonal ones where you didn't know them. You picked up bits and pieces and felt sorry, not for the person, funnily enough, but for their relatives. This is somebody's husband, somebody's son. The least I can do is give them a decent gathering together. I once had a fight with my Senior Medical Officer because our practice was to gather these blokes up and put them in a white sheet, sew it up as a shroud. And once at Gilze-Rijen, we were running short of sheets, and the SMO said that they had to be put into grey Army blankets. And I said, 'No bloody way!' It was an insult. You felt, if you ever met their relatives, you could say to them, 'I did what I could to give them this ritual we all deserve.'

When I was at Kidlington I met a wild bunch of Australians, including a big red-haired one called O'Reilly whose father was a famous spin bowler – his ears stuck out at right angles from his head. I used to get a call from the Mess Corporal, 'Get up here quick, sir. They're at it again.' I'd dash up to the mess, sometimes in pyjamas, to find O'Reilly with his head against the dartboard and Richardson and Hawkes trying to pin his ears to the board with darts.

The next time I saw Richardson was when I pulled him from a crashed Mosquito near Gilze-Rijen – he died in my arms. Those Aussies were in my life for maybe twenty days.

I was twenty-six when the war ended. It's a curious thing, I wouldn't have missed it for the world. I think it made a man of me. It made me aware of the quality of courage, though it was never put to the test with me. As a doctor, you could either choose to carry a Red Cross Certificate and wear a Red Cross arm band, or wear a gun and holster, in which case, you would be treated as an ordinary prisoner-of-war and not an MO. My little gesture to my pilots was that I wore a revolver. It was the least I could do.

Wing Commander Johnnie Johnson

My father was a police constable, and he became a police sergeant and then a police inspector, so you might say my brother and I came from a modest background. I know very well it was a struggle for him to send me to a grammar school out of a police inspector's pay.

I was always a bit of a loner in those days. When I was at school I won the cross-country. I won it because I was a boarder then and most evenings I would plough round these five and a half miles. I was on my own, I enjoyed the countryside, I enjoyed running. Later I took up shooting, I enjoyed going off with a gun. I still do it. I go fishing with my dogs on my own, down to the river. I have no trouble entertaining myself, sometimes I'm happier on my own. I have two great friends in the world. One lives in Canada and one lives in Florida – both were with me all those years ago as a fighter pilot. Maybe it's because we only see each other twice a year that we remain such good friends.

In the early 1930s I left school, and at seventeen was articled to the local borough engineer. My mother gave me five shillings a week and my father ten shillings, because as an articled pupil you didn't get any money. I ran a motorbike out of that somehow, petrol was then only about tenpence (10d.) a gallon. And I wanted a gun. I had shot a bit with farmer friends of mine. I went to the local store in Melton Mowbray, and asked for the cheapest BSA gun. They showed me a hammerless BSA for £10. I hadn't got £10, so I offered to put one pound down and pay half-a-crown a week. And they agreed.

I got permission to walk round the farms in the Waltham-on-the-Wolds area and I used to sit up in a tree with a gun and wait for the rabbits to come out on the pastures. I'd kill one stone dead with one shot, and then I had to wait another half-hour before another one came out! I'd take the rabbits home, gut them, clean them, take them to the market the next day and sell them for a bob (1s.) each. So I was in business – just. Occasionally I saw a pheasant or partridge and the farmer had said I could take a bit of game. But each shot had to count, I couldn't waste a shot. I was a much better shot in those days because I had to pay for the gun! It was great training. I used deflection shooting on rabbits in exactly the same way as I did later on shooting against Messerschmitts. It would flash through my mind that it was just the same as the deflection I'd learned years ago. All the good wartime shots were outdoor shooting men.

Of course, a real lone wolf was a rather different thing, and very rare. George Beurling came to me in 1943 fresh from Malta with all his victories and headquarters rang up and asked if I'd take him. He was a difficult man. I felt we had to give him a chance – after all, he had lots of medals. But we couldn't make a team player out of him. The wing would take off but over France he would do a half roll, disappear, come back and say he'd shot this and that down – which he had, he wasn't a liar. He'd clobber some trains and come back with bloodshot eyes from having pulled a lot of G, and there'd be rivets popping out of his aeroplane. I could do nothing with him. I made him Gunnery Officer to see if he could teach the others how he did it. I said he'd get his own wing inside a year. He wasn't interested. We should have given him a long-range Mustang and said, 'OK, go off and fight your own private war.' There were guys like that. But I liked to have a guy alongside me when I was fighting.

I'd learned that sort of team flying when I was a young man in 1941 flying with Bader. That was an apprenticeship! Douglas was a completely fearless man. He was just like a rugby three-quarter, he saw them and went straight in. We were over Lille one Sunday afternoon, and we got split up into ones and twos. I was alone at about 20,000 feet with the bombers withdrawing, and I had three or four Messerschmitts up my arse. The Messerschmitt always had the height on us in those days, they had a higher altitude than our Spitfire IIs. The Spitfire could always save your neck turning because we had the tighter turn, but I couldn't turn all afternoon, I had to get home for fuel. I was in a hell of a sweat,

I didn't know what to do. Out of the corner of my eye I saw a Spitfire going away from me about eight hundred yards away. I said, 'It's Johnnie here, I'm calling the Spitfire about eight hundred yards . . . there's four of the buggers up my arse, can you give me a hand?' It was Bader, and he said, 'OK, Johnnie, I'm turning, I can see you. You keep turning, old boy, and pretend you haven't seen them! I'll come up and we'll get one each.' 'Pretend you haven't seen them!' That was Bader, he sort of calmed the whole thing down.

He solved another problem for me too. One that had arisen before he joined us. My right hand had gone numb; the Spitfire in those days had fabric ailerons, and it got very heavy in the dive – you had to use both hands and sometimes your foot. It became difficult for me to hold it: an old rugby injury had trapped the nerve, as we found out later, and it got very sore. Eventually I went to the doctor, American chap, and asked to speak to him in confidence. At first he thought I had a dose of clap! When I explained he promised to keep it confidential and offered to try heat and massage. The next morning the CO sent for me and told me the doctor had told him and he was going to ground me. I protested that it wasn't that bad and he sent me to see the Wing Commander. It was clear what Wing Commander Stephen Hardy thought – that I wanted to get off operations. He looked very uncomfortable when he offered me the choice of going back on Tiger Moths as an instructor, or undergoing a surgical operation on the shoulder. Of course I chose surgery. I was off for two months and when I came back to the squadron, they were watching me as if to say, 'What's going to be wrong with him this time?'

Bader arrived as Wing Commander about two months later. I knew I had to make good. I'd got to make it. So I used to get down to dispersal before anybody else, sometimes I used to sleep down in dispersal. I was the first up in the morning, and I'd go round and see the Flight Sergeant and ask if he wanted any Spitfires testing. When they'd been in for some remedial work they often wanted an air test. I was there so I flew the aeroplanes.

I got a twenty-minute trip here, half-an-hour there, building up all the time – every landing gave me a bit more experience.

One morning I was up there about nine o'clock, our squadron had been night flying and hadn't come back yet, and Bader walked in. I had just flown his aeroplane for an air test because he had said it was left wing low. He wanted to go up; he was very fond of doing aerobatics, despite the fact that he lost both legs doing it. He said, 'I don't suppose my Spitfire is serviceable.' And I said I'd just flown it and it was. 'What's your bloody name?' he said, and I told him. So he took it up and twenty minutes later he came back and he said, 'What did you say your name was?' I said, 'Johnson, sir.' He said, 'Well, OK, Johnnie, it flies very nicely, thanks very much, old boy.'

That was an important step, getting your Christian name from the Wing Commander. Then the next day, at the briefing, he said, 'Who's flying with me today? I've got Sergeant Smith, Cocky Dundas, oh, Johnson, Johnnie – good show, well done.' So I was in, I was accepted! So the shoulder was in the background.

What stays with me about Bader is the great leadership and the fearlessness. There will never be anyone like him again. When we set course from Tangmere climbing up, you could feel the bonds of leadership holding you together. It was like something physical. He held us together.

And he did it with hardly a word. He'd get on the radio telephone and call the various squadrons as we left. He'd say, 'OK, Stan,' just to test the RT. Stan would say, 'OK, Douglas.' – 'OK, Ken.' 'OK, Douglas.' We'd just go, not a word did we say till over France. Our Controller, Woodall, would call and say, 'sixty plus twenty miles ahead, Douglas.' 'Bloody good show,' he'd say, and we would turn and switch the guns on to fire. We were held together by this guy, held together up there, no doubt about it. He'd take us in, bring us home. The only time we lost him was the day he was shot down. We usually came home together, because he'd call out and say where he was and ask us to join up. I think we'd done about forty ops together before

Douglas was shot down. I was flying with him when I got my first Messerschmitt. I got four kills with him.

His language was as powerful in the air as they say it was. He was a very earthy man. He used to say 'Don't fuck about, old boy.' Woodall would complain that the WAAFs could hear him. He'd say, 'I'll come and see them when I get back, old boy.'

We used to be in a lovely mess at Shopwyke House, an old stately home. On summer mornings the sun would stream down through the French windows, and we would sit and have breakfast. He always had a good breakfast, Douglas. There was a girl Corporal called Edna, who was a WAAF and always liked to serve him, and he liked her to serve him. He'd say, 'Hello, darling, how are you? Got your tin pants on today?' And he'd smack her bottom. She'd giggle, and he'd say, 'No, lads, she's not got her tin pants on today.' That was it; he never took her out. It was all part of the showmanship. He was a very earthy man. If a chap was found pranging a WAAF in his room, instead of a court martial, he'd say, 'Get him promoted. He's the right sort of chap, got a bit of spirit!'

When we lost Bader we couldn't believe it, really. We couldn't believe that the Wing Leader hadn't landed somewhere and was refuelling or at the worst might be in the Channel. We went searching for him till we were pulled out. Then when dusk came on that day, that was it, we knew. I remember his crew still looking into the evening sky, hoping that this almost immortal man might pop out. The Tangmere Wing was never the same. Another chap came down to lead us after that. He was a nice man but he just didn't have it. He was at a great disadvantage. Tangmere Wing disintegrated once Douglas was gone.

Then I moved from Tangmere to Cheshire in 1942. Crowley-Milling, who had been in France and the Battle of Britain, was one of my Flight Commanders, which was awkward, because I had been promoted over his head. I suppose Dieppe was the biggest thing we got in that year. We were up at Ludham in Norfolk doing long sea crossings over the Dutch coast. Shipping strikes, Rhubarbs and Rangers and that sort of thing. The most strenuous air fighting was over Dieppe, where I lost a few chaps and we got a few. But really it was a great victory for the German Air Force and the Fw190.

We'd first seen the Focke-Wulf 190s towards the end of 1941. We saw these square wing tips, and someone sketched them out and we sent them up to Intelligence saying we thought it was a new German fighter, and very fast. And the answer came back that it was the Curtiss Hawks which the Germans had captured from the French Air Force. That was Intelligence!

The 190 was fast because it had a radial engine in it, and it had extremely good armaments. We still had the Spitfire V. The thing just out-flew us, really. Whereas in 1941 we had been to Lille and Bethune with Bader, now we were hardly crossing the French coast because of the superiority of this aeroplane. The Spitfire could turn inside the Fw190, but you can't turn for ever.

I brought 610 Squadron down to Tangmere at the beginning of 1943 where I had been two years previously with Douglas. The AOC called me up, and I knew what he wanted me for – a promotion, a Wing Commander's job, it had to be when they called you up like that. He said I was to go and take over the Canadians at Kenley but I'd only be there a few weeks until he found a Canadian to take over. I stayed two years. I found the Canadians first-class chaps, a well-disciplined outfit. Canadians are hunters, I felt I had come home. Even the city men were hunters, outdoor men. They were always clamouring to go.

We had the very latest Spitfire IXs, which was a big technical change. After fighting for the past year against the Focke-Wulf in the Spitfire V, I took a Spitfire IX off for the first time from Kenley, and someone asked me how I liked it. I said, 'I'm going to live! I'm bloody going to live now! We've got a machine that will see them off!'

I realised straightaway that it would be wrong for an Englishman to have any disciplinary jurisdiction over Canadian aircrew. I left that entirely to the Squadron Commanders. If there was any discipline with the actual pilots that was mine of course, but except for Beurling there never was.

When I arrived the Canadians hadn't been terribly well led; they'd had a Wing Commander who wasn't a very aggressive sort of chap. He had been brought over from Canada where he had been a Wing Commander in the training organisation, and hadn't been brought up as a fighting man. That was one of the faults of the Canadians – they brought these middle-ranking chaps like Wing Commanders and Group Captains straight from Canada into operational jobs, and they usually fell down. By that time, 1943, I was on my third year and we'd been hammered by this bloody Fw190, but here was the finest aeroplane in the world, the Spitfire IX, the spring weather was just coming along, and everything was ready to go.

The first show I took the Canadians on, was on a beautiful afternoon in April, with a few cumulus clouds. The Controller, Squadron Leader Hunter, called out, 'Bandits forty miles ahead, flying from such and such. Turn so and so and I'll bring you over them.' This was bloody good stuff, right over France! He'd got the latest radars at Appledore down near the coast. He said, 'They should be below you, about five miles ahead.' And there they were, below and five miles ahead! They were a gaggle of 190s, and I was only leading two squadrons. We echeloned out and went down, and they didn't know what had hit them until they were on fire. It was classic! Chaps had been there all winter, darting about. We went out the next day and did it again. The Canadians thought I was OK. I'd learned to lead the wing from Douglas.

Another thing I'd learned in those days – from Bader – was, provided you got the results, and you were doing your stuff, everybody would back you up. We'd be flying over France and the Group Captain would come on and say we'd been airborne an hour and should withdraw soon. Then he'd ask later if we were withdrawing. I'd say we were, but would just carry on into France. Then when we got down, the Group Captain would say, 'When I told you to withdraw, the plots on the boards were still going out.' I would say, 'What an extraordinary thing, sir, I'm bloody certain we turned!' He'd say, 'I'm sure you did!'

I became more comfortable as time went on. I was utterly confident after those two shows with the Canadians. I knew that I had a good team of well-disciplined men, who would do as I told them, and I knew that we had the best aeroplane in the world. The odds, for once, were in our favour. The tide was turning. It was my most successful time as a pilot. I think that year my score went up from eight-and-a-half to twenty-four.

I remember particularly a time when we went into Normandy and I was very nearly killed. We got into a hard fight after Falaise, and what was left of the German 7th Army were withdrawing over the Seine. A Controller called up and said there were strong formations over the Seine. I only took one squadron; we were flying in squadron strength in those days because of the response time. My no. 2 turned back. I should have turned back – that was the golden rule. But I didn't, and went on with eleven aircraft and no wing man. We went into a low-level fight over the Seine – I think I shot down two that day. We all got split up and after the combat I climbed up guarding my tail very carefully, to about 14,000 feet. I heard a French-Canadian named Larry Robillard on the radio telephone, one of our Flight Commanders. I gave him my position and he said he was coming up to me, and I looked around and saw four aeroplanes coming towards me at about 1,000 yards. I waggled my wings at them, and it was four fucking 190s! The first thing I knew I was shot in the wing. I was waggling my wings in front of these buggers! They should have got me stone dead! There was brilliant sun straight overhead and I pulled the Spitfire up into the sun, put it right through the gates, gave it twenty pounds of boost, and it just hauled me straight into the sun. I went into the sun until it almost stalled and fell away and they'd gone. They couldn't see me. So that was a lucky escape.

One day when I was leading the Canadians, we were coming back from somewhere and couldn't get home and we landed at

Middle Wallop. And there was this huge man, Stephen Hardy, the chap in 1940 who had thought I was yellow. He by this time was a Group Captain. So he'd gone up one rank in those three years – from Wing Commander to Group Captain, and I had gone up from Pilot Officer to Wing Commander – four ranks. He remembered me and took me into the bar and we had a drink. He said, 'You know, I always like to think that I had something to do with your career, Johnnie. When you got that bad shoulder, I could have chucked you out of the bloody squadron, couldn't I? And put you on to Training Command. But I gave you a chance.' I said, 'I shall be eternally grateful.' He said, 'Well, you made the grade. So we were both right, weren't we?' He was terribly pleased really. He was a good man. He loved the Air Force.

Fighter Command of those days was a family. Dowding and Leigh-Mallory were father figures. We moved around a lot from squadron to squadron and from wing to wing, but our allegiance was to the Command. That was its strength. Once we were taken off operations we struggled to get back to the squadron – the family. 'Of arms and the man, I sing' wrote Virgil in his great epic about love and war – the very core of human experience; and it was this comradeship that pulled us back. The squadron was our home, our family, and the friendships were very close – closer than friends in peacetime can ever be. Once we had savoured the mystique and the affinity of a fighter squadron we had to return.

5

COASTAL COMMAND

In 1939, RAF Coastal Command had 19 squadrons of land-based aircraft and flying boats of which only the American Hudsons and the few Sunderland flying boats were modern. Its tasks were maritime reconnaissance, anti-submarine patrols cum convoy protection, and anti-shipping strikes.

Bridging the mid-Atlantic 'gap' in convoy air cover became a major priority in the desperate war against the U-boats. A squadron of Sunderlands operated from Iceland from late 1940, but the 'gap' was not closed until mid-1943 when very long range (VLR) Liberators were in operation alongside US and Canadian aircraft. Airborne radar, improved depth charges, rocket projectiles, airborne searchlights for night attacks, close co-operation with naval forces and, especially, breaking the German U-boat codes slowly contained and eventually defeated the submarine threat. The Battle of the Atlantic was the most crucial Allied victory of the war.

Coastal Command strike wings operated along the coasts of occupied Europe, often at heavy cost. The Command claimed 192 U-boats sunk (and 'shared' in 19 more with Royal Navy ships) and 478,000 tons of enemy shipping sunk in all theatres. The cost was 5,866 aircrew killed in action, and about 2,060 aircraft.

Squadron Leader Terry Bulloch

Before I arrived at 120 Squadron, I had already flown Ansons and Hudsons. From the day the war started Hudsons were under Coastal Command, in 16 Group. We did daylight raids dive-bombing Dutch harbours. The Hudson had five crew, and was a good aircraft, although not easy to handle. Landing was the main difficulty. Some people tried to teach pilots to three-point them, which was fatal: they had a tail wheel and it would swing if you landed in a three-point position. So we used to come in on the main gear, with the tail up, and then let it go down – then it didn't swing. Because if it swings, the undercarriage will come off, and it will catch fire. That happened quite a few times, because we were not on runways, we were on grass fields with old flare pots. None of this fancy runway lighting!

As far as weaponry went, nobody had heard of cannons; we had .303s, the pilot had two Brownings up front, we had a turret down the back with two, and had two Vickers gas-operated guns out the side windows. We didn't carry very much – four 250lb, and six 25lb incendiary bombs. We used to bomb the barge concentrations in the harbours at night. At this time, barge concentrations were building up in all the ports of western Europe, in Germany and Holland, ready for the invasion. We used to go to Emden quite often at night. God knows what the results were. We used to bomb the harbours anyway. We were also doing a lot of shipping forays up in the North Sea. 16 Group, from Bircham Newton, used to escort convoys down the east coast. This was extremely dull: we would fly the length of the convoy and then turn round again. We would fly patterns. This was mainly on the Hudson, in the early days of the war. But on two occasions in August and September 1940 we encountered Heinkel 115 float planes off the Dutch coast and engaged them. I shot the first one down, and we dropped a bomb close to the second. They both sank.

Then, I went to the USA and trained to fly the B-17 – the Flying Fortress. I flew the first one back home, in April 1941, to Scotland. We broke the transatlantic record then; we did it in eight hours and twenty minutes. We were at 23,000 feet, sucking oxygen out of a tube, quite primitive. We landed at Prestwick.

When I went to 120 Squadron, which was formed up at Nutts Corner, we were supplied with Liberators, thanks to Churchill's

It was not on, crazy. It was not the task that the thing was designed for: low-level, dropping a 550lb delayed-action bomb. That's where my rear-gunner got bits of shrapnel in his head, and lost an eye, all because we weren't given a proper detail or task. We also used to do photographic reconnaissance at night; we'd fly over places like Stavanger and take photographs. We were looking for the *Scharnhorst*. The photo flash showed of course, which immediately exposed us, so they used to shoot hell out of us. We soon stopped that, thank God, then we started proper anti-submarine tasking, and patterns. Each aeroplane was given a certain sector, because then they had good, reliable intelligence from the Enigma breakthrough. So we were sent out to where we would be useful, because they knew in essence where the submarine packs were. We never looked back after that.

There was a standard procedure, but it was rather ancient. We were told that, if we saw a U-boat, we should go hell for leather at it and attack it at any angle. This invariably meant crossing its track at right angles, which was stupid, because you'd only get two depth charges near it. So I devised a system whereby, if you went in and out of cloud, you could stalk it and get into position, and then either attack it up or down track at an angle of about twenty degrees. You had really to get within ten or twelve feet of its pressure hull to do any damage with depth charges. They used to go down to twenty-five feet; they were set hydrostatically by a fuse. So you had to get the U-boats either on the surface – which was difficult because if they spotted you they'd be down in sixty seconds – or just below it. If it was lower than twenty-five feet it would give them a bit of a shock, but do very little, if any, damage. I didn't work out my method properly until the end of 1941, when I started seeing quite a lot of U-boats. We used to figure it out. Mind you, I had a very good crew, well trained, and they always kept a good look-out from the side and rear-gun positions (where a mirror-attachment camera was positioned underneath, and activated when I pressed the tit to release the depth charges). The rear-gunner had a K24 hand-held camera as well, which was useful.

By 1942, I had been given several 'damaged, possibly sunk' hits, but my big day was 8 December of that year. We were operating out of Iceland, because from there we could get right down into the gap off Greenland, where the Germans had their submarine packs. This job was a convoy, twenty-five ships and five escort vessels, from Halifax to Liverpool. I spotted eight U-boats that day, and attacked seven of them. I came down at about fifty feet – we had to, because we didn't have any bombsights. I didn't worry about the sun: not in December, over the North Atlantic! I came in from the rear at an angle. The submarine looked very narrow; and as always it was just starting to submerge. I dropped off six depth charges right along the track of the U-boat. Then we saw a great patch of oil of about seven or eight hundred yards. I signalled a corvette that was near to investigate and he signalled back, 'You killed him, dead bodies seen.' Mind you, they were probably people from the conning tower – they'd left the poor buggers on top when they dived.

Our second sub that day came within half an hour. It was ahead of the convoy, off to one side, several miles away. We did an attack on it, but it had spotted us and was submerging. We only had two depth charges left, so I dropped those, but it was no good. It gave them a fright, though. Then during the next five hours we spotted six more. They were bobbing up all over the place. At one point, I was trying to eat some steak and potatoes one of the air-gunners had prepared, with 'George', the automatic pilot, in charge. A U-boat popped up. The plate went spinning off my knee; it ruined my lunch, but we dived and fired our cannons, really had a go at them, and made sure the U-boat didn't get within torpedo range of the convoy.

When we got back, our ground crew knew from our signals about our successes, so we celebrated. Because of course it was very rare indeed to sink a submarine. I reckon I sighted more than anybody else in the Command during the whole war period: twenty-eight. Of these, I attacked nineteen. The others went under before I could get into position to do anything; if I'd tried, it would only have been a waste of my depth charges. They credited me with only four destroyed, and a couple of those were marginal. We were under the Navy's control, and they wouldn't give you the skin off a rice pudding.

Over the war years, the technology improved. It was scandalous, the early charges we used, Royal Navy 450-pounders. On one of the early attacks I did, in the late summer of 1941, one of them exploded on impact with the water. I was flying over at about eighty feet, and it nearly blew my tail off. They had no ballistic qualities at all; they would just tumble over like an old oil drum. We didn't get any equipment. It was terrible – we didn't get the proper depth charges until the end of 1941 and beginning of 1942. Another technological innovation brought us a useful weapon: rockets.

By this time, summer 1943, I was attached to 224 Squadron based in Cornwall, St Eval, testing these rockets. They were involved in my fourth kill, one I really enjoyed, down at the Bay of Biscay. The rockets were solid-shot, 25lb, very primitive. They were under sponsons, little bits of metal bolted on just outside and below your window. There were four either side, and they were fired electrically. You used to get into a twenty-degree dive in a Liberator, from 2,000 feet, with cruise power on. I devised this system: you would dive down, fire the first two at 600 feet, two at 400 feet, and a stick of four at about 200 feet. Then you would pull the thing out. You had to get the trim absolutely right, or else you'd damage the wing. At the bottom of your dive, the aeroplane's nose was up in the air, but you were still sinking. It was great fun, I loved it. The rockets were very accurate. You could see them go into the water. They had ballistic qualities, believe it or not, under water. One of mine went right through the pressure hull of the U514, and straight out the other side. To make sure of it, I turned back quickly and dropped eight depth charges in a straddle and followed that up with 'Wandering Annie', an acoustic mine, and down he went to the ruddy bottom. We were tickled pink with that one. It was the first time that I'd fired that method in earnest, and of course you couldn't miss. It would have made sense to equip more squadrons with rockets, I felt, but after all my praises – and I wrote a marvellous report – they threw it out, because some idiot damaged an aeroplane, practising with them. I continued to fly with the rockets on sorties after that, until they were abandoned.

One incident occurred on 19 July 1944, in a Liberator III, a rather ancient machine by that time. It had the old-fashioned radar, which we were not allowed to use while we were operating right off the North Cape, because the Germans were triggering it off all the time. We were flying from Tain, in north-east Scotland, near Inverness, at about 200 feet, in and out of cloud. Suddenly we came out of cloud, and this U-boat, which had obviously been tracking us, was dead ahead of me. He opened up at a range of about three-quarters of a mile, and hit my two starboard engines. No. 4 was on fire, and the other one disabled, with an oil leak. He also shot away the starboard fin and rudder. We were rather taken by surprise; I flew back the nine hundred miles to Tain, on two port engines. We were throwing everything out of the aeroplane, guns, ammo, to lighten it. We went straight over Scapa Flow at about 2,000 feet. It is a wonder the Navy didn't shoot at us, because they were always very trigger-happy, but we got it in all right, though it was full of holes. It was rather an abortive sortie: fifteen hours and fifty minutes, quite exciting.

We lost a lot of people. The casualties in Coastal Command, between 3 September 1939 and 8 May 1945 were over 8,000 killed in action or accident and quite a lot missing, taken as prisoners-of-war, or wounded. They came from all parts of Coastal Command, mine-laying, anti-U-boat, photo recce, anti-shipping, attacks on land targets, fighters and so on. They lost over 2,000 aircraft, 741 in the anti-U-boat campaign. It's a lot more than people realise.

For the rest of the war, in actual fact, headquarters were getting a bit fed up with me. They had offered me command of 120 Squadron as Wing Commander. I said, 'No thanks, I want to keep flying.' And all in all, when I left the RAF, I'd done over 4,500 hours.

Flight Lieutenant Ken Gatward

I had been flying Beaufighters for some while with Coastal Command and had put up a suggestion that, instead of us just looking for targets for the Hudsons to bomb, we should go for something specific.

In the spring of 1942 an Intelligence report came in that a German parade went down the Champs Élysées every day at noon. One of our brave agents reported, 'Why don't you send an aeroplane over to beat up the parade? It would be a great morale-booster for the people in occupied Paris.' The Air Ministry agreed that this was a good idea, and that a single night-fighter could do it -- the Beaufighter. Fighter Command, however, wisely said that it was far too risky, because if the plane was shot down, the Germans would collect all our secret equipment. But Sir Philip Joubert, commander-in-chief of Coastal Command, said, 'I've got a day Beaufighter who might do it.' The next thing I heard was, Coastal Command HQ wanted to see me and my navigator, Sergeant Fern. I then had an interview with the C-in-C, Sir Philip Joubert, who said, 'There's a special mission coming along, I wonder if you'd be interested? I'm afraid it's not very safe!' I said, 'It sounds all right, sir, but what's it all about?' He said, 'It's very difficult to tell you, unless we know you're interested.' So, I said, 'Of course I'm interested.' Then he said, 'What about your navigator?' I said, 'Well, I don't think he will be interested because he's married and about to become a dad.' The navigator said, 'Oh yes I am.'

Then the AOC-in-C told us about the Paris parade. We thought it sounded an excellent idea. But he warned it could only be done with cloud cover.

We tried it two or three times in early June 1942, but over France we kept running out of cloud cover, so we thought, sod this and went tearing back home again. Eventually, we were told, 'We'd like you to collect a big Tricolour from the Navy, and when you make the run, we want you to drop it out over your target.' So we got the Tricolour, cut it in half, and got the parachute section to sew big metal bars in it. It didn't really look as though it was going to happen, anyway, because we'd be lucky to get cloud cover all the way to Paris at that time of year. But we decided that we could do it, if we went on the deck all the way, even though we hadn't been given permission to do it that way.

On 12 June we took off from Thorney Island in Hampshire, and flew very low in the pouring rain. As soon as we got to France the rain stopped, but we stayed on the deck, and eventually we saw the Eiffel Tower, sticking up like a matchstick. When we were over the Champs Élysées, flying at about fifty feet, as low as we could get, Fern threw the Tricolours out, down the flare chute like harpoons over the Arc de Triomphe. Someone, however, had got things wrong, because there wasn't a parade.

They had given us a secondary target, the Ministère Marine at the Place de la Concorde, which was the Gestapo headquarters. We swept the length of the Champs Élysées and hit the target with cannon fire. Then turned round and shoved off home.

Trouble started when flies kept smacking on to the windscreen, and pretty soon I could hardly see through it! We also got a bloody crow in the starboard oil-cooler radiator, which sent the temperature up like mad, but eventually bits started to fly off the bird, and the oil radiator cooled down again – otherwise we'd have lost an engine. Luckily, when we got to the Channel, it was pouring with rain again, and that washed all the flies off. God bless Fern. I didn't realise he was often airsick. He kept a bucket handy, but he never quit flying and kept his airsickness a secret.

Later the sortie received a lot of publicity. I think we got near enough to the Arc de Triomphe with the Tricolour. The good thing was that Fern had a heavy F24 hand-held camera, and he took pictures all the way. Otherwise, we'd have had no proof. The Germans, we heard later, said that it was one of their own aircraft that had been having trouble, but we had confirmation – about sixty photographs, and some good low-down ones including a super shot of a big notice outside the Grande Palais that read 'La Vie Nouvelle' (The New Life). That was good. The French crow, or what was left of it, was removed and laid to rest at RAF Northolt.

1943 was my busiest time, when I was working the Norwegian coast with 404 Squadron – that was the hairiest time too, because we lost a lot of crews. I was a Wing Commander by then and we were flying Beaufighters armed with 20mm cannon. Our role was chiefly anti-flak, but we carried eight rockets as well. I was usually leading, and leaders were all anti-flak, trying to subdue enemy flak ships. About nine or twelve of us would run together, flying fairly low down. We were after shipping, convoys, and we took a lot of flak, and casualties.

During the period we attacked a number of ships, mostly armed mine-sweepers. We also finished off a destroyer, although we were never there long enough to see them go down. But four mine-sweepers were definitely confirmed sunk, all in one strike.

My longest trip was six hours. Too long to sit in one position. Losses could sometimes be heavy. Normally we only lost one or two, but later on, just after I'd left 404, they lost at least six in one attack. I think they were told to hit a target that was way up against a sheer wall, in one of the fjords. They had to go around twice, and by then the wretched fighters, the 109s, had come along and caught them. But the 109s wouldn't chase you far out to sea. Most of the pilots had come from the Russian front, and they did not want to follow a Beau if you got far enough away from them out to sea so they just turned around and went home.

We tried looking for ships at night, once or twice, but without any luck. My wing man was a young American Flight Lieutenant in the RAF, and we both set off by moonlight to Norway on recce. I don't know what happened. He just disappeared. It was quite a hard war in that part of the world – and if you came down in the sea you'd basically had it. The sea was so cold in winter that, in my opinion, it was pointless to carry a one-man dinghy; I wouldn't have lasted long. I used to throw mine in the back – much better to sit on a cushion!

Flight Lieutenant John Cruickshank

I started at Harrogate on a six-week General Reconnaissance course and, on completion, in late December 1942 I joined No. 4 OTU – the flying boat operational training unit for Coastal Command at Invergordon.

I had some earlier experience on Catalina flying boats so I was directed to complete qualification on this type. This was obtained, then I met my crew and we carried out the various operational flying exercises.

On completing the course I and the crew members were posted to 210 Squadron at Pembroke Dock. The squadron was reforming and their Catalina flying boats were to be fitted with the recently developed Leigh searchlight. This was to enable the squadrons to carry out night attacks on U-boats as well as by day. We had further training to become proficient in the technique.

The squadron moved to Hamworthy to operate out of the adjacent Poole Bay in late April 1943. The operations we carried out were anti-U-boat patrols, almost all in the Bay of Biscay. This period was interrupted with a two-month detachment to Gibraltar, where we carried out similar anti-U-boat patrols in the Atlantic Ocean, west of Portugal. On one of these patrols I sighted my first U-boat. Visibility was good, so we too were sighted by the U-boat and it submerged before we could mount an effective attack.

In early January 1944 the squadron moved to Sullom Voe in the Shetland Islands to assist in covering the extensive northern flank. German submarines moved through this area from the Baltic Sea to their operational areas in the Atlantic Ocean. Also there was a flotilla of U-boats based on northern Norwegian ports patrolling the area between Norway and Spitzbergen, sinking

Allied convoys bound for Russia and to protect the German battle-ship *Tirpitz*, anchored in Altenfjord.

One operation in July 1944 was to carry out an offensive patrol for U-boats along the anticipated course of a large Royal Navy force. The force consisted of three fleet carriers, a battleship, supporting cruisers and destroyers. Fleet Air Arm aircraft from the carriers had carried out a bomb attack on the *Tirpitz* and were withdrawing from the area on their way to Scapa Flow. The German Navy's reaction to this was to concentrate their U-boats in the area to intercept the force and our task was to prevent this. A Liberator aircraft of 86 Squadron at Tain and my aircraft were assigned to the first patrols west of the Lofoten Islands.

We took off in perfect weather and, after five hours, reached the patrol area. The area was covered by dense sea fog and visibility was poor, below 600 feet or so. After three hours the radar operator reported a contact at fifteen miles and, on closing on this, it was identified as an enemy submarine. An attack was developed and although our aircraft tracked over the submarine at fifty feet, because of faulty mechanism the depth charges failed to release. The submarine was still visible so I ordered another attack and told the crew to prepare. As we came in we encountered heavy flak from the submarine which began hitting the aircraft and exploding inside. But we pressed home our attack – the aircraft tracked over the submarine and this time the depth charges were released. I then climbed up into the sea fog.

It was apparent we had suffered casualties from the flak, including myself, and a lot of damage to the aircraft, as well as a fire in the aft. The submarine was never sighted again so we set course for base. I handed over controls to the second pilot, Garnett, and retired to the rear of the aircraft to have my wounds attended to and to rest, so that when we neared Sullom Voe I would be able to resume control for landing the aircraft.

Some six hours later we arrived over base, but it was still dark and we continued to circuit the base until first light in order to ensure a safe landing. While we were circuiting the crew jettisoned all unnecessary equipment. I returned to the cockpit to assist Garnett to land the aircraft. We came down about two miles from the shoreline, taxied in, and beached the aircraft on the shore. That's all I can remember. The medical team took hold of myself and the other wounded and we were driven to hospital.

Our attack photographs showed that the depth charges on our second run had exploded within lethal range of the submarine and, much later, we were credited with the sinking of the U-boat.

6

BOMBER COMMAND

On the outbreak of war, RAF Bomber Command had 32 operational squadrons and about 480 aircraft organised into five operational Groups and a training Group. No. 1 Group (10 Fairey Battle squadrons) was sent to France in 1940 with the Advanced Air Striking Force. Blenheims, Whitleys, Hampdens and Wellingtons equipped the other front-line squadrons. Early actions – leaflet raids and attacks on German warships – proved that small numbers of bombers operating in daylight without fighter escort could not survive against the Luftwaffe. (Its first mainland targets were in Norway, 1940.) The twin-engined 'heavies' were restricted to night raids but the relatively few aircraft, primitive navigation and limited bomb-loads severely limited effectiveness. Nevertheless, in 1940, Bomber Command laid its first mines at sea (April), bombed Italy for the first time (June), and Berlin (August). But by February 1942, when Air Marshal Arthur Harris became commander-in-chief, locating targets at night was still a major problem which led to area-bombing of German industrial conurbations rather than precise targeting.

In 1942, Bomber Command made its first 'thousand bomber' raid – against Cologne in May – and developed new bombing techniques, including greater concentration of aircraft over the target, greater use of incendiary bombs, and a 'Pathfinder' force of picked crews to mark targets for the main force. From mid-1943, with radio and radar target-finding devices and a powerful main force of four-engined Stirlings, Halifaxes and Lancasters, Bomber Command could begin a remorseless campaign against Germany. Its task, decided at the Allies' Casablanca Conference, was 'the progressive destruction and dislocation of the German military, industrial and economic system and the undermining of the morale of the German people to a point where their capacity for armed resistance is fatally weakened'.

From March 1943 to March 1944 Bomber Command fought three mighty battles and a relentless technical and tactical campaign against German defences. The Battle of the Ruhr lasted from March to July. The targets could be pin-pointed with the 'Oboe' beams system and marked by the Pathfinders. About 23,000 sorties were flown against the Ruhr towns, 57,000 tons of bombs dropped and 1,000 aircraft lost. The Battle of Hamburg (July/August) devastated the city with four major raids within ten nights. The Battle of Berlin – November 1943 to March 1944 – was a grim succession of attacks. By the end of January, Berlin had suffered 14 heavy raids and the RAF had lost 384 bombers. But the city was not reduced to rubble and the Germans were not reduced to surrender. By March, after the raid on Nuremberg, known as the 'black night' when 95 bombers failed to return, with the loss of 545 aircrew, the RAF's main assault was over.

In May 1943, the specially formed 617 Squadron's great feat of airmanship destroyed the Ruhr's Mohne and Eder dams with bouncing bombs. By 1944, Bomber Command had 1,600 heavy bombers in five Groups (one Canadian), a tactical bomber Group capable of daylight precision attacks, and the Pathfinder Group. Its strategic offensive continued until the spring, when operations switched to support of the D-Day invasion. The offensive against Germany resumed in the autumn and lasted until the war's end. Combined with the US 8th Air Force's daylight onslaught the RAF's night campaign brought Nazi Germany to its knees.

From 1939 to 1945, Bomber Command flew over 307,000 night sorties, losing 7,953 aircraft, and over 80,150 daylight sorties costing 1,000 aircraft. It dropped 955,000 tons of bombs. Some 55,573 aircrew lost their lives, a figure that becomes more terrible when considered in the perspective of the RAF's final toll of 70,253 officers, NCOs and airmen killed or missing on operations.

Flight Lieutenant Roderick Learoyd

I joined the Royal Air Force on a Short Service Commission in March 1936, so by the time the war came along I had a fair bit of flying experience.

Ten days before the war started, when I was based at Scampton, Lincolnshire, I had been in the south of France. I wasn't supposed to be out of the country – nobody actually said so, but it was assumed. My father phoned and told me to get back quickly. I had to travel on a blacked-out and very crowded train.

If the war had started during Chamberlain's 'Peace in our time' business, we'd have had biplanes, and Rolls-Royce-engined Hawker Hinds as our front-line bombers with a 20lb bomb on each wing, a Browning front-gun and Lewis rear upper-gun. But luckily, the war was delayed, and the next year we took over the first squadron of Bristol Pegasus-engined Handley Page Hampdens. Of course the Hind was a much more nimble aircraft but we were very impressed with the Hampden. You could still play with a Hampden to a certain extent, much more than, say, a Wellington. In a Hampden you had a crew of four: the pilot; the navigator bomb-aimer down in the nose – he didn't stay there all the time, because it was a pretty awful position. Then there was the upper-gunner/radio operator, and the lower-gunner who also didn't sit in that position unless he was preparing for action. The Hampden was a very pleasant aircraft to fly, but they did have one fault: they used to go into what is called a 'stabilised yaw'. If you got into a spin, the rudders were blanked off by the suitcase-like fuselage, and it was difficult to correct the spin. I actually saw one spinning all the way down to a fatal crash – not a nice sight. Quite a number of aircrew (mainly in training) were killed in this manner. But we, who had a little more experience, had no real trouble.

That first day of war, I remember writing a letter to my mother and father, saying 'thank you' for everything – all that sort of stuff. One really thought something big was going to happen immediately, then of course it didn't. However, on the evening of that first day of World War II we did go out on a 'search' mission – to find the German Navy who were supposed to be en route from Kiel to Bremerhaven. And we were supposed to go and locate them. We soon lost our no. 3 in cloud and gathering darkness. My leader, George Lerwill, and I found ourselves flying in and out of cloud and I had great difficulty keeping in touch with him. We didn't find the German Navy either!

There was a longish break after that and we enjoyed our off-duty hours as, in all the pubs of Lincoln and Nottingham, we were considered operational just because we'd been out and done a trip – so it was, 'Well done, come and have a drink!' The next stage was dropping propaganda leaflets over Germany. I'm not sure that I ever read one, but they said the equivalent of, 'Give up now!'

We did a lot of mine-laying in the Skagerrak and around that area, and I can remember low-flying across Denmark once in broad morning daylight and seeing people waving to me. Denmark was not in the war at that time so nipping across that charming country in daylight at about two hundred feet was great fun. We then turned our attention to railway tunnels and marshalling yards. There was a lot of that, trying to disrupt rail transport. There was light opposition to those first raids, Bofors guns, etc. Then in August 1940 we started preparing for a low-level attack on the Dortmund-Ems canal. Our target was an aqueduct carrying the canal over the Ems river.

We had had some practice in low-level night bombing over water when mine-laying. However, a special exercise was devised for this mission – a small light was placed on a little fenland river and I had to drop my practice bomb – a small 8lb smoke-bomb – on this target. Off I went on my run, flying solo (no crew). At first I couldn't see the light, and then 'There it is!' As I approached it I suddenly realised there were houses going past my wing. I pulled up sharply, for obviously I wasn't in the right place at all. I never did find out what that light was! However, I did manage to find the right place later.

This was my first really low-level operation on the canal – I had carried out an earlier, higher, unsuccessful try. There were five aircraft, all from Scampton. We set off on 12 August, and we were supposed to go in at 150 feet, drop the bombs, each with a ten-minute delay, at two-minute intervals and swing away. I was the last one in, and so I had to be accurate with my timing, because the first bomb was due to go off very soon after I passed. I didn't want to be late!

Flight Lieutenant Pitcairn-Hill led the way in and immediately came under fire. He levelled out at about 100 feet, dropped his bomb and got away without any damage. The next two to go were great pals, both from 83 Squadron – and both Australians. Ross went first and he was hit and came down. The third to run the gauntlet was Mulligan. Before he reached his bomb-release point he was hit and one of his engines burst into flames. All four crew baled out and survived as prisoners-of-war. The next one in was Matthews who dropped his bombs – he got hit but made his way back.

I was due to bomb the aqueduct at 23:23. It was a moonlit night and you could see the features on the ground quite clearly. I came down some fifteen miles away and approached at about 1,000 feet. When I got a bit nearer to the target itself, I levelled off at about 150 feet. I had realised I was going to get a lot of flak and I knew their gunners would know what height and direction I'd be coming in, but what I hadn't reckoned on was bloody searchlights. They were shining straight into my face, I could hardly see a thing. I was trying to keep on target looking at the instruments with occasional glances out, checking the height, and all the time the navigator, Flight Lieutenant Lewis, was calling out, 'Left, left' or 'Right' or whatever, and suddenly there was a thump as we got a shell or something through the starboard wing, then another between the wing and the engine, but I managed to keep the aircraft straight. Very shortly the navigator shouted, 'Bomb gone', and I pulled up into a steep banking turn. On the way back I heard that one of the carrier pigeons had laid an egg!

Some of the hydraulics were hit and I didn't have the flaps for landing. I worried about my undercarriage, as the 'down and locked' indicators weren't working. So, when I got back over Scampton, they told me to fly around which I did for some time until most of my fuel had gone. Daylight was coming up when eventually I brought it in and, luckily, the undercarriage worked perfectly. We lost eight men on that raid, but four survived as POWs.

After that I became Personal Assistant (ADC) to Air Chief Marshal Sir Robert Brook-Popham, who at that time was the Inspector-General. I was in the mess at Mildenhall with the Air Chief Marshal when somebody said, 'Learoyd, you're wanted on the telephone.' I picked the phone up and heard, 'This is Air Vice-Marshal Harris.' And I said, 'Yes, and this is the King!' – or something equally silly. But it was him. I couldn't believe it. I mean, an Air Vice-Marshal was very senior and he was my Group Commander. He then told me I'd got a Victoria Cross and I was struck dumb. I couldn't say anything.

The next day the Station Commander said, 'Well, you probably want to go off and celebrate.'. But I didn't know a soul within a hundred miles. He lent me a Riley car and I went off to Cambridge and had a few drinks by myself. Of course, when I got to London, a day or two later, things started to move. It was in all the newspapers.

I did very few operations after the canal raid. I was posted to the Air Ministry and spent about eighteen months going round to factories spouting in canteens, etc., and 'boosting morale' – we were called the Line Shooters Squadron. There were about six of us.

When I went up to get my gong from the King, my mother and father came. The King had a slight stammer, and I did the worst thing you can possibly do, I tried to help and carried on for him when he was hesitating. Then of course he couldn't stop! I can't remember what his actual words were, but it was most unfortunate.

Squadron Leader Wally Lashbrook

All the aircrew they selected to go on the first British airborne operation, Operation Colossus at Tragino in February 1941, were reaching the end of their tours. They picked four crews from 51 Squadron, four crews from 78 Squadron – the most experienced people they could find. I had twenty-nine missions under my belt by that stage. None of us had ever dropped paratroops before.

I did six hours and forty-five minutes' total training, at Ringway, near Manchester, which included dummy drops, live drops, and canister drops by day and night. But we didn't really know what was going on until we got to Mildenhall. We stayed there for two or three days, we were briefed, and shown models of an area. The models were excellent, very well laid out, to a scale covering about ten square miles. We had to know this area by heart so that, on the actual run-in, we could recognise it even in moonlight.

X Troop, 11th Special Air Service Battalion, had actually trained with us so we'd done all our practice drops with them out of Whitleys. We thought they were marvellous fellows, ordinary chaps but so brave. They were all volunteers who had responded to Churchill's call, shortly after the fall of France, for 5,000 parachute troops. They were to be the first soldiers in uniform back into Europe. Obviously, some spies were there already, but they were to be the first uniformed people dropped.

It was planned for 11 February 1941. On board our Whitley was myself, the pilot, the second pilot, the navigator, the wireless operator, and Flight Lieutenant Williams was the tail-gunner. He was actually a professional paratrooper, teaching up at Ringway, but he came on my aircraft as a rear-gunner. We took off from Ringway on 7 February, then went on to Mildenhall where we were told our destination – the aqueduct at Tragino in Italy. Each aircraft had six paratroops, mine were led by Lieutenant Tony Deane-Drummond. We didn't really get to know them, of course. We didn't even natter to them, because they were back down in the aircraft on lilos.

Something rather amusing happened on the way out. We'd flown down over the west of Sardinia and Corsica, and were getting near the coast of Tunisia to approach Malta from the south. We'd been flying for seven hours – and I flew the plane all the way. The second pilot, Hawley, was sitting alongside me, asleep. We were 9,000 or 10,000 feet up, and there was a big black blanket in front, which I thought was just cloud. I was getting quite close to it, when Hawley suddenly woke up, and said, 'Look out, bloody mountains!' And I thought, Good God, it must be, and I pulled the aircraft into a really steep turn, kicked down the rudder and pulled back as hard as I could. As I did it I sank into the thing – of course it was cloud – but I thought I was sinking into a mountain. My stomach turned over, I can tell you. That was one of the biggest frights I've ever had. It all happened in an instant.

We arrived in Malta about eight o'clock the next morning, and did the actual operation on the night of 10 February.

Three of us flew in loose formation; Willy Tait was leading, I was on his left, and Flight Lieutenant Williams was on the right. Behind us were the other three. We flew over Sicily, up to near Naples and down towards Tragino. We turned along the valley which we had been briefed on, and everything looked more or less as it had on the model. We were losing height all the way in, down till we levelled out at 300 feet. I saw the aqueduct and, as soon as we were near the target, I switched the red light on, and the paratroops opened the exit door in the floor and two sat on either side with their legs outside ready to jump.

When we got overhead, on went the green and away they dropped. As far as I could tell, they were on the target. Flight Lieutenant Williams was singing, 'There they go, there they go, there go the canisters, there's so-and-so.' Then all of a sudden he said, 'Oh hell.' We had come too low into the steep valley. I had to turn left out over the side of the hill rather rapidly. If the wheels had been down, I swear we'd have hit the ground. I'd just managed to pull it over the top, and he saw the hill disappear underneath the tail. That was the shakiest part. We had dropped them at 300 feet, then we had to pull out over the side at about 500 or 600 feet with only a few hundred yards in which to climb. We had a quarter-flap on, to get the speed down to about 110mph for dropping. I had to use full bore to get out; we only just made it.

We'd also been given a little bomb to drop anywhere we wanted. We spotted a village down below, on a bit of a hill, but it looked such a snug little place, with its blue- and red-tiled houses. I thought, No, we can't drop bombs on these poor people. Let's go find a railway station. So we found a railway station and dropped the bombs on that. Had it been a year or two later, we would have had no compunction about bombing the village. But it was surprising how we felt then; it was too early to start doing nasty things.

Afterwards I heard that I was the first to drop. Deane-Drummond was the first down, and they were right there on target, and they blew the aqueduct. I was quite chuffed to know that my people had got down on target. At the time, though, you just had to drop and go.

We only lost one aircraft. The crew were all taken prisoner. There was supposed to be a submarine coming in to pick up the paratroops, but it was never to make it. Although they blew up the aqueduct, all the lads were captured. We didn't hear about it until after the war.

However, we did hear a lot about the success of the operation. It was well pushed up in the papers – they made a lot out of it. Psychologically it was a good thing. The fact that we could do that sort of thing made the Italians feel insecure in their bases. They had to bring a lot of front-line troops back to guard installations and bridges. At home it gave a good boost to our morale.

Leading Aircraftwoman Olive Snow

When I left home to join the WAAF there was a paratrooper from Ringway billeted in our house. I'd got quite fond of him, but when I came home on leave, he had gone off on the Tragino raid.

Then I started work as a parachute packer at Ringway. Every morning I would cycle in from Halebank in time for breakfast and then work from eight until four or five in the afternoon. It was quite a concentrated job; you'd only pack about 20 parachutes each day. Even when you'd been there a while and you might have thought you could do it with your eyes closed, you didn't; a man's life depended on each and every parachute. It was a very worthwhile job.

We were supervised by a warrant officer, Joe Sunderland – he was great. He always looked after us girls and wouldn't let anyone say anything against us. 'If my girls packed a blanket and four pieces of string, it would open.' That was him. Of course he could be very stern at times if we got chatting to the paratroops who used to come in and watch us; if you saw Joe walking down the packing room with his hands behind his back, you knew he was on the warpath.

There were a few deaths while I was there, but only one was a packer's fault. She hadn't packed the rigging right, so the parachute didn't open – it was a Roman candle. Of course they moved her from the camp straightaway, but it was a terrible thing for all of us; it could have been any of us who made that mistake. That death cast a gloom over the place for a while, and it really made us think more about the work. But you had to carry on.

We saw a lot of the paratroops of course, especially at tea-time in the YMCA where all the motherly volunteers were serving tea to the boys after they'd done their jumps. There'd be a few with bumped heads and bumped noses from the jump, but they were always cockahoop when they got their wings at the end of the fortnight's training. That evening they'd buy us a drink at the airport pub and we'd sew their wings on for them. Then the process started all over again with new trainees coming in.

We had a lot of foreign paratroopers: French, Polish, Canadian and American, and some of them were pretty cheeky. I got friendly with one Frenchman and chatted to him at teatimes for about a week. One day he came up and said, 'There's a little church up the road. Can we go down there and get married?' He was quite serious about it! But I said, 'Oh no, I couldn't do anything like that.' Things like that happen in wartime. A lot of the girls did get married to paratroopers and PJI (Parachute Jump Instructors), but I never got close to any of them, because actually we had it drilled into us: 'Don't get too involved with the paratroopers; they're only here for a fortnight and then they're off and might well get killed.'

All the men who trained for Arnhem were at Ringway. That was a fiasco if ever there was one; very few of them came back. They made a very big impact on us; we were terribly upset as quite a few girls were fond of the paratroopers who were lost. So it was a sad time and a happy time, but it's the happy memories you hold on to. You've got to keep going, haven't you?

Flight Lieutenant Nobby Clark

In March 1944 I was at 9 Squadron on Lancasters at Bardney in Lincolnshire, part of the Waddington Group. At briefing, we learned that our target was Stuttgart. We took off, flying to operational height. I had a very good aeroplane, and, although there had been plenty of flak, we hadn't flown through any. We bombed the target without incident, bomb-doors were closed, and we turned for home.

About ten minutes after leaving the target, there was a bit of flak over on our starboard side, but I wasn't too bothered about it. All of a sudden, there was a bloody great thump. The aeroplane rocked, and turned hard over to port, and it took me a little while to get hold of it again. A starboard engine had stopped, so I started to trim off and hold the two good engines down a bit. Then the mid-upper said, 'Your starboard wheel's hanging, skipper.' Because of this I had to fly left wing low, with a lot of left rudder, and trim. My legs started to ache, so after about half-an-hour I got Hughie Redmond, the bomb-aimer, down in the nose, with a scarf looped around the port rudder, just to ease my leg for a bit. While all that was happening, the engineer said, 'The starboard inner's overheating, skipper.' I had a look, and, my God, it was! So we stopped our starboard inner engine. Now, we really had trouble keeping the dead engines higher than the good engines, otherwise we'd have gone into a spiral. So we were lurching along, and weaving all over the sky. We had no idea where we were, and we were burning up gas, but everything was going fine. Hughie was hanging on to his scarf!

By this time we were down to about 8,000 feet – this was from 20,000 feet – and flying over France at a very dodgy height, because we were at a level where light flak could get us. We crossed the French coast without any incident, but we still had no idea where we were. We were running very short of fuel by now, and down to about 3,000 feet. As we crossed the English coast, still not sure where we were, I said, 'I'll try for an emergency landing and see if there's a field around here. Let's pray that was the English coast we crossed.'

So I called out, 'Mayday, Mayday, this is Short Jack B-baker, over'. Back came the reply, 'Aircraft calling Mayday, this is Tangmere. You are south-east of us. We will show our Chance light.' A Chance light is a sort of searchlight beam that goes vertically into the air and is usually blue. That came up just over on our port side.

I said, 'Tangmere, I'm on two engines. I will try to land to starboard of your runway.' Which was very optimistic, really. We were only going to get one go at it, so I told the crew to bale out, and they said, 'Arseholes.' Which was typical. They all got into crash positions. That's where two blokes brace their legs against the main spar, one bloke gets across the main spar and the other one lies on top. In other words you make a ball of fellows, so they don't bounce about.

I did a great sweeping turn to Tangmere, dropping height all the way. The girl at Tangmere said, 'B-baker, stand by.' 'Stand by?' I said. 'If you're not careful, I'll fall on top of you!' I came round over their boundary, going as fast as I could. The runway was bang ahead, little bit to port, and I was in exactly the right position to take the grass. I'd got no undercarriage; one was just hanging, and nothing happened on the other one. I lowered it down, just in case, and apparently the one wheel locked, because I came over the boundary, through the hedge. I ran along about two hundred yards on this one wheel, and then whipped it up. It broke off, hit the tail plane at the back, and we slithered along on our belly. I had switched off the engines automatically.

We slithered to a standstill, looking at Oving Church, on one side of Tangmere, with the graveyard twenty yards in front of us! Afterwards one of the crew said, 'Another twenty yards, and all they'd have had to do was dig the bloody holes.' As soon as we came to a halt, I shouted, 'Out!' The crew went scrambling up the escape at the aft end. I slithered down the side of the aeroplane, and I thought I'd sprained my ankle, because I couldn't feel my feet. I couldn't walk. Coming towards me, I'll never forget it, was the fire tender, the estate wagon, about three cars, a couple of trucks, hundreds of bikes, and lots of bods on foot – all running towards the aeroplane. Then the Doc said that I'd got something wrong with my foot, put me in the ambulance and carted me off to hospital. Apparently, we'd had some little holes in the front end of the aircraft, and an icy draught had come in and sort of frozen my feet. The Group Captain said, 'Wonderful job, wonderful job. Superb bit of flying. Get a gong for this, you know, old lad.' I said, 'Righto, sir.' And that was it, I got a DFC.

After that, I had a rest tour at Swinderby, with 1660 Conversion Unit, as an instructor on Lancasters. There was a shortage of pilots for ops, so we were worked fairly hard. We ran a six-week course, and just got them through it as quickly as we could. This was August 1944.

We were doing three-engine overshoots one day, on the short

runway, and there was a steady wind, which slows you down. I was up with a pupil pilot, and he was doing very well, and we came in on a normal approach, to practise a three-engine landing. As we got to about a hundred yards short of the runway, I looked out and, hey ho, saw the wind sock hanging like a limp cock.

Flying-control should have told me about that, but I suppose they thought I'd been at it too many years to come unstuck. On three engines you can't initiate an overshoot; when you are committed to a landing you must make it, because you've got your wheels and flaps down, and you've got too much drag – you'd never get out of it. I said, 'OK, I've got her,' and landed the thing. We were a bit high, so I'd not got anything to play with. Directly we'd touched down and run a couple of hundred yards, I said, 'Normally you wouldn't do this, but I've got no option, because we're short of runway, so we're going for the corner of the field.'

I knew that the corner of the field had no ditch, because it was the junction of the Lincoln–Newark road and the Swinderby–Morton Hall road. It all happens so quickly, you can't really describe it – all the time you're rattling along, bumping and galumphing over the grass. By the time I'd got to the Lincoln–Newark road, I was almost parallel to it. So as I turned on it I felt I was literally rolling up the runway again. Except that it wasn't the bloody runway – it was the Lincoln–Newark road! Squeezing brakes hard I pulled up outside a little pub, The Half-way House, right on the road, with about half a dozen cars up the back of me, and half a dozen in front. When I got out and had a look, the tail wheel had gone. All these guys got out of their cars, and hey ho, along comes an RAF car, and it's our dear Wing Commander Lister – a dear old boy – he really was.

He laid into me. He said, 'You are aware that you should never finish up out here on a highway. You have broken Air Ministry Orders (AMO) number so-and-so.' So I said, 'Well, thanks, sir.' 'You should have picked your undercarriage up,' he said, 'and stopped before you came across the airfield boundary.' Breaking

AMO is like disobeying the ten commandments. And of course it does say that if you are certain that you're going to overshoot the airfield, you whip up your undercarriage, and go down on your belly. Then you stop within the boundary of the airfield. Well, there I was, and I was still on two wheels. I said, 'So what? I've done it, and only you and I know. Now all we've got to do is tow the bloody thing back on to the airfield, and everybody will be happy.' He said, 'Well, I'm not bloody happy.'

We had a stand-up row in front of all these civilians. I'm not kidding. I can't even remember whether transport arrived to take us all back. And my pupil crew were watching it all from the aircraft – this arrogant Flight Lieutenant arguing with a Wing Commander in front of twenty or thirty civilians. Then the publican came out, and he really put the cat among the pigeons. 'Hey, Nobby,' he said, 'while you're arguing, would you like a pint? I've got some ale in.'

I had to go in front of the Group Captain. The old Groupy said, 'Look here, we don't want to make an incident of this. Why don't you go over to old Lister, and tell him that you're sorry, he's not a silly old bastard, he's a bloody good Squadron Commander. Why don't you just say that?' I said, 'Do you think that's the best way of handling it, sir?' And he said, 'It's my way of handling it!' So back I went to old Lister and said I was sorry and he wasn't any of the things that I said he was. He patted me on the back as though I was a small boy, and said, 'Oh, don't worry about it. It's just one of those things. We both got a little heated, all is forgiven. Off you go.' And that was the end of that.

Flight Lieutenant Lucian Ercolani

It was 7 November 1941, I was with 214 Squadron, and it was our twenty-fifth trip as a crew, our third trip to Berlin. It was 10/10 cloud most of the way. We thought we were over target and it was obviously defended, but we couldn't identify it, so we didn't know if we were doing the right thing. We had a load of incendiaries. We dropped them all, and just as we were coming back we were hit with ack-ack. What we didn't know was that one of the racks of incendiaries must have hung up inside the aircraft, and when the ack-ack hit they were set off, and of course they burn for a long time. So we were virtually alight with these things, and they gradually burned away all of the fabric. The belly of the plane was practically burned out. The fabric round the mid-part of the fuselage was gone. The fabric on the starboard wing was all burned away and both wings were badly holed and torn. The plane was nose heavy, although the trimming tabs were wound fully. My pals were marvellous, they put everything they could on the fires; when the extinguishers had run dry, they threw the rest of our coffee over it and peed on it.

There was smoke coming through into the cockpit, and I opened the two lids over my head, which was the worst thing that I could have done, because that sucked all the acrid smoke past me. I got everybody to put their parachutes on, and we were ready to jump out. I was about to tell them all to jump, but realised we were still flying. Where there's life there's hope, and we kept on flying.

We were burning all the time. We'd lost a lot of power, or rather we had a lot of increased drag, that was really the moment when we could have panicked and done all sorts of silly things. But we kept flying. It was quite difficult to hold the aircraft, all the centre section was badly gone. What made it worse was that it was difficult to find out where we'd actually got to.

We were gradually losing height all the time. As we were approaching the coast I realised that petrol was being used up faster than normal; the question was whether to jump there, or take a chance of getting through. Everybody was very good about it. They were all getting ready to jump out, and I had my parachute handy, but you want to hang on if you can. So we hung on. There was a hell of a wind blowing. We crossed the coast and we still hung on. Our wireless op. had got some sort of message through, but we didn't know where we were.

Then, of course, we were over the water, a couple of hundred feet up. There was a gadget on the Wimpy where you pulled a knob and it put both engines on to both petrol tanks. Normally, one engine ran on one, and the other engine on the other. The two engines didn't always use the same amount of petrol. So when you got right to the end, you pulled this plug and whatever petrol was left in either one, fed both engines. So I did that, and we knew that we didn't have very long to go. We weren't much above the waves. We could see searchlights about the place and were hoping that we'd cross our coast, but we didn't. We had been flying back for three hours and still the plane was ablaze. Then the engines went, and I think I remember saying good luck to everybody.

When you know that you've come face to face with the moment of truth there's almost a feeling of relief. I tried to make some sort of landing but the next thing I knew was that there was a terrific crash. Bang we came down nose first and as we went under the water I could hear the sound of things crumpling up and I saw the light of the moon shining down in the water. I felt like a spectator watching it all happen; it didn't seem to be happening to me at all. I tried desperately to get out, but the instrument panel had collapsed back on me, pinning me down. I definitely thought I'd had it then and that I was finished. Then the plane floated up again out of the water; that freed me and I was able to pull myself out through the escape hatch in the top of the pilot's cockpit.

The first thing I saw was the rear turret and the tail of the Wellington twisted right round, facing towards the front. I could see the dinghy and I could hear the rest of the crew calling to each other. I swam for the dinghy but, before we were all in, the aircraft sank.

There was an extraordinary sense of quiet, a sense of relief. We were rather glad to be alive. But at the same time sad. I felt what a pity it was for those waiting at home, particularly my dear wife.

Then, of course, you begin to wonder where you are: do we

just sit here, do we try to get back? If we're going to try and get back, what direction do we go in? Everybody was remarkably cheerful. In those days they had rum on the dinghies. We also had water flasks in the dinghy, but unfortunately the yellow stuff they had put in as a marker had got into the water. But the rum did us a bit of good.

The flares didn't work. We could see searchlights, and we thought that we were in the middle of the Channel. We had some funny little paddles, we felt that the right thing would be to try to aim towards England. We did everything we could to paddle that way. People were in remarkable spirits, we didn't actually have to do anything to keep spirits up. Everybody did it quite naturally. We just paddled and slept, paddled and slept.

We had come down at about three o'clock in the morning. It was very cold. The weather wasn't too bad at first. The next day it got quite rough. The chaps were very good, and we realised we were all in bloody trouble together. We couldn't blame each other for it or anything like that. We had a little miniature compass, an escape compass. We could see searchlights, and we heard two or three aircraft, so again we tried to let our flares off, but none of them worked.

I don't think any of us got to the stage of despair, or thought we weren't going to get out of it. That's the law of youth, of course, but I don't know how we thought we were going to get out of it. I suppose we weren't there long enough to get to the stage of desperation.

On the third day I saw what I thought was a German submarine periscope, but in fact it must have been a lobster pot marker. It appeared to be moving very fast through the water, but that was just the tide sweeping past it. Then we saw land, and I saw a bit of green, and a football post and thought this is probably England. In fact it was the Isle of Wight. Then we gradually got closer, so we paddled harder with everything we had. We suddenly saw an Air Sea Rescue launch, but to our pride we got ourselves ashore, at Ventnor. By then some people had climbed down to help us in. I stood up to walk ashore, but fell down. My ankle had broken.

I can't tell you what it was like to feel safe again. It was wonderful just to lie back in that ambulance and not have to worry about or think about anything. We were taken to the National Chest Hospital, where we were the only aircrew that they'd had, and they made a tremendous fuss of us. They sent in whisky, everything. In my room there was a wardrobe full of all the booze you could want, including lots of champagne. In the mornings, we sent out for Guinness and played cards drinking black velvet. None of the crew were badly injured. I had my ankle, and they thought that I was badly injured because I had blood all over my face, but in fact it was only a small cut.

Sergeant Robin Murray

It was 12 February 1942 and the call on that day for 214 Squadron was go for *Scharnhorst* and *Gneisenau*. We'd been on standby for some time – the powers-that-be were expecting something to happen. And when it did, of course, it was a maximum effort. So Wing Commander McFadden came as pilot. Jimmy Wood, our usual pilot, took over as second pilot, and Flight Lieutenant Hughes, the station navigation officer, took over as navigator. Squadron Leader Stephens came as the control officer for the formation, Burtwell and Harry Ward didn't come. The rest were our regular crew – Andy Everett was wireless operator/air-gunner, George Taylor rear-gunner, and I was front-gunner.

It was a cold day, overcast, 10/10ths cloud and from 9,000 feet down to about 900 feet was solid cloud, snow cloud. We took off in our Wellington, and of course we never did rendezvous with any of the other aircraft, because we just lost them. We flew out on course but we didn't see a thing because of the cloud. Then we iced up very badly. The port engine packed up, and after about twenty minutes part of the propeller broke away, came through the side of the aircraft, and demolished the hydraulics. I was in the front turret – so I had to wind the front turret round. We were coming down, and as we came out of the cloud we saw in front of us another 214 Squadron aircraft. We lost him and we picked up with another aircraft, flown by Sergeant McKenzie, who kept with us for a time. We eventually came down in the sea at about a quarter to five in the evening. I had been pulled out of the turret to act as McFadden's second pilot; he'd sent all the others to the back.

When we hit, the Perspex area behind the front turret broke and the wave took me right back up against the main spar. I came to underwater, pulled myself along on the geodetics and came up by the pilot's controls. There were four of them already in the dinghy which was still attached to the wing. I was the last one in. We'd lost Flight Lieutenant Hughes and George Taylor. We paddled around with our hands looking for them and Andy Everett swam round to the turret which was under water, because the plane had broken its back just behind the main spar, but it was no good. I had swallowed a lot of salt water and was very sick. I had bruising across my shoulders. Squadron Leader Stephens had a very bad cut and bruise over his temple. We were all sopping wet. We made ourselves as comfortable as we could. There were five of us in the dinghy, McFadden, Stephens, Wood, Everett and myself.

For the first few hours there was nothing around, just the sea. It was quite choppy, and that was very uncomfortable. Unfortunately, whoever had put the rations in the dinghy had forgotten the tin opener, so we couldn't open the tins. Then the knife fell overboard, so we didn't have that either. So all we had was Horlicks Malted Milk tablets. It was cold; the coldest winter for nearly a century.

We were hoping that somebody would come out and pick us up because the wireless operator had sent out a Mayday signal. But what none of us realised, and I didn't discover till five or six years ago, was that the navigator must have got his co-ordinates wrong. We had done a 180-degree turn and were heading out to sea again, so we landed off the Frisian Islands instead of, as we thought, twenty miles off Orford Ness.

I have always been a great reader and had read about how you mustn't go into a deep sleep when you're cold because you get hypothermia and that's it, you die. So I can remember suggesting that we always had two people awake so that we didn't all go right off into a deep sleep. And that's what we tried to do.

Everyone survived the first night and the next day being a blue cloudless one raised the spirits. We thought that any moment somebody was going to pick us up. We saw quite a few aircraft flying very high, unrecognisable of course. There were flares on the dinghy but we didn't see any aircraft that was low enough to have seen us. Once we thought we saw a ship, that was on the second day. We set off a flare but nothing happened and we tried to send off another. But it wouldn't work, it was damp. None of the flares worked at all after that. We saw quite a few aircraft that evening, just before dusk, flying very high. We came to the conclusion they were probably German.

We hadn't got a paddle on board, we were just sitting there. It was very strange, because people just went into a coma, they just sort of lost themselves. Stephens went first, on the second day at four o'clock − it was daylight. He was the injured one. He went very quickly when he went. I think he was probably badly concussed.

That second night was a very cold night. We just talked about various things, I can't remember what. Andy Everett used to like to go to Newmarket, and he used to frequent a pub near the station where the jockeys used to go. He was quite a little fellow so I suppose he felt he had something in common with them. He was talking about the people he met and how he wanted to get back and meet them again and have a nice glass of rum with the stable lads. There was no despondency, we never ever thought we weren't going to be picked up.

At dawn of that morning, Wing Commander McFadden died. He was the second one. There were no visible signs of injury.

McFadden was firmly under the impression in his last hours that he was in his car driving from the hangars back to the mess. He was the only one who got delirious in that way. People sort of went into a coma: they would be talking quite normally and they would gradually drowse off. You'd shake them to try and keep them awake but they'd gone. You could feel that they were going. But it was peaceful, there was no suffering at all. They weren't in pain, they just quietly died.

Because I'd read a great deal about survival, I suppose I was more or less in control. I realised I had to try to stop them drifting off. I was determined to survive. Pilot Officer Woods died about three hours after Wing Commander McFadden. He was very quiet.

Finally Sergeant Everett, who was very chatty most of the time, died. He went not long before we were picked up. He died at dawn also, I suppose that's when you're at your lowest ebb. I kept them all on the dinghy and was able to keep my legs out of the water by resting them on them, it sounds terrible but there was nothing I could do, they were beyond help.

The final morning was the worst time, because we drifted in towards land. The water was as calm as a mill-pond and the cliffs were about 150 yards away with a gun emplacement on the top, but when I looked down into the water I could see these masses of steel work, barbed wire with black boxes attached, so that if they were touched they might go off. That was one of my worst moments. I knew if I drifted on to one of those, I'd had it.

It was bitterly cold, I couldn't feel my hands at all, or my legs, they had gone completely. What I used to look forward to every day was to kneel up and spend a penny because my urine was beautifully warm, running down my legs. We'd had nothing to drink, and only the tablets to eat. Of course, we had attended talks about this, and you can drink your own urine up to three times before it starts affecting your kidneys. But I wasn't really thirsty. I think I was surprised Everett died, disappointed that he had gone so quickly. He just went like that, he was talking, and he sort of drifted off and he was gone. All of them – it was so peaceful it was almost unbelievable.

It was about eleven o'clock, I suppose, by the time I drifted into the shore. I got a tin lid and caught the sun and somebody came out of the gun emplacement and eventually, after five or six minutes he waved to me. So I knew they had seen me.

Then the tide started to go out. I was starting to drift out to sea. That was another bad moment. Then, I don't know how long afterwards, the German Marine Police boat with a Red Cross came out and they hauled me aboard. I was able to stand up and they got me on to the deck. They tied the dinghy on the back and came slowly back – in fact one of the Germans asked me for my home address and he gave me his. I had a watch on, a Kensitas coupons watch which had been given to me by an aunt who was a heavy smoker, and amazingly, since it wasn't waterproof, it didn't pack up until I had been on board this boat, when it just stopped. I gave it to him as a souvenir and he gave me a fountain pen.

They took me into Flushing dock. I'll never forget that moment: the deck was above the quay, and they put a ramp down, and as I walked down the ramp to the ambulance there were five or six German sailors there, and they all came to attention and saluted me.

I was taken to a hospital run by nuns where a German doctor was waiting for me. They had ten or twelve hot-water bottles in the bed, and they undressed me, dried me down, put me into pyjamas and into bed. Then he gave me a glass of schnapps and I drank it down. The last thing I remembered was holding the hand of a nun who was sitting on the bed there with me as I drifted off to sleep.

When I woke up – I don't know how long later – there was a guard sitting in the chair at the end of the bed. The officer apologised but it was law, they had to have a guard with me. They treated me very well. They bandaged my feet up and they put pads in between my toes to keep them braced. I had no feeling from the knee down, and they're still pretty dead now. I get a seventy per cent war pension for both legs. My hands were quite badly frost-bitten at the time too, but they've come back. My face and ears were all right because I had my flying helmet on.

My injuries were very minor compared to some others'. I didn't lose anything. But then I was picked up just in time. Another day and I probably wouldn't have been able to walk.

After three or four days they took me down on a stretcher to the station. They put me into a train on a long seat where I could put my feet up. I still had pyjamas on, but I had a German great-coat and some bedroom slippers that had been cut so I could get my feet inside with big socks over the top. They sat me there, and I saw the guard wave to the bloke at the end – he had seen some friends. So he went to the far end of the carriage and was sitting there chatting to them. Well, they had given me two walking sticks so I nipped out of the train and went and sat on a seat on the platform. Of course the train pulled out and all these Dutch people were killing themselves with laughter – I mean I couldn't go anywhere! The train pulled out, it went about 300 yards, then stopped and came back. Well, the poor little German guard! Germans, when they get cross, go off like a rocket, and he was waving his arms about – he went absolutely mad! His friends thought this was highly amusing and they were taking the mickey out of him something rotten.

Anyhow, we got to Amsterdam and I was taken by ambulance to hospital. They put my legs in cages and they had it all padded out, because frost-bite pulls the tendons and curls your toes and feet. My feet were smothered in thick black grease, like axle grease, which I believe was whale oil. Really, if I had been picked up by the British, I'm convinced I would have had amputations. But the Germans had learned on the Eastern front and they really knew what they were doing. The German doctor said to me, 'If you look out there, you'll see people with no noses, no ears, part of their lips or their finger tips gone, from the Russian front.' The hospital had large grounds and they had made areas where people could revolve small chalets and sit constantly facing the sun.

The trouble was I hadn't been able to pee at all, and I hadn't done a crap since I'd been picked up. That worried them and they kept giving me stuff. Well, eventually everything happened at once, and of course they had given me a bed pan and the guard had to empty it. Poor little Jerry – he had just opened the door to go out and the German doctor and all the hierarchy arrived and there he was standing there with this bloody bed pan full of good English shit, saying 'Heil Hitler!' I was then moved to Dulag Luft transit camp and another hospital. I was in bed there when a young bloke called Lieutenant Eberhardt came to interrogate me. He came in, got his briefcase out, put all the stuff on the bed, sat on the chair and said, 'Well, tell me, Sergeant – what happened?' So I told him. He said, 'What happened to the rest of the crew?' I said, 'Well, they were in the dinghy.' He said, 'With you?' I said, 'Yes, I lay on them, they kept me out of the water.' And he was violently sick! He rushed out, but left all his stuff on the bed, all the files about me, McFadden – and he knew all about us. He knew McFadden was a Wing Commander, he knew he'd been in the Cambridge University Air Squadron, he knew everything. Anyhow, he came back and interrogated me, then he went out and an older man came in and said, 'Don't worry, Sergeant, you'll be a prisoner-of-war about three years, then you'll win the war but unless you get the Poles to negotiate the peace, you'll never win the peace.' Well, he got most of that right. Eberhardt was hanged after the war for war crimes.

From the hospital I went down into the main camp. There, 'Wings' Day was the Senior British Officer, and he arranged for me to have, three or four times a day, a bucket of hot water and a bucket of cold to put my feet in to try and bring them back to life.

Then from Dulag Luft we went to Stalag VIIIB Lamsdorff. When they marched us out, Lieutenant Commander John Casson – Sybil Thorndike's son – led us. He'd had a guitar and he was playing and we were singing all the old British bawdy songs as we went down to the transport. Then we went to Lamsdorff and I was there for just over three years.

Of those three years I suppose I remember most the comradeship. Everybody mucked in when you arrived. I was lucky. When I arrived my old friend Allen was there; he had been captured in 1940. They were the first family I had met when we moved down to Brighton in 1933. As we came into the reception area he was standing at the wire, when he saw me the tears just streamed down his face. I was a link with home, and I had been home only six or eight weeks previously.

It was the largest British prisoner-of-war camp for other ranks, primarily an Army camp. We had a theatre, we had orchestras, we had football matches, you name it, we made our own entertainment. Denholm Elliott, who was a wireless operator, used to recite Shakespeare for us. There wasn't a lot of food, of course, the German rations were very poor.

There were about eight thousand of us in the camp and it was well organised by RSM Sherrif and a team of senior NCOs who had been captured at Dunkirk. We never had more than half a Red Cross parcel each a week. The parcels would have Morton's meat and vegetables, fats, cheese, cocoa, chocolate, powdered milk, that sort of stuff. Then you would get what we called bulk issues – big tins of powdered milk from Canada and packs of bully beef from Argentina. But when I say bulk issue, you got probably a slice to top up your rations. We got Ersatz mint tea, which was hot and very nice to use for shaving, and there would be potatoes and a soup which was sometimes Ling fish, sometimes swede, turnip or potato. In the afternoon we got probably a two-pound loaf of bread between six or eight of us and some more mint tea. And that was it. Then we'd cook our own meals in the evening.

Quite a few people died in the camp. We had a very bad time with hepatitis in 1943. It came up with the prisoners-of-war who had been in Italy, and it went through us like a dose of salts.

Then on 18 January 1945 the camp was evacuated. We were on the march from January right through to the middle of April. We did nearly 1,000 miles. I could cope because I'd done a lot of exercise in the camp. I had a pair of British Army boots which I had dubbined and broken in, and clumped so that the sole was about two inches thick; a balaclava made out of old socks knitted up and a handkerchief as inner lining; and I had a greatcoat. And we just marched west.

We were not far from Dresden when they did it over on the 12–13 February. We were probably about sixty kilometres away, and you could have read a newspaper by the flares they dropped. It was an incredible sight.

On the march, we were losing people at the rate of three or four a day. A lot of them got dysentery because they were going into the fields and eating the raw turnips and swedes and potatoes when they were dirty.

Eventually, we were picked up by the advancing Americans. They took us to a village where we were billeted in the Burgomeister's house. We sat down to seven fried eggs each and drank a jug of milk. We were then flown to Le Havre, where we were deloused, showered and given a new uniform and flown back to England.

I had survived.

Squadron Leader Lewis 'Bob' Hodges

In the summer of 1942 I met Wing Commander Charles Pickard in London. I had known him for some time as we had both been on the same training unit together in the early days of the war. He was still in Bomber Command and commanding 161 Special Duties Squadron at Tempsford, near Bedford, which was engaged in supporting Resistance movements in the occupied countries. He said he was looking for a Flight Commander and asked if I would like to join him. I jumped at the chance and was posted to 161 Squadron.

On arrival at Tempsford I took command of the Halifax flight. The Handley Page Halifax, which was a four-engine bomber, had been adapted for parachuting by the removal of the lower gun-turret to provide a suitable trap door through which parachutists could jump. Our task was to parachute agents, stores and ammunition into the occupied countries, supporting the Special Operations Executive (SOE).

The tactics on these operations were to cross the Channel or North Sea at medium altitude, and then come down low before reaching the enemy coast to avoid radar detection. We then flew low over enemy territory at about 500 or 600 feet; but in some cases, Norway for example, this was not possible because of the mountainous terrain.

Our objective on these missions was to find the 'reception committee' as it was called – the agents on the ground who, in most cases, had been trained in England and parachuted in. To find the 'reception committee' very accurate navigation and map-reading was required to arrive at the exact geographical location, and we needed moonlight and good weather conditions. The dropping-point was marked by a number of lights, usually in the form of a cross or the letter T, and there was always a recognition morse-code letter flashed to indicate that all was in order on the ground, and that they were not being subjected to pressure from the Germans, as happened in certain cases. We dropped agents and stores from a height of 600 feet, which was the minimum safe altitude. Dropping from a higher altitude would risk the parachutes drifting away from the dropping zone.

In the spring of 1943 Wing Commander Pickard left us to take over command of a bomber station. Then he was lucky enough to be given command of the squadron. It consisted of the Halifax flight doing parachuting, and the Lysander and Hudson flight doing landings. I then started flying Hudsons and Lysanders, landing in France and picking people up – 'pick-up' operations as they were called. The Lysander could land in a fairly small field, but the Hudson needed a landing-run of about 1,000 yards. The French agents on the ground had again been trained by us at Tempsford. They were taught how to select suitable landing-fields, how to lay out a flare path, how to judge whether the approaches to the field were safe, and about the surface of the ground, to ensure it was not too wet.

Full information about a selected field would be radioed back to London. We would then send a photographic aircraft over to France to take pictures of the proposed landing-ground so that we could satisfy ourselves about the suitability of the field, but, of course, there were incidents when things went wrong, particularly if the surface of the field was not hard enough.

The areas that we operated in were mainly in the Loire Valley, because there was suitable terrain there, but it was also possible to find fields that were suitable in the Rhône Valley, and in Normandy. Navigation was often difficult, particularly in the Lysanders where one was flying the aircraft manually and at the same time doing the map-reading. We did a lot of work preparing maps and so on – in advance – so most of the job was done before you took off. Of course after a time one got to know the country very well, because we flew over much the same routes on the day down to the Loire Valley.

We used to cross the coast normally in the Le Havre area, then climb up to identify a pin-point on the coast, to see exactly where we were; then we lost height down to about 500 feet above the ground and continued en route to the target area. Again we needed moonlight and reasonable weather to be able to map-read our way across France. The basic navigation techniques we used were to fly a compass course which had been worked out in advance, to a prominent landmark such as a river or railway, and then, by reference to the map, to identify our exact position. From that point on it was a question of setting course on a short leg to the target area – the field where we were going to land. As soon as the agents on the ground heard the approach of the aircraft they would signal the identification code and light the landing-lamps which formed the flarepath. These lights consisted of three torches in the L-shape for the Lysander, and for the Hudson there were four torches to mark out the longer landing-run. I always used my landing-lights on the approach to the field in order to illuminate any obstructions on the run-in. Once on the ground we taxied to the first light and disembarked any passengers as quickly as possible, and took on board the homeward-bound passengers. We remained on the ground for no more than five or ten minutes with the engines running all the time.

The Hudson would carry ten passengers, the Lysander was meant for only one person in the rear cockpit, but you could get two or three in at a pinch.

From time to time special 'pick-up' operations involving more than one aircraft were called for when a large number of passengers needed to be brought back to England. In the winter of 1943 I took part in a double Hudson operation. The two aircraft flew over to France together, rendezvoused over the field, and landed. We brought back twenty people.

I carried ten in my Hudson, one of whom turned out to be a future President of France – Vincent Auriol. He came on a state visit to London after the war, and he asked who the pilot was who had flown him. It transpired, looking at the records, that it had been me. I had no idea who any of the passengers were at the time, they were just agents and people who had to be brought back.

On another occasion I landed in the Loire Valley, in a Hudson, and embarked passengers. Again, I didn't know who they were, but when research was carried out recently it transpired that one was François Mitterrand. Of course at that time he was a young man and quite unknown. He returned to France in 1944 by motor torpedo boat, which landed him on the coast of Brittany. But by that time the Normandy landings were about to take place.

In spite of the risks involved in these operations, losses were remarkably light, mainly because we were able to avoid defensive positions by routing ourselves well west of Paris. Inevitably from time to time one went straight over airfields and got shot at, and we were occasionally attacked by night fighters. However, we did have some fairly major incidents: for example Wing Commander Pickard, in one of the first Hudson operations, landed his aeroplane in a field that was too soft and it sank into mud, and no-one could move it. They had to get the whole village out: oxen were produced with ropes, the Hudson was eventually towed on to the hard ground, and they were able to start up the engines and take off. By then it was very late on in the night, and they finished by flying across the northern part of France in daylight. That was fairly dramatic.

There was another, similar incident. A colleague, Robin Hooper, was flying a Lysander and he got bogged down in a field in the area south of Poitiers. They were not able to get it out and eventually had to burn it, and Hooper went into hiding with the agents. That was early in December 1943, but just before Christmas I went over in my Lysander and fetched him back.

Prior to Normandy, the Maquis were obviously going to play a major part in the liberation of France, and to do as much as they could to harass the German Army, in anticipation of the invasion. At that time our operations in the Halifaxes were augmented by Bomber Command, in a very big way. The Stirlings, for example, were withdrawn from the main bomber force and put on to parachuting. Mass drops to the Maquis in the mountains in the south of France then took place, in preparation for the Allied landings.

After Normandy there wasn't so much of a need for us, because the enemy collapse was very rapid. Our operations then were mainly on the German and Belgian borders, trying to infiltrate agents into Germany to make contact with the people in the concentration camps.

I stayed with 161 Squadron until the summer of 1944 and in my eighteen months at Tempsford I felt that we had made a major contribution to the work of the Resistance movements in the occupied countries. My next assignment took me to the Far East where I commanded a similar squadron supporting 14th Army in Burma and parachuting people behind the Japanese line in Indo-China, Siam and Malaya. I remained there until the end of the war.

Squadron Leader David Shannon

I was trained and commissioned as a pilot into the Royal Australian Air Force. After arrival in the UK I trained on Whitleys and
was posted to 106 Squadron. I did some thirty-seven or thirty-
eight ops with 106, then they wanted to take me off flying and
send me for training. I didn't like that, so I applied to go on to
Pathfinders and went off to 83 Squadron. I'd only been there
twenty-four hours when I got a call from Guy Gibson. He said,
'I'm starting up another squadron for a special raid; I can't tell
you what it is; but if you'd like to join me again I'll be only too
willing to have you back.' I said, 'Yes.' So I didn't do any flying
with Pathfinders at all.

I'd first met Guy Gibson when I was in 106 Squadron in June
1942. He'd initiated me into operations over enemy territory.
When I was flying with him I seemed to be able to read his mind
and anticipate every move he expected of me as his co-pilot and
flight engineer. He seemed to be able to relax when I was with
him in the cockpit. I was just twenty and Guy was four years
older than me. Guy and I did five operational trips together with
106 Squadron. One thing we very much shared was a hatred of
the Hun.

Guy Gibson, like Cheshire, was a magnificent leader, but in
completely different ways. Both of them were pied pipers, people
followed them. You either loved Gibson or you were scared of
him. He could be very tough. But Cheshire could be cold and
hard, yet he had a wonderful sense of humour. All told with an
absolute straight face; until you got to know him, you didn't know
how to take him. Gibson's humour was more robust, very earthy.
He had an eye for the ladies and he was, off duty, a great boozer.

617 Squadron assembled at Scampton, at the end of March
1943. To start with, Gibson just said that our brief was to practise
formation flying in threes as low as we could get. It was left to
us what height we considered to be safe. Then he said that he
wanted us to become proficient down to 150 feet. The altimeters

on the Lancasters were pretty dicey then, so this needed practice. We were flying all over the country at 150 feet; our navigation officers would just map out a route that they thought was suitable.

We didn't know what we were going to do for a long time. It must have been getting on for late April before we were told that we should start flying over lakes, and that our target would be over water. Everybody thought it was going to be U-boat pens or battleships; nobody thought that we were going to attack some bloody dams. At that time none of us, apart from Gibson, the Nav Officer and the Gunnery Officer and those people, knew what the target was to be. So we went and practised low flying over various lakes and reservoirs.

Then there were problems and Barnes Wallis scratched his head and said, 'Well, we can't use what we've got unless you can get down to sixty feet.' And that's when they put the nose and tail Aldis lamps in the aircraft: when the light beams converged on the ground, you were at sixty feet. The navigator looked out and guided the pilot. We practised doing that quite a lot at dusk and dawn over the aerodrome runway. It was fairly low for night flying; you'd be going across the middle of the aerodrome and the navigator would be saying down, down, down and you thought he'd never stop. You just had to accept that he knew what he was doing. We were more accurate over the water. We were flying over the Wash, getting down as low as we could, and were aiming and hitting targets six feet in diameter with practice bombs.

We didn't get the bouncing bombs until three days before the raids. A number of us were given the opportunity to go down and drop a dummy over the sea off Reculver to get the feel of how the aircraft would react when the 9,000lb of revolving steel was released. The vibration was the thing – you had to try and hold the plane steady. Our only target was a couple of posts on the beach. We had to fly towards them just to get down to the height and line up with them with a hand-held 'V' bombsight which would determine the distance we were away before we dropped the mine. When released the mine behaved like a flat stone that you skimmed across the water.

The briefing finally began on 16 May 1943. Contour-scale models of the Mohne Dam, the Eder Dam, and the Sorpe Dam were unveiled, and we were told to study them. We also learned what the strategic significance of the dams was, and what our flight routes were. Then Barnes Wallis explained his bouncing bomb. He told us the speed required at the time of release was 220mph, at the height of sixty feet. The distance at right angles over the water back from the dam wall was 410 yards. The bomb would then bounce three times, arrive at the dam, roll down to a depth of thirty feet and then explode. There was also the normal Intelligence briefing on enemy defences. The weather forecast was good for that evening. Security was very tight: no telephoning out, all mail censored. One chap was dismissed for breaking silence: he had telephoned his girlfriend. Guy Gibson was quite brutal, he dismissed him in front of the squadron. Security was the key thing.

In the end there were nineteen of us. As we were walking out to our aircraft Hoppy Hopgood grabbed me and we went round the back of a hangar to smoke a cigarette. He said, 'I think this is going to be a tough one, and I don't think I'm coming back, Dave.' That shook me a bit. I said, 'Come off it, Hoppy, you'll beat these bastards; you've beaten them for so long, you're not going to get whipped tonight.' At 9.30 p.m. with a full moon we took off. We were the first wave; nine of us, in three formations of three, went with Gibson. Our target was the Mohne Dam, and if we broke that, we were to go on and do the Eder Dam. The second wave's target was the Sorpe Dam.

Gibson and Martin and Hopgood went first. They were followed by me, Dinghy Young and David Maltby. Then came Henry Maudslay, Bill Astell and Les Knight. That was the first nine. Six of us got to the target area and the last three were told to hang around a bit on the outskirts of the dam at a safe height, so they could see what was going on.

Gibson went in first and made an excellent run. A huge bloody spurt of water went up hundreds of feet, but the wall was still there. Hopgood went next. He had been hit coming over with light flak and was hit again in the petrol tanks. I think the bomb-aimer was probably killed because he dropped his bomb late, and instead of skimming up and then sliding down the wall it bounced and went over the wall on the hydro-electric plants beneath. He got his plane up to about 500 feet, then it burst into flames. Hoppy's prediction had been proved right. Two people somehow managed to get out of that terrible smash and pulled their para-chutes. They were taken prisoners-of-war.

The next run of that flight was Micky Martin. While he was doing the run Gibson flew down on one side to try and attract the flak that was coming up all along the wall and on the pillars. Martin dropped his bomb and it got to the wall and exploded but didn't break it. Then Young went in. He had Guy on one side and Martin on the other side flying down. He had a very success-ful run. We thought, Christ, that must break the bloody thing, but no, it was still there. Then Maltby did a perfect run in. Gibson and Martin were still on either side, but by this time the flak-gunners were becoming a bit more subdued anyway. I think they saw the splashes and things coming at them. But still, that one didn't seem to break it. I was just starting my run in when sud-denly the wall collapsed and Gibson yelled, 'It's gone, it's gone! For Christ's sake, David, hold off.' The wall had gone. I think it was probably Maltby and Young between them who'd smashed this bloody great wall with their bombs in the right place. It was a tremendous sight, we just saw the tail end, but the water was getting more and more and faster and faster – it poured out of the lake, taking everything in front of it. After a few minutes it was just an avalanche of mud and water and stuff going down the hill.

Each time a bomb had been dropped, we'd sent a signal back to base saying, 'No go, no go!' 'Nigger' was the code word if we broke one, and after five runs on it, and the loss of an aircraft, they eventually got the 'Nigger'.

Then we flew east-south-east to the Eder Dam. The flight time was only about ten or fifteen minutes, but it was terribly difficult because by now it was well after midnight and early summer fog was coming up. It was difficult to navigate because the lake had two arms. I ran down the wrong arm to start with and said, 'I'm not there.' Gibson was right over the dam by then, and he fired a Very light. We saw that and moved over.

The Eder Dam was a bugger of a job. For a start it was much larger than the Mohne Dam. I was first to go; I tried three times to get a 'spot-on' approach, but was never satisfied. To get out of the valley after crossing the dam wall we had to put on full throttle and do a steep climbing turn to avoid a vast rock face. My exit with a 9,000lb mine revolving at 500rpm was bloody hairy! Then Gibson told us to take a breather and Henry Maudslay went in. On his third run he dropped his mine, and it was the same as with Hopgood: his bomb hit the top of the wall, bounced over, and got the power stations below. Then there was a tremendous flash as Maudslay's aircraft blew up.

Gibson told me to have another run. It seemed pretty satisfactory and we dropped. We made a breach way down under the wall and the rear-gunner shouted out that there was a bloody great hole below and the water was pouring out. But the top was still intact. Now only one aircraft remained, Les Knight. He came in, made two practice runs and hit it bang on, and we'd smashed that one. So that was two dams completely written off.

After that Gibson told us to get the hell out of it, because there was no more that we could do: we had no bombs and we didn't have enough fuel to go on to the Sorpe. The second wave had gone to the Sorpe, but the Sorpe Dam was never broken: it was an earth wall dam, and the bouncing bomb wasn't the right weapon for it.

We went back individually, not in formation. I just got down on the deck and opened the throttles and went. We landed back at 4.00 a.m. on 17 May. I had been away about six and a half hours.

But the costs were high. Out of the nineteen aircraft that had set out, only nine returned – we had lost fifty-two lives.

We had a tremendous reception from the top brass in Bomber Command when we touched down. There was Bomber Harris, Sir Ralph Cochrane, and of course Barnes Wallis. We had proved his bombs would work, but he never for a moment thought the cost would be so high. He was in tears and a more distressed figure it would have been hard to imagine by the time the last aircraft had landed.

I suppose we had become hardened to loss, we could shrug it off. We had to, otherwise we could never have flown again. We were debriefed, then we all went back to the mess and opened the bar and started drinking. The beer started flowing till late in the morning, when we struggled off to bed, and slept for a few hours. Then there was a stand-down for survivors for a week. The whole thing really took off because it got so much publicity. The press were allowed to write about it and some brilliant journalist coined the name 'The Dam Busters'.

Flight Lieutenant Bill Reid

After training and a spell of instructing I finally started my ops with 61 Squadron, flying Lancasters. The very first operation was to Rheydt, near München-Gladbach, my second-dicky trip. The target was a ball-bearings factory.

The trip after that was to Stuttgart. That was tricky because it was a job to get up to the height carrying a full bomb-load. Normally for shorter trips we had to reach 10,000 feet over the aerodrome and then set course. We could see other planes beside us, and we just kept checking up on each other. Most ops were the same, except for once when I nearly hit someone at a turning-point on the Dutch coast. This plane came right across us, which happened from time to time, because everybody would be doing the same thing, at the same time. Anyway, this plane came across, and the only way out, of course, was to shove the plane's nose down to avoid it. I didn't realise until we got back that all our shells had jammed up in the channel leading to the gun-turrets. So there might have been a bit of a job if we'd been fired at.

Out of my first six ops, we had to land away somewhere else four times, because of bad weather. Once, when we had to land at Newmarket because of low cloud, it wasn't until the next day that I discovered there was an incendiary bomb stuck in the top of one wing! On the whole, though, we seldom saw anything of the enemy aircraft. That was why one of our sayings was: 'You're better with something up your backside, because it keeps you on your toes.'

Then, on the night of my tenth raid, we'd set off as usual; we were heading for Düsseldorf. As pilot, I got the full briefing, whereas the rest of the crew only had a specific briefing for their particular section – navigation, wireless operator, etc. All pilots made sure they knew the courses roughly anyway, for safety's sake, because it sometimes happened in training that the navigator would put Red on Blue – meaning an error of 180°, and give you the wrong heading. That's how I knew the rough headings after the navigator was killed.

We had just crossed the Dutch coast, when, suddenly, there was a great bang in my face. I thought it was predicted flak. We lost about two thousand feet, and I felt blood running down my face. I pulled the plane up and then I felt this pain . . . something had hit my shoulder too, it was just like a hammer blow. The crew were all right, except for the engineer; I think he'd been hit in the forearm. I didn't see any point in saying I'd been hit, in case they panicked. So I checked that everyone was OK. I trimmed the plane and we flew on. I still thought we'd been hit by predicted flak, but Cyril the mid-upper said, 'No, it was a Focke-Wulf 190.' But the first instruction I received was, 'Dive starboard.' I think his guns had jammed, but we flew on. We were at about 19,000 feet when – WHAM – again. We were really hit this time, and we started to spin down. At about another 2,000 feet below, everything went dead in my ears. There was no intercom, nothing.

My hands were a bit bloody, skinned, really, when the windscreen had shattered. So I pulled on my silk gloves, then my leather ones, and put on my goggles because the windscreen was out. Then Jim Norris was hit in the arm, and the port elevator damaged, so there was only half an elevator holding the aircraft straight and level. Together, we held the stick back and I trimmed off as much as I could. I asked Jim to get me another heading from the navigator and he came back and signalled that Jeff was unconscious, but I felt that it was not a permanent situation.

I looked out and got the pole star and knew we were heading about 120, south-east. And I thought, Well, we'll just carry on like this. That night we were actually aiming towards Cologne, dropping spoof flares there, and then turning at the last minute for Düsseldorf. I thought we were all right for timing, and I could see other planes beside me, so I knew we were still fairly well in the stream. Then on time I saw these flares come down ahead of us, obviously Cologne, and I turned up on to 060, the bombing run. As for Les, the bomb-aimer, he didn't really know what had happened yet, because we had been keeping things going, but let him know that we were now heading for the target and he set up the bombsight and switches. I opened the bomb-doors and looked for the three target indicators which I aimed at and kept her straight and level, and held it until I felt the bombs go off. Held it for the photograph, then turned and headed back to base. I just kept going. The oxygen supply had been hit, so Jim fed me little bottles of oxygen, I occasionally slumped forward on the way back and he would change the oxygen bottle. We came down to about 12,000 feet by then. When I saw water I went down to 7,000 feet and that was below our oxygen height.

Then all four engines cut. The engineer usually kept the tanks fairly level, in case they got hit, so you didn't lose your petrol, but he'd forgotten about it in all the hubbub. He just turned them on and they started up again. My biggest problem actually, was how to hit England. Then I saw some beacons flashing, and it was a wee station, EEH or something, and we couldn't get down.

We headed off, and I spotted a big canopy of searchlights further north, and headed for that. But on the way there I saw this big aerodrome with a Drem system of lighting, and it was big enough for us to land on. So I circled there, reduced my height, and said, 'Stand by for a crash landing.' And, of course, we'd no hydraulic pressure, because the bomb-doors had stayed open. But we used the emergency air bottle and let down the undercarriage, then I flashed my landing-lamp on and off, and kept circling. They put some big sodium flares out because it was a bit foggy, and we took a low approach coming in. As we touched down, the under-carriage legs collapsed – they'd been shot through. We went along on our belly for about fifty yards, and it was only then that I realised Jefferies was dead, because he slid forward down beside me.

We'd landed at an American aerodrome, Shipdham in Norfolk. They took us into their hospital; the only thing I remember is that I was as dry as a bone, dying of thirst, and they gave me a drink of water. They stitched me up, and I went off to bed. The next morning they took us to Norwich Cottage Hospital, and two days later we were shipped down to the RAF hospital at Ely. Jim Mann, the wireless operator, died the next day.

Air Vice-Marshal Cochrane, the Base Commander, came to see me that first week. He said he'd heard my story from the rest of the crew, but he wanted to hear it from me. He asked me why I didn't turn back, and I said that I'd thought it was safer to go on, rather than turning back among all the other planes; I mean eight or ten miles of aircraft all flying in the same direction. I said if one of the engines had packed up I'd have turned round right away, but the plane was still flying. It wasn't that I was determined to drop the bombs or anything, but I just thought it was the safest thing to do at that time. Then he said, 'You know, Reid, the returns from ops have been practically nil since your raid. It's as if they all said, "That bugger, Jock, he went on even though he was wounded, so we can't turn back just because of a faulty altimeter, or something like that."'

I was at Ely for about a month, in all, but after a week or so, Jim Norris came in saying that he'd been awarded a CGM. And that was really the first time I'd thought about medals. I thought, Well, goodness, if he's got a CGM, I'll definitely get a DSO. It was only then that I really started to think about medals. On 12 December I was still in hospital, convalescing, when Cochrane rang, and he said, 'Let me be the first to congratulate you. The King has awarded you the Victoria Cross.' I nearly fainted.

I went from there on leave. My mother was so proud; my father had died just after I'd joined the Air Force, and she was alone in the house with my sister. That's something I often say: it was really a woman's war too. We'd had seven in our house when the war started: my mother and father, my elder brothers George and Jock, Jenny, my elder sister, and Lena my younger sister. By 1943, George had been killed in the Air Force, on Blenheims in 1940, my other brother was out in the Middle East in the Army, my father had died, and Jenny was married.

I went back in January to see Cochrane. He said, 'I suppose you're fed up with all the publicity? Well, now you're going to 617 Squadron.' No ifs about it.

So I went off to 617. I hadn't been there long when I was asked if I would take a cameraman back to Northolt. 'There's the plane,' they said. 'But we'll give you Squadron Leader Richardson, as your engineer, and such-and-such a wireless operator.' Of course I had no crew myself then, and I hadn't flown since 3 November, three months ago. But I wasn't worried. I flew down to Northolt, a short landing fighter drome. I came in to land, and Richardson had been doing something once or twice, and I thought he doesn't know much about the F/E's job. I was coming in to land, and I thought, Well, I'm a bit high but didn't want to overshoot. Then I thought I could make it if I cut the engines. So I came down and down, floating and floating, going off the runway and then I saw these piles of sandbags at the side of the runway. I just missed them as I got down, but the lower part of the tail fin caught them and broke off. You could look straight out the back of the plane!

We had to come back by bus! Wing Commander Cheshire was the CO then, and when he saw me, he said, 'It's my fault. After all you've been through, I should have given you a check, a few circuits before you flew off. I'm sorry,' he added, 'but I'll need to put an endorsement in your book.' So I think I'm the only pilot to get a Victoria Cross on one trip and a red endorsement on the next!

Then I started bombing trips. At that time, we were aiming at individual targets – V2s, U-boat pens, marshalling yards – and taking photographs of what we had done. I really enjoyed that. At the Saumur Tunnel, for instance, we dropped our bombs from 18,000 feet, and we got a good photograph. We were dropping 12,000lb bombs. To enable us to see the target, we used to bomb in a gaggle of planes. We aimed to have the bombs in the air at the same time, otherwise you'd need to wait maybe four minutes or so to let the dust settle. Then you could come in and bomb again. You were a bit vulnerable at that stage, because the enemy could shoot straight through, up at your aiming point, with their block barrage. That's what happened, the day I got shot down. We were on a daylight raid to Juvissy sur la Montagne, just east of Paris, aiming at a V2 bomb storage, a tunnel. We were to shut the southern end of the tunnel, by going through the roof of it with a 12,000-pounder. 9 Squadron were to shut the northern end, and then the others – there were three hundred planes on that raid – were actually bombing it with delayed-action 1,000-pounders, so that the tunnel couldn't be salvaged. It was an easy trip, and a lovely sunny day. In fact, this was the one time I took my camera with me, and I took some grand shots of us all together. We dropped our bombs, in a gaggle, and as I dropped ours Les shouted, 'Hold it!' because, of course, he wanted to take a picture too. There was flak coming up in front, but I held it there, and the next thing I knew – we'd been hit by a stick of bombs. I could smell the acrid smell from the flak. I said, 'Stand by and bale out' to the crew. The wires from the control column had been severed, so, of course, the plane started to spin out then, and a port engine, the port outer, I think, had fallen out. I couldn't get out of my seat. I pulled off my helmet, and tried to open the side window. Then I remembered the dinghy escape hatch. Chunky, my engineer, had handed me my parachute, then moved forward to go out the front with all the crew in the front. The rest of the crew got out through the back. As I clambered out, suddenly it went quiet, no noise, and I was falling through the air. I felt for my chute, and pulled the thing – it worked, and I hung on to those shrouds like grim death. Everything had happened so quickly. I was frightened in case I was hit by bits of the plane coming down. It was all probably below me already, but I didn't know. I saw these trees coming up, so I kept my legs together in case it did any damage . . . and I fell right into this tree-top. I don't know when I hit my leg, but I thought I'd broken it, it was just numb. I took my chute off, got down the tree, and took my Mae West off. My hand was broken, so I wrapped it up with my field dressing. Then, because we were supposed to act as front-line infantry if we were shot down, I got out my revolver. I'd lost the shells from my hip pocket when I'd baled out so I stuffed the revolver into the undergrowth with my Mae West. I could hear bombs going off, so I headed through the wood for about half a mile, then I sat down to check my escape kit. We were only thirty miles east of Paris, so I thought I'll go south; I could speak enough French to get by. Then I'd head west and try to catch up with the Allied troops. As I stood up again I heard, 'Hande hoch!' And so that was me in the bag. On the way back, there was this chap wearing riding breeches, who spoke better English than I do, and he thought I was American because it was a daylight raid. On the way I saw the tail part of my plane, and about fifty yards from the tail section I found the rear turret; the rear-gunner was inside it, dead. Inside the tail section I found the mid-upper-gunner dead as well. The front section of the plane was nowhere to be seen. So I thought, the lucky buggers, they've got away. But later after a doctor had looked at me, they brought in Dave Luker, my wireless operator. He didn't know what had happened to the others. We were in prison camp together, although not in the same hut.

When we were released in 1945, there was a notice up and it was only then that I found out the others had been killed. They must have been trapped in the nose. I was never very fortunate with my crews. It is very, very sad. When I see so many others who went through everything together, you know? That was the end of my war.

Just after the Gulf War I was asked to speak at a dining-in night at Leuchars, and I thought I'd make some reference to the difference between the two wars. It suddenly struck me what to say. We were schoolboys, and the majority of us looked at it as a tremendous thing to do, to get flying at all. We couldn't drive, let alone fly. And to fly a Lancaster, and a Spitfire, and all these planes was a tremendous thing. But these lads in the Gulf, they already had careers before they'd even started flying. They've all got degrees and whatnot, and wives maybe, and houses, and responsibilities. A lot of responsibility which we didn't have. And that's why we didn't have the same pressures on us. That's the main difference.

Flight Sergeant Norman Jackson

I joined the Air Force in 1939 just before the war broke out, when I was twenty. I'm an orphan, and I was brought up by a family whose name was Gunter, and I went to school under that name. On the first parade when they called out Jackson I didn't move. I got a hell of a rollocking from the Flight Sergeant. Anyway, I was a cheeky little sod in those days, so I went up to him and explained. He went to his desk, took two small bottles of light ale out, and gave me a drink. He just said, 'You know, boy, I'm convinced that you'll go a long way in this Air Force.' The name on my birth certificate was Jackson, so that's why it happened. From that day, I felt for the first time that I was somebody. I had an identity – Jackson.

First of all I was a Flight Engineer on the Sunderland flying boats in Coastal Command in Sierra Leone. I was on them for a year or two. In November 1941 I came back to Britain, and thought I'd have a bash at Bomber Command, so I volunteered. I flew in Manchesters first of all, then went over to Lancasters. I made thirteen runs to Berlin in the Lancasters; we used to do what they called spoof attacks. In other words while the main force would be going to Leipzig, we'd bomb Berlin – all those sorts of tricks. And we used to lay flares for 617 Squadron. With Berlin, you had to go straight there and more or less use the same route all the time. You had to, or you'd run out of petrol. It took about ten hours, a long journey, and we carried bomb-loads of about 14,000lb. I would sit with the pilot on take-off, at the throttle, watching instruments, checking the petrol gauges, and everything like that. Once we were up at a reasonable level I would remain on the flight deck. And then I'd be looking out for fighters.

We never had a pukka seat, just a little bit of canvas. The point was we had to be able to move quickly. I remember one occasion, when the rear-gunner was hit, knocked out, I had to go down and take over the guns, because I was trained as a gunner. Well, to do everything, really. So I took over the rear turret. As I got in there I couldn't believe my eyes. There was this Ju88 just below us. He knew he'd hit the rear-gunner, and he thought we were a piece of cake. All I had to do was more or less shut my eyes and pull the triggers. It blew up! It was that bloody close, he was right there. You see, he didn't expect a replacement so quick! But I was down there within seconds. What people don't appreciate is that the rear-gunner and the mid-upper were the eyes of the Lancaster. The crew I had was fantastic. I was with them right the way through. But now I am the only survivor.

One particular night we'd had a bloody good hiding, flak and fighters, and Christ knows what, and there was no way we could get through to the target, no way. We were losing power, everything. We dropped our bombs on an aerodrome we'd located, expecting to hit the runway or something, but we hit the ammunition dump and blew it up. They reckoned that we'd done more damage that night than the rest of our Command. It didn't half go up. The thing we tried to avoid though was getting coned. When you get coned, Christ! You were totally lit up. It was brighter than day inside the aircraft. What you had to do was get down quick, put the stick forward. They were bloody good at following you, though, there was no flies on them. You'd have to get down to what we called 'catch a train home', that low down. You wouldn't exist at 10,000 feet, they'd get you, no problem.

Some of those long raids to places like Königsberg were about eleven hours. And bloody cold it was too. Because of the distance and having to conserve fuel we couldn't carry a full load of bombs. We were after the rail yards in Königsberg; it was the only line open for supplies to get through to the Eastern front. Hundreds of aircraft went on that raid. And we got it all right. But like most raids, we lost a lot of aircraft, but you couldn't take any notice. All we wanted to do was to get back ourselves! After you've done a raid you forget it. If you weren't flying the next day you'd go home and get pissed.

The funny thing was you got used to it, took it in your stride. It was all in a day's work. You never thought about getting shot down. You just carried on doing your job. Some of the lads got a bit shaky at times. They used to call it LMF – 'lack of moral fibre'. They'd move those boys out of the squadron and put them on something else. Once you got that on your records, you were finished, no promotion, nothing, you weren't wanted. We were more scared of that than of going over to bloody Germany!

Our navigator was the bravest man I've ever met, because he was really scared, dead scared, and he carried on! I used to smell that he'd had a cigarette; his nerves had gone but he carried on. That was Frank Higgins. You see, the navigator was behind the curtain and he couldn't see what was going on. But we could. We were right in the middle of it. We could see the flak coming up, and the bullets from the fighters, and we were part of it. But all he knew was what we were saying – dive port, glide port or something like that. But he kept going. That took courage, great courage.

I was shot down on 26 April 1944. Our target was the ball-bearing factory at Schweinfurt. We'd had a lot of goes at that already. Anyway, we'd got our bombs down, and we were on the way out when we were attacked from ground and air. The flak was coming up and there were fighters all around. We all thought we were going to make it. I was sitting in the cockpit when we were hit, and I saw flames coming from the starboard inner engine, so I grabbed the fire extinguisher and put it inside my Mae West, it was smallish. We'd decided that either myself or the bomb-aimer would have to get out if there was a fire, since we were the only ones who'd been trained to deal with that sort of thing. I released my parachute inside so that the bomb-aimer and navigator could hold on to it in case I slipped. It was my duty to get out. There was a hatch behind me. I got out and slid down on to the wing. We were doing about 140–160 knots and we were at 22,000 feet. I hung on to the air intakes on the leading edge of the wing with one hand, and tried to put out the fire with the other. I'd got it under control, but the German pilot had seen me and was aiming at the engines, so the aircraft was shaking all over the place. I couldn't even jump, because they were holding on to my chute. Then I was shot off the bloody wing, and they threw the parachute out of the plane.

I was going down and watching it burn about me. It was in flames, and the holes in it were getting bigger all the time. I hit the deck fairly hard – bushes and I don't know what else broke my fall. I could hardly walk, my hands and my eyes were badly burned, and I got a couple of bullets and bits of shrapnel in my legs.

Anyway, I crawled to this village, picked a house and knocked on the door. The bloke opened the door and was bawling and shouting in German. Then two young girls came and pushed him aside. They took me inside and gave me schnapps and bathed my wounds. They were nurses from the hospital, and I thought, well, Maybe this won't be too bad, after all. The rest of the crew had been rounded up. The pilot and rear-gunner had been killed but the others were all right, so we were taken to a police station. The others were knocked about a bit, but I was in the worst shape. I could only just see. After the police station I went to a German hospital where they patched me up. I was in there for about eight or ten months. As a matter of fact, the pilot that shot us down later came into the hospital to say hello, which I thought was nice of him, the bastard. The doctor who looked after me was a captured Australian called Sherman. I was very lucky, he was brilliant. He just let my face heal, no plastic surgery, and the same with my hands. They used linseed oil to cover the burns. I could walk just about, but they had to do everything else for me. But so many people were worse off – there were people without faces there – terrible! We were treated quite well in the hospital; we used to muck in and help each other. I got better slowly and was eventually taken to a POW camp.

The POW camp was next door to Belsen. We knew what was going on there. You could smell it, and Christ, you used to see them coming through on the trains. Sometimes we'd go down to the railway, to collect the Red Cross parcels. That's when we used to see them – starving, thin people.

It was obvious the war was coming to an end, so I escaped from the camp and handed myself over to an American officer. He took me into a school, and sat me down. There was bloody eggs and bacon and Christ knows what! All of a sudden, a great big arm came across the table and swiped it away. It was a British officer who said, 'Sorry, boy. You're not touching that food until you've had a thorough medical.' I was then put on a diet of boiled eggs and lettuce!

I went to Buckingham Palace to get my VC. Leonard Cheshire was there to get his. I knew him because I used to operate with him in 617 Squadron. We were the only VCs that day. He insisted that we walk up together. I can't remember what the King said to him, but Cheshire said, 'This chap stuck his neck out more than I did – he should have the VC first!' Of course the King had to keep to protocol, but I'll never forget what Cheshire said.

The first telegram I received when I got my Victoria Cross said, 'Well done, I knew I was right. Your ex-Flight Sergeant.' No name, just 'ex-Flight Sergeant'. I was very moved by that.

Flight Lieutenant Bob Knights

I had a crash in 1942 which immobilised me. I was lucky to get out of it. It immobilised me for six months at least. I then went to a Wellington Operational Training Unit at Cottesmore. It was at OTU that one got one's crew, really, and the way in which crews were picked was a very haphazard affair. I got a crew there, but I discovered afterwards, I didn't really get the crew, they got me. The rear-gunner I got, a chap called Pop, was an old sweat who'd been in the Air Force a long time. He had a great deal of courage. At OTU, he apparently looked around at who was available, and he got himself a navigator, a bomb-aimer, and a wireless operator; and he wanted a pilot. He said to the bomb-aimer, 'There's a pilot over there who's had a crash, so he'll be more bloody careful next time.'

We picked up the flight engineer when we went to the Lancaster conversion unit at Swinderby; from there we went to 619 Squadron. We did most of a tour in 619 towards the end of 1943. At the end of a tour, one normally went to OTU to instruct. But we didn't want to go back to OTU; we wanted to do something a bit more challenging. So we thought of going to 617 Squadron. We got the agreement of the rest of the crew and I first went to see my CO. He thought it was all right; and I next had to go for an interview with Leonard Cheshire at 617, and he agreed. So we went to 617. It was an extremely satisfying period of my career. I spent most of 1944 at 617. I didn't know anything about it when I first went there, apart from the fact that it was a special squadron. And of course they'd done the Dams Raid. Unlike the main force, 617 had the SABS – a precision bombsight that gave them the ability to bomb small targets. But Leonard Cheshire had decided that the bombing accuracy wasn't good enough. He decided that one had to mark the target: to see it, and put a marker on it so that with the aid of this marvellous bombsight, the squadron could bomb it.

He tried this first on the Gnome and Rhône aero-engine factory, at Limoges. We got very strict instructions that no French people were to get killed if we could avoid it: the bombs had to fall within the target area. Leonard Cheshire flew up and down in his Lancaster, with Micky Martin, so that the workers got out of the factory. Then he put markers, 'red spot fires', on the factory. And the rest of the squadron bombed these red spot fires. Practically the whole factory was blown away, because in those days we used 8,000-pounders or 12,000-pounders. That was my first bomb raid with 617.

The next one we made was probably the only unsuccessful raid we went on with 617. We went to the Antheor Viaduct, between France and Italy which carried very important rail traffic. It was very heavily defended by light flak. Leonard and Micky weren't really able to mark it, because of the intensity of the defences.

But after that we had an almost unbroken run of success. In the raids I was on, I don't think we were ever unsuccessful. Most of the targets we attacked were either destroyed or not used again. We went for railway sidings, we did aero-engine factories, ball-bearing factories, then in the summer of 1944 we went for the U-boat and E-boat pens on the coast of France.

During this period we got the Tallboy, from Barnes Wallis, the inventor. At twelve thousand pounds, this was the perfect bomb. But no matter how well you fly the plane, no matter how good the bombsight is, bombs have an inaccurate fall path: they have what is known as trail. And depending on the altitude they're dropped from, that uncertainty could be exaggerated into a large error. A Tallboy had to be dropped at something like 14,000 feet for it to achieve its terminal velocity, but when it landed it would be exactly under the aeroplane. You knew exactly where the bomb was going to fall. So now we had the Tallboy and the SABS bombsight, which meant that with very accurate flying and the masterly, judicious movement of the bombsight by the bomb-aimer, we could bomb within a very small margin.

The first time the Tallboy was used was on the Saumur Tunnel. It was a very important railway line connecting the south of France with the beachhead in Normandy. It was important because a lot of the German troops were on the wrong side of the Seine.

Getting those troops on the wrong side of the river had been 617's task on D-Day. We had simulated a convoy sailing up the Channel towards the Pas de Calais, to make the German radar operators think that the invasion would be there. It involved very accurate flying: while the whole thing moved forward at ten knots, we had to fly round and round and drop a continuous stream of window simulating ships. This was very effective, and all these German troops were caught in the wrong place. The tunnel was most important as a way to get them across the Loire and so up to Normandy.

Well, Leonard Cheshire marked this thing with spot fires, and the first bomb that went down blew the spot fire up; it went straight through it! That was the accuracy we had.

After that, we used Tallboys all the time for the rest of 1944. The amazing thing about the Tallboy was that it would go through an immense amount of concrete. The Germans had built shelters for their U-boats and E-boats, thinking that no bombs would go through, so the E-boats and U-boats could rest in there, and then come out when they wanted them. But of course the Tallboys went right through the roofs and exploded inside and blew the whole lot to smithereens. We also went to the V1 and V2 sites, which were quite well protected, but once again the Tallboys went through the lot.

Then, of course, there was the *Tirpitz*, which was even heavier than the *Bismarck*. It was the biggest ship in the German Navy.

The *Bismarck* had been heading back to port after a naval engagement in which she was damaged. A torpedo from the Swordfish flying off the aircraft carrier *Ark Royal* crippled the steering. Attacks by *King George V* and *Rodney* mortally damaged the *Bismarck*. She was finally sunk by torpedoes from the *Dorsetshire*. Hitler was rather terrified, I think, of losing his other capital ship. So *Tirpitz* never really did anything, apart from scare the living daylights out of their Lordships at the Admiralty; they wanted it disposed of, one way or another.

It was attacked quite a number of times between 1942 and 1944. All sorts had a go at it: Halifaxes; Don Bennett, famous afterwards as the Pathfinder man, led a squadron against it; Fleet Air Arm; Midget submarines. Nobody really knew if it was damaged, or how much it was damaged, it was all assumptions. Winston Churchill was constantly being pestered by the Admirals about it. So it was decided they had to sink the *Tirpitz*. This was laid on in September 1944.

At this time the ship was moored at Alten, right up in north Norway. It was beyond our range, really, even for the Lancaster. So they decided that it would probably be a good idea to go to Russia.

We were briefed to go to an airfield outside Archangel. We flew to Russia with 9 Squadron. I remember flying over Stockholm which was the first city I'd seen lit up since the war started. Then the next thing I remember is coming out over the White Sea, in the early morning, and as it began to get light we saw another Lancaster. And I said to my navigator, 'You've done well, Terry, there's another Lanc over there. And if he knows where you're going, we know where we're going, don't we?' Eventually we came out right over the airfield at Archangel, an island in the river, a grass field, one or two Lancs had found it, and we landed. Next we were greeted by the Russians, and given glasses of vodka. Which is the last thing one wants after a ten-hour trip!

We lived on a house-boat while we were there which had bedbugs and very primitive sanitary conditions. The food was pretty primitive too, but when you're all together in a place like that you don't mind these things. You joke about them anyway.

After about a couple of days, we filled up with Russian petrol and went off to attack the *Tirpitz*. I was very conscious of saving fuel. My engineer was an old Auxiliary Air Force man and very keen on not getting lost through lack of fuel, so he had me trained on how to save fuel – get the boost up and get the revs down. We left Archangel on 15 September and as soon as we got off down went the revs, and immediately it started to pink! We had to put the revs back up. It was the Russian petrol, pretty poor low-octane stuff.

Anyway, we flew to Alten, and as we approached we could see the ship lying there. The Germans saw us just as quickly as we saw them. I suppose we must have been thirty miles away. They let off smoke which began to roll, most efficiently, and before we even got to the start of the bombing run she was obscured. Nobody could have hoped to bomb her with any accuracy, although they do say that a bomb damaged her. We lost an engine over the target, and we took our bomb back to Archangel. We were then moved back to England.

But of course the Admirals were determined to get this ship. The Germans had moved her down, fortunately for us, to Tromsø. Which was that much further south, and it meant that the Lancaster with an overload tank could get to Tromsø and back from Lossiemouth or Kinloss. At weekends we used to go up there to stand by to bomb the *Tirpitz*. This was a very pleasant interlude as they had an excellent chef in the mess!

Well, then we eventually went. We flew from Lossiemouth and Kinloss on 29 October past Orkney and the Shetlands and then turned right to cross the Norwegian coast, at low level, as fast as we could. We climbed up over the mountains, went into Sweden, up the border, and attacked her on a heading of north-west.

Just as we began the run up, low cloud came over the target. Well, we were running up nicely, all I had to do was keep the aeroplane exactly on the right height, speed, and course. So I asked the bomb-aimer, Arthur, what sort of a run he had on. He said it was absolutely magnificent, the ground speed was spot on, the drift was spot on. I said, 'Well, let it go then.' So the next thing I heard, was 'Christ, we've sunk it!' The bomb had gone right beside the ship, and turned it over on its side. Then he said, 'I don't believe it, it's come up again!'

So we didn't sink it, but apparently the bomb did a substantial amount of damage; it tore the *Tirpitz* open, and it would never sail again under its own steam. But we didn't know that at the time.

We went again on 12 November. The raid was almost identical, really, but the weather was gin clear. A fighter squadron, whose job was really to protect *Tirpitz*, didn't turn up. So we were unhindered and we had a very good run on it.

There was a line of us. Willy Tait, the CO at the time, was leading. We had a turning-point, where we had to wait for zero hour, as it were, it was a bit like a yacht race really. There were five or six aeroplanes from 617 Squadron all in a line and all converging towards this bombing position. Our bomb-aimer and engineer actually saw our Tallboy go down the side of the ship, and watched the other bombs fall as well.

They didn't have any smoke, in Tromsø, but there was plenty of flak, huge lumps of flak that came off the *Tirpitz*. We'd never seen anything like it.

You had to fly straight and level for about thirty seconds to get the bombing photograph, which I was very keen on doing. You can't get the aeroplane right over the bombing point, because obviously, when you lose 12,000lb it wants to jump forward like an unleashed greyhound. So you've got constantly to throttle it back. And it wants to climb, so you're pushing it down to 14,000 feet, which means the target photograph will be slightly off-set.

I asked Arthur to plot all the bombs he saw while we were doing this run. I was interested in what the bombing accuracy was like. So when he had dropped his bomb, he waited for the photograph to go, and he plotted what he saw after that on his chart. When the photograph had been taken I peeled off and went down lower. And we could see then that the *Tirpitz* was actually mortally wounded.

We stayed for quite a time which was rather foolish because of the possibility of fighters above and the flak below. But I felt that I had to see her go. She went very slowly. What a sight. She was a beautiful ship and well, it was sad really. That was my last trip with 617 Squadron.

Flight Lieutenant Paddy Forsythe

I went over to Bomber Command about the middle of 1944 and flew Lancasters. I did a tour of 32 raids on places like Hamburg, Dresden and Nuremberg. There were usually about 33 aircraft from each airfield on a raid. We would aim for somewhere like Paris and then divert; a spoof raid gang would go off towards a false target to take the German fighters off.

We often had great trouble at the beginning of a raid, because we had climbed to 20,000 feet with six hundred aircraft pushing through a small space. You would suddenly hear a big rumble over your head and you'd see these four engines and that was all you would see. They'd just missed you. It was quite frightening.

The weather was very frightening at times too. In bad weather the propellers used to ice up. You would hear ice coming off the propellers and banging down the fuselage. The instruments would ice up till you were flying purely on revs and artificial horizon.

The target city was lit up by chandelier flares. We were told by the master bomber what to target for. We aimed our bombs on to the chandelier flare. If we hadn't got that guidance we aimed the bomb to where we thought was the right position according to the brief. Usually we had the Pathfinder force marking the place out. Often once we got near the target area the Germans would drop chandelier flares and light up the whole area and we would see the German fighters all around us. It was just sheer luck which of us were picked out. You had to fly straight and level for a period when you were bombing and you were in great danger then because the Germans had upward-firing cannons. They could come underneath you and blast the whole bottom out.

I was coned two or three times: they'd get you pinned in a searchlight and fire up these radar-controlled rockets which you could see screaming past the aircraft. I lost a rear-gunner that way: he just completely collapsed and became a jibbering mass. We managed to get out of that cone by using the corkscrew method. We were very fortunate. But he never came back, that young man. I also lost a bomb-aimer when the aircraft was hit. There was only one aircraft hit of the 262 that went out and it was mine. He was hit by a bloody cannon shell which went through the front of the compartment. When we got back to the base they just hosed him out because there was nothing left. Your gunners would tell you there was an aircraft, and he would say, 'Corkscrew, corkscrew, starboard, go immediately!' You would peel away and you would see these bloody tracers flying past your bloody tail. You had this business of looking below you to make sure no-one was coming underneath you as well.

Once, on a raid over Nuremberg, my gunners claimed they shot down one-and-a-half fighters. I couldn't see what was happening behind me but they were absolutely certain that they got them.

I was on a daylight raid over Hamburg. It was my first one. We were always told to keep close together, and we were in what they call a gaggle. The Germans were out on either side and I saw for the first time the new German fighter, the Me262, coming down and he took these two Lancasters out just like that – bang, bang. It seemed about a minute before our fighter cover came after them; by that time the 262 was out of sight. God knows what would have happened if Germany had been able to build enough of those to have a real go at us.

The raid on Dresden was very, very long. We were in the aircraft about eleven hours. It was towards the end of the war, but we were still very conscious that we had a job to do. We were clearly briefed on that raid on Dresden to go for the marshalling yards.

We were supporting the Russians and there was no question of taking out everybody. It was a summer raid; one of these raids with our counter spoofs going to other targets. We didn't have to fight the whole way into the target as we had had to do on two or three occasions to Nuremberg. I was flying a Lancaster. That was almost the last raid. The Germans sometimes followed us right through the attack. Towards the end of 1944 they'd follow us right back to our own airfield and shoot down the chaps in the circuit.

The first thing we did after landing was to go and be debriefed. They used to list all the aircraft that had gone out on a board, under the Captains' names. So you could see by the blanks who hadn't come back. There would be blank five blank eight blank 33 or something like that. You had to wait maybe an hour or so to be certain because there were three emergency landing-places. The people back at base didn't know until a plane had landed whether it was shot down or not. It was a terrible thing because you knew who was missing. You went off to your bacon and egg breakfast and you waited till morning when you got up to see who wasn't there.

The other thing was whether the chap who was shot down was going to be a prisoner-of-war or not. Usually at debriefing, if you saw an aircraft go down, it would be corroborated by five or six other aircraft. You would have counted who got out of the aircraft. Sometimes you didn't see anyone come out at all and you knew they'd gone straight in. I remember one Hamburg raid in daylight where we saw seven of our aircrew drop into Hamburg but we never heard of them again. Not a single one. I suppose the Germans took them apart, but they never returned. I fully understood that. I think the Germans had it the other way – if a pilot baled out over Liverpool they were in deep, deep trouble. I felt mostly for the aircrew that were married with their wives living near the base. That wife would count those aeroplanes back in. She always knew there were two or three not coming back: was it her husband? It must have been absolute hell for those people, absolute hell. Thank God I was not married then.

It was a very hard war. We usually had a day off and then we were back out again, and Hitler didn't let us worry about weekends or anything. It was a seven-day week, really. We'd get a break of five or six days every now and then. That was one thing I never really agreed with. I'd like to have got the whole thing done with. It brought you back to reality and then you had to go back into it again. I've never forgiven my mother – she came over one time when I was having a pretty bad time, and she brought me back to reality.

Just towards the end of the war we went to Holland with food. Holland was very, very hungry. We put all this food on hessian underneath the bomb bays and went into The Hague and dropped it. It was quite terrifying, because we came in at two hundred and fifty feet from these Germans and all their ack-ack guns were following us about two hundred yards away. The war wasn't over; if they'd changed their minds they could have blown us out of the sky. It was quite eerie. I remember seeing a big tin of Spam being dropped in the village street below me. A little boy rushed like mad and got the Spam but he didn't have a chance because all the older people almost tore him apart to get it. That was called Operation Manna. It was a very good exercise.

Throughout the war, what never ceased to amaze me, was the tremendous spirit and co-operation of the ground crew. They wanted it right for you. You could virtually fry an egg on the floor of the Lancaster, because they had it so polished. They knew every bit of dirt would slow the aircraft down.

At the end of the war I took the ground crew to the areas I'd been to, to have a look at what had been happening. I can always remember my father saying about the First World War, that it was the war to end wars, but looking at the devastation in Germany, which was far worse than anything we'd seen in Coventry or Liverpool, convinced me that the Germans had now had a taste of what they'd never had in the First World War, and that *this* would be the war to end wars. And in fact it has been.

Squadron Leader Jimmy Malley

I joined the Royal Air Force on 3 January 1940, at the age of twenty-two. I was a civil servant pre-war, and had planned to take my law degree, but I never went back to it. After I joined in Belfast, I went to Cardington for a few days, and then for ITW I went to Hastings but we had to evacuate from Hastings and I continued at Torquay. After the training was over – that would have been about March 1941 – I went to 149 Squadron at Mildenhall, in Wellington 1Cs. I trained as an air observer. I stayed with the crew and Wellingtons the whole way through my first tour of operations.

The crew got to know each other just through day-to-day practice. We didn't live in the same hut because the pilot and I were commissioned. And we drank very little – unless you knew you were going to be on the next night, you kept away from it if possible. We came from different places: one Welshman, one Scotsman, and two Englishmen. The pilot and the rear-gunner were English. The Captain was Doug Foreman. As a crew we were damned lucky; and happy.

So we trained on Wellingtons in an Operational Training Unit (OTU) and then were given a plane. Our first plane was actually *F for Freddie* – the one that made the film, *Target for Tonight*. I heard on the radio years after that *F for Freddie* had gone to an honourable retirement, but the 'honourable retirement' was a crash-landing into a bombing range when we were on our way back from bombing *Gneisenau* and *Scharnhorst* at Brest. We were kept waiting and eventually had to crash-land into the bombing range just seven or eight miles from Mildenhall. So *F for Freddie* was completely written off.

But in the spring of 1941 our people were doing very little offensive. We were the only people that were taking any offensive action at all. My first offensive was a night raid in April 1941. Our target was Kiel. There would have been about 30 or 40 aircraft going out: Wellingtons, Whitleys and Hampdens. It was an uneventful raid; the first four or five trips were all quiet. There was flak coming up, and it looked terrifying. Of course, we were all nearly the same age in the crew; no one had any more experience than anybody else.

We spoke very little during the runs; I had to work the whole time. My job first of all was to find how accurate the forecast wind was. Once you found the actual wind you solved a lot of your difficulties. We had the triangle of forces then: to find the wind you had to find some point on the ground. Then I would give the pilot the course to steer about every half hour. Once I found a change in wind I could reckon what the other winds were going to be because I had a weather map. I'd also be telling him how long he had to go. Accuracy wasn't bad – within 10–15 minutes. We never knew what we were expecting to see, but we gradually got used to it. Mind you, a target like Kiel was quite easy; anywhere on the shore was easy. We would see the shape of the coast in the black. We used to come in at about 8,000 feet. In the Wellington there was a big hunk cut out in the nose for bombing through. It wasn't even glass underneath – it was open. I sat just behind the pilot – sideways on. Then I'd go up to the front and look down to get a landmark, and then I'd go back again. On those first few raids we did get some of the bombs within distance of the target. It was very hard to tell exactly how far you were off, but you knew whether it was successful or not. In those early days there were no Pathfinders or master bombers; it was visual sighting but the pilot couldn't really see anything. He would have to listen to me – 'turn 5 degrees starboard' or something of that nature – then bomb away. I had the bomb control as well. Once the bomb was gone you couldn't follow it down. You'd see them bursting – it took about thirty seconds from 8,000 or 9,000 feet – but you couldn't be certain that it was your own bombs. Of course, the planes were never all there together. You could be spread out over twenty minutes to half an hour. But still, you would have to bob and weave to avoid each other, and there were no navigational aids for that. But once you were clear of Kiel you were quite safe, whereas later, when we were inland, it was a different matter altogether.

After the first ten raids we had settled down completely and were a crew. Everybody knew they could rely on everybody else. We were friends – it was as much as that. We were lucky in that we had the Bird in Hand at Mildenhall, only a hundred yards from the mess. You would find all ranks in there and often the crew would drink together.

Our first five missions were to the coastal areas – the next five were inland – into the Ruhr. It was during my first thirty missions that *F for Freddie* went out on the raid on *Scharnhorst* and *Gneisenau*. They were at Brest, and we went there about three times. They were in harbour because they were slightly damaged. And of course they wanted to get out into the Atlantic as well. We got them when they were in the docks. *F for Freddie* actually got something to them. Well, we claimed we did anyway! On to the *Scharnhorst*. They were really finished as ships from then on.

I think Essen was probably our first inland target though I can't be sure. Essen was one of the toughest targets: I never did a trip where I wasn't scared and you couldn't be at all certain that you'd hit the target. If my navigation was good enough we could avoid opposition coming back where we stayed at about 8,000 feet, sometimes up to about 10,000. The Wellington's ceiling was probably about 12,000 feet. So we couldn't fly above the flak.

I think we went to Hamburg about three or four times. Hamburg was even worse than Essen. Hamburg raids always were frightening efforts, absolutely. The noticeable difference was the intensity of ground fire. We were hit over Hamburg; nothing serious and the crew remained uninjured. But most of all we hated Berlin. That was because of the length of time we were in the air. Flying time to Berlin was about nine or ten hours.

I don't have the least idea now what the target in Berlin was. If you saw fire on the ground, you checked to see if you thought that was the target. We were so spread out by the time we got to the targets, that we weren't really an awful lot of help to each other; we weren't communicating at all with the other aircraft. You usually had about two hours' spare petrol. The long trip home was the worst thing of the lot.

Sometimes, if my navigation wasn't quite good enough we would come under fire on the way out. But by then I had learned the major areas to miss. We were learning the whole time. You went more on what you experienced than on what you were briefed.

The trouble about the Wellington was, once it got to about 8,000 or 9,000 feet it froze up. All your heating went because it was water heating. We were over Berlin one night when we ran into thick cloud. We were an hour and a quarter over the city, waiting. And I stupidly had taken off my glove – and as I told you before, I hadn't even a window below me, it was open. The temperature was probably about minus 5° or 6° at that height. When eventually I saw a small gap in the clouds, I got ready to bomb, and I suddenly realised I couldn't press the tit with my right hand at all. I had to use my left hand to press the tit and my right hand has never really recovered from that. I take three praxaline a day and have done ever since. It was over Hamburg, I think, that I first saw anyone shot down. It wasn't pleasant but at that time you got hardened. I think it was worse the first time you came back to base and found you had lost a couple of crews. And especially if they were friends of yours.

After the first ten raids, I remember going over the Alps into Italy. I honestly couldn't tell you why. Milan really was our target, it was about all we could have reached. The thing I remember best of that was going over the Alps. I had never really seen a mountain, and since we were flying at about 10,000 feet, we were actually going between the mountains so you had to be sure your navigation was right.

Then we got to the stage where we could see the end. I'd say the last five or six trips of that tour we felt – well, with any kind of luck, we're getting through. Although in a way some people were more scared at that stage, there was the feeling that the luck had been good up to now, and you didn't want it to run out.

I don't remember the last one, the 35th trip. We were weary but that was the one good thing about Bomber Command: you got your regular leave every six weeks. It had taken about eight months to do the 35 trips. I went home for leave. Everybody went home and then heard that 37 of our aircraft had been lost out of the 74 operating.

Then I went to Mildenhall as an instructor for about five months, then to Harwell where I took part in two of the first 1,000 bomber operations. I was due for posting to Scotland as an instructor, but there was a fellow due to go back on ops and he didn't want to, so we agreed to change. Then we went out on Liberators to the Middle East. We worked from Tel Aviv. Our targets at first were Tobruk, Benghazi and later on in that tour, Italy. We hit Cyprus a couple of times. At Tobruk we got a destroyer, though usually there and at Benghazi we were looking for fuel dumps. We did quite a few raids there in daylight; they were my first daylight trips. It made the navigation a lot easier. The stars are different in the Middle East of course, and though in theory we used astral, in practice we weren't good enough at astral to be really accurate.

There was quite a lot of flak in Benghazi, but not terribly often did we run into fighters. The Liberator was a very flexible plane anyway. It could take on the fighters. When we did the daylights we worked in formation: you had a batch of four and your fourth aircraft was underneath – the tail-end Charlie. On the Liberators there was a rear-gunner and a top-gunner and a front-gunner, and you could move your guns to the side.

After I had completed 32 trips the four of us were rushed back to England and we came first-class on BOAC. It was most luxurious: at that time you had beds on board in first class. I had about a fortnight's leave and then I became a Squadron Leader in charge of navigation training at the OTU. I enjoyed that: 30-odd trips is more than enough at any one time. I instructed until about May 1944. And then I put in an application to get back in operations on Mosquitoes. They made me go back for a full medical, I was turned down! But I appealed against it. I went to No. 1 Medical Training Unit, then, luckily the Air Commodore was a man called O'Mally. He said, 'Well, I couldn't pass you, but I'm not going to fail you.' So I then went into training for Pathfinders.

I was with 139 Squadron then, Mosquitoes. By that time navigation was utterly important. We did all the bombing on the H2S (H2S centimetric radar was an important technological breakthrough). So you actually knew the shape of the ground, and of the town where you were putting your markers. Towards the end of my fourth tour we were marking so accurately that the whole of the mission – and there could be up to 100 Mosquitoes following you – would get there at the right time. By one hundred miles short of target I'd have found the proper wind, and I'd have to change the aiming point. You always wanted to aim up into the wind because it cut your speed down and you could be more accurate. And I then told the rest of the Pathfinders the new aiming point. We all had the same aiming point – I was a Master Bomber for the last 10–12 trips and all five dropped our markers within a two-minute limit. Then that was our job finished. These were all night-time raids, but using the H2S it was the same as working in daytime. At one time the Germans cottoned on to the fact that they could home on to the H2S beams. Luckily our people got even cleverer, and fitted up another radar in the rear of the Mosquito that put a light on any time the German beams were tracking you. So you could take evasive action in any case. The Mosquito was a wonderful aircraft in every way.

I flew 53 missions on my last tour. They were all fairly well the same, though we took a hiding once or twice. One was on a night when we had flown ten nights in a row and were heading for a world record and our Commanding Officer was very keen for us to go on. We shouldn't have taken off on the eleventh night at all because the forecast was damn bad. It was low cloud all over England, and when we got back and found it like this, we had to go down to the south of England. We lost three crews, and about five aircraft out of our ten. My crew were damned lucky to survive, because we came through at about 300 feet underneath the clouds, and found ourselves clean over the runway. It all made one angry, because it was unnecessary. And the whole lot could have gone.

I flew 127 missions in all. We didn't know our last was going to be our last because at that time we were supposed to lead a daylight raid to Berlin with the whole of Bomber Command and the Americans but luckily peace came a few days before. Then I wasn't allowed to go out to Japan.

I was always very lucky with the crews. We were always friends. That was the best part. I don't remember targets and hits any more, but I remember that: the crew were always friends and they made everything worthwhile, even the fact that I was under eight stone when demobbed and had to stay in bed for eighteen months to recover from tuberculosis.

Flight Lieutenant Lewis 'Bob' Hodges

On the outbreak of war I was based at Finningley, in Yorkshire, flying Hampdens with 76 Squadron of 5 Bomber Group. We were a fairly new squadron in that we had only recently been re-equipped with Hampdens and therefore we didn't immediately become involved in active operations. In fact we were made into a training squadron and it was not until the summer of 1940, when I was posted to 49 Squadron at Scampton in Lincolnshire, that I started flying on bombing missions over Germany. By the time, June 1940, of the attack on France we were concerned with anti-invasion targets, bombing the ports along the Channel coast and the barges being assembled by the Germans for a possible invasion of England. We also took part in bombing attacks on ports on the Atlantic coast of France, such as Brest and Bordeaux, where the Germans were concentrating their submarines for the Atlantic war.

On 5 September 1940, we were coming back from a long-range

bombing operation, to the Baltic port of Stettin, which was, for us, a very long way, at the extreme range of the Hampden. The weather was very bad, the night very black, and we had great difficulty with the navigation; we were flying in cloud most of the time and it was impossible to get an accurate pin-point of our position on the ground. In those days the navigation was very primitive indeed; it was done by 'dead reckoning' and map-reading. Unknown to us, there was a very strong northerly wind, and we were blown far south of our course so that, at dawn, I found myself with a rocky coastline on the right-hand side, which I identified as being the Cornish coast, and I realised then that we had greatly overshot our destination in East Anglia. But then I saw an airfield which I thought I identified as St Eval near Padstow on the Cornish coast. We put the wheels down and prepared to land. Suddenly all hell let loose, and I received a blasting from anti-aircraft fire. I realised then we were not in Cornwall but in Brittany which by that time was part of the German-occupied zone of France. Our fuel gauges were reading zero, and one engine then failed, and I realised we would have to make a forced landing. I ordered the crew to bale out. Two of them jumped and came down by parachute, but we were then too low, so the gunner and I made a forced landing in a small field, with wheels up. We stepped out, and saw a farmer approaching. By interrogating him in my schoolboy French, I confirmed that we were actually in France.

We had been warned, in the event of this sort of thing happening, not to go to the coast to find a boat, because the coast was very heavily guarded by the Germans. The sensible thing to do was to make for the Pyrenees and cross into Spain, a neutral country. From Brittany, it seemed a long way to go, but nevertheless I decided that that was what we should do. The two other members of my crew landed safely some distance away but were captured.

After attempting, unsuccessfully, to set fire to the aeroplane, we set off as quickly as we could in a southerly direction, to get away from the crash. We knew the Germans would soon arrive on the scene, and we wanted quickly to put as much distance as we could between us and the crash. So we set off across country. We were very tired, having flown for ten hours, and after about an hour or so of walking we hid up in a wood. We took stock of our situation and decided that we would walk by day and hide up at night. This might seem a little odd in an enemy-occupied country. However, we calculated that in the German-occupied zone of France in the north, the population would be against the Germans and pro the Allies. We were confident we would be able to get help and be able to make more rapid progress across country by day. So this became our plan, and in the evenings we knocked on farm doors, told the people who we were, and asked if we could sleep in their barns and be given food. Almost always we were received very favourably by the Breton farmers, who, although poor, would share with us what food they had; and we found that the farmers had Post Office Calendars with maps of the local area on the back, and these proved invaluable for navigating across country, avoiding main roads and towns.

In this way we worked our way across France, down towards the Loire Valley. We were still in uniform but this was not too much of a problem because RAF uniform, if you take the jacket off, with its blue trousers and blue shirt, is not unlike clothes the Breton farm people wear. We carried our jackets, which had our rank and insignia, in a sack because they were our only means of identification; otherwise we could have been taken for spies. We had a problem with our flying boots. They were not designed for walking, and they soon gave us very bad blisters, but we were able to swap them for ordinary boots at a farm, but these were still uncomfortable, and we continued to have a lot of trouble with our feet. We walked south covering about twenty miles a day.

The first major obstacle that we were going to face was the River Loire which we aimed to cross near the town of Saumur. We knew from the local people that all the main crossing-points were heavily guarded with German sentries on all road and rail bridges. We were directed to a village east of Saumur where we were told we could get a small boat, and this proved to be the case. The river was very wide at this point and we were fortunate to find a young boy who agreed to row us across.

Safely over the river we continued south-east in the direction of Poitiers, towards the demarcation line marking the frontier between the German-occupied zone in the north and the unoccupied zone in the south under the control of the Vichy government. The next challenge, then, was to cross the line. Again the main-road crossing-points were guarded but clearly that whole length of the line could not be closely watched. There were, of course, German patrols, but in the countryside, with local knowledge, one could get across without too much difficulty.

We found a farmer who said he would take us close to the line, and we travelled unobtrusively in a horse-drawn cart. He indicated to us when to jump off and we disappeared into some woods which straddled the border between the two zones.

Once we were across the line and into unoccupied France, we thought: Now we're all right, but we found that, whereas in the occupied zone everybody was very friendly, in the unoccupied zone they had seen little of the war and they were not so geared to the Allied cause. Nevertheless we still received a great deal of help.

After a few more days walking we reached the area of Limoges and were put in touch with an English lady, who was married to a Frenchman. We discussed with them the best plan of action, and they directed us down to Luchon, in the middle of the Pyrenees. I'd never been to France before, and so had no real idea of the height and ruggedness of the mountains in that part of the border area. Anyway, they gave us money and we took a train from Toulouse. We got off two stations before the border town, because we thought that there would be guards there. We walked the last few miles, hoping to go round any guard posts but it was not as easy as we thought, because there was sheer rock on either side of the road, and we had no option but to keep straight on and we could not avoid the gendarmes at a road block just before the border town of Luchon. We tried to bluff our way through by saying we were Belgians, because there were a lot of Belgian refugees in the area, but they soon discovered that we could hardly speak a word of French, and we had to admit that we were RAF airmen. After a night in the local jail we were taken to a prison camp near Toulouse which the French Army had set up for German prisoners. There we met up with thirty other British – all soldiers from 51st Highland Division – who had been cut off by the rapid advance of the German Panzers in 1940, and had been forced to surrender at St Valéry. Many of them had managed to escape and make their way south.

We stayed at this camp for a month, and then collected together in the Foreign Legion barracks. There were around three hundred of us there in what became a British internment camp. Under the terms of the armistice which the Vichy government had negotiated with the Germans, all Allied nationals of military age in the unoccupied zone had to be interned.

It was now October 1940 and we heard a strong rumour that it was not a good idea to go to Spain because, if caught, we would be likely to be interned for the duration of the war. This wasn't true, but nevertheless the rumour was going round at the time. Marseilles was still a very active and busy port and we decided to try and stow away on a ship. The gendarmes guarding the Fort St Jean were friendly and it was not too difficult to persuade them to let us out into the town. We were then able to make a reconnaissance of the docks and assess the possibility of getting on board a ship. There were ships going to Beirut which seemed to be one option; Casablanca was another; but first we needed money to bribe our way on to a ship.

The Americans were not yet in the war and there was an American consul in Marseilles who was in charge of British interests. Through him we were able to get money which they said would come out of our pay. With all the complications of war I never thought that this would be the case, but eventually, when I got back to England, I found that my bank account had indeed been debited with this advance of pay! Anyway with the help of some Poles I was able to bribe my way on to the ship, the *Ville de Verdun*, which was going to Casablanca. My plan was a simple one: as the ship went through the Straits of Gibraltar it would be stopped by the Royal Navy and I would be taken off. My air-gunner, who had been with me thus far, decided not to join me on this escape but to try and make his own way to Spain.

Once on board the ship I was hidden in a hold below the crews' quarters, and after a day at sea I was told to come up on deck and to my horror I found that the ship was full of French airmen going to Indochina. The chances of remaining undetected for long were slim indeed and I was soon arrested. I was taken before the Captain to explain myself, and they then searched the ship and found Poles, Czechs, Dutch, and all sorts in hiding. I had no idea there were so many stowaways on board. The ship was then turned round and instead of heading for Casablanca set course for Oran where we were put in jail.

After a day or two we were shipped back to Marseilles and thrown into a civil prison which was very unpleasant, and I was charged with being a stowaway.

I appeared before the magistrate on several occasions and explained that I was a military prisoner, and that it was my duty to try and escape. I stayed in the civil prison for five weeks before they agreed that I should be released, and I went back to the internment camp.

By that time, it was January 1941, and the Marseilles camp had been closed and moved to St Hippolyte-du-Fort near Nîmes, which was better for us because it was nearer the Pyrenees.

I stayed there until April 1941, when I and another colleague, who by some extraordinary twist of fate had been at school with me, decided to escape together. He was Czech by birth, and he'd been in the Czech Army fighting in France at the beginning of the war. We forged ourselves a forty-eight-hour pass to Marseilles using the Commandant's typewriter, and because we had a military pass we were able to get a railway ticket at half-price! Instead of going to Marseilles we took the train to Perpignan, which is right on the Spanish border.

The next morning we set off on foot through the vineyards to the foothills of the Pyrenees. It was a fairly easy climb through wooded country and we crossed the unguarded border into Spain shortly after midday on Easter Sunday 1941. We were following a narrow mountain road and as we went round a corner we went straight into the arms of some Spanish customs officials and were thrown into jail again. There we saw on the walls of the cell the names of lots of other colleagues from the camps in France who had passed that way before.

We were taken via a series of staging posts to the famous and rather grim concentration camp of Miranda de Ebro near Burgos, where many hundreds of foreigners were incarcerated.

There were only a handful of British in Miranda and because we had the embassy in Madrid to look after us, I was in Miranda for only five weeks. Our release was secured, and they sent a bus up to the camp and we were taken to Madrid, where we were interrogated and our clothes were taken off us and burned. We were then deloused, given new clothes, then taken by train to Gibraltar. From Gibraltar I came back to England in a flying boat, and arrived at Plymouth, Mountbatten, in a Sunderland in June 1941. It had taken me nearly ten months, from the time I crashed in France, to return to England.

I suppose the toughest time was the period in the Spanish camp, but there at least one could see a light at the end of the tunnel. One knew that one was going to get away, and that it was just a matter of time, whereas earlier on in France, although the conditions in the internment camps were not at all tough, you couldn't see exactly what you were going to do. The worst conditions of all were in the civil prison in Marseilles. I had five Frenchmen, all criminals, in a small cell with me, and very poor food. We were sleeping on straw mattresses, lousy and full of bugs. That was a very unpleasant time.

The extraordinary thing was that although unoccupied France was cut off in the war, the post office seemed to function; you could send a telegram from Marseilles and get a reply within forty-eight hours. So I was able to let my widowed mother know that I was all right. Going right back to when we crashed, we always carried two homing pigeons in a basket in each bomber aeroplane. When we landed in Brittany I thought that the first thing to do was to send the pigeons off. Well, we had a bit of difficulty. Feathers were flying in all directions, and we dropped the capsule, which was to contain the message, in the long grass, and couldn't find it. We released that pigeon. Then we got the second one and managed to get the capsule off its leg. We wrote a message to the effect that we had crashed in France and released that pigeon. On enquiring in England ten months later, I regret to say that these pigeons, because they were intended for crews who came down in the North Sea flying back from Germany, were trained to fly from west to east, and not from south to north!

When I returned to England I went back to Scampton, where I had been based before. They were surprised to see me; I had had my hair shaved off in the concentration camp in Spain and so I looked a bit odd. The sad thing was of course that most of the friends whom I had known there in 1940 had disappeared. The casualties were pretty high; there were some familiar faces, of course, but a large number were completely new to me.

After a short spell of refresher flying I rejoined the squadron. I was only twenty-two and was back on operations in a few weeks. I suffered no ill-effects from my experiences, in fact my confidence was considerably enhanced because I knew that, should I come down in enemy territory again, I would know which way to go!

Flying Officer Reg Lewis

I spent my early years beneath the shadows of the cranes in the East End of London. I was born in Poplar, and went to school on the Isle of Dogs. When the war started I was about sixteen or seventeen, and had just started work in a stockbroker's office in the City. During the Blitz we were bombed out of our house, so we moved up the road to East Ham and, exactly a month later, what the first bomb hadn't done to our family's possessions, the second one did. My parents more or less lost everything. Being from a fairly tough area we were brought up to fight back. I naturally wanted to go into Bomber Command, and joined the RAF at the outset of 1941. By September 1943, having already completed a tour of thirty operations in Stirling heavy bombers and been awarded the DFC, I was posted with my crew for another type of 'bash' with 138 Squadron.

Tempsford was a very hush-hush place – the only airfield in the country from which the two special duties squadrons operated – 138 Squadron and 161 Squadron. Churchill was responsible for the formation of the Special Operations Executive (SOE), after the fall of France. Basically, his instruction was to set Europe ablaze, and that really meant encouraging fighters throughout the enemy-occupied countries. The only way to do that was to infiltrate skilfully trained agents, saboteurs and suchlike into the Continent. To instruct the local people in the use of arms and supply them with everything they'd need to inflict damage on the enemy, and eventually to train them to form some sort of fighting force. Of course we did also drop the odd spy. On 5 November that same year we went into Germany, which was very unusual, to drop someone, God only knows who he was, but he was wearing a Luftwaffe uniform. I never found out what happened to him. You had to be careful taking these people around. You couldn't just drop them anywhere, but into a precise corner of a field if required.

Unbeknown to us, of course, the D-Day landings weren't far

away, and it was important that we got a number of agents into France to organise the Resistance and cause as much havoc as possible for the Germans. Our squadron had been trying to drop one agent in particular – I think they'd had about two or three goes. Eventually on 7 February 1944 we were called together by the Station Commander, Group Captain Edward Fielden, Captain of the King's Flight, who said, 'You're taking this man' – his code name was Jockey – 'You're going tonight. He's got to be dropped on the outskirts of Marseilles.'

We took off in our Halifax at 1930 hours, in absolutely bloody awful weather. It was foul, dreadful rain. We went straight into cloud, and had to resort to dead reckoning, hoping the cloud would break later on. We got down into Central France, where the ground gets rather high, and flying in cloud, in winter, we iced up. Eventually the starboard-outer overheated, and caught fire. So we feathered the starboard-outer, starving the fire of fuel. This meant we were on three engines, still battling against the ice. It wasn't very long before the port-inner went. We were losing height, and tossing overboard things to try and lighten the load, but it was obvious that we weren't going to deliver the agent we were carrying to the appointed dropping-point; we didn't know who he was, but we knew he was important. He baled out but it wasn't long before our pilot, Cookie (Squadron Leader T. C. Cooke) said, 'We'll have to abandon aircraft.' It was about eleven-thirty. I'd thought it would never happen to me – we thought we were fireproof!

I was the first one out, and the flight engineer was soon after me. I can still remember that awful crack as you tumble over and the parachute opens. Then I was dangling in eerie silence. I heard my wireless operator calling out, 'Rocky' – that was my nickname. Anyway, I got down a bit further and all I could see was this great expanse of water. I thought, Christ! Just our luck – we're all going to perish in some bloody frozen lake! But as it was, it was an illusion – vapour or fog, or something. In fact, I landed in deep snow.

It was a mountainous area, out in the sticks, and very cold. I buried my parachute, then I tramped off across the snowbound fields. It wasn't long before I came to a house, all shuttered up in true French style. I thought it was a bit silly to knock at the first place I came to, so I walked on, but there was nothing else in sight. It was desolate. I was somewhere in the hills above the Rhône Valley, very wild, rugged country. I went back to the house and banged on the door, and a little old lady's face appeared. I was standing there in flying kit. They hadn't taught me much French back in Poplar, but I had a smattering, and I tried to explain that I was English, in the RAF – which frightened the daylights out of her. You see, it wasn't unknown for the Germans to dress up, to try to crack these underground groups in the Resistance areas. And the French knew that if they were caught sheltering airmen it was all up for them – concentration camp, at least. They were taking great risks. But to her lasting credit, she took me in. She had a daughter who was probably twenty. There were no men in the house, they'd been sent off to do war work for the Germans. I was knackered, worn out. Just before I fell asleep I thought about my mother, my mother whom I had kidded I had a job flying VIPs around England. I thought, Now, tomorrow morning she's going to get that nasty telegram, saying that her darling, darling boy is missing. And that upset me greatly.

In the morning when I woke there was another young lady there, and she did speak a bit of English, so I was able to find out where I was – actually a few miles north-east of Valence. Meanwhile, the old girl had disappeared. They said she'd gone for help, but I wondered if she'd gone to turn me in. I was very worried, she was away for such a long time. She came back, though, with a man, both riding bicycles, and we had lunch. People were starving in France, but somehow they rustled up this food. I made them all laugh because I asked if it was horse-meat. My mother had told me that was all the Froggies ate! After lunch they produced a brown serge suit and a pair of shoes. The old lady's husband must have been a big man because his suit went over the top of my battledress. Then I was told to go with the man on the bicycle. We cycled for what seemed an eternity. We went down this bloody mountain through the snow, on and on, and eventually came to a village called St Donat. We went into the pharmacy – the name on the outside 'Jean Chancel' stuck in my mind.

The next day I was taken to a greengrocer's shop nearby, and within two days I was together with three other members of my crew – the rear-gunner, the bomb-aimer and the wireless operator.

We were then taken to a barn. We were there with some tough-looking guys, with guns – members of the Resistance. And after a while, in walks a man in the full uniform battledress of the American Marines. A Captain in the American Marines. He had hand-grenades strapped to him, knife, guns, every bloody thing! A real tough guy. He was Peter Ortiz of the American OSS, who had been walking around France in his uniform. He was highly suspicious of us, and most unfriendly.

He took our details and said, 'Look, you're going to be kept under control by these men.' And by golly they went everywhere with us. One false move and I'm quite sure we would have been despatched. The next day Ortiz came in again, and he said, 'Well, I've been in touch with London. I'm reasonably satisfied that you're who you say you are, but there's nothing I can do for you for the moment.' The next night we were taken up into the hills to a sort of logging camp; we were in with the Maquis. We could sit outside and look down at a German airfield in the valley. Their Storches used to hover around during the day – I suppose they were trying to see what the Maquis were up to. Now and again Peter would come up – always in his bloody uniform – he'd take us down to the village, for schnapps, and back up again. Very disciplined. He told us the sort of things he'd been doing – such as tying this rope between two trees across the road to pull a German motorcyclist off his bike before they shot him. He really was a soldier of fortune. He brought us some money, shaving tackle, all that sort of thing. He looked after us very well.

Not all the Maquis we were with were reliable. Apparently one of them had had a few drinks too many in the village, and shot his mouth off about the RAF chaps up in the camp. Fortunately, somebody fed the information back to us. The Maquis held a court-martial for this chap and they shot him. We felt quite bad about it, because we knew it was through us being there that all this had happened.

They were only youngsters, really, these boys. At the end of an evening we used to have sing-songs – all Communist songs, mind you. One night, we were woken up by flashing torches. Peter Ortiz was there, in his uniform, saying, 'The Germans are coming. They're on their way!' He drove us about thirty miles south, to the home of a village doctor, Doctor Sambuc, in a place called La Paillette, just outside Dieulefit, east of Montelimar, further down the Rhône Valley. By then, we'd noticed that Peter was no longer wearing a Captain's three pips, but a Major's crown. He'd been promoted. One of our own squadron aircraft had dropped the crown down with some supply packages for the Maquis. Incredible!

Doctor Sambuc had been an Army Medical Officer in French Indo-China, but he'd retired, and settled down in this village. Well, we stayed there for three weeks, never went out. I hadn't changed my clothes since baling out. We were lousy. We slept two to a bed – and we were always hungry. But somehow the doctor's wife found food for us; her stockpot was constantly on the go. They had two nieces, girls of about eighteen, who used to practise their English on us. We had to behave ourselves, with the old girl hopping around. The doctor's surgery was downstairs and people were in and out all day including the local kids who came here for Sunday School. It all went on with four RAF airmen upstairs; the family were understandably terrified and very brave. There was no sign of Peter Ortiz. We thought we were there for the duration, and it was embarrassing because, apart from the danger, Mme Sambuc had to feed us. We did have our escape maps, of course, folded silk maps, and were studying the area, so we could break out and take a chance. We knew the only way back home was to get down to the Spanish border and into Gibraltar.

After about three weeks, when we'd given him up, Peter arrived one Saturday evening. 'You're off tomorrow,' he said. He duly came, and we motored all the way to Valence, right through this damned great town – with him still in his khaki uniform, with his crowns and guns and everything else. He took us to a little terraced house, and said, 'I'll come for you this evening, and I'll take you to Valence station. You'll only have tickets, no travel passes or anything, but I'll explain what you've got to do.' When it was dark he took us to the station, put us in the waiting-room, and said, 'Separate. Scatter yourselves about. At ten o'clock a train will come in. Get into the same carriage, but sit in separate corners. It's a full night's train ride, and the Germans sometimes check the train for passes. If they do, I'm afraid you've had it unless you can bluff your way out. I'll be on the train too, keeping an eye on you.'

So, off we went, and as the hours ticked by the waiting-room filled up with people. It was a babbling mass of humanity by the time the train came in. Peter had told us not to board until the last minute. So we made our rush along this blacked-out platform – straight into a couple of German officers – knocked them arse over tit! We didn't wait. Thank God we didn't say 'sorry' or something like that! We found an empty carriage, sat down, went right through the night without any interruption at all. As daylight came we pulled into a station. To our horror on the platform were about two hundred German troops. As they boarded our carriage, we thought, Christ, what's going to happen now? But thank God, they couldn't speak French. They even offered us cigarettes. We just bluffed our way, quite frightened. Fortunately, they got off again after another station or two.

We reached Carcassonne at about nine o'clock in the morning. Peter came in and said, 'You'll make contact with a priest on the platform.' And sure enough, there was a priest on the platform. He took us on a two-track, two-carriage electric train, and after an hour or so we got out at a village up in the foothills of the Pyrenees, and we stayed in a house there until nightfall. Then we walked all night, through disused railway tunnels, past waterfalls. We walked for hours. It was very tiring. I mean we weren't fit, we'd been doing nothing for six weeks.

At about six o'clock in the morning we passed a field where there was a bonfire. We walked towards it, and as we got nearer, we could see a crowd of people. Suddenly we heard an American voice. There were a lot of Americans there, airmen who'd been shot down doing daylight raids on Bordeaux, and had somehow been filtered into this area. There were people on the run from every corner of Europe: Czechs, Poles, Greeks, a right unholy mixture. We spent the day round the bonfire, and in the evening we started walking. We'd been given a couple of loaves of bread in a brown carrier bag, and a great hunk of roast meat, so we guessed, correctly as it turned out, that some serious walking lay ahead for us.

We walked for the next week with only one night's rest. We walked, and we walked, and we walked. I was the only one of the crew who'd kept his escape pack with him when we baled out. It was a plastic container, with a bit of chocolate, condensed milk, that sort of thing . . . but it also had this wonderful drug, Benzedrine. And I was taking these tablets – to keep me awake. But, suddenly, after three days I ran out of them. I took a nose-dive, and collapsed. The guides more or less decided to leave me on the mountainside, because they were in a hurry. But, and I learned this afterwards, my Canadian rear-gunner persuaded them to give me another chance. I had a rest, and was able to carry on. You kept climbing ridges and each time you got to the top you'd see another bloody great ridge in front of you, but eventually, right in the middle of one climb – it was about midnight – this Spaniard said, 'Now, rush for it!' And we rushed, and staggered up this ridge, and he said, 'You're in Spain.' And that was a wonderful feeling. We'd made it.

Of course we didn't know that it was another two days' walking down the other side before we'd reach civilisation. Still, we found an old farm where we slept in with the sheep. We were absolutely knackered, but delighted. On the Sunday afternoon a lorry arrived, an open-backed truck, and we all clambered in. They threw a tarpaulin over us, and after about three hours that was brutal to our backsides, it stopped. Somebody said the English must get off, and we got off. There in front of us was a door with a brass plate on it, which said: British Consulate, Barcelona. Marvellous! We had lovely showers, and they gave us new shirts and vests, shoes and socks. They put us up in a flat with a Spanish family who had a beautiful daughter. We had to draw lots for the one who'd go out with her that evening. The bloody Canadian went off with her – as he would – he was the best-looking one, anyway! We spent two nights in comfort. Then, one morning, a huge car drove up with Union Jack flag on the wing, and we were driven to the embassy in Madrid. Sir Samuel Hoare, the ambassador, and Lady Hoare gave us a marvellous welcome. We stayed there a week or two, while they got false papers for us. We couldn't go out, but we had haircuts, and a bath every day.

Eventually we were given our passes and put on the train one evening in Madrid. At eight o'clock we arrived at La Linea. They'd told us that we'd see the Spanish workers, all waiting for the gates to open so that they could get into Gibraltar to do their day's work. We went through the gates with these Spaniards, and reported to the Air Force station. Marvellous moment! They got us into bloody uniforms straightaway – battledress, no insignia of ranks, they hadn't got any hats. Our nice Spanish clothes disappeared. They said, 'Right, you can go into town.' Well, we had a few beers, and were immediately arrested by the military police for not having hats, and carted straight back to camp! We spent a couple of days there and then eventually, at 0030 on 12 April 1944, we flew back to RAF Lyneham, squashed into a Liberator, while German Generals – prisoners-of-war of course – occupied the posh seats upstairs.

Wing Commander Joe Kayll

From Northolt I went to Fighter Command. Then I was made Wing Commander at Hornchurch. In July 1941, we were escorting Halifaxes on some heavily escorted daylight raids. We did one or two when nothing exciting happened. And then I was going to lead a raid to Lille, and Group Captain Broadhurst, the Station Commander, said that he would like to fly. He was going to lead it, so I said I'd go as his no. 2. I was asked to lead another squadron, but said no.

The raid was successful, we escorted the three Halifaxes in, they dropped their bombs, and we were on our way back, when unfortunately Broadhurst thought that he'd have another look. He let the wing go on, and took a section of four of us back into France. We were climbing against the sun, and we were jumped. He got back, but two were killed. I couldn't bale out because, as soon as I tried to slow down enough to open the hood and bale out, the Messerschmitts all attacked again. I had no engine – that had stopped. So I simply went down zigzagging. They left me only as I was landing. I very luckily found a nice pea field, and landed with wheels up.

I heard a rifle bullet crack over my head, and then another. I ran to a farm house while bullets flew around the Spitfire. I had landed between two canals, and there happened to be a German patrol on the far side of each canal. One saw me standing up in the cockpit, took a shot, and the bullet very nearly hit the German on the other side of the far canal. So he shot back. So while I was running away, they were shooting at each other, with the aeroplane between them.

I was a Wing Commander then, and it was customary for the Luftwaffe to ask captured senior officers round for an evening meal in the mess. But the story had been put about that I had surrendered and then had shot at the German Army, so I never got my invitation.

All the RAF captured officers went first to a place near Cologne which was a Luftwaffe Intelligence headquarters. They'd been preparing for years and had collected news stories and files on every RAF and Auxiliary pilot. They did the usual thing of leaving one with nothing for three days – nobody could speak English, all the usual stuff. I thought that the black bread I was given was a joke, I didn't realise that I was going to have to eat it!

When a Hauptman Eberhart bounced in with the standard procedure: 'Oh, Wing Commander, I'm so sorry! You should never have been left like this. I've been in Berlin, blah, blah! For you the war is over.' He spoke perfectly good English, told me how he was in the London School of Economics for a year. I've never thought much of the London School of Economics ever since. Then he started. He wasn't going to interrogate me, he knew everything already. I'd played rugger, hadn't I, against 603 Squadron in Edinburgh, yes, must have been two years ago. Anything that had appeared in the papers – even my wedding date – he knew about. He would chat away, nothing he didn't know, and then he would slip in a little question now and again. It was a good tactic. They got a bit of information one way and another.

There was one pilot who decided to kid them a bit. He told Hauptman Eberhart that they didn't realise what was going to hit them in Germany. We had a brand new aeroplane, a bomber. He gave speeds and loads, and everything else. They were very intrigued about this, and kept questioning him. When they asked the name of it, he said it was the Crosse and Blackwell bomber. At POW camp we had our own Intelligence section, run by Squadron Leader Dudley Craig, which interrogated every new inmate as they came in, as to what they'd been asked. And for a month after that, every pilot that was shot down reported that the interrogators had said they knew about our Crosse and Blackwell bomber! He had them going for at least a month before they found out.

Most people were at Stalag Luft for about five or six weeks. It didn't hold much more than about thirty, and as soon as they got a group of twenty or twenty-five, they would send them off to a semi-permanent camp. I went to a castle, called Spangenburg, a bit south-west of Berlin. It had an Army barracks down below. There were about 150 POWs. There was really no way out, it was surrounded by a dry moat with wild boars at the bottom. Of course they'd have made a noise if we tried to get through them. But we thought it would be easy to fix them. Gillette razor blades were inserted into potatoes, and thrown into the moat. The boars ate the lot and it didn't stop them at all. They were tough! So we decided that food was too valuable to waste on them, and looked for other methods.

We did manage two escapes there. Of course we explored any locked room, and up in the attics of the castle we found some civilian clothes and a German uniform. These clothes were made to fit two of our chaps. We knew the Swiss Red Cross sent an investigator every year, and that he would arrive with a German in uniform. He came, and as the senior officer in the camp, it was my job to keep him talking. I showed him around the camp and explained all our moans and groans, and generally kept him busy. These two escapees quickly got into the clothes we had found, one in uniform, one as a civilian with a little attaché case. Fortunately, the guard had changed after the investigator came in, and while I had the Swiss and the German in a far corner of the castle, these two walked out. They could speak good German, of course, and shouted at the sentry to open the gate and they walked away. It never had much chance, you didn't really have a chance if you were trying to be a German in German uniform. And all they could carry was a small attaché case, which didn't carry enough food or anything. And in those days our maps were not good. They were away for about two days, that was all, before they were brought back again.

From there we went to Warburg, Oflag VIB, which was a mixed camp, with about 120 of us Air Force, and nearly 2,000 Army, mostly 51 Division, captured at St Valéry. They were the defenders of Dunkirk who had been left behind. We dug a few tunnels from there, but only one could really be called successful. Again we had quite a few people who got out through the gates. For example, one man dressed up as a German soldier. He had a home-made, carved wooden gun, which was stained with brown and black boot polish and looked very realistic. With him he had two others dressed in long johns, as if they had been digging a tunnel. They went to the gate and he shouted that he'd caught two of them digging a tunnel, and wanted to be let out so he could take them straight to the guard-room. The sentry was fooled, and they walked out. They didn't get very far either, because they weren't very well equipped.

Then we had an over-the-wire escape that the Army organised. We had a brilliant Army officer who, in civilian life, was an electrician. This man came to see General Fortune who was the Senior British Officer, and the Army escape officer said he thought he could fuse all the lights in the camp for probably five to seven minutes. Of course the escape committee were very excited about this. General Fortune wasn't very keen. There were sentry boxes and he didn't want casualties. He wanted proof that this electrician could put the lights out, and asked for a demonstration. During the demonstration nobody was to make any attempt to get out. And there was a complete blackout for about five minutes. The Germans got very excited and immediately had a roll call. But nobody had escaped, and they assumed that something had simply gone wrong with the lights.

It was originally envisaged that we would escape with a hundred people. There were two fences about six feet apart, with coiled wire on top. We made ladders, designed with a decking: you put the ladder against the wire, pushed the decking up, and let it flop down across the six-foot gap to the other wire. You climbed up and went across on hands and knees. Then there was a bar at the end and you dropped down. We were able to practise this without being seen – it was great fun practising it – so that ten people could do it in under a minute, blindfolded. We had one RAF team and the rest were Army. It had been decided to do the escape in September, when there would be crops on the ground, apples and turnips and the like. But before the chosen date arrived the Germans decided to close the camp down gradually. Eventually it was down to four ladders, as many had left.

It did work extremely well. The lights were put out. Various people who were not escaping caused diversions by throwing grapnels with a string attached into the wire fence at points where ladders were not being deployed, shaking them and making a noise, which distracted the Germans in the boxes. About thirty-seven got out. We should have got forty out, but one ladder didn't work at all, and one broke after a few went over it. I think, in the end, two Army POWs got back home via Switzerland. That was a very good effort indeed.

I went on that one, and was out a week. I decided to walk to Switzerland, down the Autobahn. If you couldn't speak German you walked at night, and simply tried to hide up during the day. I was wearing warm clothes, and had no papers with me. Unless you could speak very good German, there was no point. Walking down Autobahns was fine, because no-one at all was allowed to walk on an Autobahn. So that was the place to be because Germans always obey the rules. There wasn't much traffic at night, and if I saw a pair of headlights I simply lay on the side, and then continued walking. And as soon as it started to get light I found a wood, and stayed in it for the day, then went off again the next evening. At the end of a week, I had made a little clearing in the middle of a wood when a wretched gamekeeper came through with his dog, and that was that.

I was sent to a camp in Poland, called Schubin. I was given forty days' solitary for escaping. Straightaway we started digging tunnels again. One never stopped digging tunnels or thinking up ways to get out of the gate. It kept one very well occupied. The successful tunnel at Schubin was dug from the lavatory. It was a long building, and was more civilised than previous lavatories in that it had about ten seats in a hut. The level was quite low, and the escape team made a cradle, and put somebody down to dig into the side wall, which was close to the wire on the outside. If any Germans came and looked, they'd just sit on the seat. That was successful; about thirty got away, including Aidan Crawley, who was later a MP. On this escape we learned an important lesson – if a large number got out, the hue and cry was so great that they really didn't have much chance. That's one of the reasons why 'the wooden horse' was so successful; only three went out. That famous escape was made from the next camp, Stalag Luft III.

The rules for escaping were that, if you thought of a new idea, you registered it with the escape committee, and it was yours so long as you made use of it within a reasonable time. It was a brilliant idea, the wooden horse, but curiously, the men who thought of it were not the two most popular, as they had not participated or helped in any previous escape attempts. They approached Wing Commander Roger Moore and persuaded him to make the wooden horse for them. Moore didn't take much active participation in escape activities. But he loved making things, and was allowed to make scenery for the camp theatre. But he had his own secret tools as well. And he made the wooden horse. It was just a box, with slightly sloping sides, and a bit of padding on top. Two bars were put through to carry it. This was a bit ridiculous, because when it was empty you could pick it up with one hand – it was made from bits of plywood from Red Cross boxes. We did the sort of thing that always fooled the Germans: we pretended to be very disciplined and we marched out with the box. Four people would carry it, one at each end of the bars, and the people who were going to jump would march behind. The Germans, of course, thought that this was absolutely right, the way things should be done, at last we were learning! So we made quite a show of carrying it out, there was a chap inside. The beauty of this was that we were able to start the tunnel so close to the wire. We would put the horse down over the trap door under the sand. The tunneller then scraped four or five inches of sand off the top, lifted the trap door, and got down inside and dug, filling up bags made from pyjama legs. He would hang those up on hooks inside the horse. We would jump over this horse until we were sick of it. When he had done his hour or hour-and-a-half of digging, he would put the lid back on, put the old sand over it, and then we would carry him and his bags of sand back. We took it inside a kitchen shed where it was kept, and the sandbags were taken out.

Then the sand had to be got rid of – that was one of the tricky bits. It was bright yellow, up against everything else which was filthy dirty. We started by putting it in the roof of the kitchen shed, that was fine except that when it dried out, it started to trickle through, which was a bit embarrassing. So then we made long sausage-like tubes out of cloth, which you could hang round your neck, down inside your trousers, to the ground. There was string attached to a pin at the bottom, and you would just walk round the camp with one or two people behind you. You pulled the pin out, and as you walked along so the sand scattered. The people behind walked in it. The guards never suspected any of that. But it took quite a lot of time, you had to make the sacks, fill them up, carry them round, and see that it didn't all run out at once. We did put a certain amount down the lavatory but that became rather obvious if you overdid it. Then the Germans would get very excited and look everywhere for a tunnel.

There was a period when everyone who was helping them went on strike. The two escapers didn't seem to appreciate what was done by other people who were disposing of all their sand and exercising on the wooden horse. The jumping and disposal teams decided that they had done enough and told the two escapees that they would have to organise their own teams. This they were not able to do. Then the escape committee realised it was far too good a thing to abandon. We had to get some people out. So we insisted they take another man on the team. Oliver Philpot was the escape officer in their hut; he was very popular and he had been digging tunnels for a year or two. We said, if they took Oliver Philpot, everybody would jump over the horse again. They demurred for a bit, but it was quite obvious that they couldn't do anything about it, so he joined.

The tunnel was finished in about a couple of months. With any tunnel, the break-out was the tricky bit, you were not quite sure where the exit was going to be. People measured, of course, and on the whole the surveyors got it pretty well right. You then left a little bit of earth for the final break-out, and dug a hole below, so that the earth would fall in and leave you room to get out. In the end, the escapees were extremely well equipped. They had civilian clothes actually sent out by Gieves. We were allowed to send two letters and postcards a month and to get a clothing parcel once a year from your family. We had ways of communicating with the Air Ministry by letter. Gieves made some uniforms for Fleet Air Arm pilots in the camp. These uniforms were so designed – we had professional tailors in the camp, of course – that if you took the buttons off, and undid certain stitching, the dark blue Fleet Air Arm uniform became a first-class civilian suit. They also had maps, railway time-tables, and lots of money.

On the final day, we carried them out one at a time. We had always varied the routine, sometimes jumping for only short sessions. We took one man out, did some jumping, then carried the horse back in, took it out again, did more jumping and then took it back and so on, until we had all three in the tunnel. The Germans never considered the wooden horse as being anything other than what it was supposed to be.

It wasn't until ten o'clock the next morning that the guards saw the hole and realised that there had been an escape. We were able to fox the count on the early-morning parade. People who were too sick to stand on parade were counted in their beds. There was a hut with a trap door at each end which we'd once made for a tunnel. The huts were two foot off the ground. So somebody in this hut was very ill in bed. He was counted and checked, then he dived through the trap door, tore along underneath, and then was counted in bed the other end as well. That was one. Another was a dummy, held up in the ranks. And somebody very cleverly foxed another count by moving. So all three were accounted for on the first appel, and by that time they were probably in Stettin. We then made a mess of the second appel, because everybody was high on adrenalin and fooling around, making fun of the Germans, which they didn't like. They called in the Gestapo, who suddenly let out a burst of gunfire through one of the huts. We sobered up very quickly and had a proper roll call. Of course they found that there were three missing.

Then they decided on our punishment. They knew we had a radio, we had always had one. It was home-made – we had some brilliant electrical people. The Germans decided to search for it in one of our huts. They happened, unfortunately, to pick the correct hut. The POW who ran the radio was a half-Italian officer, who spoke very good German and Italian, and was also one of the escape committee's liaison team. Nobody was allowed to talk to Germans unless the escape committee gave them permission. We used bribery, with cigarettes and chocolates, and it was tightly controlled. This chap had made friends with some of the guards, which was his job. As soon as he saw them going into the hut he quickly walked up to the German Commandant, saluted very smartly, and said, 'Herr Kommandant, it is all wrong that you and your officers should have to stand out here, I shall take some men and get you some chairs and a table.' And of course the Germans were thrilled to bits, here was somebody at last showing some respect. So they agreed, and he took three men in and came out with the hut's table and chairs. And of course in the table, in the legs and under the lid, was the radio! They took the hut to bits looking for the radio, and here they were sitting with their papers on it! It was a brilliant bit of work.

The escapees had gone out about eight o'clock in the evening, just as it was getting dark. It gave them time to walk to the station and catch the train. Nobody suspected them at the station at all, they were obviously smart business types. They got on the train which took them all the way up to Stettin. And from there they separated, I think, two together and Oliver Philpot on his own, and all three managed to get on to boats going to Sweden. There was a lot of traffic between Sweden and Germany. The important thing, as we had warned them, was not to declare themselves until the boat was actually tying up in Sweden. We'd had one poor chap from the Polish camp who got out, got on a boat, and he hid away in a lifeboat. When he could see the Swedish coast, he got out and went up on the bridge, and told the Captain he was an escaped POW. The Captain turned the ship round and took him back. The Germans had made it quite clear that any Captain who helped anybody to escape to Sweden would be barred from German ports.

The wooden horse escape was a great success, all three made it back to England. I think it took about a month for us to learn of their safe homecoming. A letter was sent to one of Philpot's friends simply with a pre-arranged message, that was broadcast around the camp. That was very good.

There were some people in the camp who decided that they weren't going to do any escaping. Most people played games, football or even golf with home-made balls. Softball, a version of baseball, was very popular because you could have a game in half-an-hour or one hour, and everybody got a chance. The ball was soft, we couldn't hit it very far, so it stayed in the camp. There were quite a lot of books. We played chess, bridge, and card games, and had a theatrical group who put on shows about once every month. You could learn almost any language in the camp. There were a lot of nationalities. I learned a bit of Norwegian. People ran classes on different things, we had a dentist in the camp for a bit. He would take you through dentistry; other people would take you through a clothing factory; I did sawmills. I'd been in the timber trade, and taught about timber. Nearly everybody had some civilian experience. There was an immense amount of talent.

We had a lot of striking individuals, a lot of very clever people. People with two or three languages, degrees, etc.: and we had a brilliant forgery department, who for the wooden horse and every other escape made false papers. The best forger was brilliant. He was a bank clerk!

Photographs were the most difficult thing to get, to put on the identity cards. People would remember a photograph at home, perhaps in a group which could be cut out. They would send home for it. We had some artists who could alter photographs, if an escapee hadn't got one of himself. If you got the light in a certain way, it showed up, but it was possible to make it reasonably like somebody to pass a casual inspection.

For a period the Germans sent a Nazi welfare officer to the camp whose job it was to explain and extol Nazism. Two or three potential escapers were told to make friends with him and pretend to swallow his propaganda. They were so successful that he thought he had converts, they managed to persuade him to bring in his Leica camera and to take photographs of themselves to send home to relatives. We knew that he was not allowed to bring a camera into the camp but by judicious use of chocolate and other bribes he was persuaded to do so, and he took some photographs. The escape committee decided that the next time he brought his camera in we would remove it from him and tell him we were going to take photographs, and if he didn't get them developed and bring the prints back, we would go straight to the German Kommandant and inform on him. It was something he might easily be shot for. He went as white as a sheet, and was trembling as he went out of the gate. We took the photographs, it all worked, and when he'd brought the photos in, we gave him his camera back. We had got photos of all the likely escapers. Then of course it was a big job for the forger to make identity cards from them. It took a lot of doing, each identity card took about a week, working four hours a day – it was very close work. You couldn't get a railway ticket without producing an identity card and a letter explaining the reason why you were travelling. We had one officer who could do a typewritten letter, all with brush and Indian ink, and you wouldn't know the difference.

Eventually we got the use of a typewriter, in the foodstore where the parcels arrived. We got the squad who carried the parcels out and did all the work in there to distract the German guards. We had a good typist who could go in and type the letters that were required. We found that I. G. Farben, the huge chemical company with plants all over Germany, who employed thousands of foreign workers, were a good cover. The letter would state that it was necessary for this foreign worker, Frenchman or Pole, to go to wherever it was on the train.

A tremendous amount of work was done on that. Some people said they didn't want to escape but offered to help others. There were a lot of people like that. There were always Germans in the camp called 'Ferrets', usually two of them together, who just wandered round and round the camp, looking and watching. We had a constant squad of people who had them under observation from the time they came in to the time they left. If you were digging a tunnel, there were ways of communicating where they were and which way they were heading. If they were coming your way, you shut your tunnel down, stopped people pumping. So everyone was just normal, reading or playing chess.

The Germans knew we were digging tunnels, there was no doubt about it. The only thing was where were they? And could they find them before we got out?

We had one spontaneous case of someone trying to escape. An Irish pilot. He had been a prisoner for about three years. He was a keen escaper, and suddenly one night he just went out and tried to climb up the wire. They shot him as he was halfway up. They always said they would and they did. He was one of our very few deaths.

One chap, in daylight, actually cut through the wire. He had made himself some wire cutters from skates we had had when everything was frozen one winter, that would cut through the barbed wire. Where he was going to cut through was overlooked by two boxes, and it was arranged that diversions would be staged at opposite sides of the boxes to distract the guards. One was a first-class fight, with people making a ring. Of course, the guard couldn't keep his eyes off that. The other was a fellow who went mad. He swallowed a lot of soap, was foaming at the mouth, weaving around, falling over. He would run towards the wire, people would stop him, he would struggle and run away. Of course the guard was watching him. Meanwhile, this man, with incredible courage, managed to cut the wire, used little sticks to prop it up, got through. Unfortunately he was caught after about three days.

It was in the next door camp that the 'Great Escape' took place. Squadron Leader Roger Bushel, a 601 Squadron pilot, was in charge of escaping there. We were able to help a little bit, as there was slight communication via the sick quarters. They planned to get about 150 people out. It was such a magnificent tunnel, and so many people had worked on it, there was no way they could say sorry and let half-a-dozen out. They felt that the more that got out the more chances they had of getting back home. Unfortunately the Germans recaptured a number of escapees and shot them in cold blood. That really put an end to escaping. It was getting towards the end of the war, anyway, and we simply decided that if they were going to do that, escape was no longer viable. Our chances of getting back home were about one in a hundred. It ceased to be a game, and the odds were simply stacked against us. I suppose the blackest moment of all was hearing a very shaken German Kommandant announce they had shot fifty men.

At that time one of our officers had a very clever little tunnel going. On parade, where we lined up in fives, he was in the third rank, and he made a trap door. All his friends stood in the same place each day, and we were always out on parade probably five or ten minutes or more before we were actually counted. At that time people were all wearing greatcoats. It was cold. He got down, dug away all day, and then came up again during the evening parade, passing all the sand that he'd dug up. Friends took a bag each, and he was, of course, counted. If for some extraordinary reason the Germans came rather earlier on the parade, then there would be a muddle. And the first ranks to be counted would shuffle about, and they couldn't get it right, so would have to start again, so giving him time.

Once, for some reason, they decided not to have an evening appel, and he was down. We quickly had a committee meeting. So we had the bright idea of having a rugby practice. It was an open sort of patch, so someone got some rags together to make a ball. And we scrummed and scrummed and got him out. They never suspected anything. He was very surprised. In the end he was halfway to the wire when the Great Escape POWs were shot. He was still prepared to go on, but we said it was just too risky.

We had a very good intelligence system in the camp. We had two POWs who made war maps, and kept them up-to-date. We got all the German news and we could get German newspapers, which they wanted us to have. We also had the BBC Nine o'Clock News every night. Between the two, we got very good at knowing who was winning. Very often we would realise that we had had a defeat, but nothing would be mentioned on the BBC for two or three days. Then there would be talk of strategic withdrawal. We had known three days before that they had lost in the desert. So we were extremely well informed as to what was going on. As soon as D-Day happened we had high hopes. It was quite long, though, from D-Day until the end.

We had some very good actors who put on the theatrical performances. There was Rupert Davies, who later played Maigret, and Denholm Elliott. They played *Our Town*, which I found a very emotional performance; and yet I've seen it since and it has had no effect on me at all.

The POW experience was a fascinating study of human nature. We had to some extent an advantage over the Army, and perhaps the Navy camps, in that we were all individuals. Hardly anybody knew each other, perhaps two or three who had been in the same squadron. The Army, when they were captured, were captured as a regiment, and they had their hierarchy right through. I think that the younger officers didn't have quite as much say as we did.

We were given an eye-opener when we were marched north

towards the end of the war. We were billeted in a French camp. There was dirt, disarray and low morale. But of course they'd made no attempt to escape. What kept our morale up was that we were always trying to escape. But the French simply had nowhere to escape to, and were threatened with the fact that, if they did escape, their families would get shot. So they were absolutely tied as their country was occupied.

Then the Germans marched us out of the camp. I suppose we were on the march for about three weeks. They didn't really know what to do with us, but Hitler had ideas of using POWs as hostages. In the end we were completely in control because we'd told the guards that they'd get merit certificates to say they'd been good chaps and they'd swallowed it. We finally finished up at a big farm at Lübeck, which was entirely manned by Russian women. We saw a German hitting a woman in the field. There was a shout of rage, and several people tore across the field towards him. He happened to be the owner, but he ran. The Russian women, who had never seen anyone stand up to him, couldn't do enough for us, they washed our clothes, etc. We had a very good week there.

We were brought back in Dakotas. I had been married nearly a year before I'd been captured; there were letters all the time. My wife knew I was well, and the family knew. She was without me for three years and ten months, but slowly one picked up the threads again. And I had a son whom I had never seen. He can still remember my coming home. He had been told about Daddy.

Requiem for an Air-Gunner by R. W. Gilbert

> The pain has stopped,
> For I am dead.
> My time on earth is done.
> But in a hundred years from now,
> I'll still be twenty-one.

BOMBER COMMAND

My brief, sweet life is over,
My eyes no longer see,
No summer walks,
No Christmas trees,
No pretty girls for me.
I've got the chop, I've had it.
My nightly ops are done.
Yet in another hundred years,
I'll still be twenty-one.

7

THE FAR EAST

Malaya and Singapore

The British defence plan for Malaya envisaged strong RAF forces operating from airfields in the north of the Malayan peninsula to defeat any Japanese invasion fleet at sea. In the event, there were no modern aircraft in Malaya when the Japanese invaded on 8 December 1941. The RAF's most northern airfield at Kota Bharu was abandoned the next day. Brewster Buffalo fighters – rejected for service in Europe – equipped four squadrons (1 RAF, 2 RAAF, 1 RNZAF) and were all but annihilated by superior Japanese aircraft. The few Blenheim bombers and night fighters, 1933 vintage Vildebeest biplane torpedo bombers and some Australian Hudsons were quickly overwhelmed. The Army fell back, the Royal Navy's battleship strike force, HMS *Prince of Wales* and HMS *Repulse*, operating without air cover, were sunk by Japanese aircraft on 10 December. Though some Hurricanes were delivered to Singapore at the end of December, the defence of Malaya was doomed and the British withdrew into Singapore island on 31 January. The island was surrendered after a week's fighting on 15 February 1941.

Burma

The Japanese invaded Burma on 11 December 1941 when Allied air power added up to a few RAF Buffalos, some old Indian Air Force types and a squadron of American Volunteer Group P-40s sent from China. With limited reinforcements of Hurricanes and Blenheims, the RAF (and the more experienced AVG), fought aggressively as the British and Indian troops retreated.

Outnumbered eight to one in operational aircraft, the RAF was finally forced out of its last airfields in Burma, Akyab and Magwe, late in March 1942. New RAF – and, increasingly, American – squadrons became an integral part of the eventual fight back into Burma. RAF Groups supported the Army's main Imphal and Arakan fronts with close air support, air-supply and casualty evacuation. ('Chindit' columns behind Japanese lines once had casualties evacuated by Sunderland flying boats which landed on a lake.) Heavy bombers operated from India against Japanese bases. Air supremacy slowly passed to the Allies; Spitfire squadrons arrived in Burma in October 1943. The RAF played a crucial role when the major Japanese offensive in March 1944 was fought to a standstill at Imphal and Kohima and, in increasing strength, helped drive the Japanese back to Rangoon which was recaptured in May 1945.

Wing Commander Frank Carey

I arrived in Rangoon on 19 January 1942, in the middle of an air-raid. What I remember most of the Japanese campaign is the appalling lack of facilities we had to deal with – no spares, no tools, no equipment. Sometimes, to get an engine out, we wheeled a plane under a palm tree, pulled the tree down, tied it to the engine and slowly released it. Often we cannibalised one aircraft to keep others going.

The main ops room at Rangoon was in a culvert, and we had to look out to see what was happening in the air above. Our mobile radar vehicle had barely more than a few miles' range. We had to use the ordinary telephone system to get warnings: some brave local chaps used to sit and watch the action at Moulmein airfield, because in the early days the Japanese had no other aerodrome available within fighter range of where we were at Rangoon. These chaps used to report by telephone when there was flying activity. It was important for us to know if there was any flying at all, because the Japs would often retire back into

Thailand for about a week and then come forward and throw everything they had at us again.

In the last few days in Rangoon before our final withdrawal things got interesting. The RAF element was reduced to a few dozen men – pilots and essential ground crew – and for personal safety we moved into a single building which had been a Church Mission. Martial law had been declared; the prisons had been opened and inmates set free; guns and ammunition were fairly freely available to anyone looting. Our food and provisions had to be acquired by a team of gun-toting ground crew whilst we were flying. Frequently we were potted at from the jungle cover on the road sides we drove to get to the airfield. Finally the orders were given that we were only to move in convoy with plenty of cover from our weapons.

One day at about dusk, disobeying this order for reasons I no longer remember, I went from the airfield to the Mission. About a half-mile from the Mission I came across two local men pouring gallons of oil on the road at a particularly sharp bend. Of course, everybody knew the Japanese were coming in and we wouldn't be able to stop them, and these fellows wanted a little something in the way of dead British bodies to offer them. I stopped them and chased them into the jungle, firing after them. I heard them yell, but I didn't know if I killed them. I then rushed back to the airfield to warn everyone. That was just luck again.

Once the withdrawal from Rangoon started, we had to use roughly prepared air strips on our way north from Rangoon towards Mandalay. These strips were cleared by cutting back the 'bunds' or mud wall edges of the paddy fields. These walls had been packed down like concrete over centuries and, however well they were cleared, the walls were always higher and harder than the rest of the field. It made your teeth chatter to taxi over them. An early casualty was the tail skid of the aircraft, which would hit these things and disintegrate; and of course we were short of replacement supplies. The ground crew used to cut down thick bamboo sticks and tie them at the back of the aircraft as replacement skid. That was another common improvisation forced on us.

During the retreats I was trying to set up a decent warning system at Magwe. At that time, our mobile radar was providing about a mere mile-and-a-quarter – you could see more with your eyes!

The one communication that was good in Burma was the railway. They had a wonderful telegraph system to record the movement of the trains. So we tried to make use of the facilities. We had a big conference with the rail people to organise it. We asked them to report any aircraft: height, if they knew it, direction and numbers, etc. So we sat there and waited and waited, and for four days we heard nothing. Then suddenly a bloke came in and said there was a big pile of telegrams for us reporting aircraft movements – over the last four days! We didn't have time to sort that one out before we were really clobbered. That's the sum total of the war out there, from my point of view – total lack of facilities. After that beating the RAF had to withdraw up into China by road, because they had nothing left to fly – that in itself is another graphic story.

The enemy aircraft were incredibly more manoeuvrable than ours were. If we got down and mixed it with them at low altitude we were in trouble because we couldn't accelerate away from them unless we had a bit of height to dive away and they could run rings around us. The Japs at that stage were flying fixed undercarriage monoplanes called Army 97s. They were extremely light and, for their weight, had very powerful engines, but not much in the way of gunfire. They also didn't have any armour plating behind them. If you got a good squirt at them they used to fold up.

They really worked, those Japs. One I shot down and then followed down, deliberately crash-landed trying to dive into a revetement with a Blenheim there. He missed it. We got the whole aircraft and body and everything else – he'd got twenty-seven bullets in him and he was still flying that thing round the airfield looking for a target. Incredible, isn't it? They always used to try to dive into something. That was what we were up against.

The big difficulty with the Japanese aircraft, though, was trying to find the damn things. Frequently they would seem to disappear from the area altogether and then re-appear in some strength for several days. I personally never had any success at night, not even on the moonlight nights. It used to make me mad. I just couldn't find them although other chaps seemed to have the knack. They used to fly from about half-moon through full-moon to half-moon. We used to call it a Japanese moon. Out there you could navigate easily and land without any flares at night during that period. One day we heard that they'd come to Moulmein, so I said, 'Right! We'll catch those devils – we'll have a dawn patrol.' We used to get so little warning that we could never leave our aircraft at the airfield; we had to disperse them widely. We used to taxi them down the roads away from the airfield at Rangoon or else land at small areas around Rangoon. So all we could do was to join up, in the air, at dawn. By the time we had done that, the other chap had already got his stuff together!

So there were we, trying to join up, and there they were above us! Why they didn't come down and attack us I don't know. If they didn't see us we were lucky. There was so much fine dust in those places you couldn't hide a take-off. But maybe we went off just early enough. There is also a deep thick haze at various times of the year which severely reduces horizontal visibility. I said we were all to make for Moulmein independently, chase them back down the line, and catch them short of petrol and going into land.

That's what we did. We got to Moulmein and there they were, all ready for landing – a whole mass of them like a loose hive. I saw two planes that by the time I got to them would be fifty to a hundred feet off the ground on their final approach. Which meant they would be locked in that position. My no. 2 and I went down like a couple of hawks on to these two. The first one fell into the runway. My no. 2 was quite a bit behind me, so I got tucked behind the leader – precisely the moment when he realised something had happened to the other one. He started to turn and I caught him at about nought feet. His wing got into the grass and he went round into a whacking great sweeping arc, straight into a hangar. That was an immensely lucky thing.

Then I started to look for my no. 2; I knew he'd be in a hell of a mess. I pulled hard round and there was I in the circuit with all these Japanese aircraft! So I'd got certain things to attend to. One chap came nicely across my bows and I gave him a burst and he went into the deck. So that was three. Then I had to do a 180° turn to aim back to my base and they then really hammered me! They came in from all angles and filled my plane with holes, but didn't do any serious damage! Nothing touched me. Sheer luck again!

Life out in the East was very much a pendulum between rags and riches. One minute we'd be in some awful mud hut beside a makeshift runway, and the next in some Rajah's palace. Once I was sharing the Lord Chief Justice's house on Kokine Hill, a residential area of Rangoon, with Group Captain Seton Broughall – the Justice and his lady were leaving in the face of the Japanese advance. This lady's last words to Seton and me contained a plea not to use the better quality fine china in the house! Well, she had some justification – the men used to move into one of these grand houses, stay until all the crockery was dirty, and then move on. But the Japanese were going to be coming after us, so it was really immaterial whether we used the best china or not!

Before we began to make our first advance against the Japanese down the Arakan border with Burma, I flew to a recently repaired airfield at Cox's Bazaar to test its suitability for operations. On the return journey I had to refuel at Chittagong, which had only emergency fuel supplies on it. The refuelling party were in the process of finishing their job, and I was sitting in the cockpit waiting to start up, when I noticed a number of fighter aircraft appear from behind a cloud – about twenty-seven in all. I knew they must be Japanese, because we didn't have that many aircraft in the place. Being without radar cover or any other warning was always a hazard, and here it was in large lumps! I started my engine, yelled to the ground crew to get under cover, and then had to taxi a long way to get to the end of the runway. I opened up but long before I was airborne the bullets were flying and kicking up the dust around me. I got up in the air and immediately began to jink and skid to make myself an awkward target. I was helped by my own fury with myself for having been stupid enough to take off into such a suicidal position! However, luck was with me again and I led the Japs on my tail up the river at absolutely nought feet between the river boats, finally working my way up into the hills and leading them away from their own base at Akyab. Eventually they had to break off; I suppose their fuel was getting low. I thought I saw one of them crash behind me, but that was never confirmed. I really lost a lot of weight on that sortie.

I had about seven kills against the Japanese, and finished my regular operational flying in the Far East in March 1943.

A group of us – all pilots temporarily off ops in Eastern India – formed a club called the Screechers' Club. There was a tendency for the young to hit the bottle when the pressure let up, myself included, I must admit. The idea was, you were allowed drink only as long as you remained amusing. The club also had ranks. At the bottom was Hiccough, then Roar, Scream, and Screech at the top. Everybody but me had to start as a Hiccough. I permitted myself one grade up at the beginning, since I was running the thing. Everybody else started at the bottom. You had to behave yourself because, if you went over the top, you were downgraded. The only way to move a grade up was to hang around at the bar and buy drinks for one of the higher grades. When we had graduation night – about once a week – if a chap had bought me four drinks, he was certainly worth a grade higher. Chaps would hang inverted from the ceiling punkahs and things like that, which would gain them a higher ranking as long as they weren't stupid and injured themselves.

Somebody gave us a grand piano there. We used to have sing-songs and I started to compose two pieces of music. One was called the 'Prang Concerto' and the other was the 'Symphonie

Alcoholique'. I could play the symphony all ways, you know, you didn't necessarily have to use your hands! The 'Prang Concerto' had three movements, and the last movement demanded the complete demolishment of the piano. I had to go through and play the third movement on my last day there, before being posted to the Middle East. It cost me quite a lot to replace that darned piano. Actually, I never did really complete the third movement, because it's almost impossible to break the heavier wires of a piano, even using a broken-off piano leg! Humour relieved everybody's feelings.

You couldn't survive the war without an immense amount of luck. When there are holes across the cockpit from a bullet which must have come from there to there, and if you had been leaning a bit further forward it would have hit you, it cannot have been anything else but by luck. Luck is the biggest single factor of the lot and I was very, very lucky.

Wing Commander Lucian Ercolani

There was an entirely different atmosphere flying in the Far East compared to the European show. The risk from enemy action was considerably less in the Far East, but, really, the anxiety and fear was probably worse. However badly one thought of the Germans, at least there was an element of European civilisation, as against our real fear of the Japanese and of coming down amongst them.

I had a three-year spell out there and, apart from a six-month stint at Group headquarters, I was fortunate to be on squadrons all the time. Our bases were always in the Eastern part of India, in Bengal, fifty–sixty miles from Calcutta. This meant that there was a lot of flying before we actually got to the business end, across the Bay of Bengal and, more often than not, flying over the Burmese mountains. To start with, mostly at night.

Returning back in the mornings, though, could be a joy: the sun rising behind you, a glorious gold, lighting up the tops of the mountains, the valleys shrouded in mist, still in the dark.

Although you had the worry of getting over them, they were very beautiful. The aircraft with less fuel and no bomb-load now, light to the touch, quite free and relaxed. It was quite an emotional feeling. I often thought I could hear the 'Ave Maria' being sung.

I joined 99 Squadron as a Flight Commander and, within a few days of arriving, was off over the other side. They still had the dear old Wimpys, but conditions were quite rustic. If you needed to change an engine, you had to push the aircraft under a tree and use a block and tackle from a branch.

At that time, the Japanese were pushing right up through Burma and we were involved in bombing aerodromes and communications – anything that could help the Army. They actually got as far as Imphal and it was only the leadership and strong personality of General Slim which tipped the scales against their breaking into India.

After some months, we heard that our Air Force was being built up with Liberators, that is, the American B-24, a four-engine job. They seemed very big to us in those days. They could carry probably four times as much as the dear old Wimpy and could be pushed to flights of nearly 3,000 miles. To start with they were intended to be crewed by twelve people, but we soon skimmed that down to six.

I was posted as Flight Commander to 355 Squadron and was, for some time, Senior Officer to form up the squadron. When I arrived, there were only huts on the aerodrome, quite bare of equipment. Then people started arriving. We didn't even have enough knives and forks. We went round begging, borrowing or stealing equipment. Then the great day when, one by one, the Liberators came in. We did a quick conversion course and before long, to our great excitement, we were flying them.

After a few trips over the other side, I was posted to Group headquarters in Calcutta. I didn't think I was ever really cut out to be a Staff Officer, and was only there for six months, but I learned a lot. Then I was offered the great pride of the service, the command of a squadron, and went back to my friends with

99 Squadron, where my experience with the Liberators was immensely valuable, as our first job was to convert 99 to the wonderful new Liberators.

The scene over Burma had now begun to change. Although the Army was having a very rough time indeed in the Burma jungles, they first held and then began to push the Japanese back. We changed our role and switched mainly to daylight operations and learned the art of flying these big aircraft in formation. It was a wonderful sight to be with your own squadron with twelve or sixteen aircraft all round you. Very small compared to Europe, but exciting for us. For some time, our targets were closely linked to a form of Army co-operation, clearing areas ahead of landings. We cleared the ground for the invasion of Ramree Island, off the Burmese coast, we attacked aerodromes, supply depots and generally made life uncomfortable for the Japanese troops.

It was then that we began to get involved with the infamous railway line linking Singapore right up through to Burma, built over the bodies of thousands and thousands of prisoners-of-war. It was a real 'hate' operation.

Bridges and the trains themselves were the bomb targets. The Liberators were, of course, designed for medium- and high-level bombing, but as they were the only aircraft available which could do the considerable distances involved, we had to evolve new low-level techniques. We could hardly claim ever converting a Liberator into a fighter-bomber, but we must have come fairly close!

Having flown 1,000-miles plus, to find our objective on the railway line, we would have to come right down on to the deck to try and knock out the engines. The terrible worry in our minds was that these trains, and the lines, were crowded with our own people. It was a very deep emotional experience to see your own people on the ground, right down there in those terrible places, waving to us and encouraging us on. I cannot believe that some accidents did not happen, as many were very close to the engines, but their welcome was always the same. We felt awful when we had finished and pulled up to go home again, leaving them all behind.

I was next offered the opportunity to move from 99 to 159 Squadron and to re-form the squadron into what might loosely be called the Pathfinder role. I was allowed the privilege of selecting the most experienced crews from those just being posted in and from the other squadrons. It could have caused a lot of bad feeling, but everyone was very generous and it seemed to work well.

Our squadron was made up roughly in equal proportions of British, Australians, New Zealanders and Canadians. There was probably a higher proportion of the latter. This was far better than having British, Australian etc. squadrons. By mixing us all up together, you certainly had plenty of rivalries, but healthy ones to make things go even better. We all made many lifelong friends. Fine pilots amongst many other fine pilots.

Strangely, whilst with Bomber Command, one used to do very little practice bombing, but bearing in mind our new role, we decided to work at it. Quite often we got down to 25 yards, but we used to post up the results in the mess overnight and anybody who was outside 50 yards had to buy the drinks.

This stood us in good stead when a large Japanese submarine depot ship ventured up the Gulf of Siam. We found her just south of Bangkok, scored several direct hits, sinking her under a great cloud of smoke. As we hadn't used up our bomb-load, we left her sinking and went after the escort vessels; but we missed them all, as they bobbed around like little 'water boatmen' beetles on a pond. Perhaps that taught us not to get too cocky!

Similarly, we evolved a new method for low-level bombing to knock the bridges down. Bridges are, in fact, quite difficult to hit. Amongst many other successes, our squadron led the flight that knocked down the famous bridge over the River Kwai. Great annoyance was caused later amongst the crews by the film when it was said that the bridge was too far away for the Air Force to reach!

The technique we worked out was to go as low as possible and fly slightly diagonally across the bridge, and on each run to only use three bombs. Flying diagonally gave one just a little latitude fore and aft and also sideways. We used delayed-action bombs, certainly to avoid blowing ourselves up, but particularly so that they could really settle down before exploding, trying to get them as close as we could to the bridge supports themselves.

The monsoon season used to be the season when everything stopped. Obviously we couldn't, so we had to find a way of getting through these frightening clouds. If you went in high, the up-currents had been known to break the wings off. We treated them with great respect. If we had to cross them in the middle of the Bay of Bengal, and very often they were at their worst there, we found that our best way through was to go right down on to the deck, then try to work our way along the side of the cloud. At that level, beneath these enormous cumulus clouds and flying along their edges, it was rather like flying under the overhang of a railway station. I don't know quite how wide that overhang would be, but when we flew under the edges of these clouds, about 200 feet below would be the sea, and about 200 feet above was the cloud. On one side a solid wall of rain, and on the other you could look right out across the sea, a very strange feeling. We were very frightened of them.

Out there we were rather a small Air Force, and as a result knew almost everybody. We were allowed incredible independence; once given our detailed objectives, it was left to us how we set about it.

Our squadrons were still units complete in themselves; they had not been 'rationalised' as in the UK with the squadron being flying crews only, with joint, combined, maintenance. We had the advantage of being a total unit along with all the chaps who kept our aircraft flying. There was a tremendous pride of squadron, with everybody feeling that 'together' there was hardly anything that we couldn't accomplish.

To have command of a squadron under these circumstances,

with all those exciting opportunities at twenty-seven years of age, with probably 1,000 people to be responsible for, was a very great privilege.

We had this freedom, had been wonderfully well taught to fly, but had had virtually no service training. We were presented with our job and got on with it. Where the lack of service training showed up was when we had the VE-Day celebrations and had to hold a parade. Although I was supposed to be the Commanding Officer, I hardly knew my left from my right. Fortunately for me, there were one or two people who did know what to do, so I just walked on and walked off.

Although we had this VE-Day celebration, we thought, jolly good luck to them at home, but we still had a war on. Surprisingly enough, I never detected any jealousy or envy. The truth was that it had become difficult for us to appreciate that the war could ever end. Strangely too, throughout the entire war I never saw the enemy in a personal sense. I flew against the Japanese for three years and never saw one, and I don't think I ever saw a German either. That, of course, was a joy and a blessing of the Air Force.

On a day in late August 1945, we were briefed, bombed-up and ready for take-off, when, for no apparent reason, we were told to stand down. The same happened the next day. Then the news burst on us – 'the bomb' – it was all over.

So our day arrived. VJ-Day. We certainly did have a celebration. We had one of our Liberators on the go, backwards and forwards to Calcutta, ferrying great quantities of beer, and no doubt other bottles as well. On this occasion, the Australians felt that they should come into their own and show us how they could roast a whole ox over a bonfire. Beef? It was probably old Water Buffalo. That was my most vivid memory of VJ-Day – the unpleasant smoke and a piece of dripping red charcoaled buffalo.

Frank Carey, a distinguished Battle of Britain pilot, ran a fighter training school at Armada Road, just south of us at Salbani. Quite often our Liberators would go down there to 'play' with his fighters!

On one occasion in June 1944, I just dropped in to have lunch. We had only just had our first glass, when a distraught villager burst into the mess. Would we help? A leopard had just mauled a child in their village and it was still there.

Armed with rifles we set off in Frank's jeep – one crack fighter-pilot and one bomber-boy – with the villager to show the way, and us not quite knowing what we were going to find.

We saw this poor child with a great lump torn out of her side, which they had filled with a cow pat. Apparently they had healing properties! The women-folk were in a terrible state and the men were going in all directions, armed with spears, bows and arrows, and an assortment of quite fearsome weapons!

There, in the branches of a great mango tree, in this tiny collection of huts, was this lovely great creature, draped out along a branch. The two valiant gentlemen took careful aim and fired, obviously wounding the animal but, unfortunately, not killing it. It came bounding down the tree, scattering us all as it went, and disappeared. We realised that honour was at stake and we were duty bound to track it down, but didn't quite know where to go.

The headman then took charge and pointed to the eaves of one of the huts. Apparently it had taken refuge in there. We were pushed forward by all the villagers, they were all around us, until we were only about ten yards away. There was a great roar and out leapt the leopard. We could not even lift our rifles properly with everyone crowding around us and by great good fortune, the leopard didn't touch any of us, but bounded right through between us all. Unwisely for him, he again took refuge up this tree and this time we didn't make a mistake.

As a final footnote, Frank Carey tells me that any hope he had of being regarded as a famous hunter was destroyed when the leopard skin returned from the curers in Calcutta. Apparently the skull, which had been sent with the skin in order to give the appropriate savage appearance to the ultimate fireside rug, had not been properly cleaned. The head of the rug had rotted, to become a hairless, flat and wrinkled grey mass. This prompted the story that Frank was shooting a line, hadn't shot the leopard at all, but had paid some local lads to club it to death!

By late summer 1945, I felt exhausted. I had been fortunate in flying 99 missions safely, but longed to get back home in time to see the beech trees in the Thames Valley changing to their lovely autumn colours. By good luck I did. Before I left we had a tremendous squadron party, and then I was decanted into Delhi, where the C-in-C generously offered me a lift on his plane to England.

It had been three years. My dear old father had the foresight, and kindness, to book a room in a hotel for two or three nights for Cynthia and me, so we could get to know each other again. I was terribly pleased to get home, I had a bus all to myself going up to London. They dropped me off at the Mayfair with all my battered old tin trunks. I had only just recovered from the party out in India. Most of me was still there.

Flight Sergeant David Russell

When war broke out they put up a big poster of a guy in a blue uniform with his flying helmet and his cleft chin and a Spitfire behind him, looking up at the sky: 'Wanted: young men of dash and initiative for aircrew duties in the RAF'. I reckoned that I was just as good-looking as that bugger on the poster and I went in. I only asked what an aircrew consisted of, and the next minute they had every bloody stitch of clothing off me and I'm standing on a wet towel to prove I haven't got flat feet.

I was made an air-gunner and was posted to 21 Squadron at Watton which made low-level attacks on shipping. On our first morning in the mess I was approached by a man from Northern Ireland who'd heard my accent. He said, 'Look, enjoy yourself, you've got two weeks.' Well, needless to say, I felt a certain amount of my Dutch courage begin to dissipate!

My first raid, which was on the Frisian Islands, was a baptism of fire, because I didn't see a bloody thing. I was sitting on my tin hat because I wanted to get married later and they said that you could be decapitated at the wrong end. I'd been told that I had to belt away with my Browning guns at every target I could see. Well, I saw a ship above my head and I was belting away into the clear blue yonder!

Daylight low-level ops on Two Group were far from healthy. A posting to Libya offered better chances of survival, but when Pearl Harbor took place and we were eastward bound, we flew into chaos. Landing at various places between Cairo and Singapore we found nothing but fear and uncertainty at every stop. As an operational squadron capable of attracting attention by our presence we were an embarrassment to people who had never heard a shot fired in anger. They didn't want us in Burma or in Malaya and at Singapore they told us they couldn't handle us. Little wonder, for every time the air-raid siren sounded in Sembawang the entire station disappeared into the rubber.

Wing Commander Jeudwine, our new CO, became very confused and decided we'd go to Sumatra. We landed at Medan and the Dutch refuelled us, but couldn't give us any bombs. So we flew to Palembang and there they said they could adapt some bombs and give us at least something to work with in the meantime. Jeudwine was getting all sorts of garbled orders from Singapore. Finally we were given orders to fly up to take on fuel at Medan, and do operations on Thailand, Malaya and Burma, looking for ships on the way. There was no radio contact because there were no radio stations. We sent out an aircraft now and then to look for targets. It was as bad as that. We had no ops room to work from. At no time did Jeudwine ever have more than six aircraft that he could use for operational purposes. So we'd fly up to Medan; refuel, find a target, bomb it, and then back three hundred miles to Palembang. We had to scrounge for food and fight for a bed and I was getting terribly tired and very fed up. We bombed Kuantan; then a ship when we didn't even know if it was Dutch or not. And the oil wells in Sumatra after we evacuated it.

We were setting off from Palembang one day on an operation against an invasion fleet coming into Sumatra when we saw this squadron of aircraft coming in the opposite direction. They looked like Lockheed Hudsons, but they were Japanese. I looked behind and I saw parachutes going down into the aerodrome called P2. Some of our friends were in P2. We were flying from P1. If they dropped parachutes at P1, too, we were going to come back to an infested aerodrome. We must have had a dozen aircraft at our service that day, which was great, but we bombed at too low a height and the aircraft were walloped all over the place after the bombs dropped. We came back up the river strafing their barges, which were absolutely down to the gunnels with soldiers. Of course the awful worry was not knowing if they'd already taken P1.

When we got back it was completely evacuated. There were no Japs there. Only a few RAF personnel had stayed. We found their billets empty, their clothing all over the place. The place was a shambles. It was like a ghost-town. So we went to Batavia in Java.

In the meantime, unbeknown to us, the ship *Yoma* was on its way full of squadron ground crew and spares. It came later to Sumatra and the boys were ordered off to defend the island against the Japanese invaders. Eventually the *Yoma* picked them up again and took them to the northern coast of Java and just put them off on the island where they all became prisoners, never having fought. There were thousands and thousands of guys coming in from Singapore, Malaya and Burma. Java was the only place left, and it was hiving with troops of all kinds, trying to get out.

The squadron organised raids back into Sumatra. We bombed P2 and P1, in Palembang; we bombed the oil wells. We'd been at Kalidjati in northern Java maybe two weeks when word came through that the Japanese invasion fleet was already off the north coast – fifteen minutes from our drome.

I did three operational flights that night on the fleet. We saw them dimly by the moon, but I don't think we hit anything.

When we landed at dawn we got to the dispersal point and the aerodrome was pretty well empty. Nobody came to meet us. Then three tanks came out: the Japs had already landed. They'd come in unhindered by the Dutch, through the bush, and were right on the aerodrome's perimeter. They began firing all over the place. We put a flare into the aircraft to set it alight, but the thing didn't catch! By then the Japs had opened up and we had to run like hell.

To do them justice our boys had stayed behind at the safe side of the drome to evacuate us when we landed. We were told we were to go to Bandoeng in the centre of Java. Well, that was the most humiliating experience of my service career – I saw my aircraft sitting there waiting for the Japs to take it, knowing that I hadn't helped to do any damage to anybody and that the whole thing had been just a token presence. The squadron had been sacrificed for the sake of somebody's face somewhere in the background.

I think one of the most telling moments was when an Air Marshal came to Sumatra saying there'd been far too much defeatism and we were going to fight to the last man. Sumatra had to be held, and we needed to smarten ourselves up, we needed to shave.

Within two days the Air Marshal gave orders for us to evacuate Sumatra. That's how we fought to the last man!

We knew damn well that Java was going to fall. We were billeted at the time in a huge colonial bungalow belonging to a rubber planter. He saw the writing on the wall and presented the keys of the place, including the one to the cellar, to myself and Douglas Mackillop. We owned the estate for one day only, spent sampling every bottle in the cellar. Douglas was later drowned when the prison ship he was in was torpedoed on the way to Borneo.

We joined a convoy of trucks, an old bus and a couple of

motorbikes, then we met a Dutchman who had six brand new Chevrolet cars. He gave them to us tanked up. Doug Argent took one of the Chevrolets and piled four fellows into it – with Doug and me in the front. Just outside the village on the way to Bandoeng we came across a single Englishwoman wearing a print dress, a pair of white shoes, carrying a fox terrier dog and a little handbag, her sole belongings. We stopped the car and gave her a lift. Incidentally Doug survived the war to become the producer of *Steptoe* and *Till Death*.

Bandoeng was absolutely crawling with servicemen. The Dutch Navy, the home guard, Aussies, Chinese, servicemen of all ranks and descriptions, all wondering what the hell the future was going to be. We were there three days during which the Japanese simply bombed the place to hell. We were on an aerodrome and we were trying to defend it with Lee Enfields and pea-shooters. The Air Marshal then said, you'll get some ammunition and you'll go into the jungle and fight as guerrilla fighters. Eventually we were told that that order had been rescinded and people like aircrew and senior officers were to proceed to the port of Tjilatjap where they would be evacuated on a ship that was en route from Australia.

It must have taken us nine or ten hours to get down to the south coast and into Tjilatjap. We no sooner arrived than a score of Jap Betties bombed the place to hell. It was Sumatra all over again.

There had been three or four big bombings and there were debris and dead animals in the river and dead bodies. There were ships that had been sunk and were still burning.

It was a very extensive port with a couple of oil wells, big oil holders. The CO said for our last effort against the Japanese we'd burn the bloody place. I had the night of my life, because we set fire to everything. We got pissed on Scotch whisky, I was absolutely paralytic. There were fifteen brand new American cars, and we just took the handbrakes off and pushed them all into the river.

There must have been forty-five of us left. Johnny Jeudwine got us on parade, and said, 'Look, I'm afraid it's every man for himself.' Now, that's an expression I'd never heard spoken. Of course I'd read it in adventure stories. 'Every man for himself.' 'Christ, if it's every man for himself, I haven't got a bloody chance!' I said. Jeudwine replied, 'I want you to forage. If you find a boat, try to go to Australia.' Australia! Australia was at least two thousand miles away!

But we hunted around and got two lifeboats. Everybody piled into them. There was a sail. We filled them with fresh water tins, and tins of biscuits, tins of Pabst beer, anything that could be kept.

Somebody got this little flat-bottomed river barge and three officers got into it. They were going to get rope, tie the two lifeboats on and tow them out of the estuary and out to sea. By sheer magic we would go south-east from Java and maybe, after two months, reach Australia. We had pretty poor maps but we had a compass. I was in the second boat and I was up to my knees in water. The thing was leaking like a sieve.

We got away down the estuary with this wee boat looking like the *African Queen* ahead pulling us. It was giving off fumes, the crew were out cold, and the boat was veering off course. We had to pull the rope back to get the three guys off it, and then we just cast it adrift and it just went putt-putt-putting away on its own.

The CO called us to stop and re-think. We had come to the mouth of the estuary where there was a little island. As we put in towards the island, my boat hit a coral reef and the arse came out and we all had to go overboard. I had my kit with me and managed to swim to the shore. The CO put an anchor over the side of his boat, which was safely in ten feet of water. We put all the stores on the shore, and he lined us up, about forty-five of us, and said it was obvious we couldn't all go. Twelve was the absolute limit, and with that number he hoped to get to Australia. The rest must stay on the island and find a spring. There was a banana plantation. There was a lighthouse. If he hit Australia, he would get a flying boat and come back to pick everyone up, signalling a letter P on an Aldis lamp.

My navigator Geoff and I both got our kit. After all, we'd been flying with the CO from the start. But Wing Commander Jeudwine took us down the beach a little, and told us he wasn't taking us. We had no knowledge of sailing, and a lot of the Australians did. He was going to take only Australians, and Squadron Leader Passmore and his crew. Passmore was English, but had done a lot of sailing. We were heartbroken. The CO then swam out to get on the boat and I shook hands with him. I was crying my eyes out, treading water. He wished me luck.

The next day Keene, a Canadian, saw a lifeboat floating by in the current. The thing was more seaworthy than the boat we'd lost, and about thirty feet long. It had a sail, but the mast was very badly cracked at the bottom. Keene thought it was repairable, and asked who wanted to go with him. I stepped forward, being a man of dash and initiative with a cleft chin. Two English blokes, Joe Morley and Fry, stepped forward and four Aussies. Nobody else wanted to go. The boat leaked.

We swam across to the mainland where the docks were still burning and got a big reel of wire to mend the mast. We heard firing, but we didn't know the Japs were already in the place. It turned out later that the firing we heard was two of our boys being shot by the Japanese.

The boys from my squadron coaxed me not to go. It wasn't courage that was driving me, it was the fact that I had a very vivid imagination, and I knew the Japanese hadn't signed the Geneva Convention. So that was why I was going. After five days in the boat we were bailing all day. We had sun sores, our lips were cracked, and we were arguing. There was no-one of officer rank to lead, and we were submitting decisions to a vote. After ten days on a flat sea, when we were about three hundred yards off Java, suddenly the ship began to go down into a swell and then rise again. These swells got deeper and deeper. We weren't to know that we were off one of the most dangerous beaches on the south-east coast of Java. It got terribly turbulent, and then I could see this swell of water about sixty feet high coming towards us. It hit us broadside on, the mast and everything went over the side, and somebody started screaming to get her bow on. The next wave was a huge breaker, and it just flipped us over and down we went. It was a very rocky, shelving beach. You couldn't swim, you just turned like a top all the time. Everytime I came to the surface to fill my lungs I could hear a voice screaming: it was one of the Aussies. He couldn't swim and he thought everyone else could. Nobody else was even trying. Eventually we were thrown on to the beach in total darkness and lay there exhausted until the next morning. We got into a little village, but everyone had fled when they saw us. Eventually a rather shy native came out, I think he was a headman. We told him we were British. We were all naked, our clothes had been ripped off by the water. He got us some saris and we put them round our waists. Joe Morley had kept his wallet, and had 120 guilders, which he gave to the bloke to get us a boat and supplies. So we sat there recuperating under the palm trees, and the bugger came back with Japs with him. I think he got five bucks a head for us.

We were taken to Jogjakarta and there we found an established prison camp where there were six hundred Dutch. The Dutch women were still free, but because the men had joined the home guard, they were all in the camp.

After we'd been there about two weeks three Dutchmen were caught climbing back over the wire at night, having visited their wives. A few days later we were all taken on to this football field where they had dug three graves. A Japanese Sergeant-Major got us all on parade, arranged on three sides of a square, staggered, so that nobody could miss what was going to happen. Eventually these poor creatures were led out, hands tied behind their backs, bleeding profusely from cuts and bruises all over them, staggering as the Japanese prodded them. One was placed opposite each grave. Two ranks of Japanese soldiers, none over seventeen years of age, seemed to be the firing squad. A black Dutch chap standing beside me translated the sentence read out in Malayan by a Japanese officer. He said, 'They are going to kill them, but they are not going to shoot them. They are to die by thrusting.'

While all this was going on, the Japanese officer lit a cigarette in a tortoiseshell holder, put his hands in his riding breeches' pockets and stood beside the three victims, really enjoying the scene. Then he signalled and three young Japanese left the ranks. One stood opposite each prisoner with a fixed bayonet. The officer looked to see if we were all watching, threw away his cigarette, took out another and put it in his holder. The three Dutch guys refused to be bandaged. The Japs thumped them with their rifle butts and they had to submit to the bandage. They were standing each in front of his grave.

The Japanese officer made his men practise bayonet drill – forward, retreat, forward, retreat, forward and then a lunge. Eventually they lunged for the stomach and the three men fell on the ground kicking. They kept thrusting at them and threw the men still kicking into the graves. By then my mouth was just dry.

Then we were marched into Bandoeng – a very big camp – and there were the guys who had stayed on the beach. They had been six weeks on the beach with the Japs just across the estuary. Eventually they ran out of food, and one of them had syphilis and they had to get him treated. So they had surrendered. We later discovered that the CO had reached Australia in forty-six days and had flown back, as he had promised, but the boys had already become POWs.

The camp at Bandoeng was highly organised. The officers' lines were sacrosanct – you only visited them if you knew somebody. All the ranks were kept separate. I became the camp librarian under the aegis of Colonel van der Post. We did get books. Van der Post was quite a character. He got all the talent together and started a school: a gunner called Rees, who was a lecturer in French, started giving French lessons; another guy was teaching Italian, and another Russian. My navigator friend, Ken Wibley, started Russian in prison camp and later became Senior Lecturer in Russian at Bangor University, North Wales. Van der Post spoke

Japanese, but he was getting information from all sources by pretending he didn't understand a word of it. He was a great morale builder: he would come round the Sergeants' lines and say 'Morniiing!', singing it out as if life was just perfect. He was charming and very inspirational. He'd been fighting guerrilla warfare against the Italians. He spoke fluent Dutch, French, and Italian as well as Japanese. He was well built and strong, because he had been out in the jungle so long. He would come into the library every day. But he wouldn't touch anything except cowboy stories. He said he loved cowboy stories – open-air spaces got him away from the close environment of a prison camp. He was good.

I had quite a reasonable life for four or five months and then they decided to take us to Japan. We had five days on a ship to Singapore and another twenty-eight days on a ship battened down. We lost quite a number of people on that trip. There were burials every day at sea with canvas bags overboard. It was a terrible journey. We couldn't lie down. We slept sitting up, back to back. There were rats everywhere, running over your face every night. Feeding was very difficult. They would bring a big wooden barrel full of mushy rice to the top of the gangway. The mess tins had our names on them and were passed hand over hand. When we landed I was eventually moved to a place called Ikuno where I became a copper miner. Most of my friends were there. I became a barrack hancho in Ikuno and had to learn Japanese drill.

I mined copper for a couple of years. The Japanese soldiers wouldn't come down the mine – it was only us and the civilian miners. Our job was to get great big heavy buggies and fill them with copper ore. You had a thing called a hopper, a big heavy wooden tray which you kept between your feet. You had a yamatori, a kind of hoe, with which you scraped copper ore into this hopper and you then tipped it into a buggy. We got expert at filling the buggy with pit props to take up space and covering them with copper ore.

Sometimes we got complete freedom to be by ourselves with

just this wee lamp in pitch blackness. Here would be a big pile of copper ore, and Taff and I sitting philosophising at the top. We each had a pipe with the backside nearly burned out of it, because we just peeled off bark from the pit props and put it in and lit it up. It would blow your head off. We smoked rice husks, tea leaves, anything we could get – even Japanese dog ends. There wasn't a man in the camp who didn't lose his pride by picking up the dog ends. Taff would treat me to a lecture on English Lit.

The abiding memory is the fact of starvation. The food was just minimum. We were trying to do a ten-hour shift in the mines on a few grains of rice a day. It was unpolished rice, full of weevils just scraped off the floor of some store. We stole like mad. I became a very accomplished thief. In summer time the Japanese gave us little cotton shorts, which was all we wore, and you could see everybody's ribs. We were burned black from working outside. On one day a week we worked in the gardens outside the camp, but weren't allowed to touch the produce. They grew magnificent crops of oranges, plums, breadfruit, eggfruit and rice. Sometimes they let us take the white radish tops which we put into the soup.

There was no soil. They grew everything on sand covered with manure, which we supplied. They had these huge concrete pits behind each billet, for latrines. They gave you a long pole with a big tin on the end of it and you filled the wooden barrels with loose shit – everyone had diarrhoea and dysentery, and you had this pole which you placed in hoops attached to the top of the barrel and you carried the honeypots out to the plants and you fertilised them.

Our morale was high. It's odd, you live on hope. We were getting information, and that was important for morale. We had a fellow called Arthur Brady who taught himself Japanese. We stole newspapers and he was able to translate a lot of it. We knew when Germany packed up because first of all the Japanese put us all on parade at 3.00 a.m. and beat the hell out of us. We knew something big had happened. We were delighted. Arthur got hold of a paper, and was able to translate the word Eisenhower.

We thought he was a bloody German. We'd never heard of him.

We had no library when we went to the mines. We'd each taken one book. Some fellows took the Bible. I took the *Essays of Elia*. Those were the only books we had. It was an odd funny thing in the mining camp, books became in such short supply that you took pages 1–50 of, say, *The Murder of Roger Ackroyd* and you gave it to somebody else. So you'd get guys coming round the billets saying, 'Anybody got pages 145 to 190 of such and such a book?' We read books by instalments. I managed to keep mine. No-one wanted to read it.

After the end of the war in Europe we thought maybe the Japanese would go easy. But they didn't. They were getting all sorts of propaganda: they were going to fight on the beaches. The women were out practising bayonet drill, the kids were out practising throwing hand-grenades – pieces of rock – on the sand outside the camp, and the newspapers were full of how to defend the country against the American invader. The Jap guards were saying, 'The Americans come, you die!' They cut down on the food because they were beginning to starve themselves. And they kept reminding us of what they were going to do to us. It was terrifying.

But there was one big act of kindness that happened to me after the German capitulation. I was working down the mine and Taff and I had just been given a beating for not working hard enough and we discovered that, in addition to the pit props, if you got a great big piece of copper ore into the buggy, that filled up quite a big space. I lifted this huge piece, and as I got to the edge of the buggy my stomach muscles just collapsed and the thing dropped over the edge and cut the end of my finger off. I was bleeding like a stuck pig and Taff was flapping around saying, 'You're going to die!' He went and fetched the Japanese foreman. The Japanese didn't think you were sick until there was blood all over the place. So he saw the blood and got on the blower to the surface and down came the Japanese Sergeant we called the King of Jazz, because he used pomade on his hair. He saw the blood and marched me back to camp two solid bloody miles with me leaving a river of blood behind me.

We had two Belfast doctors in that camp, both Flight Lieutenants. Harold Knox wanted to know why we hadn't brought the end of my finger, because he could have sewn it back on. He could only put a tourniquet round my arm, because he had no anaesthetic. The little bone was sticking up and had to come off. It wasn't pleasant because the nail bed was still intact and he had to get the nail to go over the end of the bone. He did it. But he had to cut the end of the bone with a pair of scissors, and I nearly went through the roof. (Later on, Taff came in after the shift had ended with this grubby piece of meat, the end of my finger. We took it to the doc. He took a look at it and rejected it.) After that a Japanese did my work for me for a solid month, wouldn't let me lift a thing. People won't believe that of the Japanese. That guy was a gentleman.

Knox loved using a scalpel. He was a physician really, but he was a surgeon manqué. He had one anodyne, and that was to recite *The Rubaiyat of Omar Khayyam*. He would go through it verse after verse while poking around with a scalpel.

The day the atom bomb hit Hiroshima was a very interesting morning. I got my barrack out as usual, at six-thirty in the morning, with the boys lined up in fours, and no Japs came to take the count! They never failed before. Dead on time you had to be there! We hung around wondering what the hell was going on. Eventually we sat down – normally the last thing we should have done. Then we saw one of the Japanese Sergeants emerging from the guard room and his head was bowed. He looked around a bit disconsolately then went back in.

Everybody was wondering what was going on. We thought the Yanks had landed and the Japs were going to kill us. The uncertainty frightened the life out of me. Then the sliding window of the cook-house was suddenly rammed aside and there was Kinsella, the cook, and his eyes were staring, and he shouted, 'The fucking war's over! The fucking war's over!' For the following two weeks we hung around, speculating about what would happen and foraging for food.

One day I was sitting on the roof looking over the curling path that led up to the camp from the way down the mountainside, and I saw this big black spider moving slowly along the road. It got bigger and bigger and turned out to be a big black Bechstein Grand Piano! Forty POWs were underneath it. They brought it in and planted it in the middle of the camp. Wilf Pooley, a Welsh pianist, got on it, and everybody gathered and sang. Then a Japanese civilian came in with a wind-up gramophone and a bunch of records and we got it up into the billet and we put it on, and there was the most beautiful music! It wasn't Japanese music, but *Clair de Lune*. Magic.

After two weeks the Americans arrived. They cleaned us, deloused us and put us on various ships and I finished up in Vancouver. All the people of Vancouver came out and were shouting at us from a distance, and gave us a tremendous welcome, but they were not allowed near us. Suddenly across the public address system came, 'Will Sergeant Russell go to the SWO's Office.' I went to the SWO's office and he said, 'There's word here from an aunt of yours in North Bay, Ontario, which this train will be going through. She just wanted to know that you're safe. You stay aboard, boy, don't be getting off at North Bay, because the train will be only stopping for water.'

I got back aboard and two girls came up the platform in blue uniforms with a tray of apples and chocolates. I think they'd chosen the prettiest ones. One came up to me and asked my name. When I told her, she said, 'Gee! You're cute. Nadine and I have got a car outside, and we've two pairs of pyjamas. Be a pal, get off the train, and we'll go and have a good time up in the mountains at my dad's cottage.' Well, talk about ready for it! They had told us we were going to be impotent, but Jesus, I wasn't impotent! I got Bill Handley and we got our kit, and the two girls stood and blocked the view down the deserted platform and put us in a little room. We were standing there and a voice comes up on the public address, 'Sergeant Russell, you're expected, North Bay, we hope you got the message, North Bay. Your aunt will be there to see you.' And I felt my heart going down. They knew I was aboard. If I didn't appear at the far end, my mother would think I was dead! I said to the girls, 'I'm sorry, girls, give me a kiss, I've got to go.' They asked if I could get them another guy! Could?? About forty of them were hanging out the windows! In North Bay the train stopped for water, and there was my old Aunt Minnie, a religious maniac, with her henpecked husband, Joe, waiting for me.

I jumped off the train and hid until it pulled out. Aunt Minnie took me prisoner. I hated North Bay and was delighted when the local MPs arrested me and sent me home.

Corporal Patricia Coulson

When I joined the WAAF in October 1942 I went with mixed feelings, but I had to go, I was conscripted. Part of me was excited at the thought of something new happening in my life, another part was apprehensive at the thought of leaving home, a fear of the unknown.

When interviewed by the Careers Officer I opted for Pay Accounts. I had been doing accounts in a commercial office.

When I left Morecambe (drilling, marching, lectures and injections) I went to the accounting school in South Wales. Five weeks' hard graft, school during the day, studying in the evenings and weekends. The Careers Officer was right, accounting in the Services is different. Nevertheless I passed the examinations and after seven days' leave I reported to Uxbridge, my first posting.

Here, I became a member of the War Casualties Accounts Unit, comprising about fifty men and girls. We kept pay records of all airmen and officers who came under the heading 'Casualties'. There were two departments, Airmen, and Officers, and these were divided into sections – Missing, prisoners-of-war; and Missing, presumed dead. I was in the prisoner-of-war section – Airmen, Europe.

Although for two and a half years these men were just names on a ledger, we had constant reminders that they were human beings. Through the International Red Cross the men imprisoned in Europe were able to fill in forms to arrange movement of some of their pay. Some would request a sum to be sent to a relative, others made what we now call 'A Standing Order' – a specific amount to be sent to a relative at regular intervals. Quite often we received letters of thanks from relatives who really appreciated what the Red Cross and we were doing to ease a financial crisis.

The powers-that-be decided at one time that, as the prisoners in the Far East did not have this facility, a Post Office account was opened for them and amounts were paid in from their accounts periodically. The Post Office books were kept in safe-keeping until their return.

After a year or so at Uxbridge the whole unit moved to a house in Harley Street in London. It was there that, in March 1945, we were told that, as the war in Europe was drawing to a close, we would be moving to Cosford in Shropshire. Here, a special unit – No. 4 MRU (Medical Rehabilitation Unit) – was opened and, as the men came home, we closed the accounts on our ledgers and transferred them to this unit.

It all began when one of the girls in our billet told us that she had to work all night in the orderly room; she would not say why, but, instinctively, we knew this was it. Nobody slept that night, we lay quietly in our beds, not speaking, just listening to the constant rumble of lorries going through the camp. The next morning, about eight o'clock, the girl returned to the billet looking utterly exhausted. When asked 'How did it go?' she just flung herself on to the bed, sobbing as if her heart would break. We stayed with her until finally, from sheer exhaustion, she fell asleep.

The more serious cases were taken straight to the hospital just outside the camp, others were billeted on the camp. One could recognise them slowly walking around the camp, painfully thin and with a certain look in their eyes. A ruling was made that they could come into the office during certain hours to enquire about their accounts. We all had a big card on our desks stating which letter of the alphabet we were dealing with. I was D–E–F. Before they arrived we had been given a talk by our Warrant Officer. The gist of it was: 'These men will be coming into the office every day. You must remember, they have been imprisoned – some for a very long time – so you must be very careful as to the attitude you adopt. Just behave normally.'

I don't think we needed to be told this, we were responsible adults. I found that my approach had to be according to the individual. Some had been able to cope with imprisonment and when they came in were quite cheerful, savouring their newly found freedom – like the one who wanted to draw out all his money, buy a car and take me out in the evening to celebrate! What he didn't know was – firstly, he would not be allowed to draw it all out in one go; secondly, petrol would not be allowed for such jaunts; and, lastly, as we were working until eight o'clock every evening, I would be too tired anyway! Other prisoners-of-war had not fared so well, and it had left its mark. They were quiet and withdrawn and needed helping along. Some had obvious injuries like the Sergeant in a wheelchair, paralysed because he had been struck on the base of the spine with a rifle butt. Keeping one's emotions in check was difficult.

I did make one terrible blunder and, even now, I squirm if I think of it. I can't remember the airman's name so let us say 'Ford, last three numbers 123'. His account was passed to me from Missing Section. His income tax was rather involved and, just when I was getting it straightened out, I got an order that there had been a mistake, pass the account back to Missing. Not long after, the documents came back to me; confirmed, prisoner-of-war. Later came further instructions, 123 Ford – confirmed missing, presumed dead. So his account was taken off my ledger. Therefore, when one day an airman came in enquiring about his account giving his name as Ford, last three numbers 123, before I could stop myself I said, 'Oh, but you're dead.' I apologised immediately and explained what had been happening. Fortunately he took it very well. He roared with laughter and said, 'Do I look as though I'm dead?'

After all the accounts had been transferred to 4 MRU we joined those who were dealing with the Far East accounts. This was slightly different because, on release, these men were taken to Canada for a few weeks' recuperation, but nevertheless, they remembered.

Two of these men stand out in my mind, George and Bill. Myself and my friend had become friendly with them, and often went to the pub in the local village for a drink and a game of darts. Bill was twenty-two and George was in his mid-forties, known to all his younger colleagues as 'Pop'. Bill was having intensive treatment for his eye injuries due to having been forced – as a form of punishment – to lie flat on his back looking up at the sun. But it wasn't about himself that Bill talked, it was George: George, who had helped keep up Bill's morale when he had been in the depths of despair; George, who had given his meagre food and milk ration to a young lad of nineteen who was dying of tuberculosis. He told us numerous stories of this nature, and it was obvious that he and many others had the greatest admiration for George, a father figure, who had done all he could for the young ones – physically and mentally.

As for George himself he never spoke of misery and suffering, his stories were always humorous. One example was: on one occasion when a guard was counting the number of men leaving the camp as a working party – counting with an abacus – the men kept moving around so that at every count the guard had a different number. Bill told us many tragic stories and it wasn't difficult to build a picture of the humiliation, degradation and misery that was suffered.

After the men came back from the Far East they were given their Post Office books. We received a letter from a mother; briefly, it read: 'My son (she gave his name), who is living with me, has been given his Post Office book. Could you please give me authority to draw out the money to look after him. He has returned minus his arms and legs.' He was twenty-three.

This sums it all up. However much I may not remember of the past as I grow older, these things I saw and heard during this period of my life will always be with me.

The End of the War . . .

The end of the war took away the purpose that for years had united young men of a dozen different countries in friendship and mutual loyalty. Flying together and fighting together, it had been a way of life and fulfilment that few would ever experience again, even if for so many it had been a way of death.

Flight Lieutenant Frank Ziegler
609 Squadron

PART THREE
THE RAF POST-WAR

Introduction: The Jet Age

Pioneering continued as soon as the war ended with ventures such as the first British flight over the North Pole (1945), a new world speed record of 616mph (1946), a new London to Cape Town speed record (1947), and the first Atlantic crossing by jet aircraft (1948).

There were also major operational commitments. In June 1948 the RAF joined Western allies in the Berlin Air Lift to sustain the city when the Soviet Union closed road and rail links. When the blockade was raised in May 1949, the RAF had flown 282,000 tons of freight into Berlin in 49,733 sorties over more than 18,000,000 miles of flying. RAF operations in the Malayan 'Emergency' which began in 1948 as 'Operation Firedog' lasted until mid-1960, and 375,849 sorties were flown.

The Korean War, which began in 1950, involved RAF Transport Command deploying large numbers of troops direct by air from the UK. Royal Navy carrier-borne aircraft played the major British role in air operations over Korea. (Indeed, there was no RAF fighter capable of countering the Russian-built MiG 15. The US Sabre was eventually bought as a stop-gap until British swept-wing designs entered service.)

In 1953, the RAF was at its strongest since the war: 277,125 men and women; more than 6,300 aircraft of all types. Some 440 jets were displayed at the Coronation review. RAF aircraft saw action in the Kenyan Mau Mau campaign of 1954 and the Suez Crisis of 1956 (when Valiant 'V' Bombers were used in a conventional role).

The advent of the four-engine, strategic, 'V' Bombers – the Valiant, Vulcan and Victor – and the development of British nuclear weapons in the early 1950s provided Britain's nuclear deterrent. The Fylingdales early warning station of 1964 provided the famous four-minutes warning of Soviet nuclear attack during which the 'V' Bombers would have scrambled. Royal Navy Polaris submarines assumed the strategic deterrent role from the RAF in 1969, and the 'V' Bombers were transferred to a NATO tactical role. (The last Vulcan squadron disbanded in 1984; Victors still serve as tankers.)

The RAF's first supersonic fighter, the English Electric Lightning, entered service in 1960 and was armed with air-to-air missiles. Techniques of air-to-air refuelling were developed to enhance the capability of deploying combat aircraft overseas in emergency, 'fire brigade' operations.

There were emergency deployments to Kuwait in July 1961, Brunei in December 1962 and Borneo in December 1963 for the protracted 'Confrontation' with Indonesia. In South Arabia, RAF ground-attack aircraft provided close support to Army units in the Radfan operations until 1967. In 1965, a Javelin fighter squadron was deployed with supporting radar and RAF Regiment troops to Zambia when Rhodesia declared independence. RAF Shackletons helped enforce the United Nations oil sanctions on Rhodesia while Transport Command's Britannias airlifted nearly four million gallons of oil to Zambia.

The 1960s saw major government cancellations in British aircraft designs intended for the RAF and substantial orders for US types. The revolutionary P1154 vertical take-off and landing, supersonic fighter was axed, though the developmental P1127 survived to become, eventually, the Harrier. The HS681 jet transport project and the advanced TSR2 supersonic strike/reconnaissance aircraft were abandoned. American F-111 strike aircraft were ordered – and later cancelled. The US Phantom strike aircraft and the Hercules tactical transport did enter RAF service. Collaboration with the French produced the Jaguar fighter-bomber. Wider European collaboration was to develop the Tornado which later became the mainstay of the RAF's strike and air defence capabilities.

The RAF's command structure saw major changes during the 1960s and 1970s. In 1964, the Air Ministry was absorbed into the unified Ministry of Defence. In 1968 the famous wartime Bomber and Fighter Commands amalgamated into Strike Command which then absorbed Coastal Command in 1969 and Air Support Command (formerly Transport Command) in 1973. By mid-1977 the RAF consisted of two Commands – Strike Command, its operational arm; and Air Support Command, its training and maintenance arm.

Royal Navy Phantoms and Buccaneers were transferred to the RAF as the large aircraft carriers were phased out. In 1975, the RAF's first-line strength was reported as 750 first-line aircraft deployed in 54 squadrons. The 1980s saw the RAF concentrated almost entirely in the United Kingdom and West Germany in NATO roles.

In 1982, during the Falklands conflict, RAF Vulcans carried out the longest range strategic bombing missions in the history of air power with attacks from Ascension Island against Stanley airfield. Harrier attack aircraft were added to the Royal Navy Sea Harrier force and a sole Chinook heavy-lift helicopter supported ground forces. A major, logistical 'air bridge' was maintained between Britain and Ascension Island and forward to the Falklands zone – a distance of 8,000 miles.

The Gulf War of 1991, sparked by Iraq's invasion of Kuwait, saw a major RAF effort. Tornado fighters were deployed within forty-eight hours of the government decision to provide a large British force. Tornado bombers, Jaguar fighter-bombers, Victor and VC10 tankers, Nimrod maritime patrol aircraft, Hercules transports, Chinook and Puma helicopters and, later, Buccaneers with special laser targeting equipment, all followed. In all, 5,500 RAF personnel served in the Gulf.

Tornado bombers flew 1,500 operational sorties including playing a crucial role in early, low-level night attacks on Iraqi airfields. Six Tornadoes were lost in action. Jaguars flew a range of Army-support missions – 600 sorties without loss. In all, the RAF flew over 6,000 sorties during the Gulf War, using 3,000 tonnes of weapons in action.

In 1999 the RAF were in action in Kosovo and the Balkans. In March 2004 the RAF were in action supporting the Coalition forces invasion of Iraq.

8

PALESTINE

Flying Officer Tim McElhaw

Just eighteen, I joined the Air Force in winter 1944, at Cambridge. The Air Force had decided that their aircrew, who were coming straight out of school, were far too naïve. They instituted a short-course scheme, whereby on leaving school you could do six months at a university as a student, also do Air Squadron stuff, then sign on for aircrew. So I had six months drinking beer at Cambridge. And, of course, I became a lot more mature in the process!

Then I learned to fly, first of all on Tiger Moths up at Perth, and then at Cranwell, though it was called 19 FTS then, because it wasn't the proper Cranwell. We were the first set of courses to go through post-war; the idea was to get the place up and running. I was on no. 4 Course with Roy Bowie and John Nicholls. I was commissioned in May 1946, and went on to a Spitfire OTU at Keevil, where I drank a lot of cider.

After training there I was posted, after two months in Italy, to the Middle East to join 208 Squadron in Palestine, at a place called Ein Shemar, where there were two Spit squadrons and a Lancaster squadron. We arrived in January 1947, when the whole terrorism business was rife, and we were all very unpopular with the local population. The Irgun Zvai Leumi (IZL) were shooting people left, right and centre. We never left camp except in fours, with guns. We wore guns day and night, even in bed. We did a lot of flying, though, especially dawn patrols to see if any ships carrying illegal immigrants had come over the horizon during the night.

Then the Mandate was coming to an end and everyone had to

be out by the end of May 1948. We were moved out of Ein Shemar, to a little airfield at Ramat David, where our two Spit squadrons were to cover the pulling-out. We were due to go on to Cyprus in May. So we took lots of photographs and escorted convoys, and flew what we called 'Scarecrows' – flying up and down over places to show that we were still a force to be reckoned with.

We were meant to move out on 22 May. On the night of 21 May, we drank the bar dry. I remember the last thing we had was some very nauseating Egyptian rum – it was the last bottle in the bar, because we were literally closing the place, smashing it up and vanishing. As a final gesture the Army Liaison Officer shot the lights out. I woke up the next morning badly in need of a pee; we were only in little tin huts. I staggered outside to have a pee and when I looked up, there were some aeroplanes above. And I thought, That's funny. The other squadron, 32, must be flying early. They flew round in a circle, then one of them came down, almost towards me, and dropped a couple of bombs. I thought, Shit! So I dived inside the door and shouted at the others and threw myself on the floor. There was an enormous bloody great bang, then another, and another. There we were under these beds, with our aircraft all neatly lined up in two rows on the concrete outside, while some bugger was dropping bombs on them! There had never been any air threat whatsoever, because the IZL didn't have aircraft and the Haganah didn't have any either. We threw our kit on and rushed outside to see these two Spits going around in a circle above, all nice and orderly. They'd shot up one line of aircraft with gunfire and dropped a couple of bombs on what was the hangar. So we all got into a little bit of a panic about this. We ran down to the aircraft, and I and three others flew down to Tel Aviv, but couldn't find anybody or anything. Of course everybody had long since gone, and we never found out who it was or what it was all about. But we thought that the Jews must have got hold of some aircraft somehow or other and come and done another bit of terrorism.

So it was decided to put up a pair of Spitfires above the airfield,

more or less constantly, in case it happened again. The first pair
had been up for about an hour or so, when it all bloody happened
again. I was in the hangar when they dropped a bomb on it. That
made me angry. I picked up my parachute and ran like hell, passed
a body on the way, and went to my aircraft. Meanwhile the
patrolling pair (Geoff Cooper and Roy Bowie) engaged a couple
of the intruding aircraft, identified them as Egyptian Air Force,
and shot both down, one each, which was very good. My partner,
Les Hully, and I took off, and we flew up and down over the
airfield, until we got a call saying there was something going on
over Haifa, about twenty miles down the valley. So we flogged
down there, but couldn't find anything at all. Then there was an
agonised cry, 'Come back, come back, we're being got at again!'
By this time the Station Commander, Wing Commander Victor
Streatfield, who had gout and had been in bed, had taken command of the whole thing, and he was sitting in a scout car,
watching his airfield as best he could, poor chap, with a stick. So
we belted off back at full throttle, and just as we were coming to
the airfield I saw aircraft orbiting quietly to the left. I think the
pilot was thinking, Ah, well, I'll just line this one up. There's
obviously no opposition. He didn't see me at all. I was going so
fast that I nearly went past him, and actually pulled up beside
him, but it was on his blind side. I noticed that he had Egyptian
markings, and because I didn't know the name of the game at
that stage, I thought, Shit, Egyptians, now what do we do? We
don't want to get into a diplomatic thing. So I called down to the
tower, and said, 'Look, it's an Egyptian, can I shoot at him?' And
Victor Streatfield said, 'Yes, yes, you hit him, boy.' So I simply
dropped back behind him and blasted him. He flipped over and
went straight down to the ground. Les Hully was watching my
tail. We had just about completed a 180° turn, and there was
another one, so I went off after him as well. He saw me and
headed due south, I overtook him without much trouble and hit
him, and he just flipped over and went into the ground. That was
the end of him. So that was two to me; Les didn't get one. A third

was shot down by an RAF Regiment gunner with a Bren gun – which was no mean feat. After this, we tidied up as best we could and flew out the next day to Cyprus.

Many years later I asked Air Chief Marshal Dawson, then our AOC, about the incident. He said, 'Oh, those buggers. I knew the C-in-C of the Egyptian Air Force, and he rang me up the same day and said that he was terribly sorry about it. Could he please fly up in his white Spitfire and come and make amends. So I said not on your nelly, mate, if you come up here you're going to get shot down like the others!' Dawson was very keen that the 'press Johnnies', as he called them, didn't hear about what had occurred. And they did actually manage to keep the whole story quiet, except for the fact that I wrote a letter to my father, home in Swindon, who told the local newspaper. I've still got the clipping – 'Swindon man shoots down two Spitfires'.

Anyway, after this odd episode, we flew out to Cyprus, stayed there for the summer of 1948, and were then going to be moved on to north Africa. But this never happened, because the Jewish–Egyptian war brewed up. We went down to Fayid in the Canal Zone, to defend it, because there was worry then that the Israelis would actually defeat the Egyptians, and take the canal. Mr Ernie Bevin was very worried about this, and he wanted to be able to show a photograph of Israeli forces inside Egypt to the United Nations, and say that this all had to stop.

So we were briefed to go up to the border. The battle was actually going on just where the Gaza Strip now is. We were briefed to fly down the battle area, low level, 500 feet, in Spitfire 18s. We belted up and down there, and got some photographs, and it was more or less all right. But at the same time, as it turned out, the Egyptian Air Force was also belting up and down in Spitfire 9s; but they were shooting up the Israelis and, of course, vice versa.

The Israeli Air Force at that stage was composed mostly of volunteers from other places, including former Royal Air Force pilots, Canadian Air Force, and Americans. They were partly mercenary; one or two were Jewish and flew for the good of the cause, but I think they were mostly mercenaries. Anyway, we flogged up and down and took photos, and everything was fine. We did it every day for seven days, until we got to 7 January. The previous trip, we saw some Egged buses among the tanks, which we recognised because we'd been in Palestine. So we thought we'd really got the photograph that Mr Bevin wanted. Anyway, on 7 January four of us went out, led by Geoff Cooper. I was no. 3, and two of us were flying at 1,000 feet, doing cover, while the others took photographs. We'd nearly got down to what is now the Egyptian border, when the no. 2, Frank Close, actually got hit by ground fire. His engine was on fire; he was at 500 feet, so he pulled straight up, rolled over and baled out.

We did a quick orbit to make sure that he was all right. At that stage, purely by chance, a couple of Israelis, actually a Canadian and an American, had taken off, heard that there was something going on over the battle area, and had come down and found these four aircraft. I think that what they'd actually been put up there for was to try and get some Egyptian Spits that had just gone through, shooting something or other up. In any case, they found us, and came straight in behind from up high. It sounds stupid now, I know, but being TAC/R trained we weren't exactly fighter-pilot-minded, we hadn't done much air combat. So because we weren't that prepared they actually jumped us, and one of them shot down my no. 2, Ron Sayers. I got one on my tail, and Geoff Cooper, the third man, got one on his. He climbed away, but eventually got shot up and baled out, and landed safely among the Egyptian Army.

I was shot up, jumped out, and came to the ground very quickly. I got out of my parachute, and ran off to hide behind a bush. And of course up comes a jeep at a great speed, with a sort of gun in the back, and some very nasty-looking people in it, dirty people – real desert soldiers. They drove straight up to me, because I'd completely forgotten that you leave footprints in sand. So there I was, pathetically hiding behind this bush, with a whole row of footprints leading straight to it. I was taken prisoner. This was some time in the morning, about eleven. And there was a truce at twelve o'clock, on 7 January, which lasted for the best part of two years. Now, nobody had told us about this truce at the briefing, and I was really pissed off later when I found out about it. However the Israelis thought, first of all, that I was an Egyptian, so they took me away as a prisoner-of-war.

I was shipped to Tel Aviv, in the back of a truck. I never saw Frank Close, who was alive, as it turned out, so there were two of us in their hands. We were very much and very clearly among the Israeli Army, whereas Geoff landed in the Egyptian side, so he got off home. But I was interrogated twice, once fairly perfunctorily, in the sense that nobody quite knew what the hell was going on, and then later in the evening quite rigorously.

Clearly they had got the idea that the British had turned on them and come in with the Egyptians. I'm sure that they were very worried. I was also very worried, because it was fairly clear that if we were inside Israel, then we were all in the wrong. My aeroplane had landed in Egypt, but I thought to myself, they could easily pick up all the wreckage and dump it in Israel. Then all they had to do was toss me in the crater with a bit of petrol, and they'd have perfect proof. As it turned out, they did this with Sayers' aeroplane, with his dead body in it. They took it well over their side and bulldozed over the hole, just in case they needed such evidence.

We were really very naïve and not prepared for war, nor certainly for becoming a prisoner-of-war. I hadn't emptied my pockets before taking off so I had everything on me – my diary, a record of lots of trips that had been done, and all sorts of things. It was a bit embarrassing. It was also very frightening. I ended up in Tel Aviv in an Arab house which had been taken over as a jail for Jewish deserters, where I had my own room. The chap who'd shot me down, or one of the others, came to see me and we had a sort of guarded chat to each other. I was cagey, because I didn't know whether we were at war, and I didn't know that there'd been a truce until he told me. I'd been thinking about whether I could break out of this place, but I didn't really think it was a good idea, so I actually hung around there for a fortnight, doing nothing except pressing my trousers, and pretending I was a military chap. There wasn't any more interrogation after the first one, because clearly everybody had realised that nothing was going to happen.

Of course, the people in the Canal Zone got terribly worried, because they'd sent four aircraft out in the morning and none of them had come back, so they got the Tempest Wing to go off, and they zoomed up to the border area. By this time there was more or less a truce, but they got bounced again by the Israeli Air Force, who were flying about. They came from high out of the sun, went straight through the formation, and shot one down; the Tempests couldn't drop their droptanks, because they'd been tightened up too tight. It was a bit of a farce: the RAF lost another aircraft and pilot – dead.

In the end it was decided that we should be shipped back to Cyprus, and I went up to Haifa. There I met Frank Close, who had his jaw wired up, because he'd broken it on landing. He was in a good state, except he couldn't eat. We were put on some little merchant ship for Cyprus, and that was the end of it, more or less. I went home fairly shortly after that, because one of the conditions of our release was that we shouldn't get involved again. Not that we were in a condition to do anything really wild.

So that's how it all turned out. Shot down two Egyptians and eight months later shot down by an Israeli, all when I wasn't expecting it.

9

MALAYA AND KOREA

Flight Lieutenant John Dowling

The first operational use of helicopters was in Malaya in 1950. Three helicopters were all we had to cover the whole of the peninsula, up to the Thai border. It was very important for the troops to know that there was a method of plucking them out of the jungle if they were wounded, and that the casualty evacuation procedure and capability was maintained.

I had trained as a helicopter pilot with the Navy. At first we were going to be sent to Westlands for training, but Westlands said that they couldn't do it. Anyway, it went off very well, partly because Jim Suthers was such an excellent instructor. At the end of his course, he placed a great big fancy stamp in the front of my logbook, and said that I was qualified to fly the Dragonfly. I had flown about twenty hours. So I was among the first one or two helicopter pilots in the Air Force. That was 1950.

Then it was off to the Far East. The helicopter went in a crate, on a boat, and probably took two or three months, so for that time I was cooling my heels in Kuala Lumpur.

Operations in Malaya started the day we got there. 'Casualty Evacuation Flight' was the title of our unit. Theoretically it had no other function, but of course that didn't last, and we were soon doing other emergency evacuations too. We were based in Kuala Lumpur, and we had to use the airfield because that was where the fuel was. That meant the full panoply of RAF regulations governed every take-off and landing which, for a helicopter, made no kind of sense. But they didn't have anybody to write new instructions. Later we found we could get the fuel ourselves. So all we had to do then was to fly. We had a little space just outside the wire, and we put the helicopter in there.

Our first casualty was in May 1950, a Malayan policeman who'd got a wound in his thigh. What happened that first time was that the helicopter went to the nearest Auster strip. If we could do a pick-up from there, of course we did. We only used the jungle clearings when necessary. So that first one was fairly simple.

The next one, which was high drama, was right up in the north of the country, near Kelantan. There they didn't believe that the helicopter would be able to get in and get the chap out, but of course they were not aware of the helicopter's capability. That was where we established the pattern we subsequently used. The pilot had another pilot as an assistant. He landed at the nearest refuelling point and made that a base for the operation. Then he sent the recce party in by air to confirm that the helicopter could get in. On this operation the Far East Air Force (FEAF) sent a Dakota to orbit the site. There was a little ramshackle hut on the side of the river bank, where the casualty was. He was a Malayan, and really quite ill by this time. We'd had to come the 400 miles from Singapore in a Dragonfly, so there had been a lot of just sitting and vibrating. However, we got there and hovered while he was loaded on. We flew to a nearby camp where he could be prepared for the Dakota and flown off. That was the way the pattern started. And really, with slight modifications, it remained like that for the whole period of the Emergency.

When the SAS arrived, they very much took advantage of our skills. In fact, in some cases the helicopter was used more than the fixed-wing aircraft. Helicopters could also be used in a non-casualty situation, although theoretically it was not allowed. But people would use their common sense. I believe the first air strike by a helicopter was actually flown from a little strip right up on the Thai border, where the casualty couldn't walk. We were in the bar, which was the headquarters of one of the Marine Commandos, and as far as we were concerned the day was over. But it turned out not to be. We heard the helicopter coming back, and it did a swift circuit and banged down unnecessarily hard, we thought. Then the pilot emerged, gibbering with rage. The terrorists were using a technique, which was quite intelligent really for them, to make an attack at the last light, about 6.30, because with any luck the security forces would not be able to get the casualties out. And that had happened on this occasion.

But the pilot wasn't going to be frustrated like that! He got his crewman, and told him to get his Sten gun, and sit on the doorsill – which he did – and then they went roaring up the road. The road didn't go very far, but it went across the border, and there must have been a very surprised group of Communist terrorists! They had ambushed a helicopter doing a casualty evacuation, and they hung around after the casualty was taken away, apparently hoping to catch it again. But within about five minutes that helicopter was back again, doing turns on the spot, in the clearing, the Sten gun being fired as the aircraft rotated, which gave it a nice spread of fire. So that really should count as an operational tasking!

There was one case in which a patrol, thirteen men strong, were operating in deep jungle swamp. They were deep in, and would require about four to five days to come out. Eventually the terrain got too much for them, and they were all falling sick, and the whole operation was beginning to disintegrate. Eventually it was decided to withdraw the patrol, and start again. So I was sent to have a look and comment on what it would be like if we tried to get these people out. The clearing was very deep, but the ranges were very short, so that was not a worry. But the Dragonfly would only be able to carry one passenger on each sortie. Refuelling each time, with ten minutes' fuel. This worked quite well. We didn't shut down at all, because of the possibility of not starting. The nightmare bit was the fear of the helicopter going unserviceable, with half the patrol still left in the jungle. But it worked like a charm; we got everyone out, including the tracker's dog. I was a bit concerned about the dog, but it behaved itself.

The handler's advice was that you must allow the dog to follow its master, and if you don't you'll have trouble. So the dog was picked up – nobody else could pick it up of course – and thrown into the helicopter, whose doorstep was about four feet up, followed by the handler himself. And I sat there for an agonising five minutes, flying back to my refuelling base, with this bloody animal and its slavering jaws! But it was all right. It must have been the first dog to have been carried in a helicopter. Of course that went down extremely well.

We used to fly the Sultans occasionally. The Sultans were in remote places like Pahang, on the east coast, and Kelantan, which were temporary bases.

We did the first helicopter mass-landing assault in a mangrove swamp, just north of Kuala Lumpur. The Navy were a squadron commanded by my old instructor Suthers, and they were introduced into the operations in Malaya, possibly in late 1952. We were given the recce task. Sometimes you've got a flat swampy type of jungle which you can't do anything with because it won't support a helicopter. And we had to do something or other about supporting it. On this occasion, right out in the open, there was no possibility of hiding, so it was a bit of a difficulty. But we devised a plan which consisted of having two helicopters with guns, and about four soldiers, and then we could repeat that if necessary. Or land and re-embark everybody, you could play it one of several different ways. That was the first time we'd actually used the helicopter with offensive troops on board. They jumped from the hovering helicopter which we could bring within two or three feet of the ground. It was the first time that the SAS had been transported by helicopter, as an offensive group.

Then that part came to an end when the Sycamore appeared, in 1953. The advantages over the Dragonfly were the speed and that you could carry one extra person in them. The Sycamore could cruise at 90 knots, lightly laden, whereas the Dragonfly was staggering at 65 knots.

There was a change in the operational emphasis when the

Sycamore arrived, because at last people were allowed to use the words 'casualty evacuation plus medical emergency lifts'. No re-supply was allowed. We did do re-supply while I was in the Malay Peninsula, but unofficially. One simply didn't have time for all the argument that was necessary, so we would describe it as 'operations'. We never said that we'd done something that we hadn't done, we just didn't specify what it was.

I can't think of an occasion when we couldn't get a casualty out. We were always able to do something, even if it was inefficient. Ideally we would look for a flight time of about ten minutes or a quarter of an hour with a casualty on board. We could push it to half an hour. The crewman would look after the casualty while we were on our way back. If you didn't have a crewman, then bad luck. I don't think any of the casualties died during the flight. There was always a hospital within some sort of range, even if it was an hour or more.

What the helicopter achieved was beyond any calculable advantage. It was survival or death. It really did advance covert operations enormously.

The frightening moments rather depended on your view of the jungle, and your view of water. It was noticeable that the new pilots who had been naval-trained would simply disappear into the sunset, out of sight of land half the time. Whereas the RAF trainee would always try to keep some ground in sight when he flew.

The casualty evacuation was the most frightening. Sometimes you found yourself going round and round a clearing trying to assess it, knowing the troops on the ground had done their best. On the one hand you didn't want to throw it away too readily, on the other hand, you weren't going to accept it as a landing-ground just because they'd cut a few branches off. It was a frightening enough experience. And one where you've really got to learn how to make the decision. We had air-to-ground communications with the troops, but of a very crude and unsatisfactory nature. We eventually found that we couldn't make it work unless we used the walkie-talkie, to say, for example, that there was an obstruction in the way. The speed at which this would be removed would depend on Mike Calvert, the CO of the SAS, because he had all the explosive. He was always blowing trees up. He used to say it was necessary for training.

Malaya was an unforgettable flying experience for me. A beautiful place, and I enjoyed working with the Malays, I found them splendid chaps. I learned the language, a very easy language which has no grammar; you string words together like beans on a string. I came back a much richer person for that experience.

Flight Lieutenant John Nicholls

While I was at Horsham St Faith flying Meteors at the end of 1951, there was a round-robin invitation for people to put their names forward to go out to Korea to fly with the Sabre Wings of the US Air Force. Four of us were chosen and told in early 1952 that we'd be going to convert on to the Sabre at the USAF base at Wethersfield. Then out to Korea directly by RAF transport for a three-month attachment.

Within about a week of starting on this exercise, we learned that it was not going to be that way. Prior to our arrival out there, the four-man team which had gone out from the Central Fighter Establishment at West Raynham had lost one of their pilots, Wing Commander Johnny Baldwin, a great wartime hero, who had flown Typhoons, but he, I suspect, had not really had the chance to get to grips with the transition from piston engines to jet aeroplanes. This wasn't as dramatic as many people made out, but it did require a different approach to flying which, in many cases, the longtime piston people hadn't the opportunity to acquire. It was mainly that things happened faster, particularly with respect to fuel. In addition, the speeds built up faster in the aeroplane; on the other hand Meteors and Vampires were a delight to land and take off. You could see where you were going.

Anyway, what happened was that Johnny Baldwin was lost. He

wasn't shot down, he was sadly lost in bad weather. As a result of losing an RAF hero, I think the USAF was very cautious about accepting any more pilots without ensuring they got the proper amount of training. So whereas previously the CFE pilots had been checked out in Britain, and then gone out, the USAF demanded that we should be properly trained in the United States. After training, as the price for taking up one of their slots, they would want us to do a full operational tour. So we went out to New York by sea in April 1952. To us, this was a breathtaking, marvellous experience. The change from wartime to peace had been dramatic anyway, but the sea journey and our subsequent arrival in America (where they were all complaining about the shortages!) was heaven to us, because we'd grown up during the war, permanently hungry. And added to that, we went to Nellis Air Force base in Las Vegas, and it took our breath away.

There were four of us. The boss was a marvellous chap, Squadron Leader John Merrifield. The rest of us were all Flight Lieutenants: myself, Alan Jenkins, and Dennis Dunlop. Our 'blooding' in Las Vegas was fascinating: the flying itself was good, the food was good and the entertainment was marvellous; the chorus girls had the longest legs we'd seen. We used to go down-town at night. We couldn't afford to do very much, but we used to save up our dollars and gamble a bit on the slot machines and the roulette tables, and if we won we'd stay there and have supper and stay late. Now and then we came back about five o'clock in the morning, changed out of a jacket into a flying suit and got straight into an aeroplane!

At the end of the course, we were entirely in the American system, we were essentially American officers. We went to Tokyo in May and, arriving there in pouring rain at 0500 hours on a Sunday, we thought, What are we doing here? There's few worse places than Tokyo in spring. And then we went on to Seoul; again we thought; God, what a place. But it had been extensively fought over for two years and it showed the scars. Two of us went to 4 Fighter Wing at Kimpo – K14. The USAF bases had the K numbers rather than names – Kimpo was K14. It is now Seoul International and quite a bit bigger. The two others went down to 51 Wing at Suwan, south of Seoul.

There were a great number of people, and a great number of aeroplanes, in the two operational wings on the base. One was 4th Fighter Wing – F-86s and some T-33s. My squadron, 335, together with its sisters 334 and 336, had been the original Eagle Squadrons manned by American volunteers in the RAF. The 4th Fighter Wing was formed from them when the US entered the European War. Then there was 67 Reconnaissance Wing, which had attached to it the Australian 77 Squadron. This was a squadron that started the Korean War flying P-51 Mustangs and then made the transition to Meteors. They were by that time flying Meteor 8s, and they had among them several RAF attached pilots, so it was a home from home for me; I could go across there and actually be understood! The 67 Wing was a vast organisation responsible for the great majority of the reconnaissance operations in Korea and some very brave crews did it night and day. With two wings there was a mass of aeroplanes on the base, running into the hundreds, and there was only a single runway. The base was about twelve miles out of Seoul itself, and the area around it looked like hell, because if you have two armies going backwards and forwards through your capital city, it ends up looking rather messy. It was precisely in that way that one saw it: there was so much devastation in what seemed, anyway, to be a very unattractive spot.

On 28 June I did my first operational sortie, which was a fighter sweep out. We didn't see a thing.

The area for operations for the Sabres was mostly what became known in press jargon as MiG Alley, a sort of quarter-circle shape bordered on the north by the Yalu River up to the areas of the dam, about a hundred or so miles in from the Yellow Sea, and then in a sweep down to the south-west to Pyongyang, the North Korean capital. It was in that area, initially, that most MiGs were found, because they operated out of two main bases immediately north of the Yalu River and also out of Mukden, which was quite some distance further in; all three were in Chinese territory. We were explicitly forbidden and reminded constantly not to cross the river into Chinese territory, because of the political implications, so we would go up there and try to find them and try to work out what tactics they might deploy. But if you did find one, you didn't care which way he'd arrived. You'd expect them to be higher than you, because they did have the advantage of taking off and climbing north of the river without interruption and they also had the double advantage of extensive radar coverage to tell them where *you* were. They could wait until we were halfway before they scrambled, that put us already 100 miles beyond the front line. The Yalu was 100 miles further.

My first actual shooting that had any effect came about almost two months after I started flying. We got among a flight of four MiGs. I was leading the flight, and I can't remember quite what the other pair did, but by the time we got close enough to start shooting they were not with us. The MiGs were just going north as fast as they could and I was slightly underneath the first chap I fired at. It was really very unrewarding, because I'd done it before and hadn't had any noticeable effect, but the first one I obviously hit because it started smoking and he was then pulling away from me. I can't remember all the details precisely, but we were above 35,000 feet and it was very likely that even the firing of the gun slowed the aeroplane down. And then I came across another one and hit that one, so I got credit for two MiGs damaged.

On 15 September, Battle of Britain day, we were on a sweep along the Yalu when I saw a wing flash far below. I dived but my no. 2 lost me and didn't say so for some time. By then I was at about 1,000 feet chasing and shooting at a MiG ahead. From the tracer I could see I wasn't hitting him, but to my surprise he flipped and flew into a small hill. At debriefing I didn't claim it as a kill, but later I learned that I'd been credited with it.

In November I had another damaged in a close fight which

started when my no. 2 called 'break' and when I did (very quickly) I came head-on to a MiG firing his cannon – happily he missed. The most memorable part of that meeting was the size of the tracer shells as they left the cannon in the MiG's nose intake and lazily came towards me.

By then I had flown an F-86F model, which had a rocket pack. This was a dream modification in an attempt to overcome the problem encountered by F-86 pilots when they got behind the MiGs. The MiGs coped with high altitude better than the F-86; they could just manage to zoom away from you – you could not stay with them. The idea was that if you fitted this rocket pack under the rear of the aeroplane just aft of the cockpit, you'd get the extra boost which would take you upwards after it. Well, some of us tried it and it either didn't operate, or else you didn't catch the MiG up rapidly enough; it really turned out to be an expensive failure, but a nice try.

Of course as you gain experience, you get more familiar, you relax more, and you can think for yourself more. You can work out your own ideas more readily and you become more self-confident as a result. And the more self-confident you are, the greater effect you have on the morale, the team spirit, of those you are leading. If the guy leading is noticeably self-confident, then everybody feels better before they take off. It has always been like that, but we had to learn it for ourselves.

The United Nations had total air superiority over the majority of Korea, including the islands way north of Pyongyang, one of which was occupied by an American radar station. So if we were in trouble we were told to head for the sea and hopefully towards this island, where there were a couple of choppers waiting. Further south, there were four P-51 Mustangs on permanent standby to give ground support cover to any downed aircrew and the activities of these rescue people were breathtakingly good. It was another major factor in the high morale we enjoyed.

One of my friends had been hit and he put out a Mayday, but he lost his fuel rather quickly, so he jumped out. When he got in the sea, he had lost his dinghy somehow, but being a US Marine, he was wearing a G-suit where the attachment pipe had been extended so that it would reach his mouth. It had a stopper like a cork and so he blew his G-suit up by mouth, inflated his Mae West, and put his stopper in the end of his G-suit. So there he was in a sort of made-to-measure-type dinghy. He lay there and put out his yellow dye marker; later he swallowed a lot of it. He was about twenty miles off the mouth of the Yalu, in the least hospitable situation. I had been on the same mission, and heard him giving his Mayday shout.

We all got back, turned around very quickly and a massive operation was launched. We went off as top cover and there were another forty or fifty F-86s, and then the middle and lower covering forces which came from the F-84 Wing to cover the helicopter flight.

The first people on the scene, however, were the four Mustangs, and they went to the area where they thought he would be and patrolled looking everywhere for him; he had lost his beacon with his dinghy. They were getting to the end of their fuel when one of the pilots saw a head in the water. The first chopper was then called up and it reached him OK. The sea was running very hard and they were just hoisting him when a particularly large wave came along and clobbered the chopper. So they dumped him quick and limped off home; then another chopper went and got him and took him safely back to the island. He stayed there a couple of days, nursing a badly bruised arm and shoulder. This illustrates how intensive the rescue operations were. That was a tremendous boost to morale of course: you knew the system would go all-out for you.

The aim we had, of course, was to destroy as many MiGs as we could, but it had been eluding me and I was furious about it. I was on my ninety-ninth mission on 8 December 1952. This time I flew as no. 3 to the Group Commander, Colonel Royal N. Baker. He was a great aviator, who had shot down a lot of aeroplanes in Europe during World War II. It was a great delight to us that the United States Air Force senior officers, all of whom flew combat operations, were so good at their jobs. At that time he had already shot down about ten MiGs, and he went on to a final total of twelve. He said to me at the briefing that morning, 'Why don't you come and fly with me and see what we can find?' Of course I couldn't resist that. We were at about 35,000 feet, flying north towards the Yalu, and about twenty or so miles south when suddenly right beneath us came a flight of four MiGs. They clearly hadn't seen us. I think I saw them first, right below us. So the Colonel said, 'You take the right-hand pair and I'll take the left-hand pair.' I latched on to mine and, with my wing man, I fell in behind this chap and started shooting at him. He didn't do what I would have anticipated and pull the stick back, he pushed it forward. I think he thought he needed to go faster, because he was close to the river and he probably thought we wouldn't follow him. And so down he went, into a very spectacular spiral. I don't quite know why he did that. I went down after him, as fast as I could, and that was really very fast. In those early days control at transonic speed was not as good as it is now. I had some difficulty getting the gunsight on to the target. I did it fleetingly, and each time I did I pulled the trigger. I could see I was hitting him, and I was determined I was going to get this one. Then my gunsight went out. A light projected on the glass screen under the windscreen and it had gone out. But we did carry a tracer, so again I fell in behind him. He was obviously slowing up, he had levelled out at about 500 feet. I sat behind him quite happily and used the tracer to hit him. But tracer tends to be misleading; you think it's going where it isn't actually going. And then I looked down and we were above the river, and I thought, Well, bugger it, I'm crossing the river even if there is a diplomatic incident. I'm going to get this one. He thought that he'd be safe when he crossed over. He had got down to about 200 feet, and then pulled up as we crossed the north bank. This enabled me to close on him and make him a better target, and I hit him again.

By the time I got him we weren't going fast at all. He had

slowed down so much that I had to pull away and climb over him and pull up to the side. I think I did a barrel roll to get back behind him, because he was obviously slowing up so much that I overshot him.

I could see the flames coming out of the back, so I took the trouble of checking with my wing man that he could see the flames, because that was as good as confirmation. At the same time, he said he was below minimum fuel, so I thought that shooting a MiG down and losing your wing man at the same time wasn't a fair swap, so we were going to have to go home. We were quite a long way away, and at low level, which was a very bad combination, particularly where we were. So I said, 'OK, let's go.' I can remember vividly that, as we turned away to the left I just dipped my wing to see where the target had gone to and I saw him flick and go straight in. He really went with a great WOOMPH! as he hit the ground.

I flew my hundredth and final mission the following day; like on my first one we didn't see a thing. I left for Tokyo the next morning.

10

THE CANBERRA, THE NEW ZEALAND AIR RACE, AND EJECTOR-SEAT TRIALS

Wing Commander Lewis 'Bob' Hodges

In 1953, after learning to fly the Canberra, I was posted to a special job to command the New Zealand Air Race Flight based at RAF Wyton, near Huntingdon. This unit had been formed to train the Royal Air Force team entered in the London to New Zealand air race scheduled to take place in October of that year; a race sponsored by the New Zealand Aero Club to commemorate the centenary of the town of Christchurch in the South Island. It was to be a record-breaking flight on the lines of the 1934 Australia race which was won by Scott and Campbell Black in the DH Comet Racer.

The RAF entered three Canberras, and the Royal Australian Air Force two Canberras, in the speed section of the race. The Royal New Zealand Air Force entered a Hastings in the transport handicap section, and there were a number of civilian entries including a British European Airways Viscount 700, and a DC-6A of KLM. Unfortunately in the months leading up to the race, the individual entries dropped out owing, I believe, to cost and organisational difficulties. The result was that, on the day, we only had eight entries left which was most disappointing.

Four RAF Canberra crews were selected, each consisting of a pilot and navigator, three to take part in the race and one in reserve. We had three Mark 3 Canberras which had been modified to carry extra fuel, and in May 1953 we started a six-month training period acclimatising ourselves to long-range flying and carrying out proving flights to test our navigation procedures.

The Canberra being fairly limited in range, we had to have a series of stops en route. We planned to fly from the UK to Shaibah in the Persian Gulf, which at that time was an RAF station, where we were to make our first refuelling stop, and then on to Colombo. From Colombo we planned to fly the long haul across the Indian Ocean to Australia, refuelling halfway at the Cocos Islands, where there was a small airfield which had been used during the war. The final stage was from Perth to Christchurch. Each stage of the flight was about three thousand miles.

Just before the race we took delivery of a newer version of the Canberra – the Mark 7 which had an increased fuel capacity and longer range. I planned to fly this aircraft in the race, and depending on its performance and fuel consumption, to over-fly the Cocos Islands and continue on a direct flight to Perth, a distance of 3,500 miles. If I was able to achieve this it would give the RAF team an advantage over the Australians who could not do the direct flight.

The race started on 8 October 1953, from Heathrow Airport. What is now the terminal building was then a small shell of girders and the passenger accommodation was in temporary huts. Our aeroplanes were parked alongside the runway. The Duke of Gloucester saw us off at five o'clock in the evening, and gave the signal for the transport aircraft to go first. Shortly afterwards I led the Canberras into the air, the other two RAF Canberras and the Australians following at five-minute intervals, and we climbed away into the setting sun.

The first leg of our route from London Airport to Shaibah was uneventful. We flew straight across Europe to Cyprus, and then across the Lebanon and Iraq to the Persian Gulf. It was of course quite dark by now and we did a night landing at Shaibah where we were rapidly refuelled. We arranged for snacks to be available at all the stopping-points and we were able to eat while the refuelling was going on. We were on the ground only for about fifteen or twenty minutes, and then took off and headed south across the Arabian Sea to Colombo. Flying at high altitude, we were doing a cruise climb up to about 38,000 feet to get the best fuel economy and maximum speed. As we let down into Colombo, the weather was good with broken cloud, and there were no problems. The worry at Colombo was always the temperature on the ground because, when taking off with full fuel and a high temperature, the performance of the aeroplane is considerably reduced. Ninety degrees Fahrenheit at Colombo; we didn't want it any hotter than that. There was no problem though, and we were airborne again, heading for Australia.

On this leg we had 3,500 miles of ocean to cross and the question – whether to land at the Cocos airfield or go straight on – depended on the fuel state at the halfway point. When we arrived in the vicinity of Cocos I decided that we had sufficient fuel to continue direct to Perth, and I arrived there in record time and well in the lead. However I now had a problem. During the last stage of our flight across the Indian Ocean a red warning-light came on, indicating a generator failure. The Canberra requires electrical power for all its systems, fuel pumps and, of course, radio, and although we had two generators I was not happy to rely on the single remaining generator for the last 3,000 miles of the flight to New Zealand. Once on the ground our engineers, who were waiting for our arrival, got to work immediately and tracked down the problem to a seized-up generator drive. This meant changing the generator and repairing the drive. When they started taking the panels off the wings I could see that things were going to go pretty slowly. This was a long job.

While this was all going on, the no. 2 and no. 3 RAF Canberras landed, and took off again on their way to New Zealand. The Australian Canberras were not landing at the same airfield at Perth; they were on a different route.

In the end it took nearly ten hours to fix the generator drive on my aeroplane. So I lost out completely because of that, but it couldn't be helped. The race continued and the first aeroplane to reach Christchurch, winning the race, was our no. 2 Canberra, flown by Flight Lieutenant Monty Burton and navigated by Flight Lieutenant Don Gannon. They covered the distance from

Heathrow to Christchurch in just under twenty-four hours, a record-breaking flight at an average speed of over 500 miles per hour.

The advent of the jet engine had certainly made its mark, and this air race pointed the way for the future of air travel.

Sergeant Jake McLoughlin

In 1958, as a Parachute Jumping Instructor, I was keen on freefall parachuting, and wrote to Sir Raymond Quilter, head of GQ Parachutes, enquiring about the purchase of a good competition parachute. He said that I should see him at the Farnborough Air Show. So I went along and we talked parachuting for a long time. He said, 'I've got just the job for you. How about going to Australia with my team, as one of the two parachutists for ejector-seat trials?' I agreed.

In the meanwhile, to save time in Woomera later, I did an ejector-seat trial, at Netheravon, from a Canberra, for the Air Force. I took off with a guy called Gabby Hayes. I was sitting in this box, as it were, with no lid on. I could hear the pilot, and there were cameras galore on the floor angled at me and various aspects of the seat. We flew to 5,000 feet, then I was given a countdown, over the air. There was a small handle above my head, which pulled down a blind to protect my face from the slipstream – and it also fired the gun which actually fired the seat. I felt as if I were in a dentist's chair with a live hand-grenade rolling about underneath it. My big fear was that, if there were a misfire, when the aircraft touched the ground I might get fired out on to the runway. Anyway, at the end of countdown, I pulled the blind, there was this terrific, terrific bang, and up I went at a rate of knots. I could see the aircraft, between my knees. Then I did a couple of fast forward somersaults, in the slipstream. So I began to do a couple of rolls forward. It was only then I came away from the seat. When I'd left the aircraft it had felt strange going up instead of down, but the seat had timers to release me from it, and a barometric system to open the parachute. I could feel the G-forces taking over, but I wasn't too worried, because at least the thing had fired, which was my only real fear. I was carrying a reserve parachute, hanging on to a very light harness under the leather suit I was wearing. But the damn thing opened with me facing forward, which was very difficult with an aircrew helmet on. I was just hanging, almost face down, suspended, it seemed, from the middle of my back, thankful to be out of the aircraft. It was also very difficult to check the canopy.

The harness was not designed for comfort, it was a clear survival harness, which was obviously functional. From there it was just a matter of waiting to land. I was carrying a survival pack on my backside, on a fifteen-foot rope, so if I'd landed in the sea, I would have had a dinghy and various other things. I thought, There is no fun in this at all. The only difference from my previous jumps was in how I got out of the aircraft: I'd been through the floor; I'd been through the door; now I had gone through the roof.

The second trial, from a Meteor, was a bit more problematic. My legs flailed as I ejected, and I lost the toecap of my boot, just as if it had been cut off by a guillotine. All the engineer said was, 'That's not quite good enough, we'll have to adjust that.' I was scared to examine my feet, I thought, Christ! Are my toes still there?

I am always so relieved and pleased when people say their lives were saved by the ejector seat, because I think, maybe I made a little contribution to it, indirectly, because certain things were changed after my and other people's reports; but looking back, I see I was perhaps stupid to stick my neck out, really. At the time it was a great adventure and great fun, with great people.

There have been a few fatalities over the years. I remember one where the problem was traced back to a tiny, tiny cartridge, which failed to fire, to initiate an important part of the system. Occasionally there have been ejections where people have ejected too low, or whatever, and the seat and chute just haven't had the

11

THE RADFAN

Squadron Leader Roy Bowie

The emergency was officially declared in the Radfan two months before we got out there in February 1964, but I don't think we quite understood how violent the tribal reaction to our presence would be.

The Radfan is a mountainous tract of country about fifty miles north of Aden. The Radfanis are a fanatically independent bunch; and warfare between the various tribes was a way of life. The caravans that passed through the Radfan along the Dhala road to Yemen – one of the traditional routes to Mecca – were made to pay and this was a constant source of friction. New laws were brought in forbidding the levy of tolls and the Qutaibis, the main tribe of the Radfan, began to cause trouble on the Dhala road. They began shooting at the caravans and mining the road. All this happened to coincide with the civil war in Yemen. So the authorities decided to do something about it.

In response to the Aden federal government request, a makeshift Aden brigade was formed, plus a squadron each of ground-support Hunters, Shackleton bombers, and Twin Pioneer transports as well as ten Belvedere helicopters. I was to act as the Brigade Air Support Officer with David Whittaker. The general task was to stop the tribal revolt and the attacks on the Dhala road.

At last light on 30 April, 45 Commando set out to capture the high ground in the Dhanaba Basin, and that same night, the Parachute Regiment was to drop from Beverleys on to the Wadi Taym. The SAS were to mark the drop zone for the Paras.

Unfortunately some chap with his goats stumbled into their 'hide' and all the locals started shooting at this nine-man patrol.

Captain Edwards, who was leading the patrol, got his signaller, Warburton, to contact their boss, Major Wingate-Gray at the SAS headquarters at Thumier, where we were also based. Major Wingate-Gray asked for Hunters to assist the withdrawal of his men. They were ordered in and, as they attacked, he was on the telephone to Whittaker and me relaying messages from the SAS patrol. While we gave fire orders over the microphone to the Hunters, 8 and 43 Squadrons were going flat out all day until it got too dark to fly. Earlier the SAS had arranged for another troop to go in by helicopter, but they had been badly hit by machine-gun fire, so they pulled that troop out and changed the plan.

That night, as the SAS patrol tried to break out, first Warburton, and then Edwards were killed. The remainder of the patrol had to leave their bodies behind. These bodies were mutilated and decapitated, and the heads were displayed in the Yemen. But we did recover their bodies later.

The Marines then went in at night and the Paras went in on foot. When dawn came, the Paras were still on the wadi floor and the Marines were up on Cap Badge. The Paras took the village at the bottom of Cap Badge and cleaned the place out. Then they were heavily fired upon and had a battle for about an hour, and two of them were killed. I called in the Hunters and they strafed the enemy and that quietened things down.

From then on the action was like the North-West Frontier of India of the 1920s and 1930s. An area would be leafleted and the locals would be told this is an area of military movement, clear out. They'd be given twelve hours' warning which meant there were very few casualties on either side. But if we got information from our agents on the ground we'd go and knock an odd house down – put a few rockets in to keep them busy, but always after we'd leafleted. The Shackletons would keep the Radfan on the move. They'd go up at night, and would sit over the top, and every time they saw a fire lit, they would drop a 25lb practice bomb at it. This meant that they couldn't cook their food and it really made life very miserable for them, which was the object of the exercise. But we weren't just going out and blasting people left, right and centre.

Of course the local political officers, who were a bit like Lawrence of Arabia, used to go round with a couple of Arab guards on the back of a camel. They were incredibly brave. They used to go out and deal with the tribes and try and keep them in order. They had a very, very big say in what was going on. They knew the score, they knew who was causing the trouble and who wasn't. The whole object of the exercise was to try and get people back to law and order.

But of course the internal security situation developed as the word came out that we were leaving. Everybody who had been friendly with us was now trying to show how unfriendly they were. At Christmas time, 1964, we had a grenade thrown into the open-air cinema at Waterloo lines. It hit somebody on the knee, rolled under a seat, and someone shouted lift your feet, and nobody was injured, which was incredible. After that I was walking back up through the camp one day, and a guy said to me, 'Ha, sir, you're a cricketer, aren't you?' I agreed but wondered at the same time what he was up to. He said, 'Take this dummy grenade, walk back fifty yards or so, and see if you can throw it into the cinema.' I kept going back until I could no longer lob it into the cinema. He then said, 'Thanks very much, sir, that's where we are going to put the fence up.'

We had a quarter about three doors down from us where there was a teenagers' Christmas party going on. Somebody threw a grenade in and killed one of the teenagers. There was also another one thrown into the mess at Steamer Point. So it was a bad period. The IS situation worsened towards the end of the time that I was out there and there was a curfew on all the time, so you couldn't be out after midnight. You couldn't have more than twelve people in a party in your quarter.

But all in all, it was a fascinating tour, some of the places we could visit out there were tremendous.

I suppose the great joy of flying out in the Radfan was to be in the Hunter. She was a beauty, a lovely aeroplane to fly, and a lovely one to look at. It was very, very strongly built, and handled very nicely. You felt when you sat in it, that you were part of the aeroplane – it was wonderful and really could shift. It had its problems – it wasn't the greatest turner in the world – but it was a joy to fly. I flew my first Hunter in 1955 and flew one on my last day of service in 1984.

12

THE FALKLANDS

Flight Lieutenant David Morgan

Beginning in 1982 I began an exchange tour with the Navy, found a house, started the conversion of the Sea Harrier and was halfway through this when, one Friday morning, I went into work and found everyone sitting around. I walked in and said, 'Hey! have you guys heard? The bloody Argentinians have invaded the Falklands.' And, to a man, they looked at their watches and said, 'Where have you been for the last four hours?' They'd all been called out at four o'clock in the morning but as I'd only been based there a short time my name wasn't on the call list.

On the Sunday I jumped in an aeroplane and landed on *Hermes* and on the Monday she sailed. I said goodbye to my wife Carol and my children on Saturday. Then it was all delayed so I went back home again and said, 'I haven't really gone, but I'm going tomorrow.' I'd always explained to the kids, while we were in Germany, what might happen if ever there was a war. We'd taken them up to Berlin and showed them the other side of the Wall and said, you know, 'That's why we're here, to stop that happening to us. We wouldn't like that, would we?' They couldn't get any chips in East Berlin and the Coke tasted horrible. Communism was way-off!

I'd always told Carol, if I actually had to go off to war, not to expect me back, because in Germany we were operating so close to the front that life expectancy would be pretty short because we would be prime targets. The kids, however, were rather confused that I was going off to war when we were back in England. I'd certainly resolved to do the best I could to stay alive but I didn't really expect to live through the campaign. There was every chance that I was going to get killed. In fact, while I was down south, Carol moved house and I came home to find all my belongings packed in boxes. But that's better than one chap I heard about whose wife said, 'Okay, he's not coming back,' sold their house, bought a smaller one, got rid of all his kit – and then he came back!

When I said goodbye to the kids for the final time my son Charles, who was five, said, 'Don't worry, Daddy. You'll be all right. They've only got tatty old aeroplanes – you've got brand new ones!'

The landing I made on *Hermes* was the only deck landing I'd ever done, apart from once in a helicopter. I didn't actually see England to say goodbye to it because by the time I got up on deck, we were out to sea, and England had disappeared. All I saw was the overhead projector screen start to swing in the briefing room. So we rattled off down the Channel with helicopters bringing things on board all the way down.

There was a lot of discussion about what we were actually going to do. We considered ourselves basically as the big stick, the big threat that probably wasn't going to be used because there would be a political solution, and I think a lot of people thought that until we got to Ascension Island. We were anchored off to re-store and bring on kit which had been flown down to us when one of the Royal Fleet Auxiliaries sighted a periscope, so we all upsticked and went very, very quickly and left the Sea Kings tracking this submarine. I don't know whose sub it was to this day, but it wasn't American, it wasn't Argentinian.

While we were heading off south the Admiral came on to the intercom and said, 'OK, we've actually left earlier than we anticipated. However, we're going now, we aren't going back and you can take it from me that we are going to war. So get settled down, sort out what you've got to do, get your house in order, as things are going to hot up from now on.' We'd already formed planning teams on the way down so we started doing quite a lot of fairly heavy training. There were some pretty heavy sessions for the next ten days or so, to make sure we'd got everything exactly right. A team of us sat down and looked at the ground-attack options. We worked out the best way to attack our first option, which was the airport at Port Stanley. We also discovered that Goose Green was being used, so we had to plan a secondary attack. Basically, we were trying to use all the aircraft on *Hermes* – we had twelve at the time – nine to attack the airfield and three in reserve to take the place of any which was unserviceable. If any two of those three were left at the end of the day, they would go and attack Goose Green. We decided early on never to send 'singletons' because that is a sure way of losing a guy.

It worked itself up gradually, the pitch getting higher and people getting more and more finely tuned. Our time from normal cruising to action stations went from about twenty-five minutes on the first try, down to a couple of minutes as we approached the zone, so things were getting pretty sharp. We started intercepting an Argentine Boeing 707 which was coming out and snooping around us and finally got clearance to fire at him if he came again. That obviously got back through the Argentine channels because they never came again.

The evening before 1 May we'd got everything sorted out and there was just the final briefings. Before dawn on 1 May the Vulcan went in and dropped a bomb in the middle of the runway and that was really the most damage they ever did with the Vulcan. We followed that up just before eight o'clock with a raid of twelve Harriers. We hit Stanley just as dawn was breaking. This was the first time we'd really been into action and everyone was very tense beforehand, very much introverted, very quiet, with the odd stupid joke at which everyone sort of cackled aimlessly and then went back into their shells again, everyone walking around, thinking very hard about what they were going to do. We got airborne and were in the air about ten or fifteen minutes before we sighted Stanley. Having had a Vulcan through, the ground defences were very alert. We ran in down the north-east coast and at Berkeley

Sound split into two lots – one lot came through between Mount Low and Beagle Ridge, and the boss and I came round the other side of Mount Low to split the fire. As I came up towards the high ground there, I got a radar lock-up because someone had detected me so I descended even lower and then ran in. Meanwhile, the other guys, two of them with cluster bombs, took out the airfield installations and aircraft.

I was the last one across and, as I ran in at about fifteen feet high, all I could see were just sand-dunes with people firing at me from the top and bombs exploding and missiles going off everywhere; there was a complete umbrella of anti-aircraft fire bursting all over the airfield. The first time I saw it I thought, Christ Almighty! My initial thought was that the cluster bombs which the guys were carrying were going off early but I then realised that that wasn't what it was; it was actually flak. I just hit as low as I possibly could and then saw the boss running in across towards the airport buildings, so I decided I would curve round and come across his path. I pulled up over the sand-dunes and the first thing I saw was a missile go straight across in front of me, chasing one of the guys who'd just gone across at right angles to me. Then I saw a Britten-Norman Islander, the light aircraft which the Falklands Islands Company use for ferrying people around, taxi-ing across the grass, so I said, 'Okay, you're the first one.' I pickled the first cluster bomb on him and blew him away. Then, as the second bomb came off about one-third of a second later, there was a great bloody explosion just behind me and my aircraft started shaking violently. This made me lift my finger off the 'Release' button and I thought, Ah Christ! We're still flying – get this other bomb off. I dropped the third bomb and that went right over the airport buildings and made a few holes there.

I then dived down, through the smoke, over the airport buildings and past the control tower, still diving down into this great ball of smoke. I thought I was about 50 feet at this stage but I had to pull up to 150 feet to release the weapons because of 'dudding'. I dived into the smoke and broke left and came out the other side, running down over the sand-dunes, and I must have come close to the hill behind the control tower. I ran out, got locked up again by another fire-control radar, did a quick manoeuvre, dropped a bit of chaff, changed my radio frequency and beetled off.

At that stage we all checked in on the radio and all nine aircraft were up. There were whoops of joy. We were all safe – that was a marvellous feeling. However, I radioed in telling them I'd been hit and might have to eject. I knew we had a search-and-rescue helicopter somewhere in the region, sitting quietly. If I had to ditch, I would have been safe, but the sea is bloody cold down there. But I climbed up and slowed down and the discomfort and the rattling became less and I started flying quite smoothly. So I cancelled the call. Later, we had one chap bang out just south of the airfield who was in the water for eight hours before he was picked up. He was a bit cold but he survived!

When I returned to *Hermes* I held off and let everyone else land first because I didn't know if I was going to be able to land the thing. I later found out there was a huge hole in the fin. I wanted to get everyone out of the way so that, if I crashed on the deck, it wouldn't harm anyone. So I brought it back and rolled it on to the deck. I didn't want to do a vertical landing because the controls may have been damaged, so I rolled it on fairly slowly and stopped. That was the end of the first mission. The whole operation had taken half an hour.

Shortly after I landed, the three from Goose Green came back, so out of the twelve aircraft we recovered twelve, and only one had a hole in the tail. Everyone was totally elated! I'd personally expected to lose three or four aircraft on that trip.

Stanley was considered a successful raid. We'd damaged the runway with two 1,000lb bombs and torn the hell out of everything that was in the area – set light to the fuel dumps, blown the tower away and taken out a lot of the Pucaras and light aircraft scattered around. Unfortunately, we didn't really have the weapons to put the airport out of action. The 1,000-pounder had to be put in from medium-level to get the penetration and the angle, because at low-level even if you toss them, they still only hit at about a thirty-degree angle and tend to skip before they explode. The Argentinians' morale must have reached rock bottom that day because they had thought Stanley was invulnerable from the air.

Day One over – jubilation. On 4 May we lost Nick Taylor at Goose Green and the *Sheffield* was hit. I was on deck when I saw this great ball of smoke; it was a ship turning, about ten miles away, with its side all glowing white. There was a hell of a lot of smoke. Then the casualties started coming back on to *Hermes* and everyone was rather subdued and gritting their teeth and saying, 'OK, this is it. Let's go and have those bastards.' I think that was when the guys suddenly realised that the Argentinians were going to fight back and we were going to lose a lot of people, so we'd really got to go for it. We'd gone into action, we'd heard of a death but we hadn't seen it; our first actual contact with war was the survivors from the *Sheffield*.

At that stage we were pulled up to sleep above the water level because of the submarine threat, which made life very uncomfortable. I was sleeping on the floor of the Captain's day-cabin with five other people. Most of us had camp beds but some of us were just sleeping on the cushions. There were about forty people sleeping in the bar. We got some sleep and, as the days progressed, you got a bit more because you were a bit more tired, but there were nearly always two or three action days to disturb you. It was irritating, but because you always knew that this might be the time you were going to get a torpedo through the side, you didn't actually get irritated. It was, however, debilitating because you never really got very much sleep. Over the first couple of weeks we all got very, very tired and people were asleep in the cockpit on the deck.

The next real action was on 9 May. During the previous four days we'd been flying patrols around the fleet and the odd harassing trip over the islands just to let them know we were still there

– nothing major and no-one was shot down for a couple of days. The weather was appalling. While I was flying on 8 May I broke cloud at 90 feet and all I could see were grey sea, grey ship and grey clouds, everything ill-defined, so I had to do a quick circuit at about 60 feet and plonk on deck. That was one of the worst days.

At this stage I went off with Gordie Batt, who was later killed, to drop high-level bombs on the airfield. We couldn't drop the bombs because there was total cloud cover and we'd been told not to drop if we couldn't see the airfield because we might put them into Stanley itself. So we turned out from there. I found a contact on the radar, went to investigate and found a big stern trawler called *Narwal*, which the Argentinians had been using to gather information. We asked what to do and the Navy said, 'Engage it.' Gordie fired a few rounds across her bows to try and stop her, unsuccessfully. So we dropped our 1,000lb bombs – we couldn't land back on board with them, so we had to drop them somewhere! The weather was pretty bad, which meant we had to drop them at low-level and since they were fused for an 18,000-foot drop we knew they probably weren't going to go off. Mine, in fact, missed and we thought Gordie's had too but it went into the fo'c'sle, down two decks, and stopped. It didn't actually go off so we didn't know we'd hit her at that stage. She still kept going, so we each emptied 200 rounds of 30mm into the side of the bridge and the engine-room. On the last pass she stopped and hove to, so we radioed back and some Sea Kings went in to capture her. Unfortunately, she was blown to pieces. The engine-room was completely knackered and there were holes below the water line from the 30mm, so we just let her sink.

So far we'd shot down nine, the Special Forces had got a Pucara, and the ships had claimed a few more. But I personally hadn't shot anything down up until then. Unlike in the Second World War, we didn't put anything on the side of the aircraft. Instead, we covered up the glass tiles behind the bar with a bit of hardboard and one of the stewards put up a stencil for everything hit.

People were coming down from sorties, rushing down to the bar and saying, 'Another A-4 on there!' So morale was pretty high.

I next got involved two days after D-Day. I was doing a CAP – combat air patrol – with John Leeming who unfortunately was killed in an accident after the Falklands. By this stage we'd moved our CAP from round the fleet to around the landings, so we were actually capping at very long range – 200 miles plus – so we were pretty short of fuel. I was capping with John over the Mount Maria area and I happened to see a helicopter fly across a lake at Shag Cove. I saw it from 8,000 feet, called it to John and asked the ship in San Carlos controlling us if we'd got any helicopters on West Falkland. They didn't know and had to check. But because of fuel problems, I couldn't afford to wait so I just dived in and took him head-on down the valley. He was flying at about fifty feet and I was slightly above him. It wasn't until I'd got within 500 yards that I realised it was a Puma and we didn't have any Pumas down there. By then it was too late to get a missile off and I couldn't actually push the aircraft down low enough to get the guns on him. So I just flew very low over the top and banked away. Meanwhile John Leeming, who was coming from the other end, had seen three more following him. As I banked away, I looked back over my shoulder to try and pick up the Puma again, to come back round and have him. All of a sudden I saw a great ball of flame shoot from the ground. Apparently, he'd been caught by my down-wash as I broke over him and this had swept him into the side of the hill. I went back later and found that he'd had 200 rounds of 120mm mortar on board which explains why he'd gone bang!

John, meanwhile, had picked up an Agusta 109 gunship and he had a go at that, then I had a go and hit it. There was another large explosion and bits were flying off it in all directions. Then, as we were pulling off, very short of fuel, John saw another Puma shot down on the ground with people running away from it, so I emptied my last few rounds into it and then went home. I handed over the position to some guys from the *Invincible*, and when they arrived they found three more lots of burning wreckage on the ground and a fourth Puma which they then wrote off. So it would appear possible that we got all four of them. It was apparently one of the major arms lifts from Fox Bay, where they'd got a supply ship. We certainly got three.

I've got my diary for the day: 'Could've been a good day but this evening Gordie Batt actually flew off the front of the carrier on a night-bombing raid, exploded and went into the water!' He was flying the aircraft in which I'd shot the helicopters down, which was also the one I'd been hit in over Stanley.

On 25 May, the *Conveyor* was hit literally hours after we'd got all fourteen Harriers off her – we were very, very lucky. The *Conveyor* was going in that night to unload the rest of the stuff when she was hit. If they'd managed to get the helicopters off, it would've made such a difference. But had the Argentinians hit it twenty-four hours earlier, things would have been very different for us. The GR3s, the Air Force Harriers, had arrived a couple of days earlier, and they'd taken over the ground-attack role from us, which was a great relief.

Our daily pattern then was flying CAP, and trying to keep the heat off the fleet while they were deploying. The GR3s did a lot of good work supporting 2 Para at Goose Green; in fact, Bob Iveson was shot down there. Then on 8 June came the disaster at Bluff Cove – it was actually at Port Pleasant which isn't the right name for a place to have a disaster. I was sitting on deck on alert when we were told there was an air-raid ashore. We scrambled but got there too late to catch the first wave. I relieved the guys who'd been there for about half an hour. My CAP area was Lively Island. As I approached it I called up the previous lot and said, 'OK, where's the action?' They said, 'Just to the north of your CAP station. We've got a problem.' I said, 'OK. Well, I can't see you, I can't see any problem. Just tell me roughly where.' They told me to head north from Lively and I'd see it. As I came in I saw the two great columns of smoke coming from the *Galahad* and *Lancelot*. Dave Smith and myself spent thirty minutes on

CAP there. The only reason we'd been sent on this particular sortie was because we needed one more night-landing to make us night-qualified. We were both fairly new guys on the machines and we'd done our three night-launches – dawn, pre-dawn and 'inky-poo' (pitch dark) launch. We'd also completed a dusk landing, and a fairly dark landing. This was the last inky-poo landing before we actually became night-qualified. Anyway, here we were on a dusk strike, we'd been out about thirty minutes and now had only very little fuel remaining. I could see below me *Fearless*'s little landing-craft coming round the coast, so I thought I would give it a two-minute orbit and then we'd have to head for home.

As I turned round I saw an enemy aircraft running in to attack the landing-craft. I'd briefed Dave Smith beforehand that if we saw anything at low-level the guy who saw it would attack and the other chap would just try and hang on and clear his tail. I was at 10,000 feet and fairly slow. I stood the Harrier on its nose and accelerated down towards this aircraft which was about eight miles away. Unfortunately, I didn't get there in time to stop him, but I locked in to the guy with my eyes and saw him miss with his bomb and disappear off. Then I saw a second guy running in from a different direction and he hit the back of the ship, which made me very, very angry. The most angry I've been in my life, because I knew from this huge great explosion that he'd killed people, and because I hadn't been able to intercept and because he'd had the audacity actually to kill somebody while I was there. So I decided that he was the guy who was going to get killed. As I was going for him, a third one appeared from underneath me and attacked the ship again, but missed. So I thought 'OK, you'll do. As I went for him, a fourth one appeared on the left-hand side of me, so I just pulled my plane across, got him in my sights and hit him with a missile. There was a colossal explosion and then a great fireball falling into the water – no chance of him getting out.

I was going very, very fast – probably around the speed of

sound. Because I was flying so much faster than the machine was supposed to be flown at and so much faster than the missile was supposed to be fired at, it rolled dramatically to the right which really took me by surprise as I was only 100 feet away from the water then. That was fairly startling. I recovered and found that the roll had pointed me directly at their third guy, so I came in behind him and fired a missile. He saw it coming and tried to reverse away but it took his tail off completely and he went into the water. I thought, That's the end of him, but about three seconds later a parachute opened right in front of me and just whistled over my port wing. I subsequently heard that his parachute was on fire and he didn't make it anyway. That left two aircraft still in front of me, flying fairly close together and beetling towards Goose Green, so I went in on those. Dave was behind me, but he couldn't see me because it was virtually dark. All he could see were the missiles going off. At this stage, my gunsight went u/s and I was just left with a blank head-up display with nothing there to aim with, which really pissed me off. Anyway, I closed in behind these two, still going fairly fast and fired a quick long-range burst at them. One of them broke across in front of me, so I just followed him in to about 300 yards, pulling my nose right ahead of him and squeezing the trigger. Then I just relaxed the nose very, very gently back down, pulled it back and tried again. I did that twice, didn't see any hits and didn't know where the bullets were going. I then ran out of bullets with this guy right in front of me, which was very frustrating. So I just rolled the wings level and pulled straight up because there was no point in hanging about there any more – I'd nothing left. Luckily Dave Smith, who was about a mile behind me, saw my bullets exploding in the water and this guy flying through them, and locked him up with his missile. He didn't know whether it was me or the other guy, but then he saw me go up through the sunset and said to himself, 'OK, whoosh!' He fired his missile and destroyed the guy – he just became a great fireball, whumff, into the ground.

By now of course, we were both very low on fuel. I went in

first on *Hermes* and landed with about two minutes' fuel remaining and he had about one minute's when he got back, so that was fairly close. We discovered that another pair who had been coming in to help us out had seen a fourth explosion. So for quite some time we thought that my stray rounds might have hit him, but in the end we reckoned it was only three and the fourth guy got back.

That really was the last bit of excitement that I had out there, the last time I actually got engaged. But we did become night-qualified! The Argentine Air Force and Navy never really came out after that. There were a couple of quick raids but that was all.

When I think about the whole campaign the most frightening fraction of a second was on the very first raid when I saw people actually firing at me and obviously trying to kill me. I think that's what really brought it home, made me absolutely scared stiff that fraction of a second. Then the old brain said, 'Sod it. We've got to get in there and drop the bombs anyway, so go do it.' I think everyone felt that on the first mission. Apart from that, the most uncomfortable times were during air attacks on *Hermes* when we were sitting down between decks with everything closed up round us, at almost perfect Exocet height, just waiting for a big rocket to appear through the wall. That was disturbing. When you're in the air, nothing matters, you're the master of your own destiny and you can do what you like, but sitting in that ship not being able to do anything was most disturbing.

My saddest moment was on Ascension Island. There were about eight of us who stayed behind on the way back and we had a service the evening we were leaving. It was a lovely, still, tropical night and the old sun was setting and we had this very, very moving memorial service. They'd flown out a whole lot of wreaths from the UK and one rose-grower had sent us a great box of roses, and we stood on the back end of the ship and said a few words, tossed the wreaths over the back, scattered the roses, and just sort of sat there with our own thoughts. When it was all over and it had all gone quiet and there was no shouting, hooting or roaring any more, we could just think about the guys who would not be going back. That was very, very sad.

I don't think I ever felt that sort of remorse and sadness during the confrontation. Obviously, when you're in the flying world, you get used to losing friends; it never gets any easier, but the effects don't last quite so long. I've lost forty or fifty people, I suppose, since I've been flying, not all close friends, but people I've been on the squadron with. I must've lost fifteen or twenty real, good, close friends and it hurts like hell, but after a day or so, it's over, you know, life goes on. It's something you live with.

And when we came back home, that was the most amazing moment of my life! We were all standing, lining the deck, and everyone had tears streaming down their faces. At long last we could actually let it all go. That I think was the most amazing moment of my life, absolutely fantastic.

13

THE GULF WAR AND AFTER

Squadron Leader Mike Williams

I became a Flight Commander not long before things started happening in the Gulf. We lost Gordon Grahame, who was then OCB, in a mid-air collision that year, so it was through unfortunate circumstances that I took over in October, and we started preparing for the Gulf shortly afterwards.

We flew constituted formations and we stuck with those formations. We almost lived and breathed together. Everybody was involved in planning, and we were doing some very new things. The squadron had never air-to-air refuelled before. We had never, of course, had the Alarm missile before. These were completely new. But it was very basic on the Alarm missile side this end; we were concentrating on getting people up to speed with the tactical side of things: air-to-air refuelling, low-flying, formation keeping, look-out, and evasion. We had done operational low-flying, but operational low-flying in peacetime is normally great fun. There is a little extra twist when you know the next time you do it, someone may be shooting at you. And I think that formations tended to draw together through the results of the individual four-ships. The crews knew that they were cracking a job and becoming quite proficient at things that they had never done before in their lives. There was a lot of hard work. If they weren't flying they were in the books learning about new systems and new threats on the enemy equipment side. We were briefed almost to death by all sorts and sundry about what equipment they had. So by the time we left for the Gulf, people were very knowledgeable and knew what they were looking for, and quite confident they were going to crack the problem when we got out there. Which all boils down to personal pride and the feeling that, 'I can do it.'

We were going down there for what looked increasingly likely to turn into a war. Now, whether we actually believed that we were going to fight a war is by-the-by. We had to be ready for it. And I think we generally succeeded in that: it came as no surprise when we had to go to war.

We had our own Combat Survival Rescue Officer, who did an excellent job. He was involved quite heavily with the Americans, and we had bits of equipment from them that were quite new to us. He also knew the terrain that we might meet in Iraq and basic survival techniques. The fundamental difference that he put over was, when you bang out of an aircraft in peacetime, you want to get found. In war the exact opposite is true. Of course we have all this bright dayglo equipment that people supposedly can see from a long way off, but all of a sudden you don't want that. So we had the sand-coloured flying suits made. There was a lot of intensive briefing on what to do, in case anything unforeseen happened and we did end up on the ground. For example, when Rupert Clarke got shot down, his first thought was apparently to steer his aircraft out to bleak terrain, where he'd get away from everybody. For him to think like that, under that sort of stress and with a crippled aircraft, means the briefings must have got through, for normally you'd want a bit of civilisation around you. So it shows that people went out there knowing what they were going to do.

If or when we are captured we are trained to give initially number, rank, name. And once the tactical period has elapsed we can then, certainly under any sort of torture, start feeding bits of information that by this time are tactically useless. Although that was not specifically briefed, it was understood. I mean, you don't want to die for the sake of 'What was your attack track?' when the attack finished four hours ago. It's pointless, dying for that. And there is always a chance that you may escape and live to fight another day, or when the war is over, get handed back. So people use common sense basically. But initially you have to keep your trap shut. As far as the men who were captured and tortured were concerned, it just galvanised the rest of us into firmer action: we vowed to hit them harder, deeper, more accurately than we ever had before.

On day one – the first mission – I was no. 2 to our formation leader. We were the first Alarm mission package in, and in fact I believe we were the first two RAF aircraft over the border. The JP233 – an airfield denial weapon – package had also got airborne and gone for the tanker. We went direct to the border and straight for the first target, Al Assad – one of their newly constructed major airfields. It's a fair way away from Tabuk and we had a long transit before we actually crossed the border, but I remember that, during the day, before the decision was made, I was just hoping and praying that we would go. I thought the element of surprise would be weakened the longer we delayed. So I was hoping that we would go on the night of 16 February or the morning of 17 February.

When we took off, just after midnight, I was very relieved. Once we did so, it was difficult to remember that this wasn't a training sortie. We'd done so many training sorties at night, by day, carrying Alarms, carrying bombs, that everything initially seemed absolutely normal. But of course then came the border. The border is almost a physical barrier and, as you cross it, there is a mixture of relief, tension, you name it. A whole host of emotions emerges as you cross it – you're terrified, and it's really going on, and of course at the same time you've got all the operational calls of the AWACS aircraft and hundreds of other formations checking in. And you can see over on the Saudi side of the border the skies full of winking aircraft lights, but of course as soon as you cross the border, all the lights go out and you know that there are many other aircraft around you, completely unlit, apart from the dim cockpit lights, going over the border in pitch black. We flew up past Mudaysis airfield and all the runway approach and perimeter lights were on. I knew then that the element of surprise was complete. We went past Mudaysis up towards Al Assad. The lights were on there, too.

Trevor Roche fired his Alarm missiles a few seconds before us and two unfortunately hit the ground. We were flying at 200 feet and I initially thought that for some reason the missiles weren't coping with the low level, so we had time to disengage the auto-pilot and climb up slightly, and we fired from about 500–600 feet hoping that would give the missiles a chance. It worked, we managed to get all three off. All that we see of our missiles is that they come off the rails and there's quite a loud whoosh!, and they go forward of the aircraft for a few seconds and then just climb vertically. At that stage they haven't locked on to target. An Alarm does most of its searching once it reaches altitude. So it's effec-tively 'fire and forget'. Then we turn to get out of the bombers' way. It's very difficult to know what the exact effect is of the missile, because the *perceived* threat from a missile is also vital. If they know that we have fired an anti-radiation missile and turn off their radars, then the missile has done its job, because they can't see without the radars. If they keep their radars on and we get a hard kill on that radar, we have no way of knowing. All we know is that the radar is not searching for us any more. But if nobody gets shot down by radar-laid missiles, to me that is suf-ficient proof that the missile did its job. On subsequent sorties, they knew that we were firing anti-radiation missiles. That had two effects: it meant that they switched off their radars, which was good; but it also brought up the flak immediately, and at low level you just see the airfield blossom into this big flower of flak. That was the disadvantage.

However, we just turned at low level. This was what we had been practising – turning, without the autopilot at low level at night, using just the terrain-following radar. Of course in the pitch black we had to be very careful. Then back home. We were first down. The thing you ask straightaway when you come in, is has everyone checked in – and they had! There was lots of back-slapping, hand-shaking and smiles all around, but inwardly one was quite reflective. It was difficult getting to sleep afterwards with a bucket full of adrenalin still rushing around the body. Everything kept coming and going in a whirling dervish of thoughts and emotions.

The second mission is worse, because you know what's coming. And certainly the worst period for me was sitting in the aircraft, engines running, before we went. The problem is everything is up and running, there's nothing going on, you're just waiting for the check-in time for the formation – and you've got time to think. That's probably the worst time, when you have to put some of the weirder thoughts out of your mind, and say to yourself, 'Come on, let's just get on with it.' But once things start happening, once you start taxi-ing and taking off, you've got too many other things to think about. This is why all aircrew ought really to be born without imagination. Because you can imagine all sorts of things.

The second sortie was slightly worse in that they were expecting us. War had been going on for twenty-four hours at this point. It was the first time that I'd seen flak and there is a cockpit tape of me saying, 'What the bloody hell is that?' It looks just like a fireworks display, and it seems a lot closer than it really is. From thirty miles away it looks as if it's almost underneath the wing tip. I was amazed at the density of it. With Alarm missiles we weren't going too close to it, although we came fairly close to another airfield that was also pushing it out, so we had to be a little careful. The flak was extremely thick. So we fired off our missiles, and then coming back again it was, you know, 'How fast will this thing go without falling apart?' Coming out the second time was a little different because we knew we were being fired at. And when there's something behind you that's going to kill you, you get away from it as quickly as you can. Everyone came back from that one as well. I can remember the first two trips, and after that for the first week it was – sleep, fly, sleep, fly – and things become a little blurred. After about a week, we went up to the medium-level option. The only reason for going low-level is to avoid a perceived SAM threat. But there is also the fighter threat. At this time the SAM threat was not as great as anticipated, apart from what was known as SAM City which was the Baghdad area. The problems you have with the Tornado are that it's a low-level beast and at medium-level it's a ship out of water. The speed and manoeuvrability that we had were very limited. If we were fired at or locked on, our capability to break that lock was diminished. Paul Goddard and I were fired at one night when we were going against a power station to the south-east of Baghdad. We'd seen SAM 8s come up and we'd then seen more missiles fired that seemed to curve over the top of the formation and down very low. We saw what appeared to be initially an explosion, but then we saw the old white light coming over, which is a missile. It goes from a long flame into a sort of pencil dot, which means, basically, it's coming towards you. That tends to concentrate your mind somewhat. I think we had five 1,000lb bombs on board and we were effectively still full of fuel. So we had to evade the missile: rolling inverted, pulling down initially, rolling back up. All the time the aircraft is shaking and juddering because you're basically taking a wing that's not designed to fly at that level, and putting it through its paces. We've got the bit on tape where I say to Paul, 'It's coming this way', and then there's a load of grunts and groans from both of us, and eventually the missile explodes behind us. Immediately then, we're concentrating on trying to get back on to the target run. We're lights out, we are only really about twenty seconds between aircraft and, although we've got maybe 1,000 feet between aircraft vertically, we've just descended down through those levels, so we are now very, very close to the guy behind us, on his bombing time – and we're below him. Which means that he's somewhere up there, dropping his bombs. Now, if he was on his planned attack track and on time we were about 5° off that, so we were happy to go ahead and bomb, hoping that his bombs would come somewhere down the left-hand side. We released the weapons and I then pulled off to the right, hoping he was left, and up and over. And as we pulled up on to the escape track I saw two after-burners light up about 100 feet beneath me – it was Glen Beresford trying to get out of it. If that had happened in peacetime, there would have been a lot of sweaty brows around. There was very little to say about it on the ground. We were avoiding a missile, we got the bombs off, we avoided everybody else and that was it.

We were told by the Intelligence staff that we were not to go for the cracking plants of refineries. The cracking plant is the tall tower where the crude oil is cracked down to its components. Very complicated bits of kit, very difficult to rebuild afterwards, and we didn't want to destroy unnecessarily the infrastructure of the country. So we were told to go, for example, for the storage or the loading facilities. On one trip, we were going way up to the north to a refinery. We couldn't actually see the refinery because of a thin layer of cloud. We pulled down and did a dive-attack – which is going in at high level, rolling on to your back, pulling about 30° nose down, and then diving down on the target. You mark the target visually and then pull the aircraft up, and the bomb computer sends the bombs off automatically. We came down through the clouds, saw the target, and aimed for the storage facilities. The bombs came off, I pulled off left and did a level turn, rather than a climbing turn to get back above cloud; a bit naughty, but like any pilot I wanted to see where my bombs had gone. And sure enough we hit smack on the cracking plant, the one place where we were told not to hit. That unfortunately is one of the penalties that you pay with this medium-level bombing: it is inherently slightly inaccurate.

The 'Hanging' Gardens of Babylon was something else we were supposed to stay away from. There was an oil refinery two miles away we had to hit, so the word was, whatever you do, don't drop your bomb short. This time, we were level-bombing. One of the aircraft had his computer kit dumped so he was flying on the wing of another aircraft and was going to pickle the bombs off when the lead aircraft dropped his bomb. We dropped ours, the second lot dropped theirs, and then the third and fourth dropped

together. Ours went effectively on target – and likewise the second aircraft's. With the third one we saw one bomb go off in the river, which was very close to the Gardens, and we thought, Oh dear! but fortunately the rest fell on to a park, and a dual carriageway. So at least we missed the Gardens of Babylon! Later, Nick Wells, one of the cards on our formation, nicknamed two of the guys 'River Killer' and 'Road Driller' in honour of that episode. I suppose it's typical of the aircrew mentality that if you can't make a joke of it, then something's wrong.

Once we went against a Scud storage site. The storage sheds went up a treat. An absolute treat! You get the initial explosion of the bomb going in and then there's just a shock wave that comes out and a huge mushroom and then these things going this way and that and screaming up – we reckon to several thousand feet. It's just like throwing a match into a box of fireworks.

The accuracy we were getting with the medium-level bombing was not sufficient to go against point targets. We went against Kabala ammunition storage, which is a huge expanse of desert with bunkers quite well revetted and spaced out: there's about 300 or 400 metres between each bunker and they were giving us individual bunkers to go for. Individual targets. In such circumstances you can almost be guaranteed not to hit that bunker. But, for such a widespread military target there is no problem as, if we miss the target, we hope to hit some other part of the facility. In this case there was virtually no collateral damage: you either hit these bunkers or you miss them. If you miss them they just end up with a bit of sand thrown over them, even a close miss. And, sure enough, we got nowhere. Didn't hit a thing. This was very disappointing. The bombs didn't go anywhere near the targets. After a couple of those trips the boys started to feel a bit disheartened – they needed results. That's why the laser bombs used in conjunction with the Buccaneer became so important.

At one point I led and co-ordinated quite a large raid into al Taqaddum, close to Baghdad. Looking back on it, I would have varied the lines of attack quite a bit more. But it's very difficult

trying to co-ordinate forty aircraft and give everyone different attack tracks. Sometimes it's just not feasible with the support that you've got. Fortunately no-one was lost to SAMs on that attack.

My blackest moments were worrying about what was going on at home. Trying to tell my wife that I was going to fly tonight but everything would be OK, knowing that she wasn't going to sleep that night.

Our formation didn't suffer any losses. The only people we lost from Tabuk were Kev Weeks and Garry Lennox – both in the same aircraft. I knew them both very well. Some of the younger guys had not lost any friends before and I think they were hard hit. Most of us who'd been around for a while had lost at least one friend in peacetime flying, and you have to learn to compartmentalise it. It was a very sad time. But it really strengthens resolve. Fortunately that trip that they were leading was a complete success, and the Iraqis had to evacuate one of their Air Defence centres. So something came of it. They didn't die for nothing.

Squadron Leader Tony Lunnon-Wood

We had spent two months before Christmas working selected crews up to laser designate over land. Our main role was maritime anti-shipping; the problems involved with overland work are different.

As Christmas approached we were told we could take the normal Christmas stand-down – we were definitely not going to the Gulf. Both squadrons were due to deploy away from Lossiemouth early in the New Year: 12 Squadron to Gibraltar and 208 Squadron to St Mawgan in Cornwall for exercises with the Royal Navy. We were in the bar at St Mawgan, discussing when we thought the war would start, when one of the guys said, 'Come in and look at the TV. It's on, it's started!' I felt incredibly pissed off, we had worked hard to work up a Gulf 'team' before Christmas and now we definitely were not going to be involved. I felt very much like

the rugby substitute, the first team was playing and all I could do was sit and watch.

We tried to get on with the routine exercises, definitely feeling like second-class citizens. We wanted to be out there with the rest of the gang – part of 'The Team'. Time seemed to pass slowly, the exercise continued, we flew to Gibraltar for a weekend ranger and met up with some of the guys from 12 Squadron. The talk was mainly about the conflict and how things were going. The Tornado boys were doing some very hairy night missions with a fairly eye-watering attrition rate. Days went by and still we were told you are not going to the Gulf. That was Tuesday night. Wednesday morning we were attacking some Navy ships in the south-west approaches, when we were recalled to St Mawgan and told to return to Lossiemouth as soon as possible. We were going to the Gulf. Marvellous! Fantastic!

Everything happened very rapidly from then on. Within an hour of being told we had a week in which to get ready, we found out some people would be leaving in a matter of days on the first Hercules. The jets had to be prepared – new modification done, a different paint scheme and irregular servicing made to ensure they wouldn't need major servicing while operating in the Gulf. Not only did the Buccs need sorting out, so did the team wills, powers-of-attorney and proxy, so that our wives could still operate if we were away for six months.

The first thing the boss had to do was decide on crews and who would fly the jets out to Bahrain. We got together and discussed it and decided the best compromise was to mix a lot of experience with relative youth in each cockpit. This proved to be a reasonable balance – but we kept six 'heavy' crews together so that if anything new or skoshey came up we would have some very experienced crews available to take it on. We had done a lot of work on the low-level role but initial reports had led us to believe we would be operating at high-level, a very alien concept to most RAF fast jet crews – it produced a different set of problems which was causing concern.

Right up to the minute we left, we were all working flat out which was extremely hard on the families. There was no going home for a week spending a bit of time with them. We worked fourteen-hour days with everybody pitching in, loading aeroplanes, sorting out kit, flying work-up sorties, and doing air tests. The day before I flew out to the Gulf I was flying with Jaguars over to RAF Leuchars, trying to work out some sort of tactics/contingency plans for high-level laser designation. The response from the whole of RAF Lossiemouth was absolutely fantastic. Nothing was too difficult and the organisation and back-up support was brilliant. I landed from the Leuchars sortie and finished some last-minute paperwork, then drove home to take the family out to dinner. We rushed our meal so I could get home, take some sleeping pills and get to bed to try and sleep before getting up at 0200 hours in the morning. It was tricky because every friend and relative was ringing up to wish us good luck, even people I'd never heard of before – lovely, fantastic.

It was a terrible night with the family, worst night of my life, not a happy bunch of bears. Babe, my wife, was fantastic and my oldest son was keeping a stiff upper lip, but my youngest son was one pissed off pixie! Going to war was one thing but being away for six months was far worse to my youngest son.

The problem was that the last five days had been so frantic there was no time to sit down and talk it through with our sons. It would have been nicer to have had a slightly gentler lead-in.

I set off very early in the morning for Bahrain happy that we had had some tactics we could use. Norman Browne, a very experienced navigator/laser operator, and the boss were already there. Norman had gone out early so he could start discussing tactics with the Tornado and the Jag boys.

Having arrived in Bahrain it became clear that our senior commanders wanted not only guidance for smart bombs, but video film of targets being destroyed to demonstrate to all back home that we were doing the job we had been sent to do. The Americans were showing some very dramatic coverage and could prove their bombs were hitting. We had nothing to show for the tremendous job the Tornado guys were doing because it was all at night! The Jag boys were also doing a splendid job but only had gunsight film.

I landed at Bahrain after an eight-and-a-half-hour trip with a bladder full to breaking point. After a series of briefs it was off to our accommodation, a palatial hotel which turned out to be an absolute godsend. A place to relax, sleep and eat properly, makes life a lot easier and you can definitely do the job better. We met up with some of the Tornado crews who had already done six or seven missions and lost friends. We definitely felt like the new boys in town.

We did some work-up sorties with the Tornadoes and Jaguars, but no-one would let us go operational until they were certain we wouldn't cock it up. Suggestions were made about a trial run into Kuwait – the Jag boys knew of some juicy targets, but that idea was vetoed. We got the definite impression that the first strike had to be deep into Iraq and it had better be successful. The computer organising the flying schedule started its programme forty-eight hours in advance. We received our tasking eighteen hours before the sortie. The lesson was clear: if you are going to play with American toys in their sandpit, you work to their timing! The toys were AWACS aircraft, Wild Weasels (defence suppression) and Ravens which are F-111s that electronically jam everything. This system does not allow for the flexible approach. You go when the computer says you go, and that's that!

Buccaneer laser designation operations need a lot of co-ordination, careful target study and, ideally, attack directions that do not point into the sun. A lot of teeth in a giant cog have to meet the chain in the correct order or it's a shambles. In essence the Buccaneer pilot must find the target using a stop watch, map and his eye-balls. That makes attack direction important; we try and pick one with some sort of lead-in feature to help us see the target. Once the pilot has identified the target he dives the aeroplane and aims the weapon sight at the target. The sight and the laser pod are already calibrated to be pointing in roughly the same area. The nav has a TV display which allows him to view what the head of the laser is seeing. The picture is extremely poor when looking into sun which is why we try to avoid into-sun attacks. Once the nav is happy he can see the target on TV, he can move the head of the laser with a small controller under his left thumb. He has a set of cross-hairs which he keeps on the target, then, at a certain time, the bomb is released. After bomb release he pulls the trigger which fires the laser. A smart bomb can see this laser spot and will now head towards it using its kinetic energy, it has no power of its own. This means that the bomb must still be dropped at an accurate range from the target, and must be able to see the spot.

We could pick the attack direction fairly often, but again, that depended on how much fuel the rest of the package had. There was little point flying an extra sixty miles to get a decent attack direction if the rest of the strike package couldn't hack it. We didn't have a fuel problem in the Buccaneer.

This whole concept was very alien to us, we had always worked autonomously with the formation leader picking his route, timing and targets. We were suddenly involved with a huge amorphous mass and were being led around by the nose. It took some fairly heated discussions to convince some folk that, no matter how big the support package was, we could not designate the target unless the pilot could visually acquire it, and the nav could see it on his TV. To allow for redundancy one Bucc would fly with two Tornadoes in the same package; this allowed for the failure of one laser. If it was a small target, the lead Bucc would accelerate in front of the main formation, dive down to decrease the slant range and call if the Tornadoes were clear to drop. We were under orders not to drop if the laser was not working to avoid wasting bombs and more importantly, hurting innocent civilians. If the first Bucc's laser failed, the second Bucc had to be in a position to take on designation duties for the whole formation. The first Bucc would orbit the target to designate for the second set of Tornadoes, should the second Bucc's laser fail. Most designation manoeuvres involved loitering around the target for from one to ten minutes if a re-attack took place. This is not healthy and should definitely carry a government warning!

The inflexibility in target times meant that we often attacked targets at the same time from the same direction. This was unfortunately necessary to deconflict the 2,000 sorties a day flying into Iraq. We became predictable, but there was more chance of having mid-air collision than being shot down by SAMs. Because the flying schedule was tasked so far in advance, you didn't have the opportunity to go back and smash a target after a partially successful attack.

So, here was the package, four Tornadoes, two Buccs, Victor Tanker support, AWACS support, Wild Weasel support, Raven support, fighter escort support, all relying on the Buccaneer pilots' navs finding the targets with their eye-balls! Runways and large bridges were relatively easy to acquire visually, but dumps and other small targets were very hard to see at more than ten miles. Ten miles was the minimum visibility we could work to. This gave us a minute to find the target, dive the aeroplane, put the sight on, let the nav look for it on TV, identify it, start tracking and give the Tornadoes a clearance to release their bombs. The word we used was 'happy'. 'Happy' meant, 'I'm tracking, the laser's working, you're clear to drop'. It was always incongruous to hear 'happy' calls coming over the radio in the middle of Iraq with people shooting at you, you shooting at them or dropping on them, and everyone absolutely shit-scared!

There is a fair amount of pressure on both members of the crew. If you cock it up, the whole world knows about it, because it's all on film. Screwing up is one thing, screwing up in front of an audience which has great expectations of you is not worth thinking about. On my first sortie I was more concerned with fucking up than being shot down! I didn't want to let the Bucc, or my mates, down, and the War Lords at Riyadh were itching to get their hands on some video film for public consumption.

Youngsters are expected to screw up occasionally, experienced guys are not.

The first Bucc sortie had gone extremely well, the target was destroyed, but a small car trying desperately to get across the bridge suffered a direct hit from one of the bombs. It was extremely unfortunate, but to show that to people sitting in their living-rooms at home would have done no good at all. So the pressure was still on.

The second target was a railway bridge deep into Iraq. We met up with the tankers on the Saudi side of the border, the tanker guys did a fantastic job on every sortie. Their attitude was very much 'can do', and they made every effort to make life as easy as possible for the fast jets. We took on gas and then left the tankers climbing to cross the border and hopefully to pick up our fighter escort. The Ravens and Wild Weasels normally tried to rendezvous with us somewhere in Iraq. They were in high demand, so they normally had to fly defence suppression for a number of packages. We checked in with AWACS and from then on received regular 'picture clear' calls. This is a call, made by the controller aboard, confirming that they could see no fighter activity. It all seemed unreal, almost surrealistic. Low-level was fast, furious and hard work – high-level flying is a lot smoother, quieter and serene. Keith Nugent, my nav, called 'Welcome to Iraq!' And then it was down to business. I began weaving the aeroplane so that both of us could search for ground activity and missile launches or anti-aircraft fire. We both nearly wet ourselves every time the RWR (Radiation Warning Radar) sounded an alarm. The RWR is a bit of kit that tells you if radars are looking at you or missiles are being launched at you.

The target area was covered with patchy cloud, so we descended below it, found the target, then danced around the cloud making sure the laser was on the target all the time. There was no ground activity and the attack went pretty much as planned. The Tornadoes' bombs hit the bridge, right under Keith's cross-hairs, and dropped a span of the bridge. We returned to Bahrain with the film, which was released around the world on CNN News. The first Bucc film was from our aircraft. Keith Nugent was suddenly famous.

We were tasked against bridges early on to try and stop troop movements to the front line but often they were in the middle of towns. On paper they looked like ideal targets – crackers – but you had to accept the risk – albeit small – that a wild bomb might go into a town, and very occasionally they did go wild. On one of our younger crews' first sorties, having done a magnificent job of finding the target and putting a laser spot on it, four bombs did not guide and landed in the town. They were extremely upset when they landed back in Bahrain. The job of the designator aircraft is to put a laser spot on the target. I often said to anyone having worries about collateral damage, 'Your job is to get to the target and to get the cross-hairs on to it. If you've done that you've done all that can be expected of you. Once the laser is pointing at the target, what happens then is up to mechanics, a reasonably accurate release point, and a final element of luck. If you get the laser on the target you've done all you can and it's not your fault if the bombs don't then hit the target.' Grand words that are not worth much to a twenty-five-year-old when he's just seen four bombs miss the bridge and go into a town. Nobody wanted to hurt innocent civilians, and even when targetting was shifted to smaller bridges away from major cities we were still getting the occasional wild bomb. It really pisses you off, having fought your way through atrocious weather to the designated target, with people shooting at you, and the bloody bombs don't work. We were then tasked against airfields to try and stop the Iraqi Air Force taking off and doing damage to our ground troops. The targets and emphasis were changing every day, and the team were starting to get a little bewildered. The big problem was spreading the word as to why targets were changing and being able to discuss changes in tactics.

The communication problem was caused by our working hours. We basically had two shifts, dawn patrol and afternoon raids.

Dawn patrol meant getting up at 0130 hours and having a snack, catching the bus, Met and Intelligence briefings, and final planning. Take-off was normally in the dark, with a night formation transit on a Tornado's wing to the tanker. This proved to be fairly skoshey! You would fly up to a four-hour mission, land at around 0930, debrief and look at the film, and get breakfast. By 1100 you would be absolutely knackered. Then back to the hotel, sleep by the pool for a couple of hours, eat dinner at 1800, pop two sleeping pills, and crash out. Dawn patrol crews were normally in bed when the afternoon mission crews returned to the hotel. The only time you could get everybody together was at 1930 or 2000 hours, which meant depriving the next day's dawn patrol of their sleeping time, or the afternoon missions of their debrief. Dissemination of information is important and, unfortunately, there was a lack of opportunity to get the whole team together. It is not fair to dictate tactics to people who are risking a lot, so I tried to get as many people as possible involved in discussing the airborne tactics. Of course the final decision always rested with the most experienced crews. The most common bitch was 'What's going on?' The normal reply was, 'I'll tell you all tonight at 2000, if you want to lose two hours' precious sleep!' Most guys chose to go to bed so we never really had the whole team together to brief them on yet another plan. Bottom line, we had to stay flexible to allow for weather and target size; and we tried to stagger the shift system so no-one did dawn patrol all the time.

After some weeks we finally got clearance to drop our own bombs. Again we had to adopt the flexible approach to this, and after two days we had worked out some parameters and had dropped some very accurate bombs. This was a major boost to morale, and we now felt we were playing an active role. You could either self-designate, which put a lot of responsibility on the navigator. It meant he was tracking the target during a 4G recovery manoeuvre which took a fair amount of skill. The other option we had was to designate for each other. As soon as the 'happy' call came from the other Bucc, you tipped in from any direction and delivered your bombs. This meant you could be far more aggressive on the recovery. It's a nice way of doing it, but of course it meant loitering in the target area for a lot longer, which wasn't healthy; however, it was then up to you to make your own decisions whether to go for it or not.

We had been told to shut down certain airfields, so we had an aim. The frustration factor caused by the weather and smoke obscuration was enormous. If we couldn't see the target, we couldn't drop. Some days the package was launched with all of us knowing full well that the target was obscured by smoke and the weather was unfit. Having to fly all the way to the target and then bring the bombs home again is not healthy for the bomb or the aircrew. Flying in cloud means you cannot see missiles being launched at you and trying to do evasive manoeuvres on instruments is impossible. The bomb also suffers, raindrops hitting the glass optic on the front of the bomb at high speed damages the glass and it ends up like a toilet window, meaning it cannot see the laser spot and will not guide. So it was very frustrating to launch day after day, knowing the target was obscured and you would probably damage the bomb. It was extremely upsetting also to break out into a clear area, having flown in cloud in close formation for two hours, to see lots of juicy targets which you could not drop on; and then go back into cloud en route to your target which was covered by smoke or cloud. We wanted to do the job, but stooging around in cloud in close formation over enemy territory is bloody stupid. Weather and target obscuration by smoke proved to be a major problem.

It was a strange existence living in a five-star hotel, leaving there in the dark, wearing civilian clothes with your gas mask, and wondering if perhaps in five hours you would be in some Iraqi prison. We all saw the pictures of the POWs but at that time didn't know what they had been through. I said to my wife before I left, 'If you see me on TV, it's good news. They can't kill me afterwards!' I think my biggest fear, and everyone had their own, was having to jump out near a spot I'd just bombed, because retribution would have been swift and merciless. Goolie chits wouldn't have been a lot of use. There were certain areas where you knew there were very skilled people disguised as trees and sheep ready to help you (if you got there), fantastic people. I take my hat off to them for what they did out there.

The trip back to the border from the target always went in phases for me. At first there was a three-week walk to the border; then the three-day walk; then, I can glide from here; and finally that fantastic sensation as you cross back into friendly territory.

On most occasions the anti-aircraft fire was well below us, like some cotton field spreading out beneath you. Some days were very hairy, with missiles shooting at us, Wild Weasels shooting at them, and us in between. I remember an airfield target close to Baghdad – it was a real bitch with loads of SAM launches on the way in. A missile was launched at us unguided and it missed the front of the aeroplane by about 300 feet. I was working hard looking for the target and all I saw was a white trail shoot past the front of the jet. I can remember thinking this is getting bloody skoshey when a HARM missile from an F-4 Wild Weasel roared over the top of the cockpit in the other direction! Keith, my nav, missed most of it, he was working hard looking for the target on his TV. Fuck this, I thought, if the bloody Iraqis don't get me the Americans will!

On another mission we were orbiting a heavily defended airfield, when some of the explosions started following our flight path and getting higher and higher. For some strange reason it irritated me to think that this particular gun crew had singled me and Keith out. You could see the muzzle flashes and I managed to pin-point his position. It was the one time it became personal and I was annoyed we didn't have any bombs. I wanted to return the gesture! I told Keith we would have that bastard next time. On the trip home my thoughts changed entirely, deep down I had a sneaking admiration for this gun crew stuck out on a ridge trying desperately to defend their airfield when the world knew it was just a matter of time before Iraq was defeated. It turned out to be only a couple of days.

Suddenly it was all over, the guys on dawn patrol were walking to their jets and were told, 'You're not going, it's all over.' For me it didn't bring a sense of euphoria or joy, just a sense of a job not completed; it was not over, we hadn't sewn this up properly. The Army had done their thing with very few losses, but I still felt we needed to finish it properly. A lot of other guys felt the same way. I wanted to see a cataclysmic finish to it all, with Saddam saying I'm really sorry, I surrender! But it didn't work out that way.

I hate to say it, but, looking back on it, it was the ultimate challenge and I enjoyed it. It was interesting to find out how you would react under pressure, how you're going to hack it when you're called on to do so. We had been training for war in a European theatre for years. The scenario here was different. The team, however, and that includes everybody – chefs, technicians, admin assistants, medics, the whole spectrum – did everything that was asked of them and more. They all worked long hours in a completely professional manner. The banter and the camarad-erie was fantastic. There were no heroes here, no false bravado, everybody admitted they were shit-scared. Working with a pro-fessional team who carried out the job despite some enormous frustrations was a real treat. We had fantastic accommodation due to Group Captain Dave Henderson, which we needed. The support from RAF Lossiemouth, who produced the goods in incredibly fast time, was fantastic. Young crews did a brilliant job in a role for which they had not trained. The expats in Bahrain were extremely kind and hospitable to us. The people at home sent letters, parcels, food, toiletries and loads of good wishes. For once in our lives, instead of people complaining about low-flying and the noise, they were telling us to go for it, and that they thought we were wonderful. It made a big difference knowing that everybody at home believed in what we were doing.

For aircrew a conflict is a very impersonal thing and we tend to aim for hard targets, not people. No-one enjoys hurting innocents and it was a desperate shame that this happened on occasions. It all added up to living in a 'Mash Movie' environment. All in all, if I had to go back tomorrow and do the same thing again, I'd do it. Having said that, we were lucky, we didn't lose anybody.

I think we learned a lot of lessons from the human side, but on the operating side, we can't learn anything, unless we go back into the same theatre. It was geared for good weather, good visibility, a very low air threat, massive support, and we wouldn't get that in Europe. The biggest lesson we learned was that we had to be flexible. We also proved the old Buccaneer could do the job – she was marvellous. If I was going to go to war again, I'd fly in a Buccaneer any time. We had finally proved that airpower can do the business. We had come into our own, the Air Force is no longer the spinster, or a bunch of little boys with grown-up toys.

I couldn't sleep much for the first two weeks after coming home, and I definitely suffered from a lack of adrenalin buzz. I'd get up in the morning waiting for some action, and this was despite two weeks off in Bahrain waiting to come home. Even so, I was delighted I was involved, that's what I had been waiting for, training for. Our youngsters did everything that was asked of them, they were very impressive, and it was a privilege to work with them. I would have hated to have been left out.

After hostilities ceased, lots of senior officers and politicians came to Bahrain to say 'thank you'. Some were very stiff and formal, and others spoke with genuine feeling. The most memorable occasion for me was General de la Billière coming down and saying, 'You've done a good job, saved a lot of casualties in the Army, and thank you very much.' He was very easy to talk to, and we all appreciated the fact he had come to talk to us personally. But the most poignant moment was when, as he left the room and departed, one of his aides, a senior officer, held back, and watched him go. He then put his head back around the door, took off his beret and said, 'Bottom of my heart, from the Army, thanks a fucking bunch – that's no bullshit. You've got no idea how thankful we are.' His sincerity was obvious in his thanks for saving a lot of his boys. For an Army man to say that to the Air Force, that was all I needed, that was the greatest compliment.

Squadron Leader Robert Ankerson

It was not until Nichol and Peters were lost that it really got home to us. Then of course we saw the video of them on TV. This really made everyone very angry. This anger was coupled with our innermost thoughts that, God forbid, this was waiting for us. So we had very mixed emotions and feelings.

By the time we took off a week after the start of the air war we had lost four aircrew, Max Collier, with Nigel Elsdon and Kev Weeks with Garry Lennox. I didn't know them closely, but we had bumped along in the Air Force together.

With my pilot, Simon 'Budgie' Burgess, we took off in the early hours of the morning; our target was an airfield and our target time was 0545. We were both as nervous as hell. As we flew towards the target we passed a few remarks between ourselves, nothing significant, all pretty trivial, but it released the tension and helped suppress fear to a level where we could get on with the job. As the navigator I had a radar screen with a moving map display, and two TV displays which kept me busy. Having done our air-to-air refuelling we climbed up to our transit and attack altitude of 20,000 feet. At that height we were certainly above anti-aircraft fire, above most of the SAMs, and anything that could get us at that height we had EW (Electronic Warfare) cover with us. We also had a fighter escort of F-15s. When we crossed the border we turned off the lights and went silent. We felt confident that we had everything we needed to cover us for a successful mission.

After we crossed the border it took us about forty minutes before we reached the target. Everything was running on rails; we did all our checks three or four times to make sure everything was OK. Then we came down to release point and felt the bombs go. I called to Simon, 'Hard left, and let's get out of here.' Seconds later there was an explosion and I could see six- or eight-feet flames leaping out of the left wing. We immediately jettisoned the fuel tanks which didn't make one iota of difference. Neither of us was in a hurry to leave the cockpit for an unknown situation on the ground. So he was saying to me, stay with it, stay with it; and I was saying, we're going to have to go, Budgie, we're going to have to go. We were turning away to the west, as we knew we were in an area of enemy deployment, so we were hoping that we might find an empty desert. Neither Simon nor I had parachuted before, neither he nor I had ejected before, and neither he nor I had been to war before.

Then the aircraft developed all sorts of failure indications. Simon shouted that the aircraft was not responding to the flying controls. He then called eject, eject, eject, and that was the start.

My head went down on to my chest, there was a tumbling, rushing sensation but somehow there was nothing terrifying about it. The next thing I knew was the jerk when the main parachute deployed. We had baled out somewhere around 15,000 feet. During the descent I could see Simon and we shouted across to each other that we were all right.

My immediate reaction on landing was to gather up my parachute. As I was doing this I found I was alongside this enormous tyre track, from the large tyres on army field transport vehicles. I realised I had come down on a sandy road. I had landed in fact on the equivalent of the M1 in the back of beyond.

Then all of a sudden a dozen people appeared, firing their guns in my direction! So I stopped pulling in my parachute and put my hands in the air. The Iraqis gesticulated to me to throw down my pistol which took me ages to reach under my life jacket. They then led me over to a bunker. Within minutes someone came over who spoke English and asked if I was hurt or if I wanted water. My hands were then tied and I was blindfolded. Over the next two hours I was moved from one bunker to the next and questioned in each. I assumed from the questioning that I was being moved up the command chain. I was asked fairly standard questions: your name? what base you operated from? what aeroplane did you fly? I replied with my name, rank and number and told them that I could not answer their other questions. I was given food and water and asked each time if I was feeling all right? Well, apart from feeling petrified, I was fine.

I was then blindfolded again and moved into another bunker. There I was asked my name, which I gave. But the interrogator said no, not you. And asked the question again and Simon gave his name. That was a great morale booster for both of us. Even though we couldn't see each other, at least we knew the other was alive.

We were then moved from that bunker and handed over to an interrogation team where things obviously began to get unpleasant because I was interrogated over a period of hours. They'd come, question me, go away and come back. At this stage they asked more operationally related questions. However, I got the feeling that there wasn't a particular direction in their questioning. It was as if there was no overall plan or particular information they were after. Having since spoken to other POWs I don't think the Iraqis ever had a plan for their interrogation.

We were moved again and for one night I shared a cell with Simon. Then we were moved to the first of the more permanent prisons where we were put into yellow prison suits. I was now in solitary confinement and, although I had a window and could see guards passing and other prisoners, I began for the first time to feel lonely. However, my spirits were cheered a little by just hearing other voices, some of which were American. We were fed in our cells three times a day; soup for breakfast, rice for midday, and then a piece of stewed 'camel' in the evening. In this first prison I had a piece of foam for a mattress and some blankets.

It was probably the only time in my life I wished I knew a bit more about football or at least had played it. You see the guards were bored out of their minds doing this job so they were happy to find that some of the POWs played football. I was taken out once for exercise, but after the parachute descent one of my knees was slightly injured which meant I wasn't running around too much. So it was back in the cell after only a short exercise period and I never got invited to play again.

There were a couple of periods of interrogation but by now I had reached the point where I had decided that saying nothing wasn't a good policy. It wasn't worth a beating not to tell them I flew a Tornado. So I answered their questions when I considered I wasn't giving away anything crucial. But when I refused to answer the beatings they gave me were pretty primitive, fist, boot or stick.

We were then moved again. This constant moving was disturbing because we were never sure why or for what reason they were moving us – we were always going to the unknown. But again it was another prison, a cold forbidding place. This time the cell had tiled floors and walls; there was a shower tray in one corner but the WC in the other had no water. Here I got one meal a day of soup, more like cabbage water. Occasionally I got some rice. After I had been there about a week I had a complaint from one of the guards that every time he opened the hatchway he could smell the stink of the toilet! So I had a go at pouring water down to flush it, but it didn't do a lot of good. But amidst the stench I got some comfort from the sunlight that came through the high window for about an hour a day to relieve the normal, very subdued, daylight.

I spent three weeks in that solitary cell. I had a couple of short sessions of interrogation but because nothing contentious came up I answered their questions. Physically I didn't feel too bad but my mental attitude was becoming a problem – what to do with my time. On a number of occasions I had to give myself a talking to because I was starting to feel sorry for myself and that wasn't going to do me any bloody good. I told myself to snap out of it and to get on with accepting and dealing with the situation. I constantly thought of my family. The first thing I did in the morning was to speak to my wife Chris and my son Gareth. I also did this the last thing at night. I would tell them what I had done that day and ask them what they had been up to. As a practising Christian I prayed a great deal. My family and my faith were an immense strength to me, particularly when things were uncertain – it was then that a quick sharp prayer made all the difference.

One terrifying event stands out: the night the prison was bombed. While the bombing was going on we were shouting to each other from cell to cell asking who was there and if they were all right. Throughout the entire bombing I felt remarkably calm – I felt I was in the hands of God and that it wasn't time for any of us. But after the bombing I remember curling up into a little ball because I got terrible stomach cramps, muscular reaction, I suppose.

The building had been wrecked by the bombing, and noise and chaos was everywhere as I was led out. I was being led out by this fellow who was about five foot and '7 stone wringing wet', who gently guided me by my elbow. We were taken out and put on to a coach where either blankets were thrown over our heads or we were told to sit with our heads down. There were no seats in this shell of a coach so I was pushed to the back next to this guy. We were really crushed together but somehow I managed to free my hand. It's not very often I have held hands with a bloke (!) but this was the right time. It was the touch of another human being – a friend – I think we all needed that.

We were transferred to another prison where I shared a cell with Robbie Stewart, Dave Waddington, John Nichol, a Kuwaiti and an Italian. John Nichol was now looking much better than when we had seen him on the video. I tell you, we just talked the night through – we just wanted to catch up on everything. You know, had we been videoed? how was the food? It really picked up the spirits. There were no beds, so when we finally fell asleep it was a case of let's not be shy, boys, let's cuddle up to keep warm.

That evening we were put back into solitary confinement, but at least I had a window. Four days later we were moved again and this time I had no window. Somehow it was about this time that things began to get me down. I got it into my mind that I was going to be kept permanently in this grim prison. I thought that, as I was now back in a military prison, I was in for a long haul. Then things began to happen. We were allowed to shave and shower, we were given a clean yellow suit, but I couldn't allow myself the luxury of the thought that we were going to be released. I rationalised it, that this was a military organisation, getting into military routine, you know, bath once a month, change of clothes etc. I was expecting nothing; I kept expectations low to avoid disappointment. I assumed I was going to be there all on my own for months.

I began to try and programme my day. I would walk round the cell fifty times, I'd pray – the simple one, the Our Father, the Glory Be, bits of the Communion service, the Lamb of God, anything I could remember over and over again. I'd then do the alphabet backwards for a while, then things like the tap code, where you have the alphabet as a matrix of 5 by 5. In my head I designed a rack to carry bikes on the back of my car, selected what motorbike I'd like to buy when I got home (they were always British!), thought up dinner party menus, tried remembering the names of the people on the squadrons I served with, who I'd been to university with. In fact anything, simply anything, to make my mind work. I wanted to be positive.

It was very early on the morning of 5 March that I heard a group of people call at the cell next to me. At the end of the conversation I heard them say, 'and today you'll be going home'. My ears pricked up and I thought, no, no I couldn't have heard that. Then they came to my cell and asked me how was breakfast and whether I needed anything and then they went away. Then I heard them next door telling him he was going home that day! My spirits sank – why them? why not me? Then I began to rationalise the situation. We had captured lots of prisoners, they'd only captured a few so it was going to be 3,000 for one or whatever, and these two guys were the first batch. Someone had to go first, I thought, and someone last – no reason why it shouldn't be me. Then twenty minutes later my cell door opened, they took down my details and told me I would be released in fifteen minutes. That was the first time I allowed myself to think I might be released – I did a lot of praying then!

I was let out and led down a corridor and there was a line of yellow suits, with John Nichol in front of me. After a short time we were led out blindfolded, given a spray of cheap aftershave then led on to a bus and driven to a hotel in Baghdad and handed over to the Red Cross. The Red Cross had been operating in Iraq during the eight years of the Iran/Iraq war, so they felt confident of their status within Iraq. I met this 5'2" Red Cross lady who was saying I will protect you; when I asked who was protecting her she said 'my badge'. All the prisoners were there from all the countries including the female American doctor – she was amazing, just one of us. That night, God bless them, the Red Cross told us that they had managed to find sufficient rooms for us to have one each. The last thing we wanted to be was alone! We just talked and talked and talked throughout the night getting through a steady supply of Swiss chocolate.

The first time I actually spoke to my wife, Chris, was on the Red Cross aeroplane as we were just approaching the Iraqi border. I was a bit surprised to get through but I told her I was on my way, and it was great to hear her voice. We had all been videoed by the Iraqis and I had assumed that, like John Peters and John Nichol, people at home had seen us and realised we were alive. It never occurred to me that she didn't know I was alive. After what seemed endless days of debriefings and medical checks I was finally united with Chris and Gareth back at the RAF base in Germany.

Wing Commander Dick Forsythe

During the last two weeks of March 1991, Saddam Hussein's aggression against the Kurdish people began to cause serious concern. Fearing further attacks, the Kurds set off for the villages along the Turkish/Iraqi border where they had been kicked out fifteen years earlier in a series of Iraqi purges. Iraqi gunships chased them right up into the mountains. By the end of March, half a million people were ready to die in squalor and cold rather than live under the dictator. They had to complete the last part of the journey on foot as they scurried up into the mountain fastness. Thus began Operation Provide Comfort.

There was considerable anxiety about the state of the Kurds, and tremendous media pressure on us to get out there and do something. So I was tasked to take three Chinooks of my unit – 240 Squadron Conversion Unit, Odiham – out to Turkey. I went with two mandates: to go and help the Kurds, which was fairly self-explanatory, and to work with the Americans. Day-to-day tasking was left to my initiative. From the time we were told to go, to getting there, was about two and a half to three days, very good going.

Coalition headquarters was set up in Incirlik, and I went out as Detachment Commander. It was relatively chaotic, because the Americans have two logistics organisations in Turkey geared to NATO emergencies, but they elected to use the headquarters that they had brought in for Desert Shield. So there were one or two problems, because loggies were not leading the ship, as it were. But we eventually got permission to operate from an airbase at Diyarbakir, the capital town of the south-east region of Turkey.

To give some idea of the chaos, when I arrived there, the world aid agencies were flying in great Russian Antonov-type planeloads full of all sorts of things, some of it useful, some of it not. The Bulgarians flew in a planeload of old uniforms, which made the refugees look like something out of *The Mikado*.

At that point, the Americans hadn't actually formulated a plan.

They were trying to find an area that the Turks would let us use as a forward operating base. Just to illustrate this chaos, a senior UN official came up to me, and asked where he should send the stuff in his charge. I said, 'Well, I believe they should be going to Salopi.' He turned round and his twenty trucks just drove past me on the basis of that one statement. The Americans had no links with the aid agencies; they didn't feel under any obligation to provide any kind of logistics for the agencies, so we ended up taking whatever we could prise out of them, sleeping bags, purified water, old uniforms, tracksuits, whatever, with, inevitably, not a lot of sensitivity as to what the people on the ground actually needed. We just moved it forward and pushed it out of the back of the Chinooks. This was very dangerous, because even a sleeping bag can do damage falling from a helicopter hovering height.

Mrs Chalker, the Overseas Minister, came out early on, and we went to the worst site. We pushed a sleeping bag at one little boy, as he was coming up quite a steep hill, and the bag came out the back and got caught in the 130-knot winds of the rotors. He met it coming down, and like a good full back, held it, but he rolled all the way back down this hill, through lumps and rocks and things. At another place I went to with Mrs Chalker, we almost got mobbed. Two women, probably seventeen or eighteen, came up to me and tried to give me their infants. And of course I said, 'No, I can't take them', but they were clearly at their wits' ends, not having the strength to look after themselves *and* their children. The smell was awful; there were no facilities available, although they were trying their best.

At Diyarbakir the Turks had an air-to-ground range. Our sleeping tents were about one hundred yards away. The tents would shake every time planes taxied out and practice bombs exploded. By this time there were 320 lads looking after twelve Chinooks. Our boys were expected to work eight hours a day in that sort of environment, when a lot of them had only been back from the Gulf for about four months. So constant noise was a major problem, and consequently we made a command decision to move out of this place to the forward operating base at Salopi. Eventually, the Americans put Special Forces teams into the camps, and they started getting a sort of system going, but they reported all the way back to the headquarters in Incirlik, where they bought food locally. And it was then passed forward by road to Salopi, which meant there was a five-day lag between requests for water or lentils and their actually appearing. We moved forward to Salopi. There we would ask at the end of the day what the people on the ground at the camps wanted. We then had people on the ground at Salopi, who'd load up what was required. Helicopters are very much more efficient if you can make the loads up and then hook them on underneath. So we carried them underslung. The Americans were very keen on internal loading because that's the way they do it on their ships.

On one occasion I took six tons of shoes, and tracksuits that the Kurds didn't like for religious reasons – they ended up just strewn all over the place. Also four tons of brownie mix. But the one that really got me for total futility was four tons of cranberry jelly.

We ended up 'robbing', with the tacit approval of the forward logistics people, the relief-convoy lorries. They were stuck, bumper to bumper, four rows of twenty-ton trucks in the middle of this highway. We just went along taking stuff off them to make into loads. The drivers were very keen for us to do this, because then they could get back and be paid for another load. What was needed was staple foods, purified water for the babies, and lentils and rice. The Kurds were very hardy. The temperature in the evenings at the start was −10°, but by the time we left it was 50°. At Salopi the sanitary arrangements left a lot to be desired: there were bacteria spores floating around in the air. We all had the runs, almost continuously.

The worst Kurdish camp was Chucurga. It was like descending into hell. I walked down this track on a muddy weekday, and saw the quagmire, the squalor and the starving children – the mortality rate was one hundred a day at the start of the problem. The stronger Kurds had got up to some of the parachute things that had been air-dropped and they were bartering what they had found. The problems involved, actually sorting out 115,000 people, can be imagined.

The air-drop and the helicopters managed to see the camps through a critical period of about four weeks when they were in trouble and the roads were impassable. The first priority was stabilising the situation; that is what 'Provide Comfort' was all about. Then they had to encourage the Kurds out of the mountains, by whatever means. The Royal Marines did that very well. One of their officers, for instance, stopped a snatch going on in the middle of Zakhu, and it ran like wildfire through the camps that somebody had at last stood up to the secret police, and so the Kurds then started to think, Maybe there is a bit of truth in what we've been told.

Our deliveries were much more specific when the marines were there. We had a clear understanding about what was required on the ground. But the camps – as there were only about ten of them, we knew where to take the stuff. There were about a thousand Kurds seeking political asylum in Turkey. And on one occasion we got 124 of them into one Chinook!

I was absolutely exhausted at the end of the operation. Yet I wouldn't have missed it for the world, but of course it wasn't entirely a pleasant trip. The boys certainly earned their crust.

Squadron Leader Chris Tingay

I joined the Hercules fleet as a pilot in 1980 and I've been with it ever since. It is a tactical aeroplane and we get involved in all theatres. In the past, Hercules operations have included everything from evacuating Aden in 1967, through supplying food to famine areas in West Africa and Nepal in 1973, getting British nationals out of Vietnam in 1975 and Iran in 1979, supplying Ascension Island during the Falklands campaign in 1982, to supplying humanitarian relief to Sarajevo in 1992.

On the Hercules, the Operational Conversion Unit (OCU) lasts about six months, including a period of ground training, simulator training, a local and then a strategic phase. So you come out of the OCU qualified to fly the Hercules from A to B but not in a tactical field. This comes later, when you've got more experience.

When I came through, they were cutting back a lot in the Air Force. Not a lot of people were coming through because we had all these experienced flyers from the Comet days and the Hastings and all these other aeroplanes that were suddenly all chopped in the mid-to-late 1970s. Consequently, when I came to Lyneham there weren't that many other youngsters about. People had been around for ever, you know, crotchety old devils, and so it was quite difficult as a youngster in those days.

Suddenly, in 1982, that changed with the Falklands conflict. The place went haywire and every man and his dog was used to get equipment down to Ascension. As the Task Force set off, we were putting the stuff forward for them to pick up on the way, at Ascension Island.

For Ascension we used to refuel at Gibraltar. Lyneham to Gibraltar: four hours twenty minutes; then Gibraltar to Dakar, six hours ten minutes. Initially that's all we did; later on we started to do the long-haul stuff. As the fleet passed Ascension on the way down, we started to air-drop the supplies, and we got further and further until we couldn't do it within the range of the Herc. So then we got ex-Andover long-range fuel tanks fitted in the freight bays, and these gave us an extra two or three hours. Then we put four tanks in, and that gave us an even longer range. Eventually, even that wasn't good enough, and we put the refuelling probes on. This was one of our great successes; it only took about four days from start to finish. Staggering!

From Ascension to the Falklands was about a fourteen-hour trip. So when we first went down there, we used to refuel twice – once a couple of hours out and another about six or seven hours out. It's a tricky operation, behind the Victors or VC10s.

The problem with the Victor is that they've got to do this at about 235 knots minimum – we normally go about 210 knots, something like that. So the only way we can do it is by doing a 'toboggan'. The Victor starts to descend and the only way we can catch up is obviously by doing a descent ourselves, so it's called a toboggan.

It takes between twenty and twenty-five minutes to refuel, depending on how much fuel you need. We used to start picking up the gas about 20,000 feet and begin at about 1,000 feet rate of descent, which gives you, basically, twenty minutes, although as you refuel you slacken the descent. So I used to try to pick up all the fuel by about 5,000 feet, but the longer you leave it, the closer the ground comes!

Initially, when we retook the Falklands, our job was unloading goodies for the fleet and troops. Then after a couple of days we put some aeroplanes in there to do all sorts of stuff: take kit in, spares, bring bodies out. After a few weeks they decided to resurface the runway with this metal matting, which stopped us from landing, so then we did quite a few air-drop sorties for resupplying. We used to fly down there, air-drop the stuff and fly back without landing. That's when Flight Lieutenant Terry Locke made the longest airborne time for the Herc – twenty-eight hours and four minutes – it's in the *Guinness Book of Records*. The standard flight time was about twenty-six and a half hours.

One of the more interesting tasks for the Herc was to drop by parachute Lieutenant-Colonel Chaundler into the sea to replace H. Jones, who'd been killed at Goose Green.

There's a triangle right in the middle which is about 1,000 miles from anywhere, and that was where I had the gearbox blow up: a big lump of metal came off, and got lodged underneath the arm that pulls the prop to stop it turning, so the prop was turning, and we wondered what the bloody hell was going to happen, so we had to divert to a place called Canoas in Brazil. On top of that we had lost the radar, which shows you where all the bad weather is. So there we were in this horrible weather with an engine that hadn't feathered properly. The Herc wouldn't fly very well on two engines when you were heavy and I was obviously having to think about ditching the load. Anyhow, the whole nightmare lasted about six hours, until we reached Brazil.

We landed there unannounced, because we also had radio problems. They weren't very happy about us, and we got arrested until they could check who we were. We eventually spent about a week there. For the first couple of days they kept us under house arrest on the base, till they checked up on us. They couldn't do us any favours, because obviously they were closely linked to the South American people. So they were trying to be standoffish and just help out in an emergency, but they had to go through the routine. They were very good, but for a couple of days we didn't know quite what was going to happen.

Another time we were flying back to Lyneham from Dakar during the Falklands campaign, but en route they diverted us to Gibraltar, which, as things turned out, probably saved us. There was water in the fuel, and the engines just went down; the fuel was icing up and not getting through. So first one engine shut down, then another and then a third. We went down like a bucket. It was one of those things that happened immediately; one minute we were just trucking along and the next we had lost three engines. There was no way it would fly on one engine, although it might have flown on two, so we just plummeted. But as we got below the icing level, the fuel came good because the ice in it melted, and the engines started up again. So we diverted to Seville, and landed safely. That was one of our worst incidents.

Long-haul sorties are fairly boring for the crews. Those, for instance, were twenty-five- or twenty-six-hour sorties. They are long! The worst thing I can remember was sitting on the runway at Ascension lining up to take off, and thinking, This time tomorrow, I'll still have a couple of hours' flying to do. You almost became a zombie. But there was some interesting stuff down the bottom end. The Joint Air Transport Establishment at Brize Norton developed a type of grappling hook to pick up mail and other things without landing, which was handy while the Stanley runway was being lengthened.

We used to pick up all sorts of things; we never knew much about it. But one day they actually put a sheep's skull inside the bag just for a laugh, and when it got to Ascension, the hierarchy saw it. They had a sense-of-humour failure, so they sent this signal back saying, 'This is not the thing to do, you must stop this, take it seriously.' The guys in the Falklands sent a signal back saying, 'This petty pilfering must stop; that was a full sheep when we sent it.'

The standard Hercules crew is five: captain, co-pilot, navigator, engineer and loadmaster. In those long sorties we also had one extra pilot and one extra navigator, which made a crew of seven. We amused ourselves in all sorts of ways. Two aeroplanes used to go down a day about an hour apart, and we used to play battleships over the radio with the other crew, and Trivial Pursuits, things like that, just to keep amused. We also all had our own signature tune for air-to-air refuelling, and we used to let the tanker know who we were by humming this tune – mine was '633 Squadron'. We also used to read a lot of books. We got very fat, too: you get bored, so you eat. We used to cook some cracking meals on a little oven we had. Guys would make cakes and all sorts of stuff; you wouldn't believe some of the things we used to do. You would have sleep periods, but you can't sleep on a Herc; it's noisy and uncomfortable. So we used to come back after twenty-six hours absolutely shattered, so they came up with some mild sleeping tablets to help us sleep. At least on long-haul civil airlines you have alcohol and pretty girls and films and things like that!

After the Falklands, the next thing that came up for me was the Ethiopian humanitarian relief. It was heart-rending; we actually got into the camps.

Initially, we saw it in the press. It seemed to me, as a layman, that this was the standard thing: the media stirring something up and then we, politically, having to get involved. Fair enough, that's right and proper. But these things had happened before, and they're still happening now. Most of the time there were two aeroplanes out there, one involved in air drops to remote areas and the other involved in the air landing of supplies. I did both, but mainly the air landing. We were based at Addis Ababa itself but we went all round the country. The food was brought into Addis Ababa by all sorts of means and we distributed it from there to the air dropping-zones, and throughout the country to all the places that weren't fighting the civil war. Personally, I don't mind getting involved in anything that will help diminish suffering, but you could argue about whether it's strictly a military thing or not.

We ended up being there for quite a while: over a year. We used to do it for about a month or so at a stretch and then fly back, so a lot of crews were involved. We often used to land on strips actually on the camps, and so you used to see people dying in front of your eyes. It was awful, it really was; you just can't describe that sort of thing. I've seen some horrific sights, during the Gulf War, for example – but to see people, especially children, wasting away like that, it really is bad, for anybody who's a parent, or anybody, full stop. Awful. The smell is staggering, and the look of despair in their eyes . . . There we were, fat and happy, because the difference between Addis Ababa and places just ten miles up the road was extraordinary. Some people in Addis didn't even realise there was a problem. You could eat in a restaurant – you could eat your fill. You could drink alcohol, very cheaply – it was staggering! And just ten miles down the road people were dying of starvation. It's difficult to get your head round that. Obviously there are feelings of guilt. But there again, if we were hungry we wouldn't be able to do our job anyway. You obviously get over it, but it is appalling and, although I was proud and pleased to be involved in that sort of relief work, it was a quite dreadful thing to see.

As far as the practicalities went, we dropped the kit out at about twenty feet. We didn't actually use parachutes; it was literally just thrown out of the back of the plane, triple-bagged-sacks of grain. We found that at that height ninety-five per cent of the bags didn't break. Of course there were difficulties due to heat and altitude: hot and high is not very good for aeroplanes. Some of the dropping-zones were also difficult; they were up a hill, for instance. The only way you could get in was by climbing, and possibly running out of power. There was one place called Gondar, a small strip – our minimum strip is about 2,500 feet if everything is going well – and this one was only about that length, but it was also hot and high, so it was quite tight. One end of it was a cliff, about 300 or 400 feet, so you had to get spot on; the other end was a village – you were actually landing *towards* a village. And of course you could land only one way as well, so if you had a bit of a tail wind it made it even worse.

To be honest, I often wonder how much good we did. We used to see things like donated Land Rovers come in, and of the three that an aeroplane brought, two would stay in Addis with the government and one might get out into the field. And the bureaucracy was such that the ships coming into Assad used to unload, and the cargo didn't get anywhere. The convoys of lorries that were supposed to take it out from the port were empty for months on end, while they got the paperwork sorted out at customs. People were dying, yet there were these empty vehicles and grain in hangars, just not moving. Most of us have these mixed feelings. These pictures from Somalia, for example, I can't watch them; they bring tears to my eyes. It's absolutely horrific.

A lot of the parachuting we do is through the Parachute Training School at Brize Norton and Weston-on-the-Green. We deal with novices, but also specialist free-fall drops. Usually these pass without incident but we went through a bad patch when we lost three people in three months from free falls. There are also odd ones, parachute twists or whatever. We lost a marine in Norway a couple of years ago. He jumped in the water but didn't release his parachute – and it dragged him down.

Of course, potentially, the Gulf War could have brought us into contact with a huge number of casualties. We had four or five Hercules based in Riyadh. They were on standby all the time for the air resupply and casevac. At Riyadh Airport, they had hospitals laid out the sight of which raised the hairs on the back of your neck: hundreds upon hundreds of beds laid out in rows, about a foot between them, because they anticipated heavy casualties. Fortunately, they weren't used. I flew the first Allied fixed-wing aircraft into Kuwait shortly after the ceasefire started. That was a sporting trip. The smoke from burning oil rigs reduced visibility to almost zero and we had to fly extremely low just to keep in sight of the ground; we didn't see the runway until half-a-mile out. On the ground, the carnage was appalling; it was just wanton destruction of anything and everything by the Iraqis. One of our tasks there was to provide fuel to British helicopters by a method called FARPing – Forward Air Refuelling Point. Basically, we act as a tanker for them. Once there, however, it soon became apparent that we were the only source of fuel and eventually, after rapidly working out a new technique of transferring fuel Herc to Herc, we off-loaded over forty tons of fuel to approximately thirty helicopters including CH-53s, Cobras, Apaches and Black Hawks. Afterwards, we got a smashing letter from a very grateful American General, having saved them from the embarrassment of having helicopters grounded for twenty-four hours while they waited for fuel to arrive.

By coincidence I was also in the first crew out to Yugoslavia and there was a lot of media interest. It was horrific, I've never seen anything like it. As I came out of the crew coach, I was literally pinned to it, swamped. Some of the things they attributed to me were simply made up, just for a sensational story. But it was satisfying to do that job, because we felt we were doing some good, using our specialist skills. We took in medical supplies and food from Zagreb to Sarajevo, usually three sorties a day. We had no idea what was going to happen, whether we were going to be shot at or whatever, but we went in with what they call the Khe Sahn approach, developed in Vietnam. Basically you go in high to avoid the small-arms fire, and then do a steep descent at the last minute. Likewise on take-off, we held it on the ground for a long while and then did a 45-degree climb out, to get above any small-arms fire. I did twenty-one sorties in and out of Sarajevo, with over 600,000 pounds of supplies delivered. We're still operating there.

Also, as in Ethiopia, the risks are high. The airfield is right in the middle of the battleground and they fight over it. All they need is a mortar to mis-fire; while I was there the tower was hit, snipers were firing at us. We have got locked-up several times by missile systems and used chaff and terrain-masking to break-lock. Not long ago an Italian G222 transport aircraft was shot down. The Hercs too are vulnerable aircraft. There are two ways you can go in: you can go in medium-level, which is the way we're doing it – and hoping you are above most of the threats – or you go scorching in at a very low level. If you start doing things out of the ordinary, that's when they start shooting. If I was out there and I needed to evacuate people, I would go in at a very low level, and bugger the consequences. But while we're doing it day in and day out, then we need to follow recognised routes and tell everybody what we're doing – which in itself has its dangers, of course, because you're telling them exactly where you're going to be at a specified time. Hopefully, they negotiate those things.

On 3 May 1992, the Herc had been in service for twenty-five years. It had been a wonderful workhorse. During the mid-1970s, the Americans looked at replacing the Herc with a more modern aircraft. Two prototypes, the YC-14 and YC-15, were developed and a fly-off organised, the winner of which would be the Herc successor. Anyway, as a control, a standard Herc was also flown, and – guess what? – it won the competition hands down. The Herc replacement was scrapped and therefore the Herc production line continued. As President Carter said at the time, 'The only true replacement for a Hercules is another Hercules.' The RAF is currently looking for a replacement for ageing Hercs and one of the main contenders is the new Hercules 'J' model. This is a swept-up version with glass cockpit, modern avionics and better airframe and engines. It has tremendous potential and, if it is selected, I just hope I am still around to fly it!

Squadron Leader Ashley Stevenson

I went to my first squadron, 4 Squadron, at Gütersloh, Germany, in 1985. I spent four-and-a-half years there, during which time I became a weapons instructor. In 1989 I displayed the Harrier for Royal Air Force, Germany, for the season.

At the end of that year I was posted back to Wittering. I converted to the GR5 Harrier, and was posted to 1 Squadron, where I'm still serving. After six months I was promoted to a Flight Commander, and since 1991 I've been the Executive Officer.

The Harrier is unique: it's very flexible, and can operate from forward sites. Its short take-off and vertical landing capabilities are outstanding. And, of course, the Americans have turned it into a formidable aircraft. Now it has greater range, can carry more weapons and has accurate, up-to-date systems, with computer technology, as opposed to analogue technology. The difference between, say, the Tornado and the Harrier, apart from the vertical movement, is its rapid reaction and ability to operate from almost anywhere. It is capable of a fast turn-round and can go rapidly back to target area, time and time again. It's the most demanding aircraft, and they only send the best out in it. That's partly why I wanted to fly it. I had this dream of being the best. It's very demanding and very, very satisfying.

The Harrier GR5 wasn't used in the Gulf, probably because the aircraft wasn't ready. It has only been in service for about two-and-a-half years, and it always takes four or five before an aircraft is truly operational. In the two-and-a-half years the RAF had been operating the GR5s, they hadn't lost one. I was returning from an exercise in Denmark, leading a four-ship. I'd been airborne about ten minutes, and was climbing through 24,000 feet, when all of a sudden the engine just packed up. There was a massive explosion. One of the low-pressure compressor fan-blades had fatigue-failed, and ripped through the engine. It was a catastrophic mechanical failure.

From 24,000 feet you can glide down for quite a while – so I became a glider for about six minutes. I made three or four attempts to relight the engine on the way down, but it wasn't having it. There's no way that you can force-land an aircraft like that, so I had to ditch it. I pulled the ejection handle at about 2,000 feet, and landed in the middle of a field. I split my lip and got muddy, and that was about it, really. I was flying again within a couple of weeks. That was the first GR5 that was lost.

Eleven months later in September 1991, we had Kate Saunders on the squadron. She was in Cambridge University Air Squadron, a student. They come into the operational stations during their summer leave to see what it's all about and get a bit of Air Force experience. She'd been with us for a week. I'd flown with her before, and this was to be her last flight. We were doing a low-level sortie on 25 September, up through the Trent Valley, into Yorkshire and then back down, with a couple of simulated targets on the way. It was really just an air experience flight for her.

On the way, I'd shown her the rudiments of how to fly the aircraft. She'd had about forty hours on Bulldogs, but they're nothing like a fast jet! We were on our way back home, heading south, about fifteen or twenty miles north of Great Driffield, on the Yorkshire Wolds. I turned it south and trimmed it out at 250 feet, and 420 knots, then I gave Kate the controls – she wanted to fly it.

I had literally just picked up my map, to look for the next turning-point, when there was a terrific bang, and something came through the canopy and hit me square in the jaw, knocking me out. When I came round I was slumped over my left knee. I thought we'd been hit by another aircraft, it had been so violent. The canopy had caved in, and we were sitting in a 420-knot slipstream. I was woken by Kate's screams. She was in the back, screaming, 'What's happening? What's happening?' It sort of brought me round.

I was blinded, whether from the blast or the actual blow or whatever had hit my face, I didn't know, but I couldn't see. I was acutely aware that we had started off at 250 feet above the ground and that she had been flying it; I could tell, from her distress, that she wasn't flying it any more. I think she'd let go of the controls, expecting me to do something, but she wasn't aware of my injuries. My visor had been knocked back and wedged into the back of the helmet. The oxygen mask had been ripped from my face, and smashed against the left-hand side of the helmet, cracking the helmet. My chin, although I didn't realise it at the time, had a horse-shoe shape ripped out through the front of it, and all my bottom front teeth were lying flat against the floor of my mouth. I was aware that we were probably plummeting earthwards. It is the normal courtesy to let the back-seater eject first, but I couldn't communicate with Kate – I had no mouth, and no oxygen mask, so no microphone. I thought, Time is of the essence, old chap. Get out, and hope to God that she follows you. It was our only chance.

I didn't even know what the attitude of the aircraft was; we could have been upside down. But the sooner I pulled the handle the more chance we had of surviving. So I pulled the handle.

The next thing I knew, I was sort of woken by the tug of the chute opening, and I got my vision back for the first time. I was about ten feet above the ground, and I quickly put my feet and knees together and hit the ground vertically, very hard. I crumpled in a heap and must have been unconscious for a minute or so, completely winded. I'd crushed a bone in my right ankle on the landing. Eventually I managed to sit up and, although I still felt very dazed, my immediate reaction was to look around and see if there was another fireball – because I'd thought we'd had a mid-air collision. Then I realised that there were flames and smoke everywhere, and a huge fire, my fireball, about twenty or thirty feet behind me.

Then I suddenly remembered Kate. I couldn't see her at all. I thought, Maybe she didn't get out! Maybe she didn't get out! I stood up and disconnected myself from my parachute, and took off what was left of my helmet. There was blood all over my face, but I wasn't too worried about it. I ran to the edge of the fire, but I couldn't see Kate anywhere. We had landed in the middle of a stubble field, and the fireball had set it alight. All of a sudden I heard screams, so I ran to the upwind end of this wall of fire, thinking that I would walk round the back of it and see Kate sitting there in a trauma. But when I got to the upwind end, I was at the corner of a square. The other side of this square went on for two more fields. So I thought, Oh shit, she's in the middle of it! I was shouting at her to call back to me. Then I heard her voice but it was very faint, so I went back to where I'd started because it seemed to be the nearest position to her. All the time, I just kept shouting and shouting to her, and she was screaming out to me. I then got to the point outside the fire which seemed nearest to her, and then hobbled my way in, picking my way through this fire until I found her. She was sitting bolt upright, her right leg was broken badly, and she was on fire. She was burning, her whole body was burning. Her helmet was off and she'd lost her gloves. Her hands were burning, her neck and her whole back and legs were burning. So I just rushed up to her.

Luckily, I still had my flying gloves on, so I did my best to put the fire on her body out with my hands. I could see her nylon life-jacket had melted to her. I had to physically tear the weld from her back. I couldn't put out the fire on that – the Mae West inside it was burning away – six- to eight-inch flames coming out of it. I had to rip it from her back. She was still screaming her head off from the pain. She said, 'I just want to lie down, I just want to lie down. I'm burning, I'm burning.' Her hands were just molten. We both started to choke from the flames and smoke, and I said, 'Look, I'm going to have to move you, Kate.' She said, 'Oh no, don't move me, don't move me, I'm in such pain.' I said, 'If I don't move you we both die. We've got to get out of here.'

Because of my injuries I couldn't pick her up. I had to slip my arms around her waist, then pick her up from behind, and drag her backwards through the fire. She was screaming her head off, because her heels were bumping over the ground and, of course, she had this broken leg. I had to stop two or three times, because I was completely exhausted and choking. Eventually we got back to the edge of the fire, and I laid her down, and tried to keep her conscious, telling her that she was OK. She was in a lot of pain. At that stage, a van appeared with a couple of guys in it. One of them rushed over to see if he could help. By then the fire had begun to move around in circles again, so he gave me a hand lifting Kate further away. Then the police and the ambulance, and the fire engines arrived. One of the firemen made me sit down and put a compress on my face to stop the bleeding. About twenty minutes later, a helicopter arrived, and it then took them another half-hour before they could move Kate because a doctor was giving her intravenous fluids. We were taken to Hull Hospital.

Later, we learned that we had ejected at about 110–120 feet. I'd got out just inside the ejection envelope, my chute opened at fifty feet. Kate had ejected at ninety feet, with something like thirty to forty degrees of bank on. Theoretically, she was outside the ejection envelope; she should not have survived. What I think happened was the aircraft hit the ground just before she did, and the blast of the fireball from the aircraft blew her sideways back towards me, and with such a force that it introduced a horizontal trajectory into her descent. It saved her life.

I landed vertically and crushed the bone in my ankle. Kate landed with such a side-force that it broke her leg. Her heel came out of the side of her boot – that shows you how far sideways she was going when she hit the ground. It was the blast, it wasn't the wind, because there wasn't any. The canopy of the parachute had caught fire in the blast, and that was what was burning her, apart from the fire which she had actually landed in. She was a very lucky girl. She shouldn't have lived.

It was a bird strike, we finally realised. A black-headed gull had smashed through the canopy and I think a large piece of canopy struck me in the face. From the second the bird hit my face to the time the aircraft hit the ground was a total of six seconds. I ejected after about three-and-a-half, and Kate ejected after about four-and-a-half – a second-and-a-half before the aircraft hit the ground. She saw me go and then pulled her own handle, which was very brave of her. A lot of people in that situation and with her experience would have just curled up and died. She showed initiative and courage. Because Kate had thirty per cent burns, she was immediately transferred to Wakefield Burns Unit in Yorkshire, the best Burns Unit in the country. She spent the next three months on her back, not even able to move her hands.

They stitched my face up. I had to grow a beard for five months, which is interesting in the Air Force. Now my face is numb. I have no feeling there. They managed to push my teeth back in, after a fashion, and I've had extensive surgery on them. But even now they're not perfect. The nerves are dead. But frankly, my injuries are nothing compared to Kate's.

She was in Wakefield until nearly Christmas. I used to drive up to see her every week. It was very emotional, extremely emotional. It's brought us together. We're very close friends – I think we will be for life. She got out of hospital late in December, and spent the next two or three months going in and out of hospital for more treatment, more skin grafts, more operations. Then she spent six months having physiotherapy at Headley Court. But she's got her flying category back now, and has just gone back for her final year at Cambridge University. Although she's not allowed to fly an ejection-seat because of her back injuries, she is up and flying.

Cadet Pilot Kate Saunders

I'd always been interested in flying, and when the opportunity came up I applied to be a Volunteer Reserve with the Cambridge University Air Squadron. I had done about thirty-eight hours on Bulldogs but only two or three of those had been solo.

I was twenty-one when I had my first experience of flying in jets. I went to Wittering, in the middle of September 1991, and was supposed to be there a week. I had about eight hours' flying with four or five different pilots. There's a compulsory emergency brief, where you have to watch a video, and someone goes through the procedure with you on a diagram, but once you're in the cockpit it isn't all that easy. You can see where the ejection handle is and also where the ejection seat pins are. Before every flight you have to take out your own pin. I had the same training as anyone else, it was standard.

On the day of the accident Ashley Stevenson and I started out at about half past nine in the morning, from Wittering. I was in the back seat, and we'd been flying for about half-an-hour, perhaps three-quarters of an hour, when there was a bright flash. I asked Ashley what was wrong, but he didn't reply, which was strange because all through the flight he'd been talking to me. I kept on asking what was wrong, although I wasn't unduly concerned, but then, suddenly, I saw him eject. We were only flying 250 feet off the ground, so I didn't have a lot of time to think about it. So, I just shut my eyes and pulled my own ejection handle. I blacked out when I ejected, and that was about one-and-a-half seconds before the aircraft hit the ground.

When I came to I was sitting up on the ground on fire. I couldn't get up – I was sitting there with one leg, which from the knee downwards looked as if it wasn't attached to me any more. But the fact that I was on fire was the menace in my mind. I tried to put the fire out with my hands and to get my life-jacket off, because it was melting on to my back. But I had to pull my helmet and my oxygen mask off first, so that I could get my jacket off. When I tried to get my arm out of my life-jacket, I knocked the glove off my right hand and that became severely burned. I knew that I couldn't save myself. I started screaming, 'Help, I'm dying.' I didn't expect anyone to hear me, but then I heard Ashley shouting. As soon as I heard his voice I knew that I was going to be safe. He told me to keep on screaming so that he could locate me. Although unable to see me for smoke he had followed my shouting and came through the fire to help me.

I remember seeing his face cut open, but it didn't seem that bad. First he beat all the flames out and ripped the jacket from my back. Then he lifted me under the shoulders and pulled me backwards. It was very painful because my leg was bouncing along the ground. I was screaming with the pain, because it was the first time that I really felt the pain. But he told me if I stayed there I'd die as the fire was moving rapidly towards me. After he'd moved me a couple of times, a guy appeared. They had to move me one more time to get me completely out of danger. Ashley picked me up under the shoulders, and the other guy tried to pick me up by the broken leg, which was a bit painful! And then other people appeared.

It seemed a long time before the helicopter came – it was actually twenty minutes. A doctor put me on a drip, but they didn't give me any painkillers until I was actually in the hospital. Then I was transferred to the Burns Unit of the Pindersfields Hospital, Wakefield.

I suffered from 28 per cent burns, an open fracture of the right tibia and fibula, an undisplaced fracture of the left side of my pelvis and a compression fracture of the twelfth thoracic vertebra. They plated my tibia and the burns on my back and my hand, left arm and legs were excised and grafted. As a result of my fractured pelvis I was unable to sit up or move from bed for several weeks.

At first I had a sort of flash burn over about two-thirds of my face, but now I've just got a bit left on my chin that is burned. My right hand, which I write with, was very badly burned. That's still the worst part. I've got bits of burn on my left fingers. My bottom is burned from the harness straps – all of me is burned in places except for my front, and many of the unburned areas had to have the skin removed to use for grafts.

I was in the Pindersfields Hospital for nine-and-a-half weeks. When I came out, I could barely walk – I was on crutches. I couldn't really sit down very well, or bend my knees. A couple of months later I had two more operations, one on my leg and a skin graft to my hand. I have to go into hospital again to have the metal taken out of my leg. I have a lot of pain in it, but I don't limp now. It's all relative!

Ashley came to see me a lot when I was in hospital; we get on very well. It was a million-to-one accident, but it happened and it happened to me. There's no point moaning about it, or feeling sorry for myself, because it's not going to change anything.

I've started flying again – flying Bulldogs with the University Air Squadron. I'm not fit enough to go back in a jet yet. But I shall be. I'm in my last year at Cambridge, and in 1993 I shall apply to join the Air Force. I want to be a pilot and make a career of it.

ENVOI

The Last Flight

Cecil Lewis flew with the RFC during the First World War, after which he went to Peking to teach flying. This extract is taken from the closing pages of his classic work on flying, Sagittarius Rising.

So the last flight came. I was up in a Vimy taking some friends to view the city from the air. It was perfect autumn weather, and we passed high over the pattern of the palaces northwards to the Great Wall. The flight had no significance for me. I did not know it was the last time I should pilot a machine. It just so happened that I never did again. Better so, for with what shrinking hearts do we approach the severing of ties. The last word, the last handshake, the last kiss, knowing that never again will the eyes meet so, nor the heart beat so, that something which once filled our lives has dwindled down to the pin-point of farewell and cannot be regained. Come back! Come back! It will be different! We will start again. I was to blame. I see it now. Forgive me! So something in us calls, ready to promise anything sooner than drink the cup, revolting that with life itself so brief, the ties within it should be briefer still. And yet we stand, like fatal oxen, mouthing the bitter word, watch that which we most desired to hold recede, and, waving, turn and go.

These are the wretched known farewells; the unknown slip by sometimes unperceived, and only after many years do we look back and say: Why, that was the last time! So with this. The fine engines roared out there on the wings. The interference beat was very slow, rising and falling like a deep sea swell, so true were they in tune. There were the Ming Tombs underneath; the broad way up to them lined with its marble monoliths, dragons and elephants, horses and watchmen, guarding that sacred road by which dead Emperors went to rest for ever in the valleys of the hills.

But had I known? Could I have seen it then, as I do now, should I not have passed the whole time in review? Should I not have thought, as I do now, of my lost friends, companions of the air: Pip blown to bits, Arthur brought down, Bill coughing as he fell back at that single senseless shot? They more than others I had known would have been happy high aloft that day, to see below the barren ridges of the hills and follow the Great Wall, fighting its stubborn way up and down the rises and the falls, lonely and strong, guarding the desolation.

And hosts of other memories would have followed, crowding: a thousand skycapes, day and night, the gay or sombre garments of the blue; the way the earth looked, falling; the wonder at first coming out above the clouds; the rush of engines starting; swallowing to stop deafness in a dive; the scream of wires; shadows of clouds on hills; rain, sweeping like veils over the sea, far off; sunlight; stars between wings; friends, close in formation, swaying, hand on throttle, as they rode ten feet away a mile above the earth. And many others: grass blown down when engines were run up; the smell of dope, and castor oil, and varnish in new cockpits; moonlight shining on struts; sunset clouds, gold-braided; the gasp before the dive; machine guns; chasing wild duck; the feel of bumps, and all the mastery over movement, pride in skill.

And should I not, had I but known, have flung the machine this way and that, once more to feel it live under my hand, have sported in the sky and laughed and sung, knowing that never after should I feel so free, so sure in hazard, so secure, riding the daylight in the pride of youth? No more horizons wider than Hope! No more the franchise of the sky, the freedom of the blue! No more! No more! Farewell to wings! Down to the little earth!

No, the truth is, had I known, I should not have felt so. Life is more savoured in its after-taste. That distant day has a significance I could not give it then, and all those days now fall into a shape, this shape I have endeavoured to set down; some things with pleasure, some reluctantly, some ill; for words straining to catch emotion have a bursting-point, they crack into heroics, platitudes. Only the rarely gifted mould them to the thought's shape, docile, so that the reader scanning the cold print feels something stir within him and take fire, and gazes stupidly upon the page, seeing the ink blurred, uplifted by the music, hardly knowing why.

So we wheeled and came back south towards the city. There were the lakes, the palaces, the spirit ways mounting between the steps, so that the unseen world might have its own way up and down unhindered by the feet of mortal men; there were the dyers' scaffolds where blue lengths of cotton cloth hung drying in the wind; there was my little house; there was the shop where I had bought an amber drop my unborn son would break. There it all was, the teeming world spread out four-square to see, and I should always be as then, apart, mostly alone, the self aside, however close the press.

The Temple of Heaven slipped by underneath, that perfect pattern in its ample park: the groves of yews, the long descending way to where the Altar, marble, white and triple-tiered, lay in the circle of its blue-tiled wall. Then the wide plain ruled to the far horizon. Soon the aerodrome.

Now shut the engines off. Come down and flatten out, feel the long float, and at the given moment pull the stick right home. She's down. Now taxy in. Switch off. It's over – but not quite, for the port engine, just as if it knew, as if reluctant at the last to let me go, kicked, kicked, and kicked again, as overheated engines will, then backfired with an angry snorting: Fool! The best is over . . . But I did not hear.

APPENDIX

Key dates in Royal Air Force history

1917
29 November. Air Force (Constitution) Bill 1917, received Royal Assent.

1918
3 January. First Air Council formed. (Secretary of State: Lord Rothermere. Chief of the Air Staff: Maj.-Gen. Sir Hugh Trenchard.)
1 April. Royal Air Force formed by amalgamation of Royal Flying Corps and Royal Naval Air Service.
1 April. Women's Royal Air Force formed.
13 May. Independent Air Force formed. (To conduct bombing attacks on Germany independently of Army or Royal Navy operations.)
3 June. Distinguished Flying Cross, Air Force Cross, Distinguished Flying Medal and Air Force Medal instituted.
June. RAF began operations at Murmansk and Archangel, Russia.
June. RAF Nursing Service formed.
11 November. Armistice. RAF strength: 133 sqns overseas: Western Front, Middle East, Italy, Mediterranean. (55 sqns in UK, 74 training sqns.)
13 December. Start of first England to India flight (Martlesham–Karachi. Handley Page V/1500).

1919

January.   Department of Civil Aviation created by Air Ministry to apply air navigation regulations, etc.

4 August.   New rank titles of RAF adopted.

23 October.   RAF Benevolent Fund created.

11 December.   Plan for Permanent Peace Time Organisation of RAF presented to Parliament. (Became: Home: 4 sqns as striking force; Army co-opn. flight attached to each Army division; 1+ sqns for artillery co-opn.; 1 recce sqn; ½ torpedo sqn; 3 aeroplane and two seaplane sqns for Fleet co-opn. Overseas: 8 sqns, 1 depot in India; 7 sqns, 1 depot in Egypt; 3 sqns, 1 depot in Mesopotamia (Iraq); 1 seaplane flight each in Malta, Alexandria, Mediterranean aircraft carrier.)

1920

Jan–Feb.   Operations in Somaliland against 'Mad Mullah'.

5 February.   RAF College, Cranwell opened.

1 April.   RAF Central Band formed.

1 April.   WRAF disbanded.

3 July.   First RAF Tournament at Hendon (later 'Pageant').

1922

4 April.   RAF Staff College opened at Andover.

1 October.   Military control of Iraq handed to RAF.

1923

9 February.   Reserve of RAF officers formed.

June.   RAF Nursing Service became Princess Mary's RAF Nursing Service.

20 June.   Interim report of Committee enquiring into National and Imperial Defence recommends home defence force of 52 sqns.

1924

3 January.   RAF Short Service Commission scheme introduced.

April. Fleet Air Arm formed. (RAF units embarked on aircraft carriers and other fighting ships.)

1925

1 January. Air Defence of Great Britain formed.

1 October. First University Air Sqn formed (Cambridge).

14 October. First two Auxiliary Air Force sqns formed (600 (City of London), 601 (County of London)).

22 October. No. 1 Apprentices Wing formed, Halton.

October. First post-war independent air action by RAF (bombing Mahsud tribe, Waziristan, North-West Frontier).

29 October. Observer Corps formed.

1927

1 January. Lord Trenchard became first Marshal of the Royal Air Force.

March. RAF's first all-metal fighter entered service (Armstrong Whitworth Siskin IIIA).

26 September. RAF won Schneider Trophy (Supermarine S5, 281.49mph).

17 October. RAF's first Far East flight began. (4 Supermarine Southampton flying boats – Egypt, India, Australia, Japan, Singapore.)

1928

February. RAF made responsible for defence of Aden.

23 December. Beginning of air evacuation of 586 civilians from British Legation, Kabul, Afghanistan.

1929

1 January. Observer Corps transferred from War Office to RAF control.

September. RAF High Speed Flight won Schneider Trophy (Supermarine S6, 328.63mph).

12 September. World Speed Record achieved by RAF Supermarine S6 (357.75mph).

1930
1 January. Far East Command formed.
5 October. Air Minister, Lord Thomson, killed in R101 airship disaster.

1931
13 September. RAF won Schneider Trophy outright (Supermarine S6B, 340.08mph).
29 September. World Speed record achieved by RAF Supermarine S6B (407.5mph).

1932
25–26 April. RAF operations against Sheikh Ahmed, Iraq.

1933
6–8 February. World Distance record set up by RAF: Cranwell to Walvis Bay, South West Africa, 5,309 miles in 52 hrs 25 mins by Fairey Long Range Monoplane.

1934
24 May. First Empire Air Day.
30 July. Government announced intentions to develop measures to protect public and essential services against air-raids.
August. RAF's first rotating wing aircraft entered service (Avro Rota autogyro).

1936
6 March. RAF's first operational monoplane with retractable undercarriage enters service (Avro Anson – which served until 1956).
14 July. Home defence organised into four Commands: Bomber, Fighter, Coastal and Training Commands.

July. First air defence exercises, assuming enemy air attacks on south-east England.

30 July. Formation of RAF Volunteer Reserve. (To train 800 pilots a year.)

1937

January. RAF's last biplane fighter enters service (Gloster Gladiator).

30 June. RAF increases its world aeroplane height record (28 Sept 1936) to 53,937ft (Bristol 138).

December. RAF's first eight-gun monoplane fighter enters service (Hurricane).

1938

1 April. RAF Maintenance Command formed.

June. Supermarine Spitfire enters service.

24 September. Munich Crisis. Emergency plans brought into operation.

1 November. RAF Balloon Command formed.

5–7 November. RAF Long Range Development Flight achieved world distance record (7,162 miles in 48 hrs, Egypt to Australia, Vickers Wellesleys).

1939

20 May. Last Empire Air Day.

28 June. Women's Auxiliary Air Force formed.

24 August. General mobilisation of RAF.

1 September. RAF Reserve (and RAFVR) called to permanent service. Auxiliary Air Force sqns embodied.

2 September. Advanced Air Striking Force (12 sqns; 10 Battles, 2 Hurricanes) deployed to France. (Air Component of British Army Expeditionary Force in France was 12 sqns: 4 Blenheim, 4 Hurricanes/Gladiators, 4 Lysanders.)

3 September. Declaration of war on Germany.

3 September. First RAF operation in Second World War. Recce of German fleet, Wilhelmshaven (Blenheim, 139 Sqn).

1940

11 March. First U-boat sunk by RAF (Blenheim, Schillig Roads).

29 April. Empire Air Training Scheme began in Canada, Australia, New Zealand.

12 May. First RAF VCs of war. (F/O D. E. Garland, Sgt T. Gray – attack on bridge at Maastricht (Fairey Battle).)

17 May. Ministry of Aircraft Production formed.

27 May. RAF Training Command replaced by Flying Training Command and Technical Training Command.

11 June. First RAF attack on Italy (Wellingtons).

22 June. Parachute Training School formed at Ringway, Manchester.

10 July. Preliminary phase of Battle of Britain.

25 August. First RAF night raid on Berlin (81 aircraft).

15 September. Peak day of Battle of Britain.

10 November. First air delivery of land planes for RAF across Atlantic (7 Hudsons – Canada to N Ireland).

1 December. Army Co-Operation Command formed.

1941

5 February. Air Training Corps formed.

10 February. First operation by RAF four-engined bombers (Stirlings, Rotterdam).

27 February. Tragino raid.

20 July. RAF Ferry Command formed.

9 October. Western Desert Air Force formed.

1942

12 January. RAF Regiment formed.

30 May. First RAF 'Thousand Bomber' raid, Cologne (1,046 aircraft, including aircraft from Operational Training Units).

15 August. Pathfinder Force formed within Bomber Command.

1943
2 February. Mediterranean Air Command formed.
25 March. RAF Transport Command formed (ex-Ferry Command).
1 April. Squadron Standards authorised to mark RAF's 25th Anniversary.
16 May. 'Dam Busters' – 617 Sqn – breached Mohne and Eder Dams, Germany.
1 June. Tactical Air Force formed (Army Co-Operation Command disbanded).
4 July. First glider crossing of Atlantic, towed by RAF Dakota.
15 November. Allied Expeditionary Air Force formed.
16 November. Air Command South-East Asia formed.

1944
14 April. Strategic bombing forces placed under command of Supreme Commander, Allied Expeditionary Forces for operations in preparation for D-Day invasion.
1 June. RAF Balkan Air Force formed.
6 June. D-Day invasion, Normandy (5,656 RAF sorties).
1 July. RAF reaches peak strength: 1,011,427 men, 174,406 women.
18 July. RAF Test Pilots School renamed Empire Test Pilots School.
4 August. First RAF jet aircraft operations. (Meteors against VI flying-bombs, southern England.)
15 September. Strategic bombing forces revert to control of Combined Chiefs of Staff.
14 October. Largest RAF Bomber Command raid of war: 1,576 aircraft despatched (Duisberg). Largest bomb tonnage on one target in one night (4,547 tons).
28 October. RAF Central Navigation School renamed Empire Air Navigation School.

1945

January. RAF Helicopter Training School formed (Sikorsky R-4s).

24 April. First RAF jet operations on Continent – Meteors against Nordholz airfield, Germany.

7 May. Last U-boat sunk (Catalina; 196th U-boat destroyed unaided by aircraft of Coastal Command).

7 May. Unconditional surrender of Germany. (RAF strength 55,469 aircraft of which 9,200 first-line).

14 August. Unconditional surrender of Japan after US atom bomb attacks.

1946

1 April. RAF Reserve Command formed – maintenance and training of RAF reserve organisations.

7 May. Central Flying School re-formed (RAF, Little Rissington).

2 June. Announcement of Auxiliary Air Force to be re-formed (20 sqns).

7 September. RAF achieves world air speed record (616.81mph, Meteor IV).

1947

10 July. Battle of Britain Memorial dedicated in Westminster Abbey.

16 December. 'Royal' prefix conferred on Auxiliary Air Force.

1948

June. Start of RAF operations against Communist insurgents in Malaya.

28 June. RAF joins 'Berlin Airlift' begun by USAAF, 26 June.

12–14 July. RAF makes first Atlantic crossing by jet aircraft (Vampires, 54 Sqn, via Stornoway, Iceland, Greenland, Labrador).

1949

1 February. Women's Auxiliary Air Force re-named Women's Royal Air Force.

1 June. Far East Air Force formed.

1 June. RAF Flying College formed from Empire Air Navigation School, Empire Air Armament School and Empire Flying School. (RAF Manby, Lincs.)

1950

1 April. First RAF operational helicopter unit formed – Casualty Evacuation Flight, Singapore (Westland Dragonfly). Later, 1953, 1st RAF helicopter sqn, 194 Sqn.

22 July. RAF Home Command formed; succeeding Reserve Command.

12 November. RAF achieves world's longest air force jet delivery flight to date (8,500 miles. Vampires from UK to Far East Air Force).

1951

May. RAF's first jet bomber enters service (English Electric Canberra).

1 September. British Air Forces of Occupation, Germany, renamed 2nd Tactical Air Force (1959: renamed RAF, Germany).

1952

19 February. First British-designed helicopter delivered to RAF (Bristol Sycamore).

15 July. The Queen's Coronation review of RAF (640 aircraft, RAF, Odiham).

1954

February. First British swept-wing fighter enters RAF service (Supermarine Swift).

October. RAF bombing operations against Mau Mau terrorists, Kenya.

1955

January. First RAF strategic nuclear bomber enters service – 'V-Bomber' (Vickers Valiant).

August. First RAF all jet ab initio training programme (RAF, Hullavington, No. 2 Flying Training School).

1956

10 February. Death of Marshal of the RAF, Lord Trenchard.

June. RAF introduces world's first jet transport squadron (de Havilland Comet 2, 216 Sqn).

11 October. Test of first British A-Bomb dropped from aircraft (Valiant, 40 Sqn, Maralinga, South Australia).

31 October. Suez Crisis. Start of RAF operations from Malta and Cyprus against Egyptian air bases.

1957

15 May. Test of first British H-Bomb dropped from aircraft (Valiant, 49 Sqn, Christmas Island).

1958

13 February. Announcement that RAF to operate US-supplied Thor Intermediate Range Ballistic Missiles in UK (First sqn, No. 77 formed August).

3 November. RAF Signals Command formed.

1959

4 April. RAF Home Command disbanded.

15 May. Last operational flight by RAF flying boat (Sunderland, 205 Sqn).

1960

17 February. Announcement that UK's first ballistic missile attack early warning station (Fylingdales) to be operated by RAF (operational 1963).

31 July. End of Malayan 'Emergency' 1948–60: 375,849 RAF sorties.

December. UK becomes one of four NATO air-defence regions. RAF Fighter Command assigned to Supreme Allied Commander, Europe, from 1 May 1961.

1961

February. Middle East Air Force renamed Near East Air Force. (Forces in Arabian Peninsula retitled Air Forces Middle East (Aden).)

1 July. RAF strike aircraft deployed to Kuwait to deter Iraqi aggression.

1962

May. RAF Near East Command disbanded.

December. Start of operations against rebels in Brunei (to 1963).

1963

December. Start of extensive operations in Malaysia and Borneo (Indonesian 'Confrontation'); to mid-August 1966.

1964

1 April. Dissident tribesmen in the Radfan effectively closed Dhala Road. Aden federal government ask Britain for assistance. Ministry of Defence formed (Air Ministry became Air Force Department).

1965

2 February. Major cancellations in British projects for RAF. (P1154 supersonic, vertical take-off/landing fighter; HS 681 transport. TSR 2 strike plane cancelled 6 April.)

December. RAF Javelin fighters deployed to Zambia on Rhodesian unilateral declaration of independence

1966

RAF Gibraltar reduced to staging post on withdrawal of Shackleton sqn.

1967

February. Announcement that RAF Bomber and Fighter Commands to merge in April 1968 as RAF Strike Command.

1 August. RAF Transport Command renamed RAF Air Support Command.

1968

16 January. Major defence cuts announced – cancellation of order for 50 US F-111 aircraft for RAF; Royal Navy fixed-wing aircraft to be transferred to RAF as carriers phased out; withdrawal from Far East and Persian Gulf by end 1971.

30 April. RAF Strike Command formed on merger of Fighter and Bomber Commands.

1 June. RAF Training Command (re)formed on merger of Flying Training Command and Technical Training Command.

12 June. Queen's Colour Sqn join The Guards in ceremonial duties at Buckingham Palace for first time as part of RAF's 50th anniversary celebrations.

1969

1 January. RAF Signals Command disbanded.

4 May. RAF Harrier vertical take-off jet makes first city centre to city centre jet flight in history (London to New York, Daily Mail Transatlantic Air Race).

1 July. RAF 'V' Bomber force hands over responsibility for British strategic nuclear deterrent to Royal Navy Polaris submarine force.

1 October. First RAF VTOL fighter sqn formed (1 Sqn, Harrier).

28 October. RAF Coastal Command merged into RAF Strike Command.

1970
1 September. First block entry of University Graduates to RAF College, Cranwell, after end of traditional cadet entry scheme.

1973 Operation Khana Cascade. 4 Hercules aircraft detached to Nepal to air-drop 1,964 tons of food in 29 days to starving people in inaccessible West Nepal.
RAF Air Support Command merged into RAF Strike Command.

1974 Coup in Cyprus and Turkish invasion: intensive airlift to extract service families.

1975 Defence White paper reduced RAF transport fleet by 50 aircraft (Britannia and Comet retired). 12 home bases closed.
RAF Maintenance Command became RAF Support Command.

1977
June. RAF Air Support Command formed when Support Command absorbed Training Command.

1979
December. Deployment of RAF element of Commonwealth Ceasefire Monitoring Force, Zimbabwe.

1982 Falklands conflict.

1984 Beginning of Operation Bushel. Hercules detachment established at Addis Ababa to conduct air–land relief for drought-stricken areas.

1990 The Gulf War.

1991   Operation Provide Comfort; Operation Haven.

1992   Operation Cheshire: RAF provides humanitarian relief to besieged city of Sarajevo.

1999   Operation Allied Forces in Kosovo.

2004   Operation Telic: in support of Coalition forces invasion of Iraq.

Index

INDEX

INDEX

INDEX